JAMES STOKES LECTURESHIP ON POLITICS

NEW YORK UNIVERSITY · STOKES FOUNDATION

THE PRESIDENT: OFFICE
AND POWERS

THE PRESIDENT
OFFICE AND POWERS

History and Analysis of
Practice and Opinion

BY

EDWARD S. CORWIN

"We elect a king for four years, and give him absolute power
within certain limits, which after all he can interpret for himself."
—*Secretary of State Seward*

SECOND EDITION (REVISED)

NEW YORK UNIVERSITY PRESS
WASHINGTON SQUARE · NEW YORK

London: Humphrey Milford · Oxford University Press

Printed in the United States of America
George Grady Press · New York

TO
M. S. C.
MY MOST ENCOURAGING
AND
CONSTRUCTIVE CRITIC

104708

PREFACE

THIS is a study in Public Law—in American constitutional law, to be precise. The approach is partly historical, partly analytical. The central theme of the work is *power* and its development—the power of the President under the Constitution; but the characteristics of the presidential office considered as a Public Law institution too are treated. Thus forewarned, the reader will not be expecting something essentially different—a work on the political or personal aspects of the Presidency, for instance, or on its day-to-day operations as an organ of government. To be sure, these other phases of the subject are not ignored altogether, for American constitutional law is not a closed system. On the contrary, it often bristles with alternatives; and particularly is this true of the section of it which is the concern of these pages. Consequently, it often becomes pertinent to raise the question as to which of two or more available theories of the Constitution is to be preferred on grounds of policy. Indeed, for reasons which the reader will discover for himself, it is only rarely that previous practice or agreed doctrine, either one, can be dogmatically asserted to have foreclosed all choice between the logical alternatives which the record of discussion concerning the constitutional position and powers of the President discloses.

While I trust I have not slighted the opportunities of this nature which have presented themselves from time to time, the reader, on the other hand, should not feel that this fact affords him warrant for demanding still more. Likewise, I have felt free to comment on the personal traits of individual Presidents when they seem to me to have materially affected the development of the office and its powers. For the Presidency unfolds a daily drama of the reciprocal interplay of human character and legal concepts which no other office on earth can quite emulate. Altogether, I suspect, I am more open to the charge of irrelevance than to that of having taken an unduly constricted view of my subject.

It is a pleasure to make certain acknowledgments. The volume is based for the most part upon a direct examination of firsthand materials, the debates of the Philadelphia Convention, debates in Congress, acts of Congress, presidential messages and papers, opinions of Attorneys General, decisions of the Supreme Court, controversial writings, and press despatches. But I have often profited by the guidance afforded by other writers in the field, Thach, Binkley, Horwill, Berdahl, Randall, Small, Warren, and others. I have also been assisted by the researches of graduate students in the Department of Politics of Princeton University, in which connection Arnold J. Zurcher's doctoral dissertation on the *Theory and Practice of the Presidency* (1928) and Turner C. Cameron's dissertation on *The Political Philosophy of Franklin D. Roosevelt* (1940) deserve special mention. Neither of these studies has been published, but is obtainable on application at Princeton University Library. All such indebtednesses are indicated more particularly at proper points in the Notes.

There is, however, *one* debt of which I must make more emphatic acknowledgment. The reader of the Notes will become aware of it at once. It is to *The New York Times,* both as a chronicle of current events and a repository of public documents. To its other great virtues in these respects has been added since 1913 its splendid Index, which renders its contents always accessible on short notice. Without the assistance of the *Times,* which I have diligently clipped for a quarter of a century, this volume would not have been undertaken; and while my readers may not regard the avowal as a recommendation for the *Times,* they will, I feel sure, concede that I have a right to feel differently on the point.

Some more personal indebtednesses are the following: To my young friends, Dr. Franklin L. Burdette and Dr. Turner C.

Cameron for data which they put at my disposal, and which appear in the Notes at the proper points; to Professor Everett S. Brown of the University of Michigan for a number of informative suggestions; to my colleagues, Professors George A. Graham and Harold H. Sprout, for reading and criticizing certain chapters; to Professor John E. Bebout of Newark University and Professor Walter L. Whittlesey of Princeton University for reading the entire volume in proof and offering a number of suggestions to its distinct improvement. My debt to the latter in this respect is especially great, thanks alike to his skill and to his characteristic generosity with his friends in rendering such services. My sister, Miss Jane Corwin, rendered valuable aid in preparing the Index, and my secretary, Mrs. Dorothy Pardee, displayed her usual speed and accuracy in the work of copyist and transcriber. And, as always, I must pay my respects to the ever courteous and helpful staff of Princeton University Library.

Lastly, it is a special pleasure to thank the authorities of New York University, the publishers of this volume, for innumerable favors. The work is an outgrowth of lectures which I gave at New York University in the autumn of 1937 on the Stokes Foundation. By far the most delightful part of the arrangement so far as I was concerned were the attentions I received from my colleagues for the time being, at whose head was Dean Marshall Brown. More recently I have had frequent occasion, in connection with the preparation of these pages for the press, to appreciate the patience and resourcefulness of Miss Barr and her assistant, Miss Geldorf. The gratitude which I have expressed orally to all the above I now gladly put in black and white.

EDWARD S. CORWIN

Princeton, N. J.
September 1, 1940

TABLE OF CONTENTS

THE PRESIDENT: OFFICE AND POWERS

CHAPTER 1

CONCEPTIONS OF THE OFFICE

THE origins of government have been sometimes traced to a monarch in the forest who gathered in his person all power. At length wearied with his responsibilities, the hypothetical potentate delegated some of them to followers who eventually became "courts," and shared others with a more numerous body of subjects who in due time organized themselves into a "legislature." The indefinite residuum, called "executive power," he kept for himself.

Thus it happens that, whereas "legislative power" and "judicial power" today denote fairly definable *functions* of government as well as fairly constant *methods* for their discharge, "executive power" is still indefinite as to *function* and retains, particularly when it is exercised by a single individual, much of its original plasticity as regards *method*. It is consequently the power of government which is most spontaneously responsive to emergency conditions; conditions, that is, which have not attained enough of stability or recurrency to admit of their being dealt with according to rule. The reversion of certain democracies within recent years in the presence of social crisis to more primitive types of government presents therefore no cause for astonishment.

Indeed, agreement is general among technical students of government that the retention of democratic institutions depends today largely upon the capacity of these to afford a matrix for strong executive leadership. What resources does our own Constitution offer in this respect? The answer brings under survey our practice and discussion for a century and a half.

The Notes to this chapter begin on page three hundred seventeen

"EXECUTIVE POWER"—A TERM OF UNCERTAIN CONTENT

Article II is the most loosely drawn chapter of the Constitution. To those who think that a constitution ought to settle everything beforehand it should be a nightmare; by the same token, to those who think that constitution makers ought to leave considerable leeway for the future play of political forces, it should be a vision realized.

We encounter this characteristic of Article II in its opening words: "The executive power shall be vested in a President of the United States of America." Do these words comprise a grant of power or are they a mere designation of office? If the former is the case, then how are we to explain the more specific clauses of grant in the ensuing sections of the same article? Some of these no doubt may be accounted for by the provision which they make for the participation of the Senate in the "executive power"; but several of them are not to be disposed of in this expeditious fashion. In the famous Oregon Postmaster Case of 1926 the difficulty is met by Chief Justice Taft with the statement that such clauses of specific grant lend "emphasis where emphasis is appropriate."[1] Not only is this an entirely novel canon of constitutional interpretation, it is one which, if it were applied to the "general welfare" clause of Article I of the Constitution, would pave the way for a complete revolution in our governmental system by converting it from a government of "enumerated" powers into one of plenary power. Yet if there *is* "executive power" which has been found essential in other systems of government and which is not granted the President in the more specific clauses of Article II, how is it to be brought within the four corners of the Constitution except by means of the "executive power" clause?

And is the President's executive power the *only* executive power known to the Constitution? This same clause seems to make an affirmative answer to this question logically imperative; but, if this is so, then what kind of power is that which Congress bestows by virtue of its power to make "all laws which shall be necessary and proper for carrying into execution" the powers of the National Government;[2] and, furthermore, what of the assumption that the President shall "take care that the laws be faithfully executed"[3]—executed, that is, by *others?* Again, is "executive power" the only kind of power which the President is capable of exercising? For, if that is the case, how can he receive power from the legislature, which, by the same course of reasoning, has only "legislative power" to confer?

Likewise, difficulty arises from the radically divergent categories into which the varied powers of the Presidency are classifiable. On the one hand are what may be termed the President's "prerogative powers," such as his power to pardon, his power to receive ambassadors, his power with the consent of the Senate to make treaties, and so on—those powers, in short, his possession of which the Constitution recognizes in fairly specific terms. As to these he is ordinarily represented as autonomous, or, as Chief Justice Marshall expressed it, as "responsible only to the country in his political capacity and to his own conscience."[4] Confronting these, on the other hand, stand such powers as answer to and are implied in the duty to "take care that the laws be faithfully executed," the immediate source whereof are acts of Congress. It hence becomes entirely possible for situations to arise in which, in order to fulfill his duty to promote the enforcement of the law, it becomes necessary that the President exercise one of his "autonomous" powers in the furtherance of ends not chosen by himself, perhaps indeed of ends of which he disapproves. How, if possible, are such paradoxes to be logically resolved—how in practice have they been resolved?

SOURCES OF THE FRAMERS' IDEAS OF EXECUTIVE POWER

The earliest American repositories of an executive power that was at all distinguishable as something other than a mere legislative agency were the governors of the royal provinces. This functionary, acting independently or with a council, was customarily entrusted with the powers of appointment, military command, expenditure, and—within limitations—that of pardon, as well as with large powers in connection with the process of lawmaking.[5] At the same time, however, he was also the point of tangency with the British Crown, and so the point of friction between the imperial interest and the local interest, the latter being represented by the colonial assembly. Gradually the assemblies in most of the royal provinces, thanks especially to their control over supplies, were able to bring the governor under a large degree of legislative control and direction; and during the French and Indian War, when the governors were in constant need of money and of men for the forces, this development went ahead with strides. The colonial period ended with the belief prevalent that "the executive magistracy" was the natural enemy, the legislative assembly the natural friend of liberty, a sentiment strengthened by the contemporary spectacle of George III's domination of Parliament.

In most of the early state constitutions accordingly we find the gubernatorial office reduced almost to the dimensions of a symbol. In these instruments the governors were for the most part elective annually by the legislature, were stripped of every prerogative of their predecessors in relation to legislation—the right to convene the assembly, to prorogue it, to dissolve it, to veto its acts—and were forced to exercise even their more strictly executive functions subject to the advice of a council of state which was also elective by the legislature and, if the latter so desired, from its members.[6] Several of these constitutions, to be sure, enunciate Montesquieu's doctrine of the separation of powers with considerable emphasis; but their actual application of the principle, when it was anything more than a caution against the same persons being entrusted with office in more than one department at a time, was directed especially against the executive. In the language of Madison in *The Federalist*:

"The founders of our republics . . . seem never for a moment to have turned their eyes from the overgrown and all-grasping prerogative of an hereditary magistrate, supported and fortified by an hereditary branch of the legislative authority. They seem never to have recollected the danger from legislative usurpations, which, by assembling all power in the same hands, must lead to the same tyranny as is threatened by executive usurpations."[7]

Finally, in the Virginia constitution of 1776 it was stipulated, as if out of abundant caution, that "the executive powers of government" were to be exercised "according to the laws" of the commonwealth, and that no power or prerogative was ever to be claimed "by virtue of any law, statute, or custom of England."[8] "Executive power," in short, was left to legislative definition and was cut off entirely from the resources of the common law and of English constitutional usage.

But while the above is a just characterization of the majority of the Revolutionary state constitutions, there were exceptions in which a more generous conception of the executive office is at least foreshadowed. Thus in the famous report of the Pennsylvania Council of Censors of 1784 the Pennsylvania constitution of 1776 is interpreted as entrusting all power not otherwise specifically provided for either to "the legislative or the executive *according to its nature*";[9] and as is pointed out by Hamilton in *The Federalist*, the New York constitution of 1777 suggested not a few of the outstanding features of the Presidency. The New York governor was not a creature of the legislature but was directly elective by the people; his term was three years and he was indefinitely re-ëligible; except in the matter of appointments and vetoes, he was untroubled by a council; he bore the designation of "Commander-in-Chief," possessed the pardoning power, and was charged with the duty of "taking care that the laws are faithfully executed to the best of his ability."[10] The first effective gubernatorial veto, however, was that set up in the Massachusetts constitution of 1780, and the designation "President" occurred in several of the state constitutions of that date.

Furthermore, the early state constitutions were by no means the only source, or even the chief source, upon which the framers of the Constitution were able to draw in shaping their ideas of executive power. Locke, Montesquieu, and Blackstone were the common reading of them all, and in the pages of these writers executive power is delineated in no suspicious or grudging terms. Especially illuminating in this connection is Locke's description of "Prerogative" in the Fourteenth Chapter of his famous *Treatise:*[11]

"Where the legislative and executive power [the passage reads] are in distinct hands, as they are in all moderated monarchies and well-framed governments, there the good of the society requires that several things should be left to the discretion of him that has the executive power. For the legislators not being able to foresee and provide by laws for all that may be useful to the community, the executor of the laws, having the power in his hands, has by the common law of Nature a right to make use of it for the good of the society, in many cases where the municipal law has given no direction, till the legislative can conveniently be assembled to provide for it; nay, many things there are which the law can by no means provide for, and those must necessarily be left to the discretion of him that has the executive power in his hands, to be ordered by him as the public good and advantage shall require; nay, it is fit that the laws themselves should in some cases give way to the executive power, or rather to this fundamental law of Nature and government—viz., that as much as may be all the members of the society are to be preserved. . . . "

Designating then "this power to act according to discretion for the public good, without the prescription of the law and sometimes even against it," as "Prerogative," Locke continues:

"This power, whilst employed for the benefit of the community and suitably to the trust and ends of the government, . . . never is questioned. For the people are very seldom or never scrupulous or nice in the point or questioning of prerogative whilst it is in any tolerable degree employed for the use it was meant—that is, the good of the people, and not manifestly against it. . . .

"And therefore he that will look into the history of England will find that prerogative was always largest in the hands of our wisest and best princes, because the people observing the whole tendency of their actions to be the public good, or if any human frailty or mistake (for princes are but men, made as others) appeared in some small declinations from that end; yet it was visible the main of their conduct tended to nothing but the care of the public. The people, therefore, finding reason to be satisfied with these princes, whenever they acted without, or contrary to the letter of the law, acquiesced in what they did, and without the least complaint, let them enlarge their prerogative as they pleased, judging rightly that they did nothing herein to the prejudice of their laws, since they acted conformable to the foundation and end of all laws—the public good. . . . "

Most readers come upon these passages for the first time with considerable astonishment, and wonder how the views which they express are to be harmonized with the doctrine advanced in the same pages that in a free commonwealth the "legislative is not only the supreme power," but is "sacred and unalterable in

the hands where the community have once placed it."[12] The
probability is that Locke himself was quite untroubled by the
inconsistency, first, because he had a special talent for incon-
sistencies; secondly, because this particular inconsistency was not
of his contrivance. For while the Glorious Revolution, which
Locke wrote primarily to justify, had settled it that the King
would be henceforth dependent on Parliament for supplies, it
had at the same time left him an unlimited veto wherewith to
protect his other prerogatives against Parliament. So what Locke
gives us in the final analysis is *not* legislative supremacy really,
but—as his Whig commentators pointed out—"a balanced constitution."

And a "balanced constitution" is also what "the celebrated
Montesquieu" had in mind when, following a hint of Locke's, he
revived Aristotle's doctrine that government comprised three
intrinsically distinct elements,[13] and reshaped it for the uses of
eighteenth-century libertarianism. In a passage which the Framers
of the Constitution regarded as embodying the greatest discovery of "political science" since the time of Adam, he wrote:

"In every government there are three sorts of power: the legislative;
the executive in respect of things dependent on the law of nations; and
the executive in regard to matters that depend on the civil law. . . .

"When the legislative and executive powers are united in the same
person, or in the same body of magistrates, there can be no liberty;
because apprehensions may arise, lest the same monarch or senate
should enact tyrannical laws, and execute them in a tyrannical manner. Again, there is no liberty, if the judiciary power be not separated
from the legislative and executive. Were it joined with the legislative,
the life and liberty of the subject would be exposed to arbitrary control;
for the judge would be then the legislator. Were it joined to the executive power, the judge might behave with violence and oppression.
There would be an end of everything, were the same man or the same

body, whether of the nobles or of the people, to exercise those three powers, that of enacting laws, that of executing the public resolutions, and of trying the causes of individuals."[14]

The doctrine of the Separation of Powers comprises, along with the doctrine of Dual Federalism, one of the two great structural principles of the American constitutional system; and from it certain other ideas follow logically, even though not inevitably: first, that the three functions of government are reciprocally limiting; secondly, that each department should be able to defend its characteristic functions from intrusion by either of the other departments; thirdly, that none of the departments may abdicate its powers to either of the others. The first two of these ideas reënforce executive power, particularly as against the principle of legislative supremacy; the last one operates the other way, and—significantly—it has today almost completely disappeared as a viable principle of American constitutional law.

Lastly, many of the Framers had also read Blackstone, another exponent of the "balanced constitution."[15] In the *Commentaries* Parliament's power is depicted in terms most sweeping:

"It can . . . do everything that is not naturally impossible; and therefore some have not scrupled to call its power, by a figure rather too bold, the omnipotence of Parliament. True it is, that what Parliament doth, no authority upon earth can undo."[16]

Likewise the subordination of the King to the law is constantly insisted upon. That, nevertheless, the law in question comprises a good deal more than acts of Parliament is amply apparent from the description given of the royal prerogative, especially in the joint fields of diplomacy and military command.[17] The passages referred to are given later in this volume.

In a word, the blended picture of executive power which is derivable from the pages of Locke, Montesquieu, and Blackstone is of a broadly discretionary, residual power which is available when other governmental powers fail; which is capable of setting bounds to some indefinite extent even to the supreme legislative power; and which, in defense of these bounds, embraces an absolute veto on legislation. How far did this picture prevail with the Framers?[18]

THE PHILADELPHIA CONVENTION AND *THE FEDERALIST*

In the problem of "a national executive"—the phrase used by the authors of the Virginia Plan—the Philadelphia Convention was faced with a difficult dilemma. The majority of the Framers ardently desired to provide an executive power which should be capable of penetrating to the remotest parts of the Union, not only for the purpose of enforcing the national laws, but also—a lesson from Shays's rebellion—for the purpose of bringing assistance to the states in grave emergencies of domestic disorder. At the same time, most of them recognized that it was absolutely indispensable that the Convention should avoid stirring up the widespread popular fear of monarchy. Nor did the vast size of the country and the difficulties of travel and transportation make the problem any easier of solution. How could a political force be provided which would be sufficient to overcome these natural obstacles and yet be safe—or at least *thought* safe—from the point of view of popular liberty?

Of those who would fain have carried over into the projected national constitution the conception of executive power which predominated in the state constitutions the outstanding representative was Sherman of Connecticut. In the words of Madison's *Notes:*

"Mr. Sherman said he considered the Executive magistracy as nothing more than an institution for carrying the will of the legislature into effect, and that the person or persons ought to be appointed by and accountable to the legislature only, which was the depository of the supreme will of the Society. They were the best judges of the business which ought to be done by the Executive department, and consequently of the number necessary from time to time for doing it. He wished that the number might not be fixed, but that the legislature should be at liberty to appoint one or more as experience might dictate."[19]

Had this conception prevailed the Convention would have anticipated the collegiate executive of the present Swiss Federation.

The leader of the "strong executive" party was James Wilson of Pennsylvania. He "preferred," Madison records, "a single magistrate, as giving most energy, dispatch, and responsibility to the office." He was also for rendering the executive "independent of the legislature," and to this end proposed that he be elected by the people at large and be vested with an absolute negative upon acts of the legislature. "Without such a defense," said he of the latter proposal, "the legislature can at any moment sink it [the executive] into non-existence."[20]

As chairman of the Committee of Detail, Wilson had the opportunity to incorporate his conception of the executive office in the preliminary draft of the Constitution. In Articles VI and X of the committee's report of August 6, the issue between a single and a plural executive was settled in favor of the former alternative; the idea was adopted of assuring the executive his principal powers by definite constitutional grant instead of leaving them contingent upon legislation; and the executive was armed, in protection of the powers thus committed him, with a qualified veto upon all legislation.[21] Not, however, till the close of the Convention was the last of a persistent and constantly renewed series of efforts to load the President with a council finally defeated;[22] and it was also at this late date that he was made a party to the treaty-making power and the power to appoint justices of the

Supreme Court and ambassadors, both of which functions had been at first lodged in the Senate alone.[23]

Lastly, from the Committee of Style, of which Gouverneur Morris, another exponent of strong executive power, was chairman, came the present form of the opening clause of Article II. The corresponding clause from the Committee of Detail had read as follows: "The executive power shall be vested in a single person. His style shall be 'the President of the United States' and his title shall be 'His Excellency'"—phraseology which designates the presidential office, but is less readily interpretable as a grant of power.[24] Curiously enough, the present form of the clause was never separately acted upon by the Convention as a whole.

But the problem of "executive independence" also involved, it was generally conceded, the problem of providing a mode for the President's election which would not bring him under the domination of the legislature, and on no other problem did the Convention expend more time and effort.[25] In the Virginia Plan it was proposed that Congress should elect the executive, and that he, or they, should be ineligible for a second term. The New Jersey Plan likewise provided for election by Congress. Another proposal, which first appeared in Hamilton's Plan, was of indirect election by Electors chosen *ad hoc,* and without stipulation regarding reëligibility. A third suggestion was Wilson's for popular election, and again without restriction as to reëligibility.

When the question first arose in committee of the whole on July 17, popular election received the vote of only Pennsylvania; and shortly afterward choice by Electors was also rejected. Thereupon election by the legislature was voted unanimously, only to be upset two days later in favor of election by Electors, who were to be chosen by the state legislatures. What were the considerations which brought about this *volte-face?* Some of them at least were set forth at the time by Gouverneur Morris in a characteristic speech worth quoting for its own sake.

"It is necessary [said Morris] to take into one view all that relates to the establishment of the executive; on the due formation of which must depend the efficacy and utility of the Union among the present and future States. It has been a maxim in political science that Republican Government is not adapted to a large extent of Country, because the energy of the Executive Magistracy can not reach the extreme parts of it. Our Country is an extensive one. We must either then renounce the blessings of the Union, or provide an Executive with sufficient vigor to pervade every part of it. . . . One great object of the Executive is to control the Legislature. The Legislature will continually seek to aggrandise & perpetuate themselves; and will seize those critical moments produced by war, invasion or convulsion for that purpose. It is necessary then that the Executive Magistrate should be the guardian of the people, even of the lower classes, agst Legislative tyranny, against the Great & the wealthy who in the course of things will necessarily compose the Legislative body. . . . If he is to be the Guardian of the people let him be appointed by the people. If he is to be a check on the Legislature let him not be impeachable. Let him be of short duration, that he may with propriety be re-eligible. . . . He suggested a biennial election of the Executive at the time of electing the 1st. branch, and the Executive to hold over, so as to prevent any interregnum in the Administration. An election by the people at large throughout so great an extent of country could not be influenced, by those little combinations and those momentary lies which often decide popular elections within a narrow sphere. . . . He saw no alternative for making the Executive independent of the Legislature but either to give him his office for life, or make him eligible by the people. . . ."[26]

Five days later (July 24) election by the legislature was voted again, a vote which was adhered to on July 26. And so matters stood till almost the end of the Convention, when the question was handed over to a committee on unfinished business which, with Morris as chairman, recommended the substance of the present method of election. There can be no doubt that the motive which chiefly influenced the Convention to make this important change at the last moment was to secure the President's reëligibility, and apparently his indefinite reëligibility, without at the same time subjecting him to the temptation of courting legislative favor. To be sure, popular election too would have done this; but the electoral method had the additional advantage that it left each state free to determine its own rule of suffrage without sacrificing its due weight in the choice of a President. It was this consideration unquestionably which turned the scale against the more democratic method, albeit it was not the only one.

"The People were liable to deceptions; the people in large areas were too ignorant of the characters of men; elective monarchies were turbulent and unhappy; people would vote for their state candidates; the people would be led by a few active and designing men (and will not be better able to judge than the legislature); 'it were as unnatural to refer the choice of a proper character for chief magistrate to the people, as it would be to refer a trial of colours to a blind man.' "

Electors, on the contrary, would be men of special discernment into the qualities demanded by the office of President; while being both a numerous and a transitory body, their choice would not excite the community in the way that the direct election of "the final object of the public wishes" would.[27]

Suppose election by the houses had been finally adopted, would "the Cabinet System" have resulted, with the President finally settling into the neutral—and largely nugatory—role of the British monarch of today? It seems extremely unlikely. The method by which the President is elected is about the least formidable barrier which the Constitution sets up to the development under it of a system like the British. Nor does the provision that "no person holding any office under the United States shall be a member of either house during his continuance in office"[28] present an insuperable difficulty although it is often cited as doing so. In the face of this provision the President might still constitute a cabinet council out of the chairmen of the principal congressional committees and then put his own powers and those of the heads of departments at the disposal of this council. A more formidable obstacle is the great power of the Senate as compared with the British House of Lords, although the equality of the French legislative chambers has not prevented the rise in that country of a modified cabinet system. Probably the greatest constitutional obstacle to the development of the cabinet system in the National Government consists in the fact that the two houses of Congress are elected for set terms which are different for the two bodies, and the further fact that the President lacks the power of dissolution. The cabinet system pivots upon the substantial agreement at all times of the executive and the legislative branches on important questions of policy, and the Constitution makes it fairly certain that such agreement will at times be lacking.

And the fact is that what the Framers had in mind was not the cabinet system or an approximation to it, but the "balanced constitution" of Locke, Montesquieu, and Blackstone, which carried with it the idea of a *divided initiative in the matter of legislation and a broad range of autonomous executive power or "prerogative."* Sir Henry Maine's dictum, that "the American constitution is the British constitution with the monarchy left out," is therefore, from the point of view of 1789, almost the exact reverse of the truth, for the Presidency was designed in great measure to reproduce the monarchy of George III with the corruption left out, and also of course the hereditary feature. And the opponents of the Constitution glimpsed this likeness to the former "despicable tyrant," albeit they greatly exaggerated in the details with which they occasionally embellished the picture.

As Hamilton wrote in *The Federalist:*

"Here the writers against the Constitution seem to have taken pains to signalize their talent of misrepresentation. Calculating upon the aversion of the people to monarchy, they have endeavored to enlist all their jealousies and misapprehensions in opposition to the intended President of the United States. . . . He has been decorated with attributes superior in dignity and splendor to those of the King of Great Britain. He has been shown to us with the diadem sparkling on his brow and the imperial purple flowing in his train. He has been seated on a throne surrounded with minions and mistresses, giving audience to the envoys of foreign potentates, in all the supercilious pomp of majesty. The images of Asiatic despotism and voluptuousness have scarcely been wanting to crowd the exaggerated scene. We have been taught to tremble at the terrific visages of murdering janizaries and to blush at the unveiled mysteries of a seraglio." [29]

Hamilton endeavored to allay these terrors, real or pretended, by pointing out how much the country had suffered under the Articles of Confederation, as well as under the state constitutions, from lack of adequate executive power. "Energy in the executive," he wrote, "is a leading character in the definition of good government"; and of "the ingredients which constitute energy in the executive" the first is "unity," [30] as it is also of responsibility; and he expressed entire agreement with Delolme's contention that,

" 'the executive power is more easily confined when it is ONE'; that it is far more safe there should be a single object for the jealousy and watchfulness of the people, and, in a word, that all multiplication of the Executive is rather dangerous than friendly to liberty." [31]

For the rest, Hamilton discharged the duties of advocacy by pointing out that if the President was beyond the menaces of Congress, so also was Congress beyond the President's power to corrupt; by emphasizing the participation of the Senate in some of the most important powers of the President, among which he included the removal power in the case of officers appointed with the Senate's consent; by emphasizing Congress's control of the purse; and, lastly, by dwelling upon the mode of election by a temporary body called into existence for the occasion and therefore not under presidential influence.[32] The role of the President as the leader of a national party was still beyond the vaticinations of either Hamilton or the opponents of the Constitution. Indeed, having disposed of corruption, they had, forsooth, forestalled parties!

THE PRESIDENCY FROM WASHINGTON TO THE 2ND ADAMS

Of the three departments of the National Government the Supreme Court, as representing the Judiciary, has been most uniformly successful in establishing its own conception of its authority and functions, the President next, and Congress the least successful. Judicial review has been, in fact, of somewhat minor importance in determining the scope of presidential powers. While the Court has sometimes rebuffed presidential pretensions, it has more often labored to rationalize them; but most of all it has sought on one pretext or other to keep its sickle out of this "dread field." This policy may be owing partly to the fact that the President has "the power of the sword," that is, immediate command of the physical forces of government; partly to the related fact that while the Court can usually assert itself successfully against Congress by merely "disallowing" its acts, presidential exercises of power will generally have produced some change in the external world beyond ordinary judicial competence to efface. Nor should it be overlooked that the same course of reasoning upon which "executive power" as conferred by the opening clause of Article II has thriven is equally favorable to the pretensions of the bearers of "judicial power" under Article III. In supporting "executive power" against Congress the Court is often fighting its own battle for "judicial power."[33]

The two earliest contests over the "executive power" of the President, indeed, were fought anywhere else than in the judicial forum. The first was the debate in 1789 in the first Congress over the location of the power of removal in relation to "executive officers" appointed "by and with the advice and consent of the Senate."[34] The second concerned the validity of the so-called "Proclamation of Neutrality" which President Washington issued in 1793 at the outbreak of war between France and Great Britain.[35] Both episodes are dealt with at some length later on in this volume; here all that is required is reference to the principal issue, which was the same on both occasions, namely, whether the opening clause of Article II was a grant of power or not. In the 1789 controversy Madison said that it was; four years later he took the opposite view, while Hamilton supported the affirmative thesis, and *practically* it was this thesis which prevailed in both instances.

But this confrontation of Hamilton and Madison in 1793 is of importance for a second reason; it signalized the early differentiation of what may be termed the quasi-monarchical and the ultra-Whig conceptions of the Presidency.[36] Under the first two Presidents the former conception prevailed as of course. The Presidency at once furnished what Walter Bagehot would have termed the "dignified element of government" and also directed the legislative process to a notable extent, although without diminishing in the least the spontaneous legislative initiative of the houses themselves; exactly as in contemporary Britain before the younger Pitt, the legislative initiative was divided. The famous Judiciary Act of 1789 was elaborated in the Senate; the acts creating the great executive departments came from the House; Hamilton's financial measures exemplified the legislative leadership of the executive. At the same time the relations of the two departments were featured by considerable ceremony. The President gave his annual "address" in person, and it was answered by formal "addresses" from the two houses, and to each of these was returned in due course an equally formal "reply"—all of which "trappings of monarchy" were incontinently consigned to the trash basket by "the Revolution of 1800."[37]

Jefferson's conception of executive power, on the other hand, was more Whig than that of the British Whigs themselves in subordinating it to "the supreme legislative power." At the time when the presidential election of 1800 was pending in the House, John Marshall predicted that if Jefferson was chosen he would "embody himself in the House of Representatives, and by weakening the office of President" would "increase his personal power. He will ... become the leader of that party which is about to constitute the majority of the legislature."[38] Better political prophecy has rarely been recorded. What we encounter in Jefferson for the first time is a President who is primarily a party leader, only secondarily Chief Executive. The tone of his messages is uniformly deferential to Congress. His first one closes with these words: "Nothing shall be wanting on my part to inform, as far as in my power, the legislative judgment, nor to carry that judgment into faithful execution."[39] His actual guidance of Congress's judgment was none the less constant and unremitting even while often secret and sometimes furtive.[40] The chief instruments of his leadership were the party caucus, which enabled the party membership to present on the floor a united front and over which he himself is alleged to have presided now and then, and his Secretary of the Treasury, Albert Gallatin, whose own influence with Congress also was enormous.[41]

Nor can there be any doubt that, despite its later repercussions upon the Presidency, Jefferson's technique, as administered by himself, was remarkably productive in terms of legislative accomplishment. Comparing in this respect Jefferson's record with Woodrow Wilson's, Dr. Small remarks:

"In according him [Wilson] a primacy in this field of Presidential activity, one ought not to underestimate the significance of Jefferson's achievement. If allowance is made for the fact that, in 1800, the Federal Government was not subjected to any centralizing influence, that, consequently, it legislated upon a smaller number of problems immediately affected with a public interest, and finally, that its legislative machinery was not capable of churning out laws with the rapidity characteristic of the present day, the disparity between the accomplishment of these two Executives is readily explainable; and, when compared on the basis of the success with which they carried out their legislative programs, the leadership of these two Presidents approaches an equality."[42]

What, then, of Marshall's prophecy that Jefferson would weaken the office of President? This, too, was justified by events when the Ulysses bow of party leadership passed to feebler hands. With the practical disappearance of the Federalist party the Republican caucus became "the Congressional Caucus," by which Madison and Monroe were successively put in nomination for the Presidency, while the younger Adams, although not its nominee, was virtually elected by it through the election being thrown into the House. So, for twenty years the plan rejected by the Framers, of having the President chosen by Congress, was substantially in operation. During this period the practice grew up of each succeeding President continuing a considerable part of his predecessor's Cabinet in office; and when he convened them in council the Chief Executive counted the votes of the heads of departments as of equal weight with his own. Hardly more than *primus inter pares* in his own sight, he was glad if Congress accorded him that degree of deference. In short, the Presidency was in commission.[43]

FROM JACKSON'S REVOLUTION TO LINCOLN'S DICTATORSHIP

With Jackson's accession this enfeebling tendency was checked as decisively as it was abruptly. Jackson's Presidency was, in truth, no mere revival of the office—it was a remaking of it. The credit, however, should not go to Jackson alone. He contributed an imperious temper, a military reputation, and a striking personality; and he had the good luck to have an admiring public in the shape of a new and ignorant electorate. But the lasting impact of the Jacksonian Presidency upon American constitutional practice also owed much to the constructive skill of his political lieutenants, and particularly to their invention of the National Nominating Convention. The precise significance of this institution is, to be sure, frequently misapprehended, as when it is said to have made the President "the Elect of the People at Large." Jackson himself did not owe his being "the People's Choice" to the national convention, which was not yet in existence when he became President; nor did the nomination of Mr. Harding by a coterie of bosses in "a smoke-filled room" at two o'clock in the morning, nearly a century later, make him the elect of the people at large in any genuine sense. The national convention is the periodic reminder of the party's unity. It dramatizes and climaxes the procedures by which a party sustains the consciousness of its nationwide character and mission. Its primary business—almost its only business— is to select somebody to carry the party standard in an approaching presidential election. If the person chosen is successful, is elected President, then, ordinarily, he remains party leader throughout his official term, and is able in that capacity to summon the party to the support of his policies, as well as to renominate himself or name his successor as party champion. When Jefferson retired in 1809 his party began at once to dissolve into local or personal followings. That the same thing did not happen on Jackson's retirement was due to the rise of the national convention and the political devices which cluster about it.[44]

And backed by a party organization which reached far beyond the halls of Congress, indeed eventually penetrated the remotest corners of the Union, Jackson became the first President in our history to appeal to the people over the heads of their legislative representatives. At the same time the office itself was thrust forward as one of three *equal* departments of government and to each and every of its powers was imparted new scope, new vitality. The Presidency became tridimensional, and all of the dimensions underwent more or less enlargement. Jackson was a more dominant party leader than Jefferson; his claim to represent the American people as a whole went to the extent of claiming to embody them; his claim to be one of three *equal* departments inferred the further claim that *all* his powers were autonomous, even his purely executive powers.

The classic statement of this tenet of his creed occurs in his famous message of July 10, 1832, vetoing Clay's bill for rechartering the second Bank of the United States. The salient passage of the message reads:

"The Congress, the Executive, and the Court must each for itself be guided by its own opinion of the Constitution. Each public officer who takes an oath to support the Constitution swears that he will support it as he understands it, and not as it is understood by others. It is as much the duty of the House of Representatives, of the Senate, and of the President to decide upon the constitutionality of any bill or resolution which may be presented to them for passage or approval as it is of the supreme judges when it may be brought before them for judicial decision. The opinion of the judges has no more authority over Congress than the opinion of Congress has over the judges, and on that point the President is independent of both. The authority of the Supreme Court must not, therefore, be permitted to control the Congress or the Executive when acting in their legislative capacities, but to have only such influence as the force of their reasoning may deserve."[45]

The Supreme Court's ratification of this doctrine so far as it bears on the President's duty to the law is dealt with on a later page.

The logical implications of Jackson's position were not exaggerated by his Whig critics, although its practical effects were. "I look upon Jackson," Kent wrote Story early in 1834, "as a detestable, ignorant, reckless, vain and malignant tyrant. . . . This American elective monarchy frightens me. The experiment, ✓ with its foundations laid on universal suffrage and our unfettered press, is of too violent a nature for our excitable people." "The President," thundered Webster in the Senate, "carries on the government; all the rest are sub-contractors. . . . A Briareus sits in the centre of our system, and with his hundred hands touches everything, controls everything." "We are in the midst of a revolution," lamented Clay, "hitherto bloodless, but tending rapidly towards a total change of the pure republican character of the Government, and to the concentration of all power in the hands of one man."[46]

Indeed, the Framers of the Constitution themselves did not escape censure for their responsibility for this state of things, as we discover when we turn to Abel Upshur's essay on *Federal Government,* which appeared in 1840. Dealing with the Presidency, Upshur wrote:

"The most defective part of the Constitution beyond all question, is that which relates to the Executive Department. It is impossible to read that instrument, without being struck with the loose and unguarded terms in which the powers and duties of the President are pointed out. So far as the legislature is concerned, the limitations of the Constitution, are, perhaps, as precise and strict as they could safely have been made; but in regard to the Executive, the Convention appears to have studiously selected such loose and general expressions, as would enable the President, by implication and construction either to neglect his duties or to enlarge his powers. We have heard it gravely asserted in Congress that whatever power is neither legislative nor judiciary, is of course executive, and, as such, belongs to the President under the Constitution. . . ."[47]

And eight years later so sober and generally well balanced a person as Reverdy Johnson of Maryland spoke in the Senate "of the overshadowing influence of power of a President," and added:

"So great a latitude of construction has not of late prevailed in relation to the power of the other departments as to the power of the President. If he adheres to the letter of the Constitution, he is to be sustained, whatever departure there might be from the spirit of the instrument, while charges of usurpation of power are constantly made against Congress. . . . It may yet be that a diadem may sparkle on the brow of an American President."[48]

This same year, 1848, the Swiss people framed a new constitution; but although imitating our national Constitution in several other respects, they steered clear of the Presidency because they felt it to be favorable to dictatorship.

Actually, prior to the Civil War, the menace was more apparent than real. For this there were several reasons. In the first place, while magnifying the powers of the Presidency, Jackson subscribed to the States' Rights doctrine of strict construction of Congress's powers. His legislative role consequently was chiefly negative, being confined for the most part to a vigorous use of the veto power.[49] In the second place, even though it had been otherwise, the further development in the houses since Jefferson's day of the committee system interposed obstacles in the way of presidential participation in legislation which had not existed at first. But the circumstance which contributed most to the temporary declension of the Jacksonian Presidency was the emergence after 1846 of the issue of slavery in the territories. For the handling of this highly charged question by the devices of negotiation and compromise, Congress, and especially the Senate, offered a far better theater than the Presidency. So the forces making for compromise systematically depressed the Presidency by taking care that only secondary and manageable personalities should be elevated to it. From the close of the Mexican War to 1861 the Presidency was in the doldrums, definitely.[50]

The last important contribution to the theory of the Presidency until recent decades was Lincoln's, whose ultimate conception of the office was as much an expression of temperament as was Jackson's. A solitary genius who valued the opportunity for reflection above that for counsel, Lincoln came to regard Congress as a more or less necessary nuisance and the Cabinet as a usually unnecessary one.[51] Nor could it have escaped Lincoln's intuition—especially after Buchanan's Message of December 3, 1860[52]—that, if the Union was to be saved, recourse must be had to some still untested source of national power, one which had not become entangled, as had Congress's, in the strangulating sophistries of States Rights. So, for a double reason, Lincoln turned to the "Commander-in-Chief" clause, from which, read in conjunction with the "executive power" clause, he drew the conclusion that "the war power" was his.[53] Originally, it is true, he appears to have assumed that his power was a simple emergency power whose *ad interim* decisions Congress must ratify if they were to be permanently valid. But, as the problems of Emancipation and then of Reconstruction loomed, he shifted ground, and his final position was, as Professor Randall phrases it, "that as President he had extraordinary legal resources which Congress lacked."[54] The practical fruitage of this theory is treated at length in a later chapter.

But, while Lincoln's invocation of "the war power" added a new dimension to the Presidency in the presence of national emergency, his incumbency was in certain other respects a calamity for the office. A frontiersman, his conceptions of the requirements of sound administration were no less naïve than Jackson's, whose record as a spoilsman he far surpassed;[55] while except for an ineffectual endeavor to interest Congress in the subject of compensated emancipation, he left the task of procuring necessary legislation to his Cabinet secretaries, and especially to Chase and Stanton, theirs being the departments most concerned.[56] The outcome in the latter case was the creation of a direct relationship between the War Department and the congressional Committee on the Conduct of the War which under Johnson brought the Presidency to the verge of disaster.

Indeed, the schism between the President and Congress which nearly cost Johnson his official life was well under way before Johnson became President. The subject of controversy was the right to determine the conditions on which the seceding states should be restored to their normal position in the Union. Lincoln professed to regard "the war power," supplemented by the pardoning power, as the constitutionally designated agency for this important task, while the Republican leadership in Congress proclaimed the paramountcy of the national legislative power, their reliance being on the guarantee by "the United States," in Article IV, section 4, of "a republican form of government" to the states.[57] The President's duty, Lincoln was warned in the Wade-Davis Manifesto of August 5, 1864, was "to obey and execute, not to make the laws ... to suppress by arms armed rebellion and leave political organization to Congress";[58] and two years later the same warning was addressed to Johnson by Thaddeus Stevens in still stronger terms:

"He [the President] is the servant of the people as they shall speak through Congress. . . . Andrew Johnson must learn that he is your servant and that as Congress shall order he must obey. There is no escape from it. God forbid that he should have one tittle of power except what he derives through Congress and the Constitution."[59]

Johnson spurned the admonition. An obstinate, ill-educated man, he took his constitutional beliefs with fearful seriousness, and points which his predecessor would have yielded with little compunction for a workable plan, he defended as if they had been transmitted to him from Sinai. First and last, no President has ever quite approached Johnson in the exorbitance of his pretensions for the office or in his inability to make them good. He is the Boniface VIII of the Presidency.

Final appraisement of Johnson's incumbency for the theory of the Presidency is, nevertheless, not easy. Johnson escaped dismissal from office by the High Court of Impeachment by a single vote, but he *escaped!* What is more, it was during his administration that the Supreme Court confessed its inability, in *Mississippi v. Johnson,*[60] to enjoin a President from exceeding his constitutional powers or to order him to perform his constitutional duties. The principle that Marshall had stated as applicable to the President's "important political powers," that "in their exercise he is to use his own discretion, and is accountable only to his country in his political character, and to his own conscience," was thus extended even to the President's duty to enforce the law. Furthermore, whatever of popular glamour the office had lost under Johnson was promptly restored to it when "the man from Appomattox and its famous apple tree" became President.

Reflecting upon all which, Henry C. Lockwood, in his *The Abolition of the Presidency,* which appeared in 1884, advanced the thesis that only by replacing the President with an executive council after the Swiss model could American liberty be preserved. He wrote:

"The tendency of all people is to elevate a single person to the position of ruler. The idea is simple. It appeals to all orders of intellects. It can be understood by all. Around this centre all nationality and patriotism are grouped. A nation comes to know the characteristics and nature of an individual. It learns to believe in the man. Certain contingencies are likely to take place. It does not require a great amount of political knowledge to form an opinion as to the course of their favorite statesman, whose character they have studied. Under these circumstances, let a person be chosen to an office, with power conferred upon it equal to that of the Presidency of the United States, and it will make but little difference whether the law actually gives him the right to act in a particular direction or not. He determines a policy. He acts. No argument that the law has been violated will avail. He is the chief officer of the nation. He stands alone. He is a separate power in himself. The lines with which we attempt to mark the limits of his power are shadowy and ill-defined. A party, real or imaginary, stands back of him demanding action. In either event, the President acts. The sentiment of hero worship, which to a great extent prevails among the American people, will endorse him. Under our form of government, we do not think so much of what Congress may do. A great multitude declared: 'Give us President Grant! We know him. He is strong! He will rule!'"[61]

These words are still as true and as pertinent as the day they were written; but fortunately they are not the whole truth, or Mr. Lockwood's gloomy prognostications would have been realized long ago.

Recent accessions to the theory of the Presidency are dealt with at appropriate points later in this volume. They embrace: (1) The first Roosevelt's effort, by means of his "Stewardship Theory," to incorporate Locke's notion of prerogative in the constitutional grant of "executive power"; (2) The revival under Cleveland, Wilson, and the two Roosevelts of presidential leadership in legislation; and (3) a vast extension of the President's law-enforcing powers through delegations of power by Congress. Of this last development, however, the President has been by no means the sole beneficiary, for much of this legislatively delegated discretion, what has come to be termed "administrative power," has gone to the so-called "independent commissions" and similar bodies; and hence the issue has been raised within recent years whether the unity of the "executive power" is not being undermined. We shall return to this question in a later chapter.

Taken by and large, the history of the Presidency is a history of aggrandizement, but the story is a highly discontinuous one. Of the thirty-one individuals who have filled the office only about one in three has contributed to the development of its powers;[62] under other incumbents things have either stood still or gone backward. That is to say, what the Presidency is at any particular moment depends in important measure upon who is President. Yet the accumulated tradition of the office is also of great importance. Precedents established by a forceful or politically successful personality in the office are available to less gifted successors, and permanently so because of the difficulty with which the Constitution is amended. Hence the rise and spread from the Jacksonian period onward of the doctrine of popular sovereignty operated very differently upon the Presidency than it did upon the governorship in the states. In the case of the latter there was for years a progressive splitting up of the executive power, accompanied by the transference of its component parts to elective officials over whose tenure and conduct the governor had no control. In the National Government, on the contrary, the dogma of popular sovereignty had to adapt itself to the comparative rigidity of the national Constitution, and this it did by exalting and consolidating the power of the one national official who is—in a sense— elective by the people as a whole. The claim set up by Jackson to be the "People's Choice" has been reiterated, in effect, by his successors many times, and with decisive results for the presidential office.[63]

CHAPTER II

QUALIFICATIONS, ELECTION, TENURE

THE one hundred and fiftieth anniversary of the Constitution naturally evoked many encomiums of it. Especially was Gladstone's famous eulogy of the document of 1787 as the "most wonderful work ever struck off at a given time by the brain and purpose of man" repeated many times. The provisions of the Constitution which are to be considered in this chapter would certainly blush if they had ears to hear such words, and a proper moral sensibility. For this portion of the Framers' work the only thing to be said is that it represented their conscientious belief that they had done the best they could in the circumstances. To it applies emphatically the astringent estimate voiced by Gladstone's contemporary Bagehot of the entire instrument: "The men of Massachusetts could work any Constitution."

WHO MAY BE PRESIDENT—THE BAN ON THIRD TERMS

Paragraph 5 of the first section of Article II of the Constitution reads as follows:

"No person except a natural-born citizen, or a citizen of the United States at the time of the adoption of this Constitution, shall be eligible to the office of President; neither shall any person be eligible to that office who shall not have attained to the age of thirty-five years, and been fourteen years a resident within the United States."

Do the qualifications here stipulated need to be possessed at the time of a person's being chosen President, or is it sufficient if he possesses them at the time of entering upon the office? Etymologically "eligible" means *choosable*; but state courts, in inter-

---

preting analogous provisions of the state constitutions,[1] have often defined the word as meaning *qualified,* and following this reading of it the provision just quoted is satisfied when a President-elect possesses the qualifications stipulated for at the time of taking office.

"A citizen of the United States at the time of the adoption of this Constitution." It has been conjectured that it was the purpose of this clause to render Wilson, Hamilton, Robert Morris, and a few others, who had been born abroad, eligible to the Presidency. Indeed, Wilson, a member of the Committee of Detail, seems to have felt strongly the need of such a clause in his own behalf. But the fact is that nobody old enough to become President in 1787, or for a long time afterward, was a "natural-born citizen of the United States"; all, like the men just mentioned, had been *born* British subjects, and had become American citizens in consequence of the casting off of allegiance to the British monarch by the Declaration of Independence. The clause may, therefore, have been inserted with that entire generation of Americans in mind, and not merely a few individuals thereof.[2]

But who are "natural-born citizens"? By the so-called *jus soli,* which comes from the common law, the term is confined to persons born on the *soil* of a country; and this rule is recognized by the opening clause of the Fourteenth Amendment, which declares to be citizens of the United States "all persons born or naturalized within the United States and subject to the jurisdiction thereof." On the other hand, by the so-called *jus sanguinis,* which underlay early Germanic law and today prevails on the continent of Europe, nationality is based on *parentage,* a principle which was recognized by the first Congress under the Constitution in the following words:

"The children of citizens of the United States that may be born beyond sea, or outside the limits of the United States, shall be considered as natural-born citizens of the United States; provided that the right of citizenship shall not descend to persons whose fathers have never been resident in the United States."[3]

And the general sense of this provision has been continued in force to this day by succeeding legislation.[4] The question arises, whence did Congress obtain the power to enact such a measure? By the Constitution Congress is authorized to pass "an uniform rule of naturalization,"[5] that is, a uniform rule whereby *aliens* may be admitted to citizenship; while the provision under discussion purports to recognize a certain category of persons as citizens from and because of *birth*. Probably the provision is to be referred to the fact that Congress is the legislature of a nation which is sovereign at international law, and hence possesses the right of any sovereign nation in determining who shall be members of its body politic and who not.[6]

At any rate, should the American people ever choose for President a person born abroad of American parents, it is highly improbable that any other constitutional agency would venture to challenge their decision—a belief which is supported by the fact that Mr. Hoover's title to the Presidency was not so challenged although he had not been fourteen years a resident of the United States immediately preceding his assumption of office.[7]

Lastly, the question arises whether the above stipulated qualifications might be added to by act of Congress. The mere fact that the subject is one dealt with by the Constitution is not necessarily conclusive. For example, as I point out below, Congress at an early date passed legislation to supplement the provision made by the Constitution itself for the case of the Presidency falling vacant.

Certainly, it would not be safe to assert dogmatically that anybody who possesses the constitutional qualifications of a President is under all circumstances qualified to be President in the contemplation of the Constitution. Thus a number of sections of the national Criminal Code contain the provision that any one who is convicted under them shall, in addition to other penalties, "be incapable of holding office under the United States." One convicted of treason finds himself in this situation; also one convicted of inciting rebellion or insurrection against the United States; also any officer of the United States convicted of taking a bribe; and so on.[8] Would it be questioned that such provisions are capable of excluding an otherwise qualified person from the Presidency?

Quite different is the question which arose in 1920 when the Socialist party nominated Mr. Debs, while he was residing in a federal penitentiary for violating the Espionage Act. As his supporters pointed out, this act did not contain the disqualifying clause among its penalties, from which it was a fair deduction that Mr. Debs was still in full possession of his civil rights, including eligibility to the Presidency. To be sure, his place of abode would not have been the most convenient one from which to administer the presidential office; but the situation would not have been irremediable, for once Mr. Debs had taken office, he would have possessed the pardoning power, and I see no reason why he should not have exercised it in his own behalf, supposing his predecessor had lacked the magnanimity to spare him this embarrassment.

The term of four years during which the President "shall hold office" was, prior to the adoption of the Twentieth Amendment, reckoned from March 4 of the alternate odd years beginning with 1789. This came about from the circumstance that under the Act of September 13, 1788, of "the Old Congress," "the first Wednesday in March," which was March 4, 1789, was fixed as the time "for commencing proceedings under the said Constitution." Although as a matter of fact Washington was not inaugurated until April 30 of that year, by an act approved March 1, 1792, it was provided that the presidential term should be reckoned from "the fourth day of March next succeeding" the date of election. And so things stood until the adoption of the Twentieth Amendment by which the terms of the President and Vice-President end at noon on the 20th of January.

As was pointed out in the preceding chapter, the prevailing sentiment of the Convention of 1787 favored the indefinite reëligibility of the President, a sentiment which was owing in considerable part to the universal expectation that Washington would be the first person to be chosen President, and that he would live practically forever. The custom which limits any individual's tenure of the presidential office to two terms was initiated by Washington himself, although purely on grounds of personal preference and without seeming thought of creating a precedent; but that did not prevent Jefferson, when making public his own decision in 1807 to withdraw at the end of his second term, from stressing Washington's example. Indefinite reëligibility, Jefferson argued, would so undermine the elective system that, while the office would remain "nominally elective," it would "in fact be for life" and "degenerate into an inheritance." Considering how universal monarchy was at that date—to say nothing of the common law concept of property in office which had just received countenance from the Supreme Court's decision in *Marbury v. Madison*—the argument possessed contemporaneously a good deal of force, and would have doubtless possessed more if either Washington or Jefferson had had a son.[9]

Sanctioned by the examples of Washington, Jefferson, Madison, Monroe, and Jackson, the "no-third-term" tradition had become by the Civil War a generally accepted tenet of the American constitutional credo. Indeed, Jackson while President had called repeatedly for a constitutional amendment which should render the President directly elective for a single term of four or six years. Although his crusade failed of its immediate purpose, yet fol-

lowing his retirement no other President was reëlected till 1864—
the ban on third terms had become in effect one on second terms
as well.

The "no-third-term" taboo was first definitely challenged in
1876, when a coterie of Republican politicians broached the idea
of running President Grant again. The popular reaction was
strongly adverse; and when four years later a similar movement
was launched, Grant being now in retirement, its sponsors professed the greatest deference to the principle but contended that it
applied only to a third consecutive term.

Within recent years the scope of the tradition has become
involved in uncertainty repeatedly, and this circumstance has
undoubtedly contributed to loosening its hold on popular regard.
The prestige of the tradition was never higher than when the first
Roosevelt, following his election in 1904, construed it as covering
the term which he was then completing in consequence of Mc-
Kinley's assassination and death in September 1901. "The wise
custom," he said, "which limits the President to two terms regards
the substance and not the form." "Under no circumstances will I
be a candidate for or accept another nomination." And, when later
a strong "third-term" movement developed in his behalf, he
declared himself to be still of the same determination. All of
which, however, did not hinder his running for President in 1912,
and justifying himself for doing so by the argument that if at
some time he had declined "a third cup of coffee" nobody would
suppose that he had meant never to take another cup. Nor, apparently, would Mr. Wilson have been averse, had health permitted, to seeking a third term in 1920,[10] a course which would
have been in harmony with his conception of the Presidency as
the American equivalent of the British premiership.[11]

Roosevelt's succession to McKinley was matched in August

1922 by Coolidge's succession to Harding; but there was the difference that the segment of term which remained to Mr. Coolidge was considerably less than that which had fallen to his predecessor. The question was thus sharply provoked, when is a President to be regarded as having had a "term" in the sense of the custom which condemns a third term for the same individual? Does a third "term" mean a third period of full four years, or a third time? This question Mr. Coolidge coyly side-stepped by not choosing "to run for President in 1928." Whether he would choose to run at some other date was a question left open, as was also the question whether he might not *be* run even in 1928 without his choosing to. At least we have Mr. "Ike" Hoover's word for it that those who indicated to Mr. Coolidge an opinion that his statement was really no obstacle to his being "drafted" in 1928 were generally invited to the White House again while those who took the other view were apt not to be.[12] That Mr. Coolidge, had he chosen to run, would have been reëlected, seems highly probable.

Meantime, the doctrine that a President shall have no more than two terms has produced the inverse doctrine that he is entitled to a renomination at the hands of his party. This, to be sure, is less the consequence of the taboo upon a third term than of the position of the President as party leader. If a President in power is a failure, then the party which is responsible for having put him there is a failure too, and for it to refuse him a nomination is to confess both failures. Nor is a President on completing his second term forbidden by the tradition to name his successor. Jefferson did this, so did Madison with Jefferson's assistance, so did Jackson, so did the first Roosevelt, and so might Woodrow Wilson have done in 1920 had he desired.

Today, it being at long last settled that President Roosevelt will seek a third term, the country is confronted with the question whether it wishes to part with the tradition in its most unambiguous form which forbids a third consecutive, elective term for a President in office. What are the merits of this question? To begin with, it is argued that the people are nowadays cold toward the tradition, and in this connection it is pointed out that of all the proposals which have been brought forward in Congress within the last fifty years—a hundred or more in number—to limit the presidential term, not one has ever reached first base.[13] However, it is just possible that this outcome is to be explained not by popular indifference toward the tradition, but by popular reliance on it —why amend the Constitution when custom has already done the job satisfactorily? Again, it is contended that eight years may be too short a time to permit a President to establish a needed program. This, obviously, is but the "indispensable man" argument, to accept which, some one has wittily said, is next door to despairing of the country. Yet the rejoinder cannot be conceded for all circumstances, for it is also obvious that political talent is not at all times equally plentiful, nor necessarily most plentiful just when there is most need for it. Still, the failure of a President to develop talent capable of carrying on should not ordinarily be a reason for continuing him in office; for that is the business of an executive, of its very essence. And an untried President may be better than a tired one; a fresh approach better than a settled one.

In this matter, as in most others of such scope, it is impossible to adjudicate at all nicely between the contending arguments, inasmuch as the values which they oppose to one another are frequently incommensurate. One thing is nevertheless fairly certain: if the anti-third-term taboo is once set aside, it will take a long time for an anti-fourth-term or anti-fifth-term taboo to develop. In a word, the presidential term will become indefinite —just what in 1787 it was expected to be![14]

THE ELECTORAL COLLEGE—DANGEROUS BREAKDOWNS

The so-called "Electoral College"—actually a congeries of "colleges"—is provided for in the Constitution in the following terms:

"Each State shall appoint, in such manner as the legislature thereof may direct, a number of electors, equal to the whole number of Senators and Representatives to which the State may be entitled in the Congress; but no Senator or Representative, or person holding an office of trust or profit under the United States, shall be appointed an elector."[15]

The power to determine the manner in which the Electors from any state shall be chosen is thus delegated to the legislature thereof for its exclusive determination, and the most diverse methods have been at various times resorted to. The history of practice in this matter is extensively reviewed in the Court's opinion in *McPherson v. Blacker,* decided in 1892.[16] In summary, the Court says, Electors have been chosen

"by the legislature itself on joint ballot; by the legislature through a concurrent vote of the two houses; by vote of the people for a general ticket; by vote of the people in districts; by choice partly by the people voting in districts and partly by the legislature; by choice by the legislature; by choice by the legislature from candidates voted for by the people in districts; and in other ways, as, notably, by North Carolina in 1792, and Tennessee in 1796 and 1800."[17]

Lot, it is true, seems not to have been resorted to so far, although this method of choosing Electors from Congress itself was actually proposed in the Philadelphia Convention.[18] Nor has any state legislature as yet delegated to a President the right to cast the state's vote for his successor.

In the first three presidential elections choice by the legislature itself was the usual method. In the election of 1824, when the choice fell eventually to the House, Electors were chosen by popular vote, either by districts or by general ticket in all but six states; and from 1832 till the Civil War they were chosen by popular vote and by *general ticket* in all states except South Carolina, where the legislature still chose. Since the Civil War there have been but two departures from the general ticket system. In 1876 in Colorado, which had been recently admitted into the Union, choice was by the legislature; and in 1892 Michigan, whose legislature was then in the hands of the Democrats, who however had no hope of retaining their hold on the state as an entirety in the approaching presidential election, choice was by districts, some of which went Democratic.[19] And there have been cases in which individual Electors have, on account of personal popularity, been chosen by the minority party.

It was the belief of the Framers of the Constitution that the Electors would exercise their individual judgments in the choice of a President, a belief which the universal understanding that Washington would be the first President, and probably for an indefinite number of terms, went to sustain. But the requirement that the Electors meet "in their respective states," which reflected the poor condition of travel in those days, destroyed the possibility of a deliberative body from the outset; and with the first avowed appearance of party organizations on a national scale, in consequence of Washington's announcement in 1796 that he would not stand for a third term, the Electors became promptly transmuted into party dummies, a character they have retained ever since. Probably the last independent Elector was William Plumer, Sr., whose vote for John Quincy Adams in 1821 prevented Monroe's unanimous reëlection. It has been customary to explain this apparently eccentric conduct of the New Hampshire Elector as arising from his unwillingness to see Monroe honored as only the great Washington had ever been thus far. But Plumer himself asserted at the time that it was his desire to bring the younger Adams to the notice of the country, which he did to such good purpose that four years later Adams became Monroe's successor.[20]

A half century later occurred the disputed election of 1876, and James Russell Lowell, who had been chosen by the Republicans as an Elector from Massachusetts, was besought to save the country from threatened civil war by casting his vote for Tilden. Lowell refused on the ground that he had been elected not as an individual but solely as a party representative.

"I was nominated [said he] and elected by my fellow-citizens of the Republican party to give effect to their political wishes as expressed at the polls, and not to express my own personal views. I am a delegate carrying a definite message, a trustee to carry out definite instructions; I am not a free agent to act upon my own volition; in accepting a place on the Republican ticket I accepted all its limitations and moral obligations. . . . My individual sympathies and preferences are beside the matter; to refuse to comply with the mandate I received when I accepted my party's nomination would be treacherous, dishonorable, and immoral."[21]

Indeed, it was a former President's considered opinion that "an Elector who failed to vote for the nominee of his party would be the object of execration, and in times of very high excitement might be the subject of a lynching."[22] That, on the other hand, the Electors retain their discretion as against any outside *legal* control would seem to be unquestionable; and any attempt on the part either of a state or of Congress to confine their choice of a President to persons put in nomination in a specified manner would therefore be invalid.

But, although composed of political automata, the intervention of the Electoral College in the choice of a President remains a matter of importance—at times, of decisive importance. Because of the state-wide ticket system, each state's representation in the College is ordinarily a party unit; yet because of the intervention of the College the plurality by which it is chosen is, however large or small, operative only within the state's boundaries. The result is that the discrepancy between the size of a candidate's vote in the Electoral College and that of his so-called "popular vote" is often enormous; and particularly is this apt to be so when more than two considerable parties take the field. Thus in 1860 Lincoln and Hamlin received 180 of the 303 electoral votes, but only about two fifths of the total popular vote; and in 1912 Mr. Wilson, while receiving 435 of the 531 electoral votes, was the choice of but few more than six million of the sixteen million voters voting; and in both cases the discrepancy might conceivably have been increased, for many thousands of the votes cast for Lincoln in 1860 and for Wilson in 1912 were cast in states which went for their opponents, and so did not contribute to the choice of members of the Electoral College. Nor should it be overlooked that every state has two Electors who correspond to its representation in the Senate and so are assigned to it without reference to popular voting strength.[23]

The manner in which the Electors originally exercised their function is described in paragraph 3 of section 1 of Article II.[24] The failure of the Electors, however, under this method to distinguish their choice for Vice-President from that of President having produced a tie in the election of 1800 between Jefferson and Burr, this part of the Constitution was presently superseded by Amendment XII, which reads as follows:

"The Electors shall meet in their respective States, and vote by ballot for President and Vice-President, one of whom at least shall not be an inhabitant of the same State with themselves; they shall name in their ballots the person voted for as President, and in distinct ballots the person voted for as Vice-President and they shall make distinct lists of all persons voted for as President, and of all persons voted for as Vice-President, and of the number of votes for each, which lists they shall sign and certify, and transmit sealed to the seat of the government of the United States, directed to the President of the Senate; the President of the Senate shall, in the presence of the Senate and House of Representatives, open all the certificates and the votes shall then be counted; the person having the greatest number of votes for President shall be the President, if such number be a majority of the whole number of Electors appointed; and if no person have such majority, then from the persons having the highest numbers not exceeding three on the list of those voted for as President, the House of Representatives shall choose immediately, by ballot, the President. But in choosing the President, the votes shall be taken by States, the representation from each State having one vote; a quorum for this purpose shall consist of a member or members from two-thirds of the States, and a majority of all the States shall be necessary to a choice. And if the House of Representatives shall not choose a President whenever the right of choice shall devolve upon them, before the fourth day of March next following, then the Vice-President shall act as President, as in the case of the death or other constitutional disability of the President.

"The person having the greatest number of votes as Vice-President shall be the Vice-President, if such number be a majority of the whole number of Electors appointed; and if no person have a majority, then, from the two highest numbers on the list the Senate shall choose the Vice-President; a quorum for the purpose shall consist of two-thirds of the whole number of Senators, and a majority of the whole number shall be necessary to a choice. But no person constitutionally ineligible to the office of President shall be eligible to that of Vice-President of the United States."

But the Twelfth Amendment was itself far from settling all dangerous questions. Thus, who was to count the electoral vote; what powers did this function carry with it; and when was an

Elector to be considered as definitely "appointed"? All these questions were involved in the famous Hayes-Tilden election dispute of 1876.[25]

It was conceded by everybody that Mr. Hayes had 165 votes in the Electoral College and that Mr. Tilden had 184 votes, or one vote less than a majority of the College and so of the number necessary for a choice. The House at this time was in the control of the Democrats, the Senate of the Republicans. Although the latter set up the claim that the counting was to be done by the President of the Senate, that functionary discreetly declined to assume a power which none of his predecessors in office had ventured to assert. Custom at least had settled that the counting was to be done by the houses, and by the houses as separate entities and not as composing one joint assembly.[26] Furthermore, under the so-called "Twenty-second Joint Rule," which had been followed in the counting of the electoral vote since 1864, the consent of both houses was necessary to count the vote of any state. That is to say, under this rule either house was in a position to exclude the electoral vote of any state from being taken into account in determining "the whole number of Electors appointed." In the existing situation the rule was obviously favorable to the Democrats; but, not having been reënacted by the houses in 1876, it was binding only by acquiescence, and the Republicans, although they were the original authors of the rule, naturally refused acquiescence.

The really vital question in 1876, however, concerned the scope of the power of the houses in *counting* the vote in relation to power of the states to *appoint* Electors. By one theory the two powers were exclusive and coterminous, and the function of the houses was the purely ministerial one of counting the votes of persons who were formally authenticated to them as Electors of a state by the state's election officials. By the other theory the func-

tion of the houses overlapped that of the state in some measure,
and involved the right on their part to enter into the question
whether the appointment of the Electors of a state was tainted
with fraud or violence. Again we note a curious reversal of constitutional creeds in the respective attitudes of the two parties.
Controlling as they did the election boards of the states involved,
the Republicans were all for States Rights in this matter, while
the Democrats took the diametrically opposed position.

The dispute was eventually put in the way of settlement by
what is undoubtedly the most extraordinary measure in American legislative history. The two houses being hopelessly at logger-
heads in the matter of counting the electoral vote, Congress, by an
act approved by the President January 29, 1877, created an Electoral Commission, to which, in practical effect, it delegated the
power of the houses, as well as power to determine what that
power was.[27]

As constituted under the act the Electoral Commission con-
sisted of five members of the House chosen thereby; five Senators
chosen by the Senate; and five Justices of the Supreme Court, four
of whom were designated in the act itself by reference to their
circuits, while the fifth was to be chosen by these four. The House
contingent comprised, naturally, three Democrats and two Republicans; the Senate contingent comprised three Republicans
and two Democrats; while the four Justices designated by the act
were divided equally as to earlier party affiliations. The fifth Justice would therefore presumably be the pivotal member of the
commission; and it was originally supposed that this post would
be filled by Justice David Davis from Illinois, whose political
record was sufficiently ambiguous to suggest a fair possibility of
impartiality, or at least the appearance of it. Justice Davis, however, "loved his ease" and was little disposed to assume so arduous
a role. When, accordingly, the Democrats of the Illinois legisla-

ture, with singular maladroitness from the point of view of party advantage, elected him to a seat in the Senate, he quickly resigned his justiceship and took the proffered post. Thereupon, the judicial members turned to Justice Joseph P. Bradley of New Jersey as the remaining member of the Bench most likely to pursue an unbiased course. In fact Bradley, a Republican, voted with his party throughout on all crucial issues before the commission, though this is not to say that partisan bias was the only consideration determining his decision. The line of reasoning which Justice Bradley developed in his opinions was, save in one instance, consistently adhered to, and was furthermore supported by a practical consideration of the greatest weight. What the Democrats had wanted the houses, and now the commission, to do was to institute an inquiry into the circumstances surrounding the choice of Electors in Florida, South Carolina, and Louisiana. To have done so would have been to postpone any possibility of electing a President far beyond March 4.

Bradley's attitude on the crucial issue before the commission is given in the following passage from his opinion on the reception of the Louisiana vote as attested by the board of canvassers of that state:

"I cannot bring my mind to believe that fraud and misconduct on the part of the State authorities, constituted for the very purpose of declaring the final will of the State, is a subject over which the two Houses of Congress have jurisdiction to institute an examination. The question is not whether frauds ought to be tolerated, or whether they ought not to be circumvented; but whether the Houses of Congress, in exercising their power of counting the electoral votes, are entrusted by the Constitution with authority to investigate them. . . . Evidently no such proceeding was in the minds of the framers of the Constitution. The short and explicit directions there given, that the votes should first be produced before the Houses when met for that purpose, and that 'the votes shall then be counted,' is at variance with any such idea. An investigation beforehand is not authorized and was not contemplated, and would be repugnant to the limited and special power given. What jurisdiction have the Houses on the subject until they have met under the Constitution, except to provide by law for facilitating the performance of their duties? An investigation afterwards, such as the question raised might and frequently would lead to, would be utterly incompatible with the performance of the duty imposed."[28]

In short, the houses, and hence the commission, were unauthorized to go behind the returns as authenticated by the state election officials. In a later paragraph Bradley added, nevertheless: "Whether the legislative power of the government might not, by law, make provision for an investigation into frauds and illegalities, I do not undertake to decide. It cannot be done, in my judgment, by any agency of the Federal Government without legislative regulation."[29]

And thus were nineteen of the disputed electoral votes disposed of. The twentieth was that of an Oregon Elector. That the three Republican Electors of that state had received a majority of the votes cast was not questioned. But one of them, named Watts, had unfortunately at the time of his appointment held "an office of trust and profit under the United States," to wit, that of postmaster. Having resigned his postmastership, however, he had been promptly rechosen by the two remaining Republican Electors under a provision of the Oregon law for the filling of "vacancies" in the post of Elector. But had there been a vacancy? The highest Democratic Elector, one Cronin, claimed not, his contention being that he was the third Elector. Furthermore, Cronin had been able to convince the secretary of state and the governor of the correctness of his view, and they had issued him a certificate of election. Notwithstanding their previous emphasis upon the sanctity of the election certificate, the Republican members of the commission rejected Cronin and recognized Watts.

The act establishing the Electoral Commission contained a proviso reserving any right existing under the Constitution to question before the national courts the titles of the persons who should be declared elected President and Vice-President. Despite the intensity of feeling which the contest had produced no action of the sort was brought, although Justice Field expressed the hope that one would be.[30]

By the Act of February 3, 1887, passed to prevent a recurrence of the episode of 1876 but not until eleven years later, it is provided that if a contest arises in any state over the appointment of any of its Electors, the state itself is authorized to determine such contest, provided it does so at least six days before the time for the meeting of the Electors; and all determinations of such contests made pursuant to state law shall be "conclusive, and shall govern the counting of the electoral votes as provided in the Constitution" when duly certified to the houses by the executive of the state under the seal thereof. But if a state neglects to provide machinery for this purpose, in other words, fails to comply with the act, then the electoral vote of such state is not to be received unless both houses of Congress are favorable.[31]

Paragraph 4 of section I of Article II of the Constitution empowers Congress to "determine the time of choosing the Electors and the day on which they shall give their votes, which day shall be the same throughout the United States." Under the Act of March 1, 1792, previously mentioned, the Electors are chosen on the Tuesday following the first Monday in November of every fourth year; while by the Act of June 5, 1934, enacted to give effect to the Twentieth Amendment, the Electors of each state meet and give their votes the first Monday after the second Wednesday in December following the November election, and the two houses meet to count the votes in the hall of the House of Representatives on the ensuing January 6 at one p.m.[32]

Has Congress any further powers with respect to the choice and functioning of the presidential Electors? On first consideration it would seem not, inasmuch as the Court has more than once characterized Electors as "state officers." To begin with, however, the accuracy of the designation is open to serious challenge. At least the mode of choice would not determine the question—United States Senators were not state officers even when they were chosen by state legislatures. The office of Elector is created by the Constitution of the United States and the function which Electors perform is a national function. In the face, therefore, of the proposition that Electors are "state officers," the Court held shortly after the Civil War that Congress had power to protect the right of all citizens entitled to vote to lend aid and support "in any legal manner" to the election of any lawfully qualified person as a presidential Elector, and recently it held that Congress may enact legislation calculated to protect the choice of President and Vice-President from corruption. "That a government," the Court declared in the earlier of these cases,

"whose essential character is republican, whose executive head and legislative body are both elective, whose most numerous and powerful branch of the legislature is elected by the people directly, has no power by appropriate laws to secure this election from the influence of violence, of corruption, and of fraud, is a proposition so startling as to arrest attention and demand the gravest consideration.

"If this government is anything more than a mere aggregation of delegated agents of other States and governments, each of which is superior to the general government, it must have the power to protect the elections on which its existence depends from violence and corruption.

"If it has not this power it is left helpless before the two great natural and historical enemies of all republics, open violence and insidious corruption."[33]

The Court then quoted with approval the following words from Chancellor Kent's *Commentaries:*

"The government of the United States was created by the free voice and joint will of the people of America for their common defence and general welfare. Its powers apply to those great interests which relate to this country in its national capacity, and which depend for their protection on the consolidation of the Union. It is clothed with the principal attributes of political sovereignty, and it is justly deemed the guardian of our best rights, the source of our highest civil and political duties and the sure means of national greatness."

And the recent decision in *United States v. Burroughs*[34] is grounded on like doctrine.

But why may not this reasoning be given an even wider application? Why may not Congress, taking account of the fact that presidential Electors are today mere party dummies, turn its attention to the political activities which really determine the choice of Presidents, and indeed regulate such activities to the extent which it deems necessary for the purpose of keeping them open and aboveboard and free from corrupt manipulation?[35]

On no problem did the Convention of 1787 expend more time and effort than that of devising a suitable method of choosing a President. With no other feature of the Constitution did they express greater satisfaction than on the method finally devised. It is, Hamilton declared in *The Federalist,* "the only part of the Constitution not condemned by its opponents."[36] Actually, no feature of the Constitution has raised more difficulties in the past, or remains at this moment a graver menace to our domestic peace. Based on the theory that George Washington was going to live practically forever, the scheme has remained workable since his demise only in consequence of the rise of national parties, a development which the Convention did not foresee and would have deplored. And even with the national party organizations to supplement it the system was confronted with serious breakdown in 1800, 1824, 1860, and 1876. The same sort of breakdown may easily occur again, with results that are unpredictable. Suppose a fairly even division of the electorate among three parties today —either the Electoral College would be forced to choose a minority President as in 1860 and 1912, or the election would be thrown into the House as in 1825, and Nevada would have equal voice with New York in choosing a President. One feature of this preposterous arrangement is mitigated by the Twentieth Amendment—a new House of Representatives would do the electing instead of one possibly under the control of a defeated party. But this reform is only a short first step in the revision which must be effected sooner or later of this vital feature of our constitutional system.

Serious consideration ought, therefore, be given a current proposal which has the support of Senator Norris. By this plan, while the Electoral College would be abolished, each state would remain an electoral unit with the same relative strength as at present in the choice of a President, which, however, would be divided among the contesting parties in proportion to their popular vote in the state. Also, a plurality of electoral votes would elect. Thus, the danger would be obviated of the election ever being thrown into the House of Representatives, which is the outstanding peril of the present arrangement.

ANOTHER DANGER SPOT—PRESIDENTIAL DISABILITY

Article II, section one, paragraph six of the Constitution reads as follows:

"In case of the removal of the President from office, or of his death, resignation, or inability to discharge the powers and duties of the said office, the same shall devolve on the Vice President, and the Congress may by law provide for the case of removal, death, resignation, or inability, both of the President and Vice President, declaring what officer shall then act as President, and such officer shall act accordingly until the disability be removed or a President shall be elected."

Who is authorized to say whether a President is unable to discharge the powers and duties of his office? When he is unable to do so, does the said office become vacant? What is it to which the Vice-President succeeds when the President is disabled, or is removed, or has died—to the "powers and duties of the said office," or to the office itself? Or does he succeed to the former when the President is disabled, and to the latter when the President has vanished permanently from the scene? And what is the election referred to in the last clause of the above provision—is it the next regular presidential election or a special election to be called by Congress? Finally, suppose a vacancy to exist in the Presidency for some reason not mentioned above, as it would if the Electoral College, and then the House and Senate, respectively, failed to elect either a President or Vice-President or if both President-elect and the Vice-President-elect died before their assumption of office—what provision does the Constitution make for such a situation?

Twice in the history of the country Presidents have been unable to discharge their official duties for extended periods. President Garfield was thus disabled from July 2, 1881, when he was shot by Guiteau, till his death the following September 19; and President Wilson was disabled for many weeks following his collapse September 26, 1919.

Out of each of these episodes an extended discussion arose as to how such a situation was to be dealt with constitutionally. Apparently the most widely held view was that it was the duty of the Vice-President alone to decide the issue of "inability," since if inability existed it was he who must act; but the case must be a clear one, otherwise the Vice-President would be a mere usurper and punishable as such. Another theory conceded that the *initial* responsibility lay with the Vice-President, but urged that his action must receive the ratification of Congress, as in effect it had in the case of both Tyler and Fillmore; and until such ratification was forthcoming a succeeding Vice-President was, it was contended, only "acting President *de facto*," while following it he became "acting President *de jure*." A third view put the initial responsibility on Congress to provide beforehand for the determination, on the basis of evidence, of a President's alleged "inability" by the Supreme Court, or the President's own Cabinet, or by the houses of Congress themselves, acting by concurrent resolution. And of course there were variants of these views, some people urging that the Vice-President could be compelled by mandamus to take action, others that any action he took would be subject to judicial review, and yet others that Congress was entitled to define "inability," and so on.[37]

In point of fact, in the case of neither Garfield nor Wilson did either Congress or the Vice-President act. In both cases alike the official powers and duties of the disabled President were left to be discharged in such manner and by such devices as his immediate family and personal entourage had a mind to contrive. To all intents and purposes it was they who determined the issue of disability and determined it contrary to apparent fact.[38]

All Vice-Presidents—six of them—who have succeeded to the Presidency have done so in consequence of the death of the President, and this fact has made easy the establishment of the idea that they were entitled to succeed to the presidential *office* rather than merely to "the powers and duties of the said office." But the question still remains whether this result, sanctioned though it now is by repeated usage, is harmonious with the original intention of the Constitution; and also the more important question practically, whether the usage established for the only kind of case that has hitherto arisen should be considered as applying to all possible occasions of vice-presidential succession.

The first instance of a Vice-President succeeding was that of Tyler to the elder Harrison, in 1841. Certain circumstances in connection with the event are worth recounting. Harrison died April 4 and two days later Tyler took the oath prescribed by the Constitution for the President, but only, as he explained at the time, for "greater caution," his own conviction being that he was fully "qualified to perform the duties and exercise the powers and offices of President . . . without any other oath than that which he" had taken as Vice-President. In other words, it was clearly Tyler's original belief that he was Vice-President acting as President, and not President. But as was apt to be the case with Tyler, reflection enhanced his self-assurance and stiffened his attitude, and in the "inaugural address" which he published on April 5 he boldly proclaimed that he had been called to "the high office of President of this Confederacy," though by whom called he did not say. In other quarters, nevertheless, some doubt seems still to have lingered. For when, with the convening of Congress nearly two months later, the customary resolutions were introduced into the two houses to inform "the President" that they were in session, amendments were promptly offered to substitute the term "Vice-President," but were with equal promptitude voted down, that in the Senate by a vote of thirty-eight to eight.[39]

And unquestionably it was malice pure and simple which a quarter of a century later would fain have seen Andrew Johnson impeached as "Vice President discharging the powers and duties of the office of President of the United States"; and the move was ineffectual, for the impeachment ultimately voted was of "Andrew Johnson, President of the United States."[40] Nor was the question again mooted outside of books till 1927, when a Republican advocate of a third term for Mr. Coolidge informed the latter that it would not be a third term, inasmuch as following Mr. Harding's death he had been only "acting President."[41]

But is the outcome of usage regarding this matter harmonious with the original intention of the Constitution? In his *Usages of the American Constitution,* Mr. Henry W. Horwill asserts confidently that it is not, but his argument is not altogether persuasive.[42] The constitutional provision on which Mr. Horwill most relies is the provision quoted above, in which, he contends, "the powers and duties of the said office" is "grammatically" the antecedent of "the same." To the contrary, as it seems to me, the requirements of *grammar* are better met by making "the office" the antecedent, this alone being mentioned in the opening clause of the paragraph. Also, we may note the care which the Twelfth Amendment manifests to require the same qualifications for the Vice-Presidency as for the Presidency, although the original Constitution did not. That the Vice-President succeeds permanently when the President dies, resigns, or is removed is not disputed; and this being so, he may well be held to succeed to the office of President, for what is the difference between an "office" and "the powers and duties" thereof when to the latter is joined a guaranteed tenure? What is more, when the Vice-President succeeds he also succeeds, by uncontroverted practice, to the salary of "the President"—a circumstance which President Coolidge regarded with pronounced complacency.[43]

On one point, nevertheless, Mr. Horwill's argument is conclusive. The existing precedents do not, and should not, apply in the case of a temporary disability of the President; and this also seems to be the theory of Amendment XX.[44]

If the President leaves the country, does his absence disable him from exercising the powers and duties of his office? The question was raised by critics of President Wilson when he went abroad following the war with Germany. President Washington, the critics pointed out, had refused even to enter Rhode Island until that stiff-necked little commonwealth had joined the Union; and while President Taft had visited the Canal Zone in 1910, being absent from November 9 to November 23, he had been scrupulous to travel on an American war vessel and to remain on soil subject to American jurisdiction. But then, President Wilson also traveled on a government vessel; and if such technicalities avail it would seem that wherever an American President treads is for the moment American soil.[45]

Even more extreme was the implication of a resolution adopted by the Democratic House of Representatives in 1876, that the President must perform his official acts at the "seat of government established by law." President Grant, who was the target of the resolution, had the satisfaction of demonstrating to his Democratic critics that of all Presidents Thomas Jefferson was the one who had been most persistently absent from the Capitol, his record of absenteeism being 796 days, or more than one fourth of his eight years in office;[46] and any significance that the issue thus raised may have had in the past has been pretty well eliminated by modern ease and speed of travel.

In enforcement of its power to provide for the lack of "both a President and a Vice-President," Congress has passed two "Presidential Succession Acts" so-called. That of 1792 provided for the succession first of the President *pro tempore* of the Senate and then of the Speaker, who however were to hold office only until a new President could be chosen for another four years. The act thus violated the principle of the separation of powers by investing an officer of the national legislature in his quality as such with the full executive power; while by the provisions which it made for an intermediate election for a full term it set at naught the synchrony evidently demanded by the Constitution in the choice of President with that of a new House of Representatives and one third of the Senate. Furthermore, it failed to deal with the possibility of there being no President *pro tempore* or Speaker, which would be the case if the Congress in office had not yet organized; and it also overlooked the possibility that neither the Speaker nor the President *pro tempore* is an "officer" in the sense of this paragraph of the Constitution.

The Act of January 19, 1886, at present in force,[47] provides for the succession of members of the Cabinet in the order of the establishment of their respective offices, provided the incumbent possesses the constitutional qualifications for the Presidency. Inasmuch as the officer "acts as President" by virtue of his post in the Cabinet, he continues in the latter—a member of his own Cabinet. The statute also requires that if Congress is not already in session when such a contingency arises or is not scheduled to meet within twenty days, it shall be convened in extraordinary session; but the question of an intermediate election is not touched upon. Whether Congress is empowered to provide for such an election is matter for debate; but, if it is, then the position is at least plausible that it could limit the term of the President chosen to the unexpired term.[48]

But while the Act of 1886 makes adequate provision for that type of vacancy in the presidential office which occurs *within* a presidential term, it does not provide for several other possibilities, and it is to these deficiencies that sections 3 and 4 of Amendment XX are addressed:

Section III

"If, at the time fixed for the beginning of the term of the President, the President elect shall have died, the Vice-President elect shall become President. If a President shall not have been chosen before the time fixed for the beginning of his term, or if the President elect shall have failed to qualify, then the Vice-President elect shall act as President until a President shall have qualified; and the Congress may by law provide for the case wherein neither a President elect nor a Vice-President elect shall have qualified, declaring who shall then act as President or the manner in which one who is to act shall be selected, and such person shall act accordingly until a President or Vice-President shall have qualified."

Section IV

"The Congress may by law provide for the case of the death of any of the persons from whom the House of Representatives may choose a President whenever the right of choice shall have devolved upon them, and for the case of the death of any of the persons from whom the Senate may choose a Vice-President whenever the right of choice shall have devolved upon them."

Without supplementary legislation by Congress these provisions are only partially efficacious for their purpose. By section 7 of Article I all bills, resolutions, and so forth, which are intended to have the effect of law must be laid before the President for his approval, and presumably the requirement would still hold if there were only an acting President. So in the absence of either there could be no legislation. If, therefore, Congress should fail to exercise the powers which Amendment XX confers upon it with respect to a situation in which "neither a President elect nor a Vice-President elect shall have qualified" *and taken office,* it would then be too late—the legislative power would be paralyzed. Nor does the above language make it clear whether a President who qualified at some date after "the term fixed for the beginning of the term of President"—fixed, *i.e.,* by the Amendment— would hold only until the end of that term, or for the full four years which are stipulated in the opening paragraph of Article II. Manifestly, Congress should clear up these difficulties.[49]

Paragraph 8 of section 1 of Article II of the Constitution reads:

"Before he enter on the execution of his office he shall take the following oath or affirmation:

"'I do solemnly swear (or affirm) that I will faithfully execute the office of President of the United States, and will, to the best of my ability, preserve, protect, and defend the Constitution of the United States.'"

Is the President already in office when he takes the above oath, or is taking it a necessary step in his assumption of office? The former would seem to be the correct theory. It is "the President" who is required to take the oath; the Act of March 1, 1792, referred to on an earlier page, assumed that President Washington became President on March 4, 1789, although he did not take the oath till the following April 30; and in the parallel case of the coronation oath, the royal succession is not dependent on the heir's taking it. The ceremony is, in fact, sometimes deferred for years.[50] In short, the President's first official duty is to take the above prescribed oath, and his refusal to do so would be a violation of the Constitution.

The question whether the oath confers upon the President powers which he would not otherwise possess, especially in connection with interpreting the Constitution, is dealt with in a later chapter.

Paragraph 7 of section 1 of Article II reads as follows:

"The President shall, at stated times, receive for his services a compensation, which shall neither be increased nor diminished during the period for which he shall have been elected, and he shall not receive within that period any other emolument from the United States or any of them."[51]

A decision of the Supreme Court, rendered in 1920, held that the salary of a judge of the United States would be "diminished" contrary to Article III, section 1, by the application to it of a general income tax which was levied after the judge took office; and a later case held the same as to an income tax which was in force when he took office.[52] Clearly, the same rule would apply to the President's salary; and furthermore, since this may not be "increased" during his term, and he may receive no "other emolument from the United States," a general income tax in force when he took office would have to be maintained at the same rate during such term, and not only as to his salary but also as to his income from private sources, even though repealed as to everybody else's income! Awareness of these absurdities was probably one of the reasons why the Court recently overruled the second of the decisions referred to and laid the ax to the roots of the other.[53]

A further word or two should be added regarding the Vice-President.[54] In the first Senate a debate sprang up over how the President should be addressed. "His High Mightiness" was one proposal, "His Excellency" another. Thereupon, the further question arose of how the Vice-President should be addressed, and some one suggested "His Superfluous Excellency." From that date to this the Vice-Presidency has been a theme for disparagement even by its incumbents. "My country," wrote the first Vice-President to his wife, "has in its wisdom contrived for me the most insignificant office that ever the invention of man contrived or his imagination conceived";[55] and a century and a quarter later another Vice-President compared his official condition to that of "a man in a cataleptic fit. He is conscious of all that goes on but has no part in it."

Actually the first Vice-President played no inconsiderable role. As president of the Senate he exerted a control over its proceedings which its later rules were to make impossible. He also had occasion to exercise his constitutional prerogative of giving the casting vote to break a tie no less than twenty times—a record which no successor has approached. President Washington, too, frequently consulted with him, as he did with the Chief Justice and many others in the interval before the definite appearance of the Cabinet. Besides, prior to the Twelfth Amendment, the Vice-President was in a sense—a fact not overlooked by Adams—"the constitutional equal of the President," having been voted for by the Electors, not for "Vice-President," but for "President."[56] He was, in other words, the second political figure in the country, and due as such to succeed the existing incumbent of the Presidency, as in fact the first two Vice-Presidents did.

Following the retirement of Washington, however, the office received a succession of blows. President and Vice-President were now of opposed parties, with the result that official intimacy ceased. Then came the Twelfth Amendment, and along with it the practice of "the Virginia School of Presidents" of making their Secretaries of State their successors-designate. Thereafter the Vice-Presidency was ordinarily a somewhat secondary pawn in the game of choosing a President. Lastly, Calhoun, who had aimed for higher things, had his revenge on the office by his famous ruling in 1826 that as presiding officer of the Senate he was not entitled to call a Senator to order—those proud ambassadors of the Sovereign States—thereby pointing senatorial procedure toward its present individualism.

The inherent feebleness of the office was never better exemplified than in the negligible role which it played in 1881 and again in 1919. Yet this is not without its element of compensation; at least we have never seen the country plunged into civil war by a scheming Vice-President. And latterly the office has shown some signs of revival—not dangerous, yet promising. The succession of the first Roosevelt and of Coolidge, occurring as they did within a few years of each other, conveyed a warning of the potentialities of the office which has not gone altogether unheeded by the party Warwicks. At the same time Presidents have also given thought to making the Vice-Presidency an instrument of presidential leadership, though thus far with varying success. Mr. Coolidge by Mr. Harding's invitation sat in the latter's Cabinet, but could not persuade Mr. Dawes to follow suit. Mr. Garner sits in Mr. Roosevelt's Cabinet, not always to the entire satisfaction of either, it may be suspected. Perhaps Gouverneur Morris had the right of the matter in the Philadelphia Convention. Objecting to the proposal to make the Vice-President president of the Senate, Elbridge Gerry had said: "We might as well put the President himself at the head of the Legislature. The close intimacy that must subsist between the President and the Vice President makes it absolutely improper," to which Morris retorted: "The Vice President then will be the first heir apparent that ever loved his father!"[57]

While the foregoing pages hardly require summarization, it may be appropriate to recur to one or two matters of current interest and importance. The Framers devised the Electoral College with the intention of rendering the President indefinitely reëligible. Conversely, they assumed that the College would prove workable because they believed the President would be indefinitely reëligible, and that when one retired the incumbent Vice-President would usually succeed him. Granted these assumptions, and the adoption of the Electoral College becomes understandable. However, the Jeffersonian ban on indefinite reëligibility must soon have put matters in a different light, had not Jefferson been able to offset his work of destruction with one of construction—I mean his creation of a national party. For a quarter of a century following his election a single political party dominated the country and hence the College, and by so doing kept the latter workable. Nor, thanks to the rise of the

Jacksonian Democracy, did the breakdown which occurred in 1825 long continue.

The verdict of actual practice is that the Electoral College provides a feasible method of choosing a President so long as there is a continuously dominant party in the country, as was the case from 1801 to 1825, and again with two interruptions from 1829 to 1861, and again from 1861 to 1873. Moreover, it remains a more or less feasible method in the presence of two fairly equal, alternating parties, despite the fact that the majority party in the college may be the minority party at the polls—even overwhelmingly so. But should a strong third party ever spring up the scheme would be confronted with the dangerous possibility of entire collapse. Although just such a danger has impended several times already, the lesson of the situation has been obscured each time by a fortuitously fortunate dénouement. But we should not continue to rely solely on the intervention of that Providence which is said to have fools and the American people in its special care. Hence serious attention ought to be given the proposed constitutional amendment, sponsored by Senator Norris, to which reference was made early in this chapter. Nor should another case of presidential disability be permitted to occur without some procedure for handling such situations having been enacted; nor should the Twentieth Amendment be left longer without proper supplementing legislation. In a word, Congress should wake up to its responsibility in keeping the Constitution a workable instrument of government.

CHAPTER III

ADMINISTRATIVE CHIEF

LOGICALLY, and in some measure chronologically, the President's first duty is to constitute an "administration," that is to say, a more or less integrated body of officials whose chief duty should be the enforcement of the acts of Congress. The President's own duty in connection with the enforcement of the laws is phrased by the Constitution as follows: "He shall take care that the laws be faithfully executed." But what precisely is the scope of the *power* which this *duty* implies? The truth of the matter is that the Constitution is ambiguous as regards this most interesting matter. The opening clause of Article II carries the inference that the sum total of executive power which is known to or recognized by the Constitution belongs to the President. The clause just quoted suggests, on the contrary, that there is, or can be, in connection with the enforcement of the laws, an executive power which does not belong to the President, although he must supervise it to some extent.

What, then, is the scope of the President's supervisory powers over his "subordinates," and is it subject to any extent to determination by Congress? Also, what is the scope of the President's power to appoint to office; and of his power to remove therefrom? Obviously, all these questions are more or less related; and particularly is the question of the scope of the President's removal power closely connected with that of the scope of his supervisory power—whom the President may remove he may dominate.

It is the purpose of the first three sections of this chapter to deal with the above questions. A final section will then bring some of

The Notes to this chapter begin on page three hundred forty-three

the results arrived at to bear on a recent phase of the question of presidential supervision.

"OFFICE" AND APPOINTMENT THERETO

It was formerly, and within limits is still, an element of the royal prerogative in England to create offices as well as to appoint to them.[1] At the outset, in fact, the two things were indistinguishable. Etymologically, an "office" is an *officium,* a duty; and an "officer" was simply one whom the King had charged with a duty. In the course of time certain frequently recurrent and naturally coherent duties came to be assigned more or less permanently, and hence emerged the concept of "office" as an *institution* distinct from the person holding it and capable of persisting beyond his incumbency.

The Constitution, however, by the "necessary and proper" clause assigns the power to *create* offices to Congress, while it deals with the *appointing power* in the following words of Article II, section 2, paragraph 2:

"And he [the President] shall nominate, and by and with the advice and consent of the Senate shall appoint ambassadors, other public ministers and consuls, judges of the Supreme Court, and all other officers of the United States, whose appointments are not herein otherwise provided for and which shall be established by law; but the Congress may by law vest the appointment of such inferior officers as they think proper in the President alone, in the courts of law, or in the heads of departments."

An appointment is, therefore, ordinarily to an *existing* office, and one which owes its existence to an act of Congress.[2] The contention has nevertheless been advanced at times that certain offices are the creation of the Constitution itself. This is obviously so as to the two great elective offices of President and Vice-President.

How, then, is it as regards membership on the Supreme Court, which is an appointive office? The Court has voiced the theory more than once that it derives its existence directly from the Constitution,[3] an idea which logically infers that membership on it arises from the same source, it being rather difficult to imagine a court without members. The size of the Court would then be for the appointing power—the President acting with the advice and consent of the Senate—to determine, although in point of fact Congress has always done this. On the other hand, until 1855 Congress left it entirely with the President, subject to the advice and consent of the Senate, to appoint such "public ministers and consuls" as in his judgment the national interests required, the theory being, as stated by Attorney General Cushing, that the designations of such officers were "derived from the law of nations and the authority to appoint from the Constitution."[4]

Furthermore, beginning with Washington, Presidents have, practically at discretion, despatched "secret" agents on diplomatic or semi-diplomatic missions without nominating them to the Senate;[5] while at other times they have, with or without the consent of the Senate, designated members of that body or of the House to represent the United States on international commissions and at diplomatic conferences; and this in face of Article I, section 6, paragraph 2, of the Constitution, which reads:

"No Senator or Representative shall, during the time for which he was elected, be appointed to any civil office under the authority of the United States, which shall have been created, or the emoluments whereof shall have been increased, during such time; and no person holding any office under the United States shall be a member of either house during his continuance in office."

How, then, are the above mentioned practices, which have long since become an established usage of the Constitution, to be reconciled with these provisions? Only on the theory, apparently, that such diplomatic assignments are not "offices" in the sense of the Constitution, being only for specific, temporary purposes and carrying with them, in the case of Senators and Representatives, no extra compensation.[6]

And a like explanation is probably available to vindicate a practice, first resorted to on any scale by President Theodore Roosevelt, of constituting "volunteer unpaid commissions" for the purpose of investigating certain factual situations and reporting their findings to the President.[7] Eventually Mr. Roosevelt's enthusiasm for this method of informing himself concerning "the state of the nation" came to be denounced in Congress as "unconstitutional," and an amendment to the Sundry Civil Act of 1909 undertook to forbid the practice.[8] Mr. Roosevelt signed the measure but proclaimed his intention of ignoring the restriction. "Congress," he argued, "cannot prevent the President from seeking advice," nor disinterested men from giving their service to the people,[9] and that this view of the subject has won out appears from the fact that Mr. Hoover when President appointed literally dozens of fact-finding commissions, most of which were without statutory basis.[10]

Finally, Congress has on a few occasions endowed the President with its own power to establish offices and has merged therewith the full power to appoint to such offices, that is, without consulting the Senate. Thus Title II of the National Recovery Act of June 16, 1933, authorized President Roosevelt to create the post of Federal Administrator of Public Works and to "establish such agencies . . . to appoint, without regard to the civil service laws, such officers and employees, and to utilize such Federal officers and employees . . . as he may find necessary"—provisions which still govern the rendition of work relief and the construction of public works by the National Government.[11]

President Wilson's creation of the War Industries Board and the Committee on Public Information during the war with Germany, both of which exercised vast powers in the President's name, must however be credited to the general expansion which presidential authority always undergoes in war time.[12]

The Constitution distinguishes three stages in appointments by the President with the advice and consent of the Senate. The first is the "nomination," which is by the President alone; the second is the assent of the Senate to the "appointment"; and the third is the final appointment and commissioning of the appointee by the President.[13] The only limitation which is imposed by the Constitution itself on the President's freedom of choice in nominating or appointing to office is the one, already noted, which results from the disqualification of Senators and Representatives in certain instances. This restriction came recently under scrutiny in connection with the appointment of Senator Hugo L. Black of Alabama to the Supreme Court shortly following the passage by Congress of an act improving the financial position of Justices retiring from the Court at the age of seventy. Although Mr. Black's term had still some months to run, his appointment was defended by the argument that, inasmuch as he was only fifty-one years old and so would be ineligible for the "increased emolument" for nineteen years, it was not *as to him* an increased emolument.[14] Similarly, when in 1909 Senator Knox of Pennsylvania wished to become Secretary of State in President Taft's Cabinet, the salary of which office had been recently increased, Congress accommodatingly repealed the increase for the period which still remained of Mr. Knox's senatorial term.[15] In other words, a Senator or Representative—and especially a Senator—may, "during the time for which he was elected, be appointed to any civil office under the authority of the United States, . . . the emoluments whereof shall have been increased during such time," *provided only* that the increase in emolument is not available to the appointee "during such time."

Much more extensive is the control which is exerted over the President's freedom of choice by a set of usages which go by the name of "senatorial courtesy." If the President in nominating to an office within a state fails to consult the preferences of the Senator or Senators of his own party from that state, he is very likely to see the appointment defeated upon an appeal to the Senate by the slighted member or members. Reciprocally, the Senate will ordinarily interpose no objection to the President's nominees for Cabinet or diplomatic posts. While any attempt to find basis in the written Constitution for this interesting understanding would be disappointing, since it is the advice and consent of the Senate which the Constitution requires and not that of individual Senators,[16] yet there is no usage of the Constitution affecting the powers of the President which is more venerable. As early as August 6, 1789, we find President Washington addressing to the Senate the following message:

"My nomination of Benjamin Fishbourn for the place of naval officer of the port of Savannah not having met with your concurrence, I now nominate Lachlan McIntosh for that office. Whatever may have been the reasons which induced your dissent, I am persuaded they were such as you deemed sufficient. . . . "[17]

Actually the reason which induced the Senate's dissent was the dissent in the first instance of the Senator from Georgia, and this apparently had nothing to do with the question of Fishbourn's fitness.

The practical importance, nevertheless, of this interesting institution in curtailing the President's power over appointments has often been a good deal exaggerated. The number of nominations for a given vacancy rejected by the Senate on this score has never apparently exceeded two, while the talent from which a President bent on making a sound appointment may choose is by no means ordinarily so limited. If Hamilton's prediction in *The Federalist* that the Senate would concern itself only with the merits of suggested appointees has not been realized, neither on the other hand has James Wilson's prediction that the President would be "but the minion of the Senate."[18]

But by far the most important limitation upon presidential autonomy in this field of power is that which results from the fact that, in creating an office, Congress may stipulate the qualifications of appointees thereto. First and last, legislation of this character has laid down a vast variety of qualifications, depending on citizenship, residence, professional attainments, occupational experience, age, race, property, sound habits, political, industrial or regional affiliations, and so on and so forth. It has even confined the President's selection to a small number of persons to be named by others.[19] Indeed, it has contrived at times, by particularity of description, to designate a definite eligible, thereby virtually usurping the appointing power.[20]

For the proposition is universally conceded that some choice, however small, must be left the appointing authority.[21] Thus the Civil Service Act of 1883 leaves the appointing officer the right to select from *"among* those graded highest as the result of" the competitive examinations for which the act provides,[22] and supplementary executive orders have customarily further restricted choice to the *three highest*. The Foreign Service Act of 1924 is notable in that it extended for the first time the principle of competitive examinations to certain offices appointment to which was formerly made with the advice and consent of the Senate,[23] although logically there would seem to be no reason why this should not be done in all cases, the appointive power being the same power whether it is exercised by the President with the Senate, or by the President alone, or by a head of department.[24]

Another power of Congress which must be distinguished from the appointing power is that of determining the powers and duties of officers of the United States. In the case of an existing office Congress may increase these to an indefinite extent without necessitating a reappointment to the office;[25] but it appears to be the Court's opinion, and is certainly a logical one, that new duties should be "germane" to the existing office, at least to the extent that their assignment shall not transgress the principle of the separation of powers.[26]

Another characteristic of the President's power of appointment is that while the power connotes a choice among eligibles, it involves ordinarily no choice whether there shall be an appointment. This results from the fact that the vast majority of civil offices under the National Government are instrumentalities for carrying into effect one or more of Congress's delegated powers and represent its views of what is "necessary and proper" to that end. The President's duty therefore to make an appointment to such an office flows from his duty to "take care that the laws be faithfully executed." But if the President fails to make an appointment there is, of course, no legal remedy, any more than there is when he fails to exercise any other of his powers. Mr. Roosevelt's success therefore in keeping the office of Comptroller General unfilled for many months following Mr. McCarl's retirement is of more than passing interest, suggesting as it does the possibility of a usage which would transfer the question of the need for continuing an existing office to the final discretion of the President.

Except the President and Vice-President, all members of the civil service of the National Government are appointive and fall into one of three categories, those who are appointed by the President "by and with the advice and consent of the Senate"; "inferior officers" whose appointment Congress has vested by law "in the President alone, in the courts of law, or in the heads of departments"; and *employees*.

As here used, the term "employee" bears a very special meaning. Ordinarily the term denotes one who stands in a contractual relationship to his "employer," but here it signifies all subordinate officials of the National Government receiving appointment at the hands of officials who are not specifically recognized by the Constitution as capable of being vested by Congress with the appointing power.[27] The concept thus affords a way of circumventing the apparent purpose of the Constitution to confine the power to appoint "inferior officers," by the authorization of Congress, to the President alone, the courts of law, and the heads of departments. As used in the statutes the term "officers" is frequently construed to cover "employees" in the above sense.

What, however, are "inferior officers" in the sense of the Constitution? Thanks to the jealous vigilance of the Senate, Congress has exercised its power in the vesting of appointments quite sparingly, and so the question just put has never been adjudicated by the Supreme Court. The term seems to suggest in this particular context officers intended to be subordinate to those in whom their appointment is vested, and at the same time to exclude the courts of law and heads of departments. If this is so, then it is at least highly doubtful whether the suggestion advanced in 1930 that the power be lodged in the Supreme Court to appoint the Comptroller General, an officer whose functions lie entirely outside the judicial field, was constitutionally sound.[28]

The sole case in which the Supreme Court has had occasion to pass directly upon the participation of the Senate in the appointing power is the fairly recent one of *United States v. Smith*,[29] which grew out of an attempt by the Senate early in 1931 to recall its consent to certain nominations by President Hoover to the Federal Power Commission. In support of its course the Senate invoked a long-standing rule which permits a motion to reconsider a resolution of confirmation and to recall the notification thereof within "the next two days of actual executive session of the Senate." Inasmuch as the nominees involved had meantime taken the oath of office and entered upon the discharge of their duties, President Hoover denied the request, which he stigmatized as an attempt "to encroach upon the executive function by removal of a duly appointed executive officer under the guise of reconsideration of his nomination."[30] The Senate thereupon voted to reconsider the nominations in question, again approving two of the nominees but rejecting the third, against whom by the Senate's order the district attorney of the District of Columbia forthwith instituted *quo warranto* proceedings. From an extensive review of previous occurrences of the same general nature the Court, speaking by Justice Brandeis, concluded that the Senate's rule as heretofore applied did not reach the case of an appointee who had already been installed in office on the faith of the Senate's initial consent and notification to the President, and that this interpretation bound the Senate in the instant case.

Just how the Court became entitled to construe the Senate's rules, which it conceded were subject to change by the Senate without notice, does not appear from Justice Brandeis's opinion; but at any rate the expedient enabled the Court to evade the question whether the rule governing the reconsideration of nominations is *constitutionally* valid once notification has gone forward to the President. Jefferson in his *Manual* asserted unqualifiedly that "If, after the vote, the paper on which it [the Senate] passed has been parted with, there can be no reconsideration." But, as already indicated, practice has been far from supporting this sweeping assertion; nor is its logic inescapable, for it may with equal logic be contended that the senatorial consent is only "a warrant of attorney, valid until revoked," or that it is akin to a proffer and hence may be withdrawn at any time before acceptance. In Smith's case the revocation or withdrawal—depending on the analogy adopted—clearly came too late.

The latest precedent bearing on this subject is furnished by President Roosevelt's refusal on July 13, 1939, to honor the request of the Senate that he return its resolution consenting to the appointment of Elmer D. Davies to be United States judge for the Middle District of Tennessee. "I regret," the President wrote, "that I cannot accede to this request as before its receipt I had signed and sent out a commission appointing Judge Davies, by and with the advice and consent of the Senate." It is not impossible that Mr. Roosevelt's action was influenced by the reflection that if Mr. Davies was in office he would be irremovable, but that fact hardly lessens its value as a precedent—and a very sensible one.

May the Senate attach conditions to its approval of an appointment, as it frequently does to its approval of a treaty? The entire record of practice under the Constitution negatives the suggestion, as also does that of opinion. Madison, Hamilton, Jefferson, and Story all expressed themselves to the effect that the Senate's role in relation to appointments is only that of rejecting or confirming nominations without condition.[31] Moreover, the conditions which the Senate would attempt to attach would be apt either to invade the powers of the office, which come from the law, or to limit the officer's tenure, which also comes from the law or is subject to determination by the removal power. And in principle at least the Senate's pretensions would extend to judicial no less than to executive appointees.

Although the Constitution says that the President *"shall* commission all officers," etc., this, as applied in practice, does not appear to mean that he is under constitutional or legal obligation to commission those whose appointments have reached that stage, but merely that it is he and no one else who has the power to commission them. The sealing and delivery of the commission is, on the other hand, in the case both of appointees by the President and Senate and by the President alone, a purely ministerial act which has been lodged by statute with the Secretary of State, and the performance of which may be compelled by mandamus unless the appointee has been in the meantime validly removed.[32]

A further element of the appointing power is contained in the following provision of Article II, section 2, paragraph 3:

"The President shall have power to fill up all vacancies that may happen during the recess of the Senate, by granting commissions which shall expire at the end of their next session."

The significant word is "happen." Setting out from the proposition that the very nature of the executive power requires that it shall always be "in capacity for action," Attorneys General came early to interpret this to mean "happen to exist," and long continued practice securely establishes this construction.[33] It follows that whenever a vacancy may have occurred in the first instance or for whatever reason, if it still continues after the Senate has ceased to sit and hence cannot be consulted, the President may fill it in the way described. But a Senate "recess" does not include holiday or temporary adjournments,[34] while by an act of Congress, if the vacancy existed when the Senate was in session, the *ad interim* appointee may receive no salary until he has been confirmed by the Senate.[35] Also, there appears to be an informal understanding, although it is not always observed, that the President will not extend a recess appointment to a rejected nominee.[36]

To be distinguished from the power to make recess appointments is the power of the President to make temporary assignments of officials to the duties of other absent or incapacitated officials. Usually a situation of this nature is provided for in advance by a statute which designates the inferior officer who is to act in place of his immediate superior, but, in the lack of such provision, theory and practice alike concede the President the power to make a designation.[37]

THE PRESIDENT AS SUPERVISOR OF LAW ENFORCEMENT; THE CABINET

The acts of the British monarch are judicially noticeable only as the acts of his agents. "The King can do no wrong" because, in strict law, he can do nothing. In the case of the President, on the contrary, there are many acts which to be done constitutionally must presumably have been done by him personally or in the exercise of his personal judgment.[38] In the words of an opinion rendered by Attorney General Cushing in 1855:

"It may be presumed that he, the *man* discharging the Presidential office, *and he alone,* grants reprieves and pardons for offenses against the United States."

And again:

"No act of Congress, no act even of the President himself, can, by constitutional possibility authorize or create any military officer not subordinate to the President."[39]

May this type of obligation be created by statute? Dealing with this question in a case before the Civil War, which grew out of a statutory provision expressly prohibiting the advancing of public money to the disbursing officers of the government except under "the special direction of the President," the Court said:

"The President's duty in general requires his superintendence of the administration; yet this duty cannot require of him to become the administrative officer to every department and bureau, or to perform in person the numerous details incident to services which, nevertheless, he is, in a correct sense, by the Constitution and laws required and expected to perform. This cannot be, 1st, Because if it were practicable, it would be to absorb the duties and responsibilities of the various departments of the government in the personal action of one chief executive officer. It cannot be, for the stronger reason, that it is impracticable —nay, impossible."[40]

It is true that the Court once held a certain decree of a court-martial void because, although it had been confirmed by the Secretary of War, it was not specifically stated to have received the sanction of the President as required by the 65th Article of War; but later decisions call this holding into question.[41] Such legislation is at any rate quite exceptional. The general rule is stated by the Court to be that when any duty is cast by law upon the President it may be exercised by him "through the head of the appropriate department," whose acts, if performed within the law, become the President's acts; and, in point of fact, most orders and instructions emanating from the heads of the departments, even when in pursuance of powers conferred by statute on the President, do not mention him.[42]

Suppose, however, that the law casts a duty upon a subordinate executive agency *eo nomine,* does the President thereupon become entitled, by virtue of his "executive power" or of his duty to "take care that the laws be faithfully executed," to substitute his own judgment for that of the agency regarding the discharge of such duty? An unqualified answer to this question would invite startling results. An affirmative answer would make all questions of law enforcement questions of discretion, and the discretion moreover of an independent and legally uncontrollable branch of the government. By the same token, it would render it impossible for Congress, notwithstanding its broad powers under the "necessary and proper" clause, to leave anything to the specially trained judgment of a subordinate executive official with any assurance that his discretion would not be perverted to political ends for the advantage of the administration in power. On the other hand, a flatly negative answer would hold out consequences equally unwelcome. It would, as Attorney General Cushing quaintly phrased it, leave it open to Congress so to divide and transfer "the executive power" by statute as to change the government "into a parliamentary despotism like that of Venezuela or Great Britain, with a *nominal* executive chief or president, who, however, would remain without a shred of actual power."[43] Or, in different words, it would leave it open to Congress to destroy unity of administration in the National Government, as it has long since been destroyed in the state governments. There are some critics, indeed, who profess to believe that this has already occurred in a measure. The subject is dealt with later in this chapter.

The earliest discussion of this crucial issue is to be found in the argument which was made by Madison in the first Congress in behalf of attributing the removal power to the President. It was "the intention of the Constitution," Madison contended, expressed especially in the "take care" clause, that the first magistrate should be responsible for the executive departments, and this responsibility, he urged, carried with it power to "inspect and *control*" the conduct of all subordinate executive officers.[44]

Yet when in the same year it organized the first executive departments, Congress itself adopted a radically different principle. The acts creating the Departments of State and of War specifically recognize the responsibility of the heads of those departments to the President, but not so with the act organizing the

Department of the Treasury. "The Secretary of the Treasury," this act read, and indeed still reads,

"shall from time to time . . . make report and give information to either branch of the legislature in person or in writing, as may be required, respecting all matters referred to him by the Senate or House of Representatives, or which shall appertain to his office; and generally shall perform all services relative to finances as he shall be directed to perform—"[45]

directed, that is, by Congress. Nor is the reason underlying this difference far to seek. The State and War Departments are principally, although not exclusively, organs of the President in the exercise of functions which are assigned him by the Constitution itself, while the Treasury Department is primarily an instrument for carrying into effect Congress's constitutional powers in the field of finance. For like reasons, when in 1794, the Post Office was established on a permanent foundation, it was not placed under the control of the President, nor was the Interior Department when it was formed in 1849; although the Navy Department, established in 1798, was so placed.[46]

And meantime, in *Marbury v. Madison,* Chief Justice Marshall had suggested a parallel distinction between the duties of the Secretary of State under the original act which had created a "Department of Foreign Affairs," and those which had been added by the later act changing the designation of the department to its present one. The former were, he pointed out, entirely in the "political field," and hence for their discharge the secretary was left responsible absolutely to the President. The latter, on the other hand, were exclusively of statutory origin and sprang from the powers of Congress. For these, therefore, the secretary was "an officer of the law" and "amenable to the law for his conduct."[47]

Nor is the doctrine which was advanced by Attorney General Wirt in 1823 of substantially different import when it is confined to the field of Congress's delegated powers, which is evidently what Wirt was thinking of. It is that the President's duty under the "take care" clause requires of him scarcely more than that he should bring a *criminally negligent* official to book for his derelictions, either by removing him or by setting in motion against him the processes of impeachment or of criminal prosecution,[48] an opinion which voiced the point of view of "the Virginia School of Presidents," including the later Madison. The doctrine, on the other hand, that Congress is unable to vest any executive agency even within the field of its own specifically delegated powers with any legal discretion which the President is not entitled to appropriate to himself is, of course, the very hallmark of the Jacksonian conception of the Presidency, although the groundwork for it was prepared much earlier, first, by "the decision of 1789," which is treated below; secondly, by the rise of the President's Cabinet.

Like its British namesake, the American Cabinet is entirely extra-constitutional.[49] The President, the Constitution states, "may require the opinion, in writing, of the principal officer in each of the executive departments, upon any subject relating to the duties of their respective offices."[50] The consultative relationship thus suggested is an entirely one-sided affair, is to be conducted in writing with the "principal officers" separately and individually, and is to relate only "to the duties of their respective offices." If an executive council was needed, it was the general idea in 1789 that the Senate would serve the purpose.

The Cabinet may be said to have emerged as a definite institution of the National Government from the diplomatic crisis of 1793. Washington had previously called the three Secretaries and the Attorney General into assembled consultation, but now such meetings became frequent. "The most notable of these was the meeting of April 19 of that year, at which the issuance of the so-called 'Neutrality Proclamation' was agreed upon. Writing at this time, Jefferson refers to the meetings as occurring 'almost every day'"; and so matters continued more or less till the close of the year.[51] Two years later "the Cabinet," as it was now generally termed, underwent another notable stage in its evolution when Washington, as a result of Secretary of State Randolph's equivocal attitude in the fight over the Jay Treaty, proceeded to reconstruct his Cabinet on the avowed basis of loyalty to his own policies, and in so doing created a precedent which, with negligible exceptions, has guided Presidents in their choice of departmental heads ever since. And meantime, by "the decision of 1789," the President had been endowed with an unqualified power of removal over the heads of the executive departments.

Thus from the first the heads of these departments have occupied, when exercising powers delegated them by statute, a dual role and have been subject to a dual responsibility. The inevitable clash between these two roles came in 1833 as an incident of Jackson's "War on the Bank." Convincing himself by a characteristic process of self-hypnosis that the Bank was an unsafe depository for the national funds, Jackson ordered Secretary of the Treasury Duane to transfer them, which Duane had power under the law to do. As it happened, however, the House of Representatives had recently expressed its confidence in the Bank by formal resolution, and Duane's own instructed judgment was to the same effect. He accordingly refused to comply with Jackson's demand, was promptly removed, and his successor Taney at once gave the desired order.[52]

Although in commenting on this episode writers are apt to treat it as the outcome solely of the President's possession of the removal power,[53] this was far from Jackson's own theory of the matter. The latter, as stated in his Protest Message of April 15, 1834, was "that the entire executive power is vested in the President"; that the power to remove "those officers who are to aid him in the execution of the laws" is an incident of that power; that the Secretary of the Treasury is such an officer; that "the custody of the public property and money is an executive function" exercised through the Secretary of the Treasury and his subordinates; that "in the performance of these duties he [the Secretary] is subject to the supervision and control of the President"; and finally that the act establishing the Bank "did not and could not change the relation between the President and Secretary—did not release the former from his obligation to see the law faithfully executed nor the latter from the President's supervision and control."[54]

In short, *the Constitution knows only one "executive power," that of the President, whose duty to "take care that the laws be faithfully executed" thus becomes the equivalent of the duty and power to execute them himself.* The removal of Duane was, therefore, the constitutionally ordained result of that officer's attempt to usurp the President's constitutional prerogative; or, in broader terms, the President's removal power, in this case unqualified, was the *sanction provided by the Constitution for his power and duty to control all his subordinates in all their official actions of public consequence.*

Five years later the case of *Kendall v. United States*[55] arose. The United States owed one Stokes a sum of money, and, when Postmaster General Kendall at Jackson's instigation refused to pay it, Congress passed a special act ordering payment. But Kendall still proving noncompliant, Stokes sought and obtained a mandamus in the United States circuit court for the District of Columbia, and on appeal this decision was affirmed by the Supreme Court.

While *Kendall v. United States,* like *Marbury v. Madison,* involved the question of the responsibility of a head of department

for the performance of a ministerial duty, the discussion by counsel before the Court and the Court's own opinion covered the
entire subject of the relation of the President to his subordinates
in the performance by them of statutory duties. The lower court
had asserted that the duty of the President under the "faithfully
executed" clause gave him "no other control over the officer than
to see that he acts honestly, with proper motives," but "no power
to construe the law and see that the executive action conforms to
it."[56] Counsel for Kendall attacked this position vigorously, rely-
ing largely upon statements by Hamilton, Marshall, Wilson, and
Story having to do with the President's power in the field of
foreign relations.[57]

This argument the Court rejected with calculated emphasis.
"There are," it pointed out,

"certain political duties imposed upon many officers in the executive
departments, the discharge of which is under the direction of the President. But it would be an alarming doctrine that Congress cannot
impose upon any executive officer any duty they may think proper,
which is not repugnant to any rights secured and protected by the
Constitution; and in such cases, the duty and responsibility grow out
of and are subject to the control of the law, and not to the direction of
the President."[58]

In short, the Court recognized that the underlying question of
the case was whether the President's "executive power," coupled
with his duty to "take care that the laws be faithfully executed,"
made it constitutionally impossible for Congress ever to entrust
the construction of its statutes to anybody but the President; and
it answered this question with an emphatic "no."

How does this exceedingly important issue stand today? The
question is particularly worth discussing in connection with certain features of the President's proposal of January 12, 1937, for

the reorganization of the executive branch of the National Government and their possible implications. First, however, we need to consider the President's removal power and the effort of the Court in recent years to equate this power with his supervisory powers; in other words, to stamp upon the removal power the character of a sanctioning power in relation to these, and on the other hand to confine it to that scope.

THE REMOVAL POWER—THE MYERS AND HUMPHREY CASES

Except for the provision which it makes for a power of impeachment of "civil officers of the United States,"[59] the Constitution contains no reference to a power to remove from office, a situation in which early resort to the judicial divining rod would seem on first consideration to have been highly likely and necessary. Actually, until its decision in *Myers v. United States,*[60] October 25, 1926, the Supreme Court had contrived to side-step every occasion for a decisive pronouncement regarding the removal power, its extent and location.

How explain this strange hesitancy on the Court's part to advance the cause of judicial review? Two reasons suggest themselves. The first is the strong course taken by the first Congress under the Constitution in undertaking to settle the removal issue by legislation. Throughout the ensuing one hundred and forty years the initiative thus asserted, at first in favor of the power of the President and later against it, was respected by the Court.

But in the second place, it may be surmised, the Court has always been uneasily distrustful of its ability to intervene effectively in this primarily political field. So long as Congress chooses to permit it to do so the Court is free to decree that an official who has been ousted contrary to its view of the constitutional proprieties shall be paid his salary, but as the statutes stand today that is ordinarily the full extent of its competence in such situations.[61] Curiously enough, in the two principal cases which are reviewed below—the first being the Myers Case—the ousted official died while his suit for salary was pending, with the result that the inadequacy of the Court's remedial powers was conveniently obscured.

The point immediately at issue in the Myers Case was the effectiveness of an order of the Postmaster General, acting by direction of the President, to remove from office a first-class postmaster, in view of the following provision of an act of Congress passed in 1876:

"Postmasters of the first, second and third classes shall be appointed and may be removed by the President with the advice and consent of the Senate, and shall hold their offices for four years unless sooner removed or suspended according to law."[62]

A divided court, speaking by Chief Justice Taft, held the order of removal valid, and the statutory provision just quoted void. Standing by itself this disallowance does not necessarily imply more than that so long as Congress chooses to leave the appointment of an inferior officer with the President, acting with the advice and consent of the Senate, it may not make the officer's removal dependent also on such consent. But with this comparatively narrow holding the Court was not content, and in the Chief Justice's elaborate opinion the sweeping doctrine was advanced that the President is endowed by Article II of the Constitution with a power of removal which, so far as "executive officers of the United States appointed by him" are concerned, is not susceptible constitutionally of any restraint or limitation by Congress, and that all such officers are intended by the Constitution to be left removable at the President's will.

The Chief Justice's main reliance was upon "the decision of 1789" previously alluded to. The incident may be briefly described.[63] On June 16 of that year the first House of Representatives under the Constitution went into committee of the whole to consider a bill proposed by Madison for establishing a Department of Foreign Affairs, the opening clause of which provided that the principal officer of the new department was "to be removable from office by the President of the United States." In the debate which ensued three fairly equal groups disclosed themselves: first, those who, headed by Madison, argued that the power of removal was an inherent element both of "executive power" and of the duty to "take care that the laws be faithfully executed"; secondly, those who, headed by Sherman—also a former member of the Philadelphia Convention—contended that the power of removal was conferred as an incident of the power of appointment jointly on the President and Senate; and, thirdly, those who held that the Constitution had left it with Congress, by virtue of the "necessary and proper" clause, to locate the power of removal where it thought fit. A fourth group, comprising only three or four members, urged that unless removed for misbehavior in office by the power of impeachment, or by judicial process known to the common law, an officer had a vested right in his office for the term of his appointment as fixed by law.

The mode in which the theoretical issue thus raised was disposed of is somewhat confusing. The objection having been raised to the clause "to be removable by the President" that it represented an attempt by Congress to confer power on the President which was not otherwise provided for in the Constitution, the clause was stricken out, and in its place were inserted the words "whenever the said principal officer shall be removed from office by the President of the United States," which were thought to infer that the President already had the power of removal, in certain cases at least, without grant from Congress. Subsequently the Senate ratified the action of the House by the casting vote of Vice-

President Adams, and like action was later taken with regard to the Secretary of the Treasury and the Secretary of War.

Was the "decision of 1789" capable of sustaining the sweeping conclusions of the Chief Justice's opinion? It seems very questionable. While the decision undoubtedly avoids the direct implication that the President owed the power of removal to a grant by Congress, yet this outcome was brought about by the indispensable aid of those who throughout the debate had championed the doctrine that Congress could determine the question of the scope and location of the removal power in any way it saw fit. What is more, the question related, as was repeatedly emphasized in the debate by the champions of presidential power, to a high political office, one which was to be the instrument of the President in the principal field of executive prerogative and whose tenure was, for this very reason, being left *indeterminate*. While, therefore, the decision may be fairly considered as ascribing to the President alone the power to remove executive officers appointed with the consent of the Senate whom Congress chooses to leave removable *by not fixing their terms,* it certainly did not establish the proposition of the Myers Case that Congress is without power to *fix the terms* of any executive officers whatever as against the President's power of removal.

Nor does the record of opinion respecting the power of removal under the Constitution, prior at least to the Civil War, generally support the results arrived at in the Myers Case. In *The Federalist* Hamilton had stated explicitly that the Senate would be associated with the President in the removal of officers, although he seems later to have retracted this opinion.[64] Neither Marshall, Kent, Story, nor Webster regarded the decision of 1789 as reaching offices of determinate tenure; and all but Marshall were quite clearly of the opinion that the correct reading of the Constitution located the power of removal in both the President and Senate in the case of officers appointed with the Senate's consent, although they were willing to concede the binding effect of the decision of 1789 as "a practical construction of the Constitution" till Congress should choose to revise it.[65] And that the Supreme Court of the period shared these views is indicated by its opinion in *ex parte Hennen*[66] in 1839.

The literary source of the Chief Justice's opinion is Jackson's famous Message of Protest, which was dealt with in the previous section.[67] There all the essential elements of the Chief Justice's doctrine were assembled for the first time, and, it may be added, for the *last* time until the Myers Case was decided. Other partial sources are certain opinions of Attorneys General, although the real preponderance of opinion from this source by no means supports the sweeping propositions advanced by the Chief Justice. Still another source is the debate stirred by the Tenure of Office Act of 1867, while a fourth source is to be discovered in the arguments developed by President Johnson's counsel at the time of his impeachment trial. Yet even these gentlemen, it is worth noting, generally contented themselves with asserting that Johnson, assuming that he had violated the Tenure of Office Act, had acted in good faith, not that he had beyond peradventure acted constitutionally.[68]

But apart from the verdict of past opinion, the Chief Justice also urged the theory that the power of removal was inherently "executive" on its own merits. His contention was based on the two grounds of history and of necessity; and in assertion of the former he instanced the power of "the British Crown" in the appointment and removal of officers. The argument proves too much. The power of the British Crown in the appointment and removal of officers, as we saw earlier, is an historical outgrowth of and is still intimately involved with a much wider prerogative in the creation of offices, while the only offices normally known to the Constitution of the United States are those "which shall be established by law."[69]

The ultimate basis, however, of the decision in the Myers Case is to be sought far less in constitutional history and legal theory than in certain practical considerations which naturally loomed large in the mind of a Chief Justice who had once been President himself. That this is so is clearly indicated in the following salient passage of the opinion:

"There is nothing in the Constitution which permits a distinction between the removal of the head of a department or a bureau, when he discharges a political duty of the President or exercises his discretion, and the removal of executive officers engaged in the discharge of their other normal duties. The imperative reasons requiring an unrestricted power to remove the most important of his subordinates in their most important duties must, therefore, control the interpretation of the Constitution as to all appointed by him."[70]

That the President ought to be able to remove at will all subordinates whose discretion he is entitled by the Constitution or by the laws of Congress to control, and for whose conduct he is hence responsible, must be granted, as we have seen. But the Chief Justice's conclusion that this fact "must control interpretation of the Constitution as to all appointed by him" was much too drastic and resulted in the paradox, conceded by the Chief Justice himself, that, while the Constitution permitted Congress to vest "duties of a quasi-judicial character" in executive officers in the performance of which they were to exercise their own independent judgment, it at the same time permitted the President to guillotine such officers for exercising the very discretion which Congress had the right to require!

Nor was the menace of this paradox a merely theoretical one. For, as was pointed out earlier, recent decades have witnessed the establishment of a number of "administrative tribunals" outside and independent of any department. The Interstate Commerce Commission was thus established in 1887, the Federal Trade Commission in 1914, the Federal Tariff Commission in 1916, the Federal Power Commission in 1920 (revamped in 1930), the Federal Communications Commission (succeeding the Federal Radio Commission) in 1934, and the Securities and Exchange Commission in 1934. The members of all these bodies are appointed by the President and Senate *for fixed terms,* while the members of the first three are removable by the President for "inefficiency, neglect of duty or malfeasance in office"—a provision which is not repeated as to the last three, possibly because of the influence of the Myers Case.

And meantime, in the Act of 1920 creating the Railroad Labor Board, Congress had taken a further step. In an endeavor to confer upon the members of this body a quasi-judicial status, it provided that they should be removable by the President "for neglect of duty or malfeasance in office, but for no other cause"; and a similar tenure was bestowed upon the members of the Board of General Appraisers and the Board of Tax Appeals by the Acts of 1922 and 1924, respectively.[71] Nor should the enactment in 1921 of the Budget and Accounting Act, whereby Congress inaugurated an almost revolutionary reform in methods of national financial legislation, be overlooked in this connection. The act sets up the office of Comptroller General of the United States and endows this functionary with a fifteen-year term during which, save upon impeachment, he is removable only by joint resolution of Congress and then only after a hearing which shall establish to Congress's satisfaction his incapacity, inefficiency, neglect of duty or malfeasance, or "conduct involving moral turpitude."[72]

There can be little doubt that all these measures, so far as they purported to restrict the President's power of removal, were by the Chief Justice's opinion in the Myers Case constitutionally ineffective, and that the Court would have been compelled sooner or later, had it adhered to that opinion, either to set aside the restrictive provisions or to have interpreted them away. In point of fact, it has since recanted much of the Taft opinion in its decision in 1935 in *Humphrey v. United States*.[73]

The material facts of this case were as follows: Humphrey, a member of the Federal Trade Commission, was reappointed to his post by President Hoover, by and with the advice and consent of the Senate, on December 10, 1931, for a term of seven years. On July 25, 1933, and again on August 31, President Roosevelt wrote the commissioner requesting his resignation on the ground that the two entertained divergent views of public policy, but at the same time disclaiming any reflection on Mr. Humphrey personally or on his official conduct. Said the President:

"You will, I know, realize that I do not feel that your mind and my mind go along together on either the policies or the administering of the Federal Trade Commission, and, frankly, I think it is best for the people of this country that I should have a full confidence."

Humphrey having declined to resign, the President on October 7 notified him that he was from that date "removed" from office; and in due course Humphrey brought suit for salary.[74]

The principal basis of the Court's unanimous decision sustaining Humphrey's claim that he was wrongfully removed from office is indicated in the following paragraphs of Justice Sutherland's opinion. Distinguishing the Myers Case, the Justice says:

"A postmaster is an executive officer restricted to the performance of executive functions. He is charged with no duty at all related to either the legislative or judicial power. The actual decision in the Myers Case finds support in the theory that such an office is merely one of the units in the executive department and hence inherently subject to the exclusive and illimitable power of removal by the chief executive, whose subordinate and aid he is. . . . It goes no farther;—much less does it include an officer who occupies no place in the executive department and who exercises no part of the executive power vested by the Constitution in the President.

"The Federal Trade Commission is an administrative body created by Congress to carry into effect legislative policies embodied in the statute. . . . Its duties are performed without executive leave and in the contemplation of the statute must be free from executive control. . . .

"We think it plain under the Constitution that illimitable power of removal is not possessed by the President in respect of officers of the character of those just named [the Interstate Commerce Commission, the Federal Trade Commission, the Court of Claims]. The authority of Congress, in creating quasi-legislative or quasi-judicial agencies, to require them to act in discharge of their duties independently of executive control, cannot be well doubted; and that authority includes, as an appropriate incident, power to fix the period during which they shall continue, and to forbid their removal except for cause in the meantime. For it is quite evident that one who holds his office only during the pleasure of another cannot be depended upon to maintain an attitude of independence against the latter's will."[75]

Elsewhere in his opinion Justice Sutherland takes pains to point out that "the decision of 1789" concerned an office which "was not only purely executive" but an officer "who was responsible to the President and to him alone, in a very definite sense."[76]

That this holding, considered in the light of this opinion, goes a long way toward scrapping the Myers decision is fairly clear. Not only does the opinion entirely ignore Chief Justice Taft's invocation of the opening clause of Article II, but it employs the term "executive power" throughout either in the sense of the President's constitutional prerogatives or in the narrow sense of non-discretionary powers. All other powers which grow out of or succeed to legislation by Congress within the field of its delegated powers are comprised, when they do not fall to the regular courts, under the captions of "quasi-legislative" and "quasi-judicial." It seems to follow that the President's constitutionally illimitable power of removal reaches only two classes of officials: (1) those whose statutory powers are ministerial merely; (2) those who exercise the President's own powers, whether of statutory or constitutional origin."

And in getting rid of a constitutional limitation upon Congress's power in a field which is essentially political in nature—in which, properly speaking, no vested rights except the right of an officer to salary earned are or can be involved—this decision is undoubtedly to be applauded. But this does not mean that the doctrine of the case is invariably sound. The truth is that some of Justice Sutherland's dicta are quite as extreme in one direction as some of Chief Justice Taft's dicta were in the opposite direction; and especially does he provoke wonderment by his assertion that a member of the Federal Trade Commission *"occupies no place in the executive department."* Taken literally, this statement would mean that the Court was ready to scrap the principle of separation of powers as the formal principle of classification of governmental functions under the Constitution. I say *"formal* principle," since I see no reason for supposing that Justice Sutherland had any intention of challenging the power of Congress to vest the functions of the Federal Trade Commission in a departmental officer if it chose to do so, functions of like nature having been so vested again and again. The dictum seems to have been the product of hasty composition, for certainly it is not to be squared by any verbal legerdemain with more deliberate utterances of the same Justice, as, for example, his statement in *Springer v. Philippine Islands* that "legislative power, as distinguished from executive power, is the authority to make laws but not to enforce them or appoint the agents charged with the duty of such enforcement. The latter are executive functions."[78] Moreover, if a Federal Trade Commissioner is not in the executive department, where is he? In the legislative department; or is he, forsooth, in the uncomfortable halfway condition of Mahomet's coffin, hovering 'twixt Heaven and Earth? The latter is, I should say, just about the condition of the Comptroller General, but the anomaly is based on historical grounds which do not hold for Federal Trade Commissioners and the like.[79] Nor is Justice Sutherland's endeavor to make out that the latter are any more "agents of Congress" than is a postmaster at all persuasive. Both officials get their powers—such as they are—from an exercise by Congress of its constitutionally delegated powers—there is no other possible source.[80]

Still another phase of the general question of the constitutional basis and scope of presidential removal power emerged recently in connection with Mr. Roosevelt's removal of Dr. A. E. Morgan from the chairmanship of the Tennessee Valley Authority for the latter's refusal to produce evidence in support of statements which he had made to the detriment of his fellow directors. The act of Congress creating TVA contains two provisions regarding removal,[81] the first of which says that "any member of the board may be removed at any time by a concurrent resolution of the Senate and House of Representatives"; while the other provides that any member of said board found to be guilty of applying "political tests in the selection or promotion of the corporation's employees and officials" "shall be removed from office by the President of the United States." The question raised by Morgan's dismissal is whether the latter provision should be given an exclusive construction. The answer is both "yes" and "no." Inasmuch as it was the obvious intention of Congress that the board of directors of TVA should be an independent body, the President has no right to construe their legal duties for them, and hence no right to remove them for a refusal on their part to permit him to do so. But the President was not attempting to construe Dr. Morgan's legal duties for him. He was merely requiring his coöperation in attempting to clear up charges which had called into question the honesty of the other directors and which had virtually brought the activities of the board to a standstill. To deny the President the power of removal in such a case would be to make it impossible for him to discharge his duty to "take care that the laws be faithfully executed" under the most modest interpretation of that duty.[82]

But the provision which purports to make the directors of TVA removable by a concurrent resolution of the houses also challenges a moment's attention. Since a concurrent resolution is not submitted to the President for his approval, and hence can effect no legal change under the terms of Article I, section 7, of the Constitution, the question arises, on what theory can such a resolution remove from office one who was appointed thereto by legal or constitutional authority? Only on the theory, I should say, that Congress's power to create suitable agencies for carrying into effect its delegated powers embraces the power—as the dictum in the Humphrey Case suggests—of locating them in the legislative department; and, secondly, that Congress acting in its legislative capacity—as, of course, it was doing when it created TVA—may delegate this power to the two houses.

To consider the second proposition first—it is undoubtedly true, as the history of practice under the Constitution amply demonstrates, that Congress may delegate to the houses powers which it might have exercised itself. That, on the other hand, it had power in this case to delegate seems to me most questionable. Certainly the holding in the Myers Case, that when the law permits the removal of an officer in whose appointment the President has participated, the power of making such removal belongs to the President alone, has never been overruled—although again the case of the Comptroller General may be the exception which *proves* the rule.

One further point—What has been said above boils down to this: (1) as to agents of his own powers, the President's removal power is illimitable; (2) as to agents of Congress's constitutional powers, Congress may confine it to removal for cause, which implies the further right to require a hearing as a part of the procedure of removal.[83] Need, however, the maintenance of the distinction between the two kinds of removal power be left exclusively with the President's unaided sense of duty to the law? Apparently not, there being no constitutional reason why it should not be stimulated, if Congress wishes to make provision to that end, by *quo warranto* proceedings for testing the title to office of successors to officers who claim to have been wrongfully removed.[84] And, of course, in the case of officers appointed with its consent, the Senate is always in position to uphold the distinction when it is minded to do so.

ADMINISTRATIVE REORGANIZATION AND THE CONSTITUTION

It will now be in point, in the light of the foregoing, to endeavor to evaluate the two outstanding proposals of the President's Committee on Administrative Management for the reorganization of the executive branch of the National Government—its recommendations respecting the independent commissions and the Comptroller General. Congress has not as yet acted on these, it is true, but it is by no means improbable that it will do so some day in one way or another; and meantime the problems both of constitutional law and of public policy which they pose are well worth discussing for their own sake.[85]

National governmental practice has been characterized within recent years by two highly important developments: (1) extensive delegation by Congress of broadly discretionary powers to the agencies of law enforcement; (2) extensive employment of independent commissions as such agencies. The constitutional problem raised by the first of these developments, its effect upon the maxim against the delegation of legislative power, is treated in the following chapter. It is the problem raised by the second development, that of the dispersion of responsibility for the enforcement of the laws, which furnished the President's Committee its principal concern.

The Committee's point of view is thoroughly Jacksonian.[86] The Constitution, it says, "places in the President, and the President alone, the whole executive power of the Government of the United States," a thought which Mr. Roosevelt emphasizes in his message transmitting the Committee's report to Congress in the following words: "The Presidency as established in the Constitution of the United States has all the powers that are required. In spite of timid souls in 1787 who feared effective government the Presidency was established as a single strong Chief Executive office in which was vested the entire executive power of the National Government, even as the legislative power was placed in the Congress, and the judicial in the Supreme Court." And surveying the independent commissions from this angle, the Committee sees them as constituting "a headless 'fourth branch' of the government, a haphazard deposit of irresponsible agencies and uncoordinated powers," a constant obstruction to "effective over-all management of national administration." The Committee then continues:

"The commissions produce confusion, conflict, and incoherence in the formulation and in the execution of the President's policies. Not only by constitutional theory, but by the steady and mounting insistence of public opinion, the President is held responsible for the wise and efficient management of the Executive Branch of the Government. The people look to him for leadership. And yet we whittle away the effective control essential to that leadership by parceling out to a dozen or more irresponsible agencies important powers of policy and administration."

Moreover, the worst is yet to come, since

"Congress is always tempted to turn each new regulatory function over to a new independent commission. This is not only following the line of least resistance; it is also following a 50-year-old tradition. The multiplication of these agencies cannot fail to obstruct the effective over-all management of the Executive Branch of the Government almost in geometric ratio to their number. At the present rate we shall have 40 to 50 of them within a decade. Every bit of executive and administrative authority which they enjoy means a relative weakening of the President, in whom, according to the Constitution, 'the executive Power shall be vested.' As they grow in number his stature is bound to diminish. He will no longer be in reality *the Executive,* but only one of many executives, threading his way around obstacles which he has no power to overcome."

What, then, does the Committee propose should be done about the matter? "Any program," it answers, "to restore our constitutional ideal of a fully coordinated Executive Branch responsible to the President must bring within the reach of that responsible control all work done by these independent commissions which is not judicial in nature." More definitely, the Committee proposes to replace the independent commissions with two sorts of agencies, both to be organized within one or other of the departments, whose heads are subject to the President's discretionary power of removal. In one of the agencies would be lodged the "quasi-judicial" functions of the present commissions, and it would exercise these just as the commissions do, without being responsible to any higher authority in the administrative hierarchy. The other agency, however, would be accountable for all its acts to the head of department, and through him to the President. Thus any discretion not classifiable as "quasi-judicial" which Congress chose at any time to repose in any administrative agency of the National Government would be at the ultimate disposal of the President.

So far as the Committee's case rests on historical grounds it is far from impregnable. From data assembled in earlier pages of this volume it appears extremely probable that most people qualified to pass on the matter would have said, whether in 1787 or forty years later, that Congress was entitled, by virtue of its power "to make all laws which shall be necessary and proper for carrying into execution the foregoing [that is, its own constitutional] powers," to create executive agencies *ad libitum,* and to vest in them powers not controllable by the President. While Madison anticipated the later Jacksonian thesis when the office of Secretary of State was under discussion in the first Congress, yet he shortly afterward abandoned it as to the Comptroller of the Treasury, and indeed in implication as to the Secretary of the Treasury as well; and Hamilton's arguments in support of Washington's "Neutrality Proclamation" of 1793 had only to do with presidential prerogative in the "political field." Neither Madison nor Hamilton appears at any time to have had clearly in mind that executive power which results from an exercise by Congress of its own delegated powers. Still less if possible would the Committee be able to draw support from acts or words of "the Virginia School of Presidents," including the later Madison. Nor is the very development of which the Committee complains without evidential value for the historical issue. This began with the creation of the Civil Service Commission in 1883, that is to say, nearly sixty years ago—and sixty years is two fifths of our national existence. We are compelled, therefore, to conclude that when it is viewed simply in the perspective of history, the establishment by Congress of the independent commissions within the field of its granted powers does not represent, as the Committee contends it does, "a relative weakening of the President"; but that, on the contrary, it may only represent a disinclination on the part of Congress to let the increased use of its own powers serve as a source for a relative augmentation of the presidential office—relative, that is, to what the Presidency had been.

And in this connection it is pertinent to comment briefly upon the Committee's use of the words "responsibility," "irresponsible," and the like. The independent commissions are said to be "irresponsible agencies," and to "enjoy power without responsibility." But this can mean only that they are not responsible to the President. It is not shown, nor could it be, that they are less responsible to the law, or less disposed to observe it according to their own conscientious interpretation of it than is the President himself, or that their acts are less readily subject to judicial review. The President is, to be sure, "responsible" to the electorate in a general way, while the commissions are not, but this kind of responsibility is certainly a frail reliance when private rights are concerned. What the Committee really means undoubtedly by "responsibility" is *capacity for effective action,* not accountability to the law; and it is the former, not the latter, which its proposals are intended to promote.[87]

Is, then, centralized administration necessarily the best administration for so vast an area as the United States? The Committee itself looks forward, it says, to the regional decentralization of administration; but before this can take place, it contends, the principle of "over-all management" centering in the President must be securely established. Its prima facie case is no doubt a strong one. The principle of hierarchy appeals to one's demand for symmetry, one's sense of order. Why is it, moreover, that the National Government has come to fill the vast role that it does today in the economic field if not for the very purpose of mitigating the conflicting policies of Big Business on the one hand and of the local governments on the other? And how is this purpose to be realized if the translation of the legislative policy of the government into terms of administration is to be the work of multiple independent agencies?

Yet, there are powerful considerations on the other side too. From the very nature of things a considerable part of the administrative tasks of government will always have to be performed by the functionaries who are immediately charged with them, without there being any opportunity for what the Committee terms "over-all management" to be consulted or, in fact, intelligently applied. In other words, the world of administration is a *pluralistic* rather than a *monistic* world, and reposes on the loyalty and competence of individual bureaucrats, qualities which thrive best in conditions making for independence of judgment and pride in a job well done.[88] Certainly, to conceive of the President as a potential "boss of the works" save in situations raising broad issues of policy would be both absurd and calamitous; and for such issues the legislative process is still available, a field in which presidential leadership is today a more vital factor than ever before.[89] At the same time, however, it is not even today the only factor; and the Committee's complaint that the commissions produce "confusion" and "conflict" "in the execution of the President's policies" is, consequently, only partly valid. For the broader policies which these commissions were created to carry out are laid down in the law itself, in the making of which Congress still shares.

While the problem of the independent commission may be, as some have contended, the "Gordian knot" of the administrative problem as a whole, yet the application to it of one single, slashing solution without further experimentation would be of doubtful wisdom; although, of course, this does not mean that the problem should be ignored, nor in fact has it been. Despite the suggestion of the Committee to the contrary, Congress has not always within recent years taken "the line of least resistance" and turned "each new regulatory function over to a new [independent] commission." Thus the Secretaries of Agriculture and Commerce constitute a "commission" for the enforcement of the Grain Futures Act of 1922, while the Secretary of Agriculture is a "commission" all by himself for the enforcement of the Packers and Stockyards Act of 1921 and of the Agricultural Adjustment Act of 1938. Likewise, the enforcement of the Fair Labor Standards Act of 1938 has been entrusted to an administrator who is an officer in the Department of Labor; while the National Bituminous Coal Commission, which enforces the Coal Conservation Act of 1937, is located in the Department of the Interior, although this may be only a nominal relationship. Also, in several cases, the President has been given the power to designate which member of an independent commission shall serve as its chairman. This is so in the case of the Federal Communications Commission, the Federal Power Commission, and the National Labor Relations Board; and the device is one evidently designed to facilitate administrative collaboration. Nor should we overlook the vast powers of a regulatory nature which Congress, first and last, has vested in the President directly, or indirectly through the heads of departments. Thus its control of banking credit is one of the greatest powers of the National Government. By the law creating the Federal Reserve Board this power was largely vested in that body, which is independent of presidential direction. Today, nevertheless, the powers which have within recent years been delegated to the Secretary of the Treasury, and so are ultimately controllable by the President, virtually render the competing powers of the Federal Reserve Board nugatory. Things are not always what they seem.

One method of promoting administrative collaboration Congress does appear to have neglected, and that is to require the independent commissions and similar agencies to report to the President at his request. Exaction of such a duty would work beneficially in two ways: (1) it would bring divergent tendencies in administration to the light of day and put them on justification; (2) it would inform the legislative judgment of the President. The hierarchical principle, it has been suggested, may be less important for its authoritative than for its communicative aspects.[90]

We turn now to the constitutional issues which were referred to earlier. The first of these offers little difficulty. The decision in the Humphrey Case makes it clear that Congress has the constitutional power to shield members of administrative commissions from the President's discretionary removal power. The question arises, whether it could do the same thing in the case of a subordinate of a head of department, or of the head himself. The latter portion of the question may be dismissed as academic, since—to make nothing of the political relationship which has grown up in the course of time between the President and the heads of departments—every head of department today exercises powers, whether of statutory or constitutional origin, over which the President enjoys the broadest supervisory control, and over the immediate custodians of which he may consequently claim a corresponding power of removal. But these considerations would not necessarily apply in the case of the head of a departmental bureau. It may be argued, to be sure, that such a functionary, being housed in an "executive department," would be "a purely executive officer," in the sense of the dictum in the Humphrey

Case. But, as we have seen, the distinction can hardly be maintained except on the theory that the independent commissions are an extension of the legislative department, an idea which scraps the principle of the separation of powers. This historically untenable theory being dismissed, Congress is free, it seems clear, to protect any agency of its constitutional powers *except* a head of department from the President's discretionary removal power, provided such agency is not at the same time an organ of presidential prerogatives.

The second constitutional issue provoked by the Committee's recommendations respecting independent commissions arises out of the distinction between the "quasi-judicial" functions of such bodies and their "sublegislative" functions, and the accompanying proposal that the latter, which are described as "policy determining," be entrusted to a departmental bureau directly responsible to the Secretary and through him to the President. In more precise terms, do the words "sublegislative" and "quasi-judicial" denote two distinct administrative functions or does the former word designate a *function* and the latter the *method* of its performance? The answer appears to be that sometimes it is the one thing and sometimes the other. By "sublegislation" is meant the making of orders, rules, and regulations in elaboration of and in conformance with principal legislation, such as acts of Congress. Whenever Congress or the Constitution requires that exercise of the "sublegislative" function be attended by a hearing for the interests which it is proposed thus to regulate, then the term "quasi-judicial" designates the method and the term "sublegislative" designates the result. Furthermore, in every such case the "quasi-legislative" activity must be performed by the agency giving the hearing and hence is not properly subject to superior control, a fact of which Presidents have more than once been apprised by their own Attorneys General.[91]

Thus in the recent case of *Morgan v. United States*,[92] the Court overturned an order of the Secretary of Agriculture setting a schedule of rates for certain marketing agencies under the Packers and Stockyards Act of 1921, the ground of the holding being that the private interests involved had not been given the kind of hearing to which the Act of Congress entitled them. Said the Chief Justice:

"Congress, in requiring a 'full hearing,' had regard to judicial standards,—not in any technical sense but with respect to those fundamental requirements of fairness which are of the essence of due process in a proceeding of a judicial nature."

And he continues:

"The answer that the proceeding before the Secretary was not of an adversary character, as it was not upon complaint but was initiated as a general inquiry, is futile. It has regard to the mere form of the proceeding and ignores realities. . . . It is idle to say that this was not a proceeding in reality against the appellants when the very existence of their agencies was put in jeopardy. Upon the rates for their services the owners depended for their livelihood and the proceeding attacked them at a vital spot."[93]

Also, it may be noted in passing that the Chief Justice at one time speaks of the Secretary of Agriculture's powers under the Packers and Stockyards Act as "quasi-legislative" and at another time as "quasi-judicial," having in mind in the latter instance the process, and in the former instance the product.[94]

So, while the Committee's assumption that the "quasi-legislative" function can always be separated from the "quasi-judicial" function and lodged in a different agency, subject to outside control, is erroneous, at least so far as rate-making is concerned,[95] yet this fact does not render its proposals to supersede the independent commissions with departmental agencies constitutionally impracticable even in such a case. In *Morgan v. United States* itself we see a head of department engaged in rate-making, and no objection being raised on that score. Furthermore, following the Myers Case, while a head of department could not be legally directed by the President in the performance of such a function, yet having performed it, being *functus officio,* he could straightway be removed for the way in which he had performed it.

Besides, cases of rate-making by no means exhaust the possibilities; and nothing can be more certain than that not all administrative legislation need be attended by a "quasi-judicial" hearing. Thus the Commissioner of Immigration is not obligated when making "rules and regulations" for the carrying into effect of the naturalization laws to notify and hear prospective citizens. Nor is the Secretary of the Interior obligated to consult prospective users of the national parks and public grazing lands before issuing "rules and regulations" with which such users will have to comply. Nor need a head of department give his subordinates an opportunity to be heard on rules by which their official conduct will be directed.[96]

Indeed, the law creating an administrative agency sometimes delimits two distinct fields for the operation respectively of the "quasi-legislative" function and the "quasi-judicial" function, thus supporting the Committee's dichotomy from the point of view both of *method* and *result.* For example, the Securities and Exchange Commission is empowered to issue "rules and regulations" under the act setting it up for the purpose of ensuring fair dealing on the exchanges and to protect investors. At the same time it is authorized, after appropriate notice and opportunity for a hearing, to bring to book any exchange which it finds to have violated any provision of the statute or any of the rules and regulations issued under it, and "by order" suspend the culprit firm for a period not exceeding twelve months or to withdraw its registration, without which it is not permitted to use the mails or the facilities of interstate commerce.[97]

In short, the principal questions raised by the Committee's proposal are not questions of constitutional law strictly speaking, but questions of constitutional theory, involving especially the principle of the separation of powers, and questions of sound public policy.

And this brings us to the Committee's recommendations with regard to the Comptroller General. It is this official's duty, which he is ordered to perform "without direction from any other officer," to audit the accounts of the spending agencies of the National Government. Sometimes the auditing is done prior to payment, though after the obligation has been incurred, which is termed "pre-audit." Much more frequently it is done after payment— which is "post-audit." Through the pre-audit function the first incumbent of the office, Mr. McCarl, was able at times to block expenditures which the spending agency thought it was legally authorized to make, and thus to obstruct the administrative process. What the Committee proposes, in brief, is that all accounts be settled in the Treasury, whose head is directly responsible to the President, and that the Comptroller General be replaced by a functionary who would be vested with the post-audit power and would be called Auditor General.

Whether Mr. McCarl was the watchdog he evidently took himself to be, or the dog in the manger which the Committee thinks he was, is unnecessary to determine. Unquestionably the practical disadvantages of the present arrangement are considerable, although they could probably be relieved by better staffing of the General Accounting Office. What, however, of the Committee's constitutional objections? These are substantially the same as those which it levels against the independent commissions. It says:

"The removal from the Executive of the final authority to determine the uses of appropriations, conditions of employment, the letting of contracts, and the control over administrative decisions, as well as the prescribing of accounting procedures and the vesting of such authority in an officer independent of direct responsibility to the President for his acts, is clearly in violation of the constitutional principle of the division of authority between the Legislative and Executive Branches of the Government. It is contrary to article II, section 3, of the Constitution, which provides that the President 'shall take Care that the Laws be faithfully executed.'"

To what has been said earlier that bears upon this general position, two comments ought to be added. The first is that there is always a serious objection—logically, at least—to any endeavor to set up the President's duty to the law as an independent limitation on the lawmaking power, which is increased in this instance by the fact that the element of executive power most immediately concerned—the power of expenditure—is a constitutional dependent of the legislative power most immediately concerned— the power of appropriation. The second comment is that the Committee's argument for its proposals is disappointing in failing to consider the question of the value of the Comptroller General's present powers and independent position as a defense of Congress's control of the purse, and of the check which this provides against the executive. For while a presidential veto may be overridden by a two-thirds vote of both houses, and an impeachment can be effected by a majority vote of the House and a two-thirds vote of the Senate, supplies can be withheld by a simple majority of either house. The check is not one that should be lightly sacrificed. Finally, the Committee suggests in effect that its proposed Auditor General be appointed by the President and

Senate and that the former participate in his removal, as he does in the case of the present Comptroller General. Is such an arrangement constitutionally required? Why not proceed on the theory that an official possessing only the post-audit function would be purely an arm of Congress's, and especially of the House of Representatives', control of the purse, and so could be made appointable and removable by the two houses acting concurrently, or indeed by the House alone? The history of the equivalent British office would support this theory—a history which long antedates the American conception of the separation of powers.[98]

To sum up briefly: From the outset the relation of the President to the remainder of the executive establishment of the government has been influenced by two more or less conflicting ideas. Originally the notion of legislative supremacy enjoyed a preponderating influence, but under Jackson the notion of presidential domination underwent a great accession of power. *En revanche,* to escape the operation of an uncontrolled presidential removal power—the result for constitutional doctrine of the Duane ouster in 1833—Congress fifty years later set up the Civil Service Commission outside the executive departments, although not outside the Executive Department, unless we reject the principle of the separation of powers as an underlying doctrine of our constitutional system; and thus was inaugurated an experiment from which have latterly issued a considerable number of executive agencies not subject to presidential direction in the performance of their functions.

The Myers Case was decided by a former President under the influence of Jacksonian concepts, and went to such lengths that Congress was stripped of all power to protect the independence of these bodies even when exercising their "quasi-judicial" functions. This result, however, was soon perceived by the Court to clash with the doctrines which it had been building up since about 1890 with regard to "a fair hearing" in connection especially with rate regulation; and in the Humphrey Case it beat a precipitate retreat from the ideology of the Myers decision.

Yet, despite their contradictions one common purpose can be perceived in both these decisions; namely, to make presidential removal power and presidential supervisory power march abreast. The great problem awaiting solution today is the one raised by the recommendations of the President's Committee on Administrative Management as to the "sublegislative" functions of the independent commissions: Can these be brought under presidential direction and control, and ought they be? They *cannot* be altogether, so long as a "fair hearing" is a constitutional requisite of their performance, not so long as the Court declines to distinguish between the "quasi-judicial" and the "quasi-legislative" functions when they touch vested rights. They *ought not* be, save in full recognition of the dangers of political interference with tasks which often require a trained judgment for their satisfactory performance. Besides, the national legislative power, in which the President's part is very important these days, is always available to correct the more serious aberrations of its administrative agents.

CHAPTER IV

CHIEF EXECUTIVE

VIEWED from the angle of the principle of the separation of powers the governmental process assumes a striking resemblance to the "assembly line, conveyor belt" technique of a modern factory. The President and his advisers formulate a legislative proposal, which is then put through the usual parliamentary processes, including approval by the President. But the formal enactment of the measure is only the first stage in its history. A law is made, presumably, to be enforced, and enforcement involves as its first step interpretation; enactment and interpretation are a continuous process. But interpretation, too, proceeds through different stages, for while the initial stage falls often within the executive department, the final stage usually belongs to the judiciary. Thus the executive function, so far as it is juristically creative, may be defined as what occurs between the time when Congress passes and the President approves an act, and the Supreme Court announces the reading of it which the national judiciary will support with the sanctions at its command. Originally this intermediate role was a narrow one, since statutes were couched in fairly definite terms, or if more general terms were employed they were drawn from the common law of which the courts were the recognized interpreters. Very different is the situation today, when Congress finds it necessary to leave more and more to executive discretion, and consequently less and less to the interpretative art of the judiciary. So what happens to a congressional act nowadays between its formal enactment and its judicial explication is a great deal.

In this chapter I shall deal, first, with executive practice and constitutional doctrine touching congressional delegation of power to the national executive; secondly, with those assertions of presidential power which are evoked by situations for which no legislative provision has been made, in a single word, "emergencies"; and, thirdly, with the President's prerogative of pardon, which supplements his executive powers, sometimes indeed at the expense of the other departments. Finally, I shall discuss briefly the question whether the President's constitutional oath is an additional source of power, or simply of obligation. The vast enlargement which presidential executive power underwent under Lincoln from the President's prerogative as Commander-in-Chief I reserve in the main for the following chapter.

THE PRESIDENT AS LAW INTERPRETER; DELEGATED LEGISLATIVE POWER

Whenever the courts are employed in the enforcement of the law their view of it is final for the situation submitted to them. There is no doctrine of American constitutional law which is more securely established. All executive readings of the laws are, therefore, when they give rise to litigation, subject to review by the courts, and so ultimately by the Supreme Court.[1] Yet even in such instances the Court is free to retire behind the maxim, which also goes back to an early date, that great weight ought to be accorded an executive interpretation, particularly if it has been uniform and is of long standing.[2]

Certain acts of the first Roosevelt in promotion of his "conservation policy" are illustrative in this connection. As the statutes then stood the President was specifically authorized to withdraw from private entry all lands in which "mineral deposits" had been found, and so inferentially *only* such lands. In the teeth of this provision Mr. Roosevelt withdrew, "pending legislation," many parcels of land for forest and bird reserves, or because they were supposed to contain oil, coal, or phosphate, or for other reasons.[3] Later with the advent of the Taft administration many of the above orders were cancelled as being invalid, but eventually President Taft himself withdrew a large tract in California in which oil had been discovered, asking Congress at the same time to ratify his action. The Act of June 25, 1910, however, which Congress presently passed, while it gave the President *carte blanche* as to future temporary withdrawals, made no reference to past withdrawals.[4] In *United States v. Midwest Oil Co.*,[5] nevertheless, the Taft order was upheld on the ground that it was supported by long-continued usage which Congress had had ample opportunity to correct but never had. Prior to 1910, the Court pointed out, there had been scores of executive orders establishing or enlarging governmental reservations of various sorts, and all without definite statutory warrant. Indeed, the Court itself had nearly fifty years previously justified this very practice on the ground of its having existed from "an early period in the history of the Government."[6] In short, the executive was recognized as being able to acquire authority from the silences of Congress as well as from its positive enactments, provided only the silences were sufficiently prolonged.

Furthermore, whenever executive constructions of a statute assume a negative shape every possibility of their coming under judicial scrutiny is obviated automatically. Indeed, the very kernel of the power to interpret a statute preparatory to its enforcement is the power to determine whether a prosecution or other positive act shall be attempted under it. While at the outset of the government this power was apparently regarded as being dispersed among the various United States district attorneys, it was another of Jackson's achievements, facilitated by the ever compliant Taney, to make good the right of the President to the final voice in all such matters when he chooses to assert it. The point arose in connection with some jewels which had been stolen from the Princess of Orange and seized by officers of the United States Customs in the hands of the thief. A request was thereupon filed by the minister of the Netherlands for the restoration of the booty, but not before the local United States district attorney had begun condemnation proceedings on behalf of the United States which, as he soon indicated, he was indisposed to discontinue. In this dilemma Attorney General Taney informed the President that since the district attorney had the option under the law to discontinue the suit, the President had the constitutional right to compel him to exercise that option or to effect his removal and appoint a more responsive successor.[7] Subsequent legislation has, in effect, ratified this doctrine. By the Act of August 2, 1861, the Attorney General, a member of the President's Cabinet, was endowed with power of supervision and direction of all marshals and district attorneys of the United States, while by the Act of March 3, 1887, he was authorized to determine in all cases whether appeal should be taken from decisions adverse to the United States;[8] that is to say, the President was so authorized.

Theoretically, to be sure, the decision of the designated agents of national law enforcement, at whose head stands the Chief Executive, whether or not to enforce a statute in a given situation or situations, may not be based on mere grounds of expediency but must be required by the statute in question, or at least have its sanction. Actually, any particular statute is but a single strand of a vast fabric of laws demanding enforcement; nor—simply from the nature of the case—can all these be enforced with equal vigor, or with the same vigor at all times. So the President's duty to "take care that the laws be faithfully executed" has come to embrace a broad power of selection among the laws for this purpose; and that this power is today without statable limits the history of the Sherman Act alone is sufficient proof. In a word, the President's very *obligation to* the law becomes at times an authorization to *dispense with* the law.[9]

Nor is it alone in prosecutions that executive interpretations of statutes may flower. Nowadays—and more and more so—they give rise to proclamations, orders, ordinances, rules, and regulations to supplement the law as it comes from the hands of Congress, and to give it definiteness—in a word, to *executive lawmaking*.[10] We are thus brought face to face with the maxim, derived immediately from John Locke's *Treatise on Civil Government,* more remotely from a passage of Justinian's *Digest* having nothing to do with legislative power, that "the legislature may not delegate its power."[11]

By the strict logic of the principle of the separation of powers, the only power which the legislature possesses to delegate is legislative power; yet by the maxim just quoted it is this power precisely which the legislature cannot delegate. Conversely, by the principle of the separation of powers the executive should be incapable of receiving or exercising anything but executive power, from which it must follow either that the executive can never receive any power from the legislature or that when power passes it is automatically transmuted from legislative into executive power. But the former alternative is obviously contrary to fact, and the latter opens the way to delegation by the legislature of all its power to the executive. Nor is it sufficient to urge that executive power is a mere capacity to act within limits set by the legislature. For the obvious answer is that, on this assumption too, the maxim against delegation loses all its virtue unless there is some intrinsic limitation to the capacity of the executive thus to act, which again would render the maxim superfluous.[12]

First and last, we find it to be the fact that the legislature has always been acknowledged to have the right to pass three kinds of laws, every one of which represents a delegation of powers which the legislature itself might exercise. These are: (1) laws delegating to local units powers of local self-government; (2) laws to go into effect upon the happening of some future event to be ascertained by some other authority; (3) laws delegating a considerable measure of choice or discretion as to the actual content and application of the law. The first category has always been recognized by American courts as furnishing an exception to the maxim, but as being justified by the fact that local self-government is "fundamental" to the American constitutional system.[13] All the cases accordingly which have arisen under the maxim touching the relation of legislative to executive power represent an endeavor to set limits either to the practice of "contingent" legislation—category (2); or to the not always distinguishable practice of vesting executive discretion regarding the application of the law to a situation deemed to be already in existence—that is, category (3).[14]

The earliest case bearing upon the relation of the legislative power of Congress to national executive power was that of *United States v. Brig Aurora*,[15] which arose out of the Non-Intercourse Act of 1809. This act, in forbidding trade with Great Britain and France, authorized the President to suspend its provisions when in his judgment certain events had taken place, and likewise to revive them upon the occurrence of certain other events, of which also he was to be the judge. The *Aurora* was seized for attempting to trade contrary to the provisions of the act after it had been revived by presidential proclamation. Counsel for claimant argued: "To make the revival of a law dependent upon the presidential proclamation is to give that proclamation the force of a law." "Congress cannot transfer the legislative power to the President." The Court, nevertheless, upheld the government, saying, "We see no sufficient reason why the legislature should not exercise its discretion in reviving the act of 1809, either expressly or conditionally as its judgment should direct."

The precedent thus established was followed in 1891 in the case of *Field v. Clark*,[16] in which the point at issue was the validity of a provision of the Tariff Act of 1890 empowering the President to suspend certain other provisions of the act in described contingencies to be ascertained by him. The Court cited an imposing list of similar provisions from earlier statutes and of presidential proclamations in pursuance thereof, and concluded that both on the basis of precedent and of principle the provision in question was unassailable. "That Congress cannot delegate legislative power to the President," Justice Harlan asserted,

"is a principle universally recognized as vital to the integrity and maintenance of the system of government ordained by the Constitution. The act of October 1, 1890 . . . is not inconsistent with that principle. . . . Nothing involving *the expediency or just operation* of such legislation was left to the determination of the President. . . . Legislative power was exercised when Congress declared that the suspension should take effect upon a named contingency. What the President was required to do was simply in execution of the act of Congress."[17]

The stress of the argument, it should be noted, is on the alleged *definiteness* of the "fact" to be ascertained by the President, for it was this which precluded the executive power from varying the application of the will of Congress in accordance with considerations of expediency, and so kept it strictly *"executive."* Evaluated by this test, subsequent acts of Congress in the same field have gone much further. By the Tariff Act of 1922 the duty was imposed upon the President of determining, with the aid of advisers, differences in costs of production here and abroad, and of making increases and decreases in the customs rates in order to equalize such costs; and by the Tariff Act of 1930 he was authorized to raise or lower the rates set by the statute as much as fifty per cent. In *Hampton v. United States*[18] the former provision was attacked on the ground that "the difference in cost of production at home and abroad cannot be found as a fact without using ... *choice* between results at every stage, thus expressing the exercise of the legislative will." The Court overruled the contention, but in so doing found it necessary to supplement the reasoning in *Field v. Clark* with precedents and arguments of a radically different tendency—which brings us to the final and most significant of the three categories distinguished above.[19]

From its very beginning railway rate regulation was characterized by the courts as a "legislative" function. How then could it be denied that in delegating the same function to commissions, legislatures were delegating "legislative power"? The question first emerged in certain of the state courts in the early 80's, and was met with a significant modification of the maxim against delegated legislation. Instead of saying flatly that the acts creating these commissions did not constitute delegations of legislative power, they said that they did not constitute *invalid* delegations thereof, the power involved being of such a nature that the legislature could not itself "satisfactorily" exercise it.[20] Subsequently the Supreme Court came to adopt closely similar language in sustaining delegations of authority to certain of the departmental heads to make regulations of a statutory character, and later still it advanced an even more elastic test.

The cases I have especially in mind are *Buttfield v. Stranahan, United States v. Grimaud,* and *Clark Distilling Co. v. West Maryland Railway Co.,* which were decided respectively in 1904, 1911, and 1917.[21] The first mentioned involved an act which authorized the Secretary of the Treasury to fix "uniform standards of purity, quality and fitness for consumption of all" teas to be imported into the United States. Said the Court, speaking by Justice White:

"Congress legislated on the subject as far as was *reasonably practicable,* and from the necessities of the case was compelled to leave to executive officials the duty of bringing about the result pointed out by the statute. To deny the power of Congress to delegate such a duty would, in effect, amount but to declaring that the plenary power vested in Congress to regulate foreign commerce could not be efficaciously exercised."[22]

In short, Congress may delegate its powers when it is necessary to do so in order to achieve the results which it desires.

To the same effect is the lesson of the Grimaud Case. Here defendants had been indicted for grazing sheep in the national forest reserves in violation of regulations which the Secretary of Agriculture had promulgated under authority conferred by Congress. The trial court held the statute in question to be an unconstitutional delegation of legislative power; and on appeal the Supreme Court originally sustained this holding by a divided vote,[23] but a rehearing convinced it of its error and its final decision sustaining the government was unanimous. Speaking for the Court, Justice Lamar relied in part upon a distinction between "legislative power to make laws" and "administrative authority to make regulations." When allowance is made for the fact that the latter must always conform to the former, the distinction is obviously only verbal, a begging of the question. The real basis of the decision is to be found in the Justice's recognition that "in the nature of things *it was impracticable for Congress to provide general regulations*" for the "various and varying details" of the situation which had called for its intervention. For quoting again:

"What might be harmless in one forest might be harmful in another. What might be injurious in one stage of timber growth, or at one season of the year, might not be so at another.... Each reservation had its peculiar and special features...."[24]

The mental image conjured up by these words is symbolic of the all-pervasive complexity of the conditions with which governments have to deal today and in the presence of which the Lockian aphorism has fought a losing rear-guard action.

Indeed, in the Clark Distilling Company Case the Court

seemed to be on the verge of chucking the maxim entirely. The statute involved was the Webb-Kenyon Act of 1913 which subjected interstate commerce in intoxicants to the police powers of the states. To the argument that this amounted to an unconstitutional delegation by Congress of its legislative power, Chief Justice White answered simply that Congress could at any time recover the power which it had delegated.[25] By this reading the maxim does little more than reword the truism that legislative power is not diminished by exercise, and what it forbids is merely outright and complete abdication.[26] It may be added that, in all probability, this was precisely the sense which Locke intended to give the maxim.

More recently, to be sure, the Court has appeared to retreat from this latitudinarian position. I refer to its decisions in the "Hot Oil" and Poultry Cases, in which for the first time in our history legislation by Congress was disallowed as contravening the maxim, and to certain dicta in the Curtiss-Wright Case.[27] How are these later holdings to be evaluated?

The "Hot Oil" Cases involved a provision of the NIRA which empowered the President to prohibit the shipment in interstate commerce of oil produced in violation of state quota laws. The two grounds of the decision were, first, that neither the provision in question nor any other relevant provisions of the NIRA furnished a "standard" to guide presidential choice in the matter; and, secondly, that the President had made no finding of facts to justify his order. The second ground may be ignored as superfluous inasmuch as a finding of facts could only have been relevant to a controlling standard; and this apart from the consideration that—at least as far as I have been able to discover—the Court has never ventured to traverse a presidential finding of facts, whether it was expressed or merely implied from the order or regulation before the Court.[28]

The proposition yielded by the case does not necessarily go beyond asserting that Congress may not delegate its *entire* power to the President even as to a fairly definite subject matter—in this instance, oil-produced-in-violation-of-state-quota-laws. Either there are or there are not previsible circumstances in which, and in which alone, the power ought to be exercised. If there are, Congress should condition its delegation upon the occurrence of these; if there are not, then it should wait until there are, or else assume the responsibility of exercising the power regardless of results. Persisted in, this doctrine might easily prove embarrassing, but it is not likely to be persisted in. For one thing, the decision has a good deal of the appearance of a makeshift whereby the Court was enabled to side-step for the time being the more fundamental constitutional issue of Congress's power to prohibit interstate commerce. Also, there were certain peculiar features of the case which were well calculated to irritate and disconcert the Justices, one being the sudden discovery by the government that one of the regulations which it was asking the Court to sanction had been withdrawn some time before! In the footnote which I give below a certain amount of judicial irritation is unmistakably visible.[29]

Likewise, there were special circumstances which influenced the Court's attitude in the Poultry Case. One of these was the huge *number* of delegations represented by five or six hundred "codes of fair competition"—"delegation running riot," Justice Cardozo called it. Another was the fact that these codes, while resting ultimately on the President's approval, were usually drafted in the first instance by private persons or organizations— a procedure, said the Chief Justice, which was "unknown to our law." That the Court should have been startled by both these aspects of the situation confronting them is hardly surprising; and the maxim against delegation afforded them the best words they knew with which to express their dismay.[30]

In the Curtiss-Wright Case[31] the Court sustained the Joint

Resolution of May 28, 1934, which authorized the President to prohibit the sale of arms and munitions of war to the countries then "engaged in armed conflict in the Chaco" if and when he found that such action would "contribute to the reëstablishment of peace." The case is dealt with more at length in a later chapter. The important feature of it in the present connection is the implication which seems to run through Justice Sutherland's opinion that all previous delegations by Congress of comparable scope occurred like this one in the field of foreign relations in which Congress's power over commerce is absolute and wherein the President enjoys large "cognate" powers in the conduct of foreign relations.[32] We have only to recall the Grimaud Case, however, to discover the fallaciousness of any such evaluation of the precedents; nor is it borne out by more recent developments.

Fairly typical of the New Deal legislation in the matter of delegation is the Agricultural Marketing Agreement Act of 1937, by which the Secretary of Agriculture is authorized to set the prices of certain agricultural products, including milk, with the end in view of restoring their purchasing power to what it had been during a previous "base period."[33] Furthermore, in the particular case of milk, the Secretary was ordered to take into account the price and supply of feed in the "marketing area" for which the price was fixed, as well as "other pertinent economic conditions"; but in any event was empowered to set a price which would "provide adequate quantities of wholesome milk and be in the public interest." And along with this delegation of power to the Secretary went supplementary delegations of power to producers to approve a marketing order without an agreement by handlers and to coöperatives to cast the votes of producer patrons. In *United States v. Rock Royal Cooperative,* decided June 5, 1939, this entire scheme of legislation was sustained against all objections to its delegative features, and at the same time a price-fixing order of the Secretary of Agriculture was upheld as tending to "effectuate the declared policy of the act."[34]

The importance of the holdings in the "Hot Oil" and Poultry Cases is today moral rather than legal. The former particularly is still a wholesome caution to both Congress and administrative authorities—to the former, to clarify as far as possible the objectives in furtherance of which it is legislating; to the latter, to render their supplementary legislation accessible to those who are entitled to be informed concerning it.

And so much for the Lockian aphorism in those fields of power in which it is recognized as applying in full force. But if we may generalize from the Curtiss-Wright Case, there are other fields in which there is even less application, if indeed any at all; the fields, namely, in which congressional power and presidential prerogative merge into each other. One such field, undoubtedly, is that of expenditure. The pertinent provision of the Constitution reads thus: "No money shall be drawn from the Treasury, but in consequence of appropriations made by law. . . ."[35] Inasmuch as this provision could have been intended to operate only on the executive branch, it assumes that expenditure is primarily an executive function, and conversely that the participation of the legislative branch is essentially for the purpose simply of setting bounds to executive discretion—a theory which is confirmed by early practice under the Constitution. Thus the first appropriation act under the Constitution, which received Washington's approval September 29, 1789, read as follows:

"An act making appropriations for the present year; Section I. Be it enacted by the Senate and House of Representatives of the United States of America in Congress assembled, That there be appropriated for the service of the present year, to be paid out of the monies which arise, either from the requisitions heretofore made upon the several states, or from the duties on impost and tonnage, the following sums, viz. A sum not exceeding two hundred and sixteen thousand dollars for defraying the expenses of the civil list, under the late and present government; a sum not exceeding one hundred and thirty-seven thousand dollars for defraying the expenses of the department of war; a sum not exceeding one hundred and ninety thousand dollars for discharging the warrants issued by the late board of treasury, and remaining unsatisfied; and a sum not exceeding ninety-six thousand dollars for paying the pensions to invalids."

And the second appropriation act (March 26, 1790) proceeded in the same general categories as the first, although it also contained some more specific items. The third act (February 11, 1791) contained only the same general categories as the first, and the grant for "the civil list" was stated to be based on estimates from the Secretary of the Treasury. The entire act fills about two thirds of a page.[36]

Beginning with the second Congress, however, the annual appropriation acts became more and more detailed; those voted by the twenty-fourth Congress (May 9 and 14, 1836) filling more than fourteen pages of minute specifications.[37] Even so, there were still certain fields in which Congress long left executive discretion a nearly free hand in this matter. Thus the provision made in the annual appropriation acts during Jefferson's two administrations and during Madison's first administration "for the expenses of intercourse with foreign nations" was voted in lump sums. In the words of Attorney General Cushing, "Just those words, and nothing more, disposed of the whole question during the time of Mr. Jefferson."[38] Indeed it was not until 1855 that Congress began to assign definite diplomatic grades to named countries with a specified annual compensation for each.

The latest chapter in this history is supplied by the Budget and Accounting Act of 1921,[39] which, following similar reforms in municipal government in various cities of the United States, represents an effort to restore to the national executive the function of planning expenditure, while leaving to Congress its proper function of consent and grant. In the words of Professor Willoughby, the act makes the President "the working head of the administration in fact as well as in name. The budget serves as his plan of operations."[40]

Of course, I am not suggesting that Congress may not stipulate any terms it chooses as the condition of making an appropriation and thereby limit the effective scope of the inherently executive prerogative of planning and directing expenditure. But, if the above argument is correct—and it is supplemented by best modern practice—Congress is not *required* to stipulate *any* terms beyond directing that its grants be applied in promotion of the "general welfare."[41]

The most recent aspect of the question of delegation is an outcropping of congressional consideration of the President's reorganization proposal, which was mentioned in the preceding chapter. By the Reorganization Act approved April 3, 1939, the President is authorized in the interest of economy and efficiency to regroup certain executive agencies and functions, but no "plan" of reorganization may take effect except on the expiration of sixty calendar days following its transmission to Congress, and then "only if during such sixty-day period there has not been passed by the two Houses a concurrent resolution stating in substance that the Congress does not favor" it. The provision was defended in Congress as a conditional delegation of power to the President, the condition being the expiration of the sixty-day period without adverse action by the Houses. "That the taking effect of action legislative in character may be made dependent on conditions or contingencies is well recognized," said a spokesman for the provision; nor did it make any difference that the required contingency was proof that somebody's opinion was favorable to the action in question. The argument is persuasive, especially in view of recent decisions of the Court sustaining delegations of power to the Secretary of Agriculture which were qualified by the requirement of a favorable referendum among marketers of certain agricultural products. In the leading case this feature of the act before the Court was specifically declared not to "involve any delegation of legislative authority."[42] The device—borrowed from British practice—suggests the constitutional possibility of the complete reversal of the role of the President and Congress in legislation.

All in all, it is easy to see that the maxim has passed its heyday, along with the *laissez-faire* conception of governmental function of which it is a reflection. For underlying it is the idea that any situation, in order to be brought under governmental control, should receive definition in a nearly automatic rule of law, applied through a nearly nondiscretionary magistracy. With present-day conditions such a theory is glaringly out of touch. The only question is whether the augmented powers of government shall continue to find expression and modulation through broadly flexible statutory rules announced beforehand. The minimization of the taboo upon delegated legislative power, by keeping legislation a still feasible technique of government, answers this question affirmatively.[43]

EMERGENCY POWERS OF THE PRESIDENT— THE "STEWARDSHIP THEORY"

While he was a preëminent exponent of the idea of "a government of laws and not of men" and hence of the supremacy in the English constitution of the lawmaking organ, this fact did not, as we have seen, deter John Locke from claiming for the executive in its own right a broad discretion capable even of setting aside the ordinary law in the meeting of special exigencies for which the legislative power had not provided. Nor did he regard this prerogative as limited to war time, nor even to situations of great urgency. It was sufficient if the "public good" might be advanced by its exercise.[44] To what extent has this doctrine received recognition in constitutional law and theory appertaining to the President's power?

The most important utterance of the court which is relevant in this connection is to be found in the opinion of Justice Miller delivered in 1890 in the case of *in re* Neagle.[45] The material facts of the case were as follows: Because of threats against the life of Justice Field by one Terry, a resident of California, the Attorney General had detailed Neagle, a United States marshal, to act as Field's bodyguard while the latter was traveling on circuit in that state. In the discharge of his duty Neagle shot and killed Terry and was taken into custody by the California authorities for so doing. The question before the Supreme Court was whether Neagle was entitled to his release on a writ of habeas corpus under section 753 of the Revised Statutes, which authorizes the writ to issue in the case of a prisoner in jail "for an act done or committed in pursuance of *a law* of the United States."

The difficulty of the case arose from the fact that Neagle's assignment was not traceable to any definite statutory provision. The Court held, nonetheless, that the order of the Attorney General, being with the presumed consent of the President, had adequate basis in the duty of the latter to "take care that the laws be faithfully executed" and hence should be treated as "a law" in the sense of section 753. The broad doctrine was stated by Justice Miller that the President's duty is not limited "to the enforcement of the acts of Congress or of treaties of the United States according to their express terms," but embraces also "the rights, duties and obligations growing out of the Constitution itself, our international relations, and all the protection implied by the nature of the government under the Constitution."[46] He further cited the act of Congress which clothes marshals of the United States with the same powers in each state "in executing the laws of the United States" as its sheriffs have in executing the laws of the state; and asserting that "there is a peace of the United States" which was violated by an assault on one of its judges, he held that Neagle was as much entitled to protect this peace as a California sheriff would have been in analogous circumstances to protect the local peace.[47]

The Neagle Case brings to focus the implications of executive actions and of opinion in confirmance thereof in a variety of fields. As early as 1818 it had been recognized by the Court that the United States had, in the absence of statutory provision to the contrary, a common-law right to sue on a bill of exchange which had been endorsed to the Treasurer of the United States;[48] and a few years later the broad general doctrine had been laid down "that the United States, being a body politic, as an incident to their general sovereignty, have a capacity to enter into contracts" "within the general sphere of their constitutional powers" through the instrumentality of the appropriate executive department "whenever such contracts . . . are not forbidden by law."[49] In the latter case, moreover, the Court had listened to argument by the Attorney General that in the performance of the trust enjoined upon him by the "take care" clause, the President "not only may, but . . . is bound to avail himself of every appropriate means not forbidden by law";[50] and, while the Court does not advert to this contention, the immediate and inevitable result of its holding was the location in the executive department of the power which it ascribed to the United States Government in its corporate capacity.[51]

A series of opinions handed down by Attorney General Cushing in the years 1853 and 1854 are also significant in this connection. One of these claimed for the President the power, as growing out of his duty, to "take care that the laws be faithfully executed," to institute investigations and incur expenditures therefor which it became the moral obligation of Congress to meet.[52] Another held that although no statute made it the duty of the United States to assume the legal defense by counsel of marshals and other ministerial officers of the law when they were sued for their official acts, yet it was within the discretion of the President to do so if he was persuaded that such officers were being harassed by suits on this account.[53] Pertinent too was Cushing's holding a little later that a marshal of the United States, when opposed in the execution of his duty by unlawful combinations, had authority to summon the entire able-bodied force of his precinct as a *posse comitatus,* comprehending not only bystanders and citizens generally but any and all organized armed forces, whether militia of the state, or officers, soldiers, sailors, and marines of the United States.[54] Interestingly enough, this opinion, the basis of which was the same act of Congress as Justice Miller relied upon, is the immediate source of the theory invoked by President Lincoln in justification of his call for volunteers of April 15, 1861, the theory that they constituted a species of *posse comitatus* to repress combinations too powerful to be dealt with by the ordinary processes of law enforcement.[55] I shall return to this phase of the subject in the following chapter.

Five years after the Neagle Case *in re* Debs[56] was decided along parallel lines. The case grew out of a strike of railway unions which was alleged to interfere with the transmission of the mails and the carrying-on of interstate commerce. Against the violent protest of the governor of Illinois, President Cleveland despatched a considerable body of troops to Chicago, and at the same time the United States district attorney obtained an injunction from the United States circuit court against the strikers. The question before the Supreme Court was whether this injunction, for violation of which Debs had been jailed for contempt of court, had been granted with jurisdiction.

The Court conceded, in effect, that there was no statutory basis for the injunction, but sustained it on the ground that the government was entitled thus to protect its property in the mails, and on a much broader ground which is stated in the following passage from the Court's opinion:

"Every government, entrusted, by the very terms of its being, with powers and duties to be exercised and discharged for the general welfare, has a right to apply to its own courts for any proper assistance in the exercise of the one and the discharge of the other.... While it is not the province of the Government to interfere in any mere matter of private controversy between individuals, or to use its granted powers to enforce the rights of one against another, yet, whenever wrongs complained of are such as affect the public at large, and are in respect of matters which by the Constitution are entrusted to the care of the Nation and concerning which the Nation owes the duty to all the citizens of securing to them their common rights, then the mere fact that the Government has no pecuniary interest in the controversy is not sufficient to exclude it from the courts, or prevent it from taking measures therein to fully discharge those constitutional duties."[57]

Taken in conjunction with the doctrine of the Neagle Case that "there is a peace of the United States," this later ruling embraces possibilities which ex-President Taft did not exaggerate when he interpreted it as signifying that the national executive may seek an injunction in the national courts in any case "involving a wide-spread public interest." And he might have added that it is a situation in which the discretion resting with the national courts is entirely equal to making good the Scriptural promise, "ask and it shall be given." A century earlier the Court had refused to concede that the Attorney General had a right *ex officio* to move for a writ of mandamus.[58]

And thus we are brought to the first Roosevelt's so-called "Stewardship Theory" of the Presidency, as set forth in the following passage from his *Autobiography*:

"The most important factor in getting the right spirit in my Administration, next to the insistence upon courage, honesty, and a genuine democracy of desire to serve the plain people was my insistence upon the theory that the executive power was limited only by specific restrictions and prohibitions appearing in the Constitution or imposed by the Congress under its Constitutional powers. My view was that every executive officer, and above all every executive officer in high position, was a steward of the people bound actively and affirmatively to do all he could for the people, and not to content himself with the negative merit of keeping his talents undamaged in a napkin. I declined to adopt the view that what was imperatively necessary for the Nation could not be done by the President unless he could find some specific authorization to do it. My belief was that it was not only his right but his duty to do anything that the needs of the Nation demanded unless such action was forbidden by the Constitution or by the laws. Under this interpretation of executive power I did and caused to be done many things not previously done by the President and the heads of the Departments. I did not usurp power, but I did greatly broaden the use of executive power. In other words, I acted for the public welfare, I acted for the common well-being of all our people, whenever and in whatever manner was necessary, unless prevented by direct constitutional or legislative prohibition. I did not care a rap for the mere form and show of power; I cared immensely for the use that could be made of the substance."[59]

Mr. Roosevelt's own justification of his policy relating to land withdrawals, which was discussed earlier, involved reference to the above theory. He also tells us that at the time of the anthracite coal strike of 1902 he stood ready on the same reliance to take over the mines and work them, had he not succeeded in bringing about a satisfactory settlement between the miners and the operators.[60]

A vigorous critic of the "Stewardship Theory" was ex-President Taft, who, in his book *Our Chief Magistrate and His Powers,* warmly protests against the notion that the President has any constitutional warrant to attempt the role of "a Universal Providence." Later, to be sure, as Chief Justice he was to appeal in his opinion in the Myers Case to the opening clause of Article II as a grant of power; but in 1916 his view was substantially different. "The true view of the executive functions," he then wrote, "is, as I conceive it, that the President can exercise no power which cannot be fairly and reasonably traced to some specific grant of power or justly implied and included within such express grant as proper and necessary." Mr. Roosevelt's theory of "a residual executive power" he thought thoroughly "unsafe."[61]

The "Stewardship Theory" must be assessed, first, for the scope of the power which it ascribes to the President even in normal times; and, secondly, for the relationship which it impliedly sets up between this power and the legislative powers of Congress. From either point of view it is unquestionably disruptive of conventional views. What Mr. Roosevelt asserts, in effect, is that if and when Congress itself lacks the constitutional power to act for the public good its deficiency becomes a mandate to the Executive to act, and, by the same token, that the Executive's action is not subject to congressional control. Thus by one and the same stroke the National Government loses both its normal character as a government of limited powers, and also its character as "a government of laws and not of men."

To consider here only the latter point—Locke could attribute to the King an undefined prerogative to act for the public good even to the derogation of the standing law because such prerogative was overmatched in his mind by the equally undefined scope of Parliament's supreme power; but to treat the opening clause of Article II as comprehending a similar prerogative is frequently to put the decisions arrived at in its exercise beyond even the theoretical possibility of legislative correction. That the National Government has "the inherent power" to meet grave national emergencies has been proved in fact many times. By the same sign, pending action by Congress, the President may, if the emergency is sufficiently pressing as in 1861, adopt temporary measures calculated to meet it, which measures are "law" until superseded by congressional action. But the existence of emergency powers is by no means to be squared with conventional constitutional theory by throwing around them the phrase "executive power" in the opening words of Article II and thereby putting them out of the control of Congress. The power of dealing with national emergencies is an inherent power in the National Government *as a whole,* not in a part thereof, and it is subject in its exercise to the methods and procedures which are laid down in the Constitution.[62]

Yet while all this is true it is not the whole truth. Historically, executive power *is* residual power, Mr. Taft to the contrary notwithstanding; and the idea that the opening clause of Article II is a grant of power affords this conception an open route into constitutional law and theory. Moreover, the principle of the separation of powers as applied in the Myers Case sets up a barrier against legislative interference with executive power however defined. Seventy years before Roosevelt certain of Jackson's followers were proclaiming the thesis on the floors of Congress "that whatever power is neither legislative nor judiciary is, of course, executive, and, as such, belongs to the President under the Constitution." Two generations earlier Gouverneur Morris had apotheosized the executive, in the Federal Convention, as "the protector of the masses." Still farther back looms the benevolent figure of Bolingbroke's Patriot King, and before Bolingbroke the Tory was Locke the Whig.

Nor should we overlook the natural affinity of democracies always for executive power. Unwieldy, more or less aware of their own incompetence, they turn inevitably to simple solutions—and executive power is such a solution. There have been, moreover, epochs when the simple solution seemed the only solution, the only alternative to social disintegration. It is perhaps a comfort to know that if such a day should ever dawn in America, Theodore Roosevelt's theory of executive power would be at hand to provide the new regime its decent clout of legalistic justification.[63]

Finally—and by way of linking this section with the preceding one—a moment's attention must be given certain acts of Congress which—to use the Court's expression in the Curtiss-Wright Case—supplement the "cognate" presidential prerogative in situations of emergency. By the Alien Act of 1798, Congress delegated to the President virtually unlimited power to "direct the conduct" of nationals of hostile countries whenever the United States should be engaged in a declared war or its territory threatened with invasion, and this enactment, somewhat amended, still remains on the statute books. Indeed, for nearly one hundred and twenty years it was almost the only provision of its kind. The approach of war with Germany, however, the war itself, and finally the economic situation which confronted the country in 1933 and the years immediately following have produced a considerable crop of statutory provisions delegating powers to the President to be exercised by him "in cases of emergency," of "extreme emergency," "sufficient emergency," "in time of war or similar emergency," in "a state of public peril," and so on. In the presence of such a contingency, of which he is of course the sole judge, the President may today increase the Army and Navy beyond their authorized enlisted strength; prohibit transactions in foreign exchange; forbid the Federal Reserve banks to transact business except under regulations to be made by the Secretary of the Treasury with his approval; take over power houses, reservoirs, and so forth, for the purpose of manufacturing munitions of war, "or any other purpose involving the safety of the United States"; alter the monthly apportionments of appropriations among the various departments and agencies of the government; suspend or amend the rules and regulations governing the transmission of communications by radio or wire—not to mention any number of lesser delegations of power.[64]

Actual use of such powers by Presidents has rarely occurred except in the precise emergency which Congress had before it in making the delegation. The emergency, however, which was proclaimed by President Roosevelt on September 8, 1939, "in connection with and to the extent necessary for the proper observance, safe-guarding and enforcing of the neutrality of the United States and the strengthening of our national defense within the limits of peace-time authorizations"[65] hardly falls within this description, although the steps which have been taken by the administration on this justification do not seem excessive. The principal one has been an effort to bring the Army and Navy up to their peacetime strength, whereas the statutes authorize the President to exceed this limit in case of emergency. It is true that in carrying out its policy the administration has had to resort to deficit spending in anticipation of congressional approval; but such expenditures in furtherance of measures authorized by Congress cannot fairly be termed "unauthorized."[66]

At the same time, it seems to me very questionable whether such delegations of power are usually necessary or desirable. Many of the provisions referred to above are obvious leftovers from periods of actually existent emergency, and do not represent the considered judgment of Congress that they ought to be retained permanently. Moreover, as we have just seen, the President has ample authority in his own right to meet temporary emergencies, even serious ones, without being empowered to set aside the usual limitations and procedures which are imposed by the statutes and the appropriation acts; and whenever an emergency does arise in which these need to be set aside, Congress can be readily summoned to do the job.

PARDONS, AMNESTIES, REPRIEVES

In a peculiarly complacent passage of the *Commentaries,* Blackstone asserts it to be "one of the great advantages of monarchy in general, above any other form of government, that there is a magistrate who has it in his power to extend mercy wherever he thinks it is deserved," adding that "in democracies . . . this power of pardon can never subsist, for there nothing higher is acknowledged than the magistrate who administers the laws."[67] In the very face of this warning the Framers provided that "he [the President] shall have power to grant reprieves and pardons for offenses against the United States, except in cases of impeachment"![68] Their temerity was due partly to the fact that whereas Blackstone was thinking of pardon as an instrument only of clemency, and so more or less opposed to the law, the Framers regarded it as also an instrument of law enforcement. This is shown by the fact that when it was moved in the Convention to confine the power by inserting in the clause the words "after conviction" objection was at once offered that "pardon before conviction might be necessary in order to obtain the testimony of accomplices," and the motion was withdrawn. Likewise, an effort to transfer the power to the legislature in "cases of treason" failed.[69] As Hamilton explains in *The Federalist,* "in seasons of insurrection or rebellion there are critical moments when a well-timed offer of pardon to the insurgents or rebels may restore the tranquillity of the commonwealth," and "the dilatory process of convening the legislature," if it was not in session, would mean the sacrifice of a golden opportunity.[70] The development of the power by usage and adjudication has been influenced by similar considerations.

By the theory of the common law, as summed up by Chief Justice Marshall in the early case of *United States v. Wilson*,[71] a pardon is like a deed, to the validity of which delivery and acceptance are essential; nor may it be known judicially, being "the private though official act of the President," unless it be pleaded by its intended beneficiary.[72]

In short, the granting of a pardon is an essentially man-to-man transaction, from which it would seem to follow that the power of granting it does not embrace the power to issue a general amnesty, of which the courts would be obliged to take notice. From the first, nevertheless, the contrary was assumed. General amnesties were issued by Washington in 1795, by Adams in 1800, by Madison in 1815, by Lincoln in 1863, by Johnson in 1865, 1867, and 1868, and by the first Roosevelt—to Aguinaldo's followers—in 1902. It is true that Johnson's enemies in Congress made a half-hearted effort to challenge his power in this respect, but without avail. In cases decided in 1871 the Court declared that "pardon includes amnesty," and that a proclamation of amnesty by the President was a public act of which "all courts in the United States are held to take notice and to which all courts are bound to give effect."[73]

Other limitations on the pardoning power arising from the conception of it as "private though official" were slower to be removed. The starting point is the Burdick Case,[74] the circumstances of which reduced the doctrine of the Wilson Case to palpable absurdity. Burdick, having declined to testify before a federal grand jury on the ground that his testimony would tend to incriminate him, was proffered by President Wilson "a full and unconditional pardon for all offenses against the United

States" which he might have committed or participated in in connection with the matter he had been questioned about. Burdick, nevertheless, refused to accept the pardon and persisted in his contumacy with the unanimous support of the Supreme Court. "The grace of a pardon," remarked Justice McKenna sententiously,

"may be only a pretense involving consequences of even greater disgrace than those it purports to relieve. Circumstances may be made to bring innocence under the penalties of the law. If so brought, escape by confession of guilt implied in the acceptance of a pardon may be rejected."[75]

And this, in face of the fact that it was Burdick himself who first suggested the idea that he was guilty of a crime! Nor did the Court pay any attention to the fact that the President had accompanied his proffer to Burdick with a proclamation, although a similar procedure had been held to bring Johnson's amnesties to the Court's notice.[76]

For rescuing the Court from the entanglements of this pedantical nonsense principal credit should go to President Coolidge. In 1923 Coolidge "remitted" the sentence which had been imposed for contempt upon one Craig by the United States district court for the southern district of New York. Craig, evidently bent on martyrdom, had already given notice that he would refuse a pardon if it was tendered him, but the President's action, which merely closed the jail against him, left him nothing to reject.[77] In other words, the pardoning power was found to embrace a previously undiscovered attribute, the power to *remit* sentences—at least jail sentences—without consultation of the other party.

Two years later occurred a similar episode involving the poet-gunman, Gerald Chapman, who had escaped from the Federal penitentiary at Atlanta. On his recapture Chapman found himself confronted with a Connecticut indictment charging him with murder, and an order by President Coolidge "commuting" his Federal sentence to the portion of it which he had already served and handing him over to the Connecticut authorities, who promptly tried and convicted him and sentenced him to hang. Again a discriminating choice of phraseology proved decisive. In an application for a writ of habeas corpus in the United States district court for Connecticut, Chapman's counsel vainly urged that the alleged commutation of sentence was a pardon which, to be valid, must be accepted by their client.

"To speak of a 'right' [said Judge Thomas] to be imprisoned is to invest that word with a significance not to be found in common parlance nor in legal definition. If there is such a thing as a 'right' to incarceration, it is certain that it is not one of the rights guaranteed by the Fourteenth Amendment to the Constitution of the United States nor by any other provision of that document."[78]

An appeal to the Supreme Court only evoked an order declining review.

This long-standing issue was finally disposed of in 1927 in the case of one Perovich,[79] who in 1909 had a sentence of death "commuted" by President Taft to one of life imprisonment. Repenting now nearly twenty years later his choice of life, Perovich assailed the Taft order on the ground that it was the equivalent of a pardon and that he had never accepted it. That he—and Chapman as well—had a pretty solid argument on the basis of the Burdick Case can hardly be gainsaid, nor in fact did the Court attempt to gainsay it. It simply discarded outright the common law theory of pardon. Said Justice Holmes speaking for the Court:

"A pardon in our days is not a private act of grace from an individual happening to possess power. It is a part of the constitutional scheme. When granted it is a determination of the ultimate authority that the public welfare will be better served by inflicting less than what the judgment fixed. . . . The only question is whether the substituted punishment was authorized by law—here, whether the change is within the scope of the words of the Constitution, Article II, Section 2. . . . By common understanding imprisonment for life is a less penalty than death."[80]

In short, the Constitution knows nothing of "*private* official acts" done in exercise of the powers granted by it. From this it follows that not only need a pardon not be accepted to be valid, it need not to be known judicially to be pleaded, being the official act of a coördinate department of government. But the President is not authorized to *add* to sentences imposed by the courts—he may only *mitigate* them, such being the common understanding of a pardon. And the question whether an alleged pardon does the one thing or the other and so is a pardon or not, is a question ultimately for the Court.

But while the common law has been largely abandoned as a disabling factor of presidential pardoning power, in other respects it remains in full force, as we discover when we turn to certain questions concerning the *scope* of the power and of its *effect*. The leading case dealing with the first of these aspects is *ex parte* Grossman,[81] which was decided in 1925. Grossman had been enjoined under the National Prohibition Act from further violations thereof and had violated the injunction, for which he had been sentenced to a year's imprisonment and a fine for contempt of court. President Coolidge, seeing an opportunity to save the government Grossman's board bill, commuted the latter's sentence to the payment of the fine; and Grossman with reasonable promptitude paid up, despite which he was committed by the offended tribunal to the Chicago house of correction. The question before the Supreme Court was whether he was entitled, in view of the President's order, to his release on a writ of habeas corpus.

The argument most stressed in support of the district court's action is that set forth in the following passage from Judge Wilkerson's opinion:

"The power to punish for contempt is inherent in and essential to, the very existence of the judiciary. If the President is allowed to substitute his discretion for that of the courts in this vital matter, then truly the President becomes the ultimate source of judicial authority. Such a holding would be a distortion of that cardinal principle of American institutions that the executive, legislative and judicial branches of government are coordinate and proudly independent."[82]

But it was also argued that the only "offenses against the United States" known to the Constitution were offenses in violation of some definite statute of the United States, that the term was interchangeable with "crimes" and "criminal prosecutions" in the Constitution, and that a contempt of court was not such an offense but *sui generis*—all which assertions had considerable support in judicial dicta.[83]

The Court ordered Grossman's release on the basis of the twofold proposition that the President's pardoning power extends to "criminal" contempts, as above defined, but "may not interfere with the use of coercive measures to enforce a suitor's rights." Chief Justice Taft's opinion deals largely in historical data. The pardoning power, it urges, having been conferred upon the President in the light of English practice, must be defined by common law standards. "The King of England, before our Revolution— had always exercised the power to pardon contempts of court, just as he did ordinary crimes and misdemeanors."[84] "Moreover, criminal contempts of a federal court had been pardoned for eighty-five years. In that time the power had been exercised twenty-seven times" and with repeated approval by Attorneys General.[85] Nor was any new or special danger to be apprehended from this view of the pardoning power. "If," says the Chief Justice, "we could conjure up in our minds a President willing to paralyze the courts by pardoning all criminal contempts, why not a President ordering a general jail delivery?"[86] Indeed, he queries further, in view of the peculiarities of procedure in contempt cases,

"may it not be fairly said that in order to avoid possible mistake, undue prejudice, or needless severity, the chance of pardon should exist at least as much in favor of a person convicted by a judge without a jury as in favor of one convicted in a jury trial?"[87]

On the other hand, the opinion continues, the President's prerogative does not reach "civil contempts," that is to say, noncompliance with orders issued in support of the rights of private litigants. The distinction is vaguely supported by Blackstone but hardly, if at all, by the opinions of Attorneys General which the Chief Justice cites in behalf of his main proposition.[88] Indeed, the terms "criminal" and "civil" contempts are set in opposition to each other for the first time in an opinion of the Supreme Court in 1904.[89]

The practical significance of the Grossman Case is that it clearly recognizes a pardoning power which is able to cope with "government by injunction." The recognition is important not only in the field of labor law, but in that of the ordinary criminal law, whose sanctions are nowadays—as in the Grossman Case itself—frequently supplemented by the injunctive process. Furthermore, the holding arms the President with a power which might conceivably become of great importance in enabling him to protect his official subordinates against judicial interference.

Finally, the case has a certain theoretical interest, for, contrasted with the Perovich Case, which was decided only two years later, it illustrates the variety and diversity of the materials which are often available to the Court in its highly selective work of constitutional interpretation.[90]

The third dimension of the pardoning power is supplied by the doctrines of the Court concerning the *effect* of a pardon. Under this heading the leading case is still *ex parte* Garland,[91] decided in 1867, although not everything said on that occasion is still good law. By an act passed in 1865 Congress had prescribed that before any person should be permitted to practice in a federal court he must take oath asserting that he had never voluntarily borne arms against the United States, had never given aid or comfort to enemies of the United States, and so on. Garland, who had been a Confederate sympathizer and so was unable to take the oath, had however received from President Johnson the same year "a full pardon for all offences committed by his participation, direct or implied, in the Rebellion." The question before the Court was whether, armed with this pardon, Garland was entitled to practise in the federal courts despite the act of Congress just mentioned.

A closely divided Court held with Garland. The position of the majority, speaking through Justice Field, was that the act of Congress was intended to punish past acts, that it was therefore *ex post facto,* and that, furthermore, to give it operation in Garland's case would be to deny his pardon by the President its constitutional efficacy. "The inquiry arises," the opinion runs,

"as to the effect and operation of a pardon, and on this point all the authorities concur. A pardon reaches both the punishment prescribed for the offence and the guilt of the offender; and when the pardon is full, it releases the punishment and blots out of existence the guilt, so that in the eye of the law the offender is as innocent as if he had never committed the offence. If granted before conviction, it prevents any of the penalties and disabilities consequent upon conviction from attaching thereto; if granted after conviction, it removes the penalties and disabilities, and restores him all his civil rights; it makes him, as it were, a new man, and gives him a new credit and capacity."[92]

The minority, speaking by Justice Miller, challenged both the majority's view of the intention of the act of Congress and its view of the efficacy of a pardon. As to the former point he said: "Attorneys are often deprived of this right [to practise in court] upon evidence of bad moral character, or specific acts of immorality or dishonesty, which show that they no longer possess the requisite qualifications"; and he asked what qualification could more properly be demanded of an attorney than fidelity to the government in whose tribunals he sought to practise. The oath prescribed by the act of Congress being, therefore, no more than a test of professional fitness, was in no wise affected by Garland's pardon. That relieved him "from all the penalties . . . which the law inflicted for his offense," but it could not relieve him from meeting appropriate tests of fitness laid down by the law for the pursuit of his profession. This, Justice Miller continued,

"is not only the plain rule as between the legislative and executive departments of government, but it is the declaration of common sense. The man who, by counterfeiting, by theft, by murder, or by treason, is rendered unfit to exercise the functions of an attorney or counsellor at law, may be saved by the executive pardon from the penitentiary or the gallows, but he is not thereby restored to the qualifications which are essential for admission to the bar."[93]

The merits of the question are somewhat divided as regards both earlier law and later.[94] Justice Field's latitudinarian view of the effect of a pardon undoubtedly still applies ordinarily where the pardon is issued *before conviction*. He is also correct in saying that a pardon restores a *convict* to his "civil rights"; and this is so even though simple completion of the convict's sentence would not have had that effect. One such right is the right to testify in court, and in *Boyd v. United States*[95] the Court held that "the disability to testify being a consequence, according to principles of the common law, of the judgment of conviction, the pardon obliterated that effect."

Indeed, this discrepancy between the effect of a pardon on the one hand and a completion of sentence on the other has given rise to frequent applications to the President for pardons by one-time offenders under the national statutes who have discharged the penalties laid upon them by the national courts, but still find themselves denied their civil rights in the states of their residence on account of their former conviction. So common, in fact, have such applications become in recent times that the Department of Justice has adopted a regular procedure for sifting them before bringing them to the President's attention. And while the immediate source of the disabilities which are thus removed is state law, state courts never fail to give full effect to such presidential pardons, a fact which testifies to the continued influence of Justice Field's opinion.[96]

Notwithstanding which, Justice Field's unqualified assertion that a pardon "blots out of existence the guilt, so that in the eyes of the law the offender is as innocent as if he had never committed the offense" must today be set down as much too sweeping. A case immediately in point is *Carlesi v. New York*,[97] decided in 1914. Carlesi was convicted in the New York courts and sentenced as a "second offender," his prior offense having been one against the United States for which he had been pardoned by the President. His contention in the later case was that in thus taking account of this prior conviction, the New York courts were unconstitutionally denying the presidential pardon its full operation. The Court rejected the argument. The New York statute, it said, did not purport to authorize additional punishment for the act pardoned, but only prescribed such penalties as were appropriate "in view of the nature of the [later] offense and the character of the offender, taking in view his past conduct"; and it intimated that Congress could validly do the same thing without infringing in any way upon the President's power of pardon.

That is to say, a pardon does not necessarily blot out the fact of guilt *if it has been established by previous conviction*. That fact thus established may be validly treated as evidence of habitual criminality whether it was the occasion of an exercise of the pardoning power or not. But, if this is true, it is difficult to see how a pardon can qualify a man for a pursuit from which those convicted of crime are validly excluded. In the one case as in the other the pardoned man would appear to stand in the same situation as the man who has served his sentence—the holding in the Garland Case to the contrary notwithstanding. The ultimate question, therefore, regarding the effect of a pardon in the case of a convicted offender is this: what line will the courts draw between the "civil rights" of which his conviction deprived him and the power of the legislature—national or state—to lay down suitable qualifications for certain pursuits?[98]

Other phases of the subject may be dismissed rather briefly. It is only "offenses against the *United States*" that the President may pardon; and the offense must have been already committed, that is, it may not be anticipated, otherwise the power to pardon would be a power to dispense with observance of the law. On the other hand, pardon may precede trial, and so dispense with it. Also, pardons may be absolute or they may be conditional, and may cancel the entire sentence or may commute to a lighter sentence.[99] Where the penalty takes the form of a fine or forfeiture a pardon by the President restores to the offender so much of his property as has not become vested in third parties, or covered into the Treasury, whence no money may be paid out "but in consequence of appropriations by law."[100] While Congress may not restrict the pardoning power, it may itself, under the "necessary and proper" clause, enact amnesty laws remitting penalties incurred under the national statutes, and may stipulate that witnesses before the courts or other bodies qualified to take testimony shall not be prosecuted by the National Government for any offenses disclosed by their testimony.[101] It may also authorize judges of the United States to suspend sentences, action which without such authorization is an invasion of the President's prerogative.[102]

Finally, by the words of the Constitution itself, the pardoning power does not extend to "cases of impeachment." What does this mean? As it stood in the Report of the Committee of Detail of the Convention which framed the Constitution, the original of this clause read "his [the President's] pardon shall not be pleadable in bar of an impeachment," which is taken from the English Act of Settlement of 1701, although the principle it states had been asserted by the Commons as early as 1679.[103] The evident purpose in the form finally adopted is not only to prevent a presidential pardon from constituting a bar to impeachment proceedings, but also to prevent it from relieving one thus convicted of the penalties imposed by the court of impeachment, it being elsewhere provided that these "shall not extend further than to removal from office, and disqualification to hold and enjoy an office of honor, trust, or profit under the United States."[104]

Thus the development of the President's power to pardon has proceeded along two different, even conflicting lines: (1) the power has been augmented by drawing into it certain positive elements of what Blackstone terms "the most amiable prerogative" of the British Crown; (2) it has been released from certain cramping restrictions upon that prerogative. And both these developments are in harmony with the undoubted outlook of the

Framers, who regarded the pardoning power as a very positive adjunct of the law-enforcing machinery of government.

THE PRESIDENTIAL OATH—JOHNSON'S IMPEACHMENT

The President takes an oath to "preserve, protect and defend the Constitution" "to the best of my [his] ability." Two questions arise: (1) Does the oath add anything to the President's powers? (2) Does it add anything to his reading of these powers? The latter question has an important bearing on the President's role as legislative leader, as we shall see later; here we are interested in the bearing of the above questions on his powers and prerogatives as Chief Magistrate.

Logically, there is obvious difficulty in claiming for the President powers which the Constitution otherwise withholds from him simply on the score of his obligation to protect and preserve it. Nor does history prior to the establishment of the Constitution aid the case for treating the oath as an independent source of power. The Philadelphia Convention in elaborating the oath drew upon the constitutions of Pennsylvania, Georgia, and South Carolina in which the oaths required of the governors of these states were certainly not regarded as augmenting their powers. Nor was a word spoken in the Convention, or afterwards while ratification of the Constitution was pending, so far as I have discovered, which lends any countenance to the idea that the oath would increase presidential powers. And even more clearly, if possible, does the coronation oath of the English King, from which the President's oath is lineally descended, refuse to lend itself to any such interpretation. By it the King swore to "confirm to the people of England the laws and customs granted to them by the ancient kings of England," and to "hold and keep the righteous customs which the community" of the realm should have chosen and to "defend and strengthen the same."[105] Its purpose, definitely, was to put the King's conscience in bonds to the law.

The notion that the President's oath adds indeterminate cubits to his constitutional stature is a phase of the Jacksonian conception of the powers of the office as autonomous, and the *locus classicus* of the idea is Jackson's Bank Veto Message of July 10, 1832.[106] Jackson's primary intention was to assert his right to veto, on the ground that it was unconstitutional, a measure which by existing decisions of the Court was clearly constitutional; but he used language, or Taney—the real author of the message—used language which was construable as claiming for the President the right to refuse to enforce both statutes and judicial decisions on his own independent finding that they were not warranted by the Constitution. Many years later Taney, now Chief Justice, in a letter to Van Buren, vigorously repudiated this reading of the message. "General Jackson," said he, "never expressed a doubt as to the duty and obligation upon him in his executive character to carry into execution any act of Congress regularly passed, whatever his own opinion might be of the constitutional question."[107] Whether the Taney of 1832—let alone the Jackson of 1832— would have endorsed this interpretation of their words must be left to conjecture.[108]

The outstanding precedent, however, for treating the oath as a source of power is not of Jacksonian but—ironically enough—of Whig provenience. I mean Lincoln's invocation of it on his message of July 4, 1861, in partial defense of his suspension of the writ of habeas corpus without obtaining congressional authorization, "Are all the laws *but one*," he inquired, "to go unexecuted, and the Government itself go to pieces lest that one be violated? Even in such a case, would not the official oath be broken if the Government should be overthrown when it was believed that disregarding the single law would tend to preserve it?"[109] He straightway added, it is true, that he did not believe the question he had put "was presented" or that "any law was violated"; but if anything can be certain it is that by previously established tests of constitutionality the law *was* violated, and not alone with respect to the suspension of habeas corpus. Furthermore, Lincoln's apology is immensely weakened by his failure to summon Congress long prior to this date, for it is this which made necessary the acts which the apology was intended to justify. Nor can there be any doubt that in proceeding as he did Lincoln permanently recruited power for the President—recruited it, that is, from the presidential oath.

The question raised by Jackson in 1832—perhaps inadvertently —was brought forward deliberately, albeit with some caution, by Johnson's counsel in his impeachment trial in 1868. The main charge against Johnson was that in removing Stanton from office as Secretary of War he had deliberately violated the Tenure of Office Act of 1867. Conceding for the sake of argument that the act had been violated, Evarts contended for Johnson that the latter's course was justifiable as a bona fide attempt to bring before the Supreme Court the question whether the act did not unconstitutionally invade the powers of his office; and he pointed out that in no other way and by no other person could this question have been submitted to judicial determination.[110] Another of the President's counsel, Groesbeck, seems indeed to have gone even further. "Shall he [the President]," Groesbeck queried, "execute all laws?" and answered:

"No. If a law be declared by the Supreme Court unconstitutional he should not execute it. If the law be upon its very face in flat contradiction to plain express provisions of the Constitution, as if a law should forbid the President to grant a pardon in any case, or if a law should declare that he should not be Commander-in-chief, or if a law should declare that he should take no part in the making of a treaty, I say the

President, without going to the Supreme Court of the United States, maintaining the integrity of his department, which for the time being is intrusted to him, is bound to execute no such legislation; and he is cowardly and untrue to the responsibilities of his position if he should execute it."[111]

The position of Johnson's impeachers was stated by one of them in the following uncompromising terms:

"If a law be in fact unconstitutional it may be repealed by Congress, or it may, possibly, when a case duly arises, be annulled in its unconstitutional features by the Supreme Court of the United States. The repeal of the law is a legislative act; the declaration by the court that it is unconstitutional is a judicial act; but the power to repeal, or to annul, or to set aside a law of the United States, is in no aspect of the case an executive power. It is made the duty of the Executive to take care that the laws be faithfully executed—an injunction wholly inconsistent with the theory that it is in the power of the Executive to repeal, or annul, or dispense with the laws of the land. To the President in the performance of his executive duties all laws are alike. He can enter into no inquiry as to their expediency or constitutionality. All laws are presumed to be constitutional, and whether in fact constitutional or not, it is the duty of the Executive so to regard them while they have the form of law."[112]

And another of the impeachers answered Groesbeck thus: "It is not a supposable contingency that two-thirds of both houses of Congress will flatly violate their oaths in a clear case."[113] That is, it is not "a supposable contingency" that the President should be more conscientious than two thirds of both houses. The argument from the "clear case" does not apply.

The outcome of Johnson's trial, his acquittal by a single vote— not to mention the political maneuvers which account for this outcome—make the episode of slight value as a precedent. But viewing the question from the angle of the actual record of practice under the Constitution, it seems clear that the impeachers had the better of the argument for all but the most urgent situations. No one doubts that the President possesses prerogatives which Congress may not constitutionally invade; but neither does any one doubt that he is under obligation to "take care that the laws be faithfully executed." And, he was endowed by the Constitution with a qualified veto upon acts of Congress with the idea among others in mind that he might thus protect his prerogatives from legislative curtailment. But this power being exercised, this power of self-defense is at an end; and once a statute has been duly enacted, whether over his protest or with his approval, he must promote its enforcement by all the powers which are constitutionally at his disposal unless and until enforcement is prevented by regular judicial process. And his oath, far from diminishing this obligation, on the contrary reënforces it.[114] These conclusions apply, however, only to his executive capacity; in his legislative capacity the President stands in all respects on a constitutional level with Congress.

A word or two of summary: The Framers of the Constitution, in an endeavor to realize the eighteenth-century idea of a balanced constitution, cast the President for a role that was in some respects self-contradictory. They endowed him with certain monarchical and more or less autonomous prerogatives, but at the same time made him the principal instrument of law enforcement. Until Jackson's period no serious conflict resulted from this assignment of functions; not at first, because the Federalist leaders thoroughly understood its implied obligations of self-restraint; not later, because of the ultra-Whiggism of the Jeffersonian party. Jackson's violent reconstitution of the executive, however, obliterated the theoretical line separating the two aspects of presidential power; or, in other words, as I pointed out in Chapter I, the

President's obligation to the law lost its character of *legal* obligation and became one of *constitutional* obligation, of which the
presidential oath—impeachment being ordinarily out of the question—is the principal sanction; and Lincoln's course confirmed
and amplified this result with a wide-ranging conception of
executive prerogative in times of emergency. But long before this
Congress itself, veering away from the original conception of the
law-enforcing power as narrowly nondiscretionary, had enacted
legislation whose enforcement was left to presidential judgment
as to the mode and extent of its applicability; and the practice
thus begun has in recent years, with the vast expansion of the
powers of the National Government, become a dominant feature
of national legislation. Today the twentieth-century conception of
the state as primarily *administrative* is more and more exemplified by the trends of government under the Constitution. Legislation emerges out of administrative experience and comes to
fruition in enlarged *administrative powers*.

CHAPTER V

COMMANDER-IN-CHIEF

"THE king," remarks Blackstone, "has the sole prerogative of making war and peace. For it is held by all writers on the law of nature and nations, that the right of making war, which by nature subsisted in every individual, is given up by all private persons that enter into society, and is vested in the sovereign power." Also, the king "is considered," he continues, "as the generalissimo, or the first in command, within the kingdom," and in this capacity "has the sole power of raising and regulating fleets and armies"; and he quotes with approval the declaration of a post-Restoration statute that "the sole supreme government and command of the militia within all his majesty's realms, and dominions, and of all forces by sea and land, and of all ports and places of strength ever was and is the undoubted right of his majesty. . . and that both or either house of parliament cannot, nor ought to, pretend to the same."[1]

In *The Federalist* Hamilton minimizes the power of the President as Commander-in-Chief in the following words:

"The President is to be commander-in-chief of the army and navy of the United States. In this respect his authority would be nominally the same with that of the king of Great Britain, but in substance much inferior to it. It would amount to nothing more than the supreme command and direction of the military and naval forces, as first general and admiral of the Confederacy; while that of the British king extends to the *declaring* of war and to the *raising* and *regulating* of fleets and armies,—all which, by the Constitution under consideration, would appertain to the legislature."[2]

Yet if one were to ask today which of the two writers represented by these statements comes nearer to describing the powers which have first and last been attributed to the President as Commander-in-Chief, the answer would have to be that it is the Briton rather than the American, and this although the latter was also one of the Framers of the Constitution.

What was said in the previous chapter on the President's emergency powers bears of course on this subject, and another aspect of it appears in the following chapter, on the President as "Organ of Foreign Relationship." In the present chapter we shall be chiefly interested in the President as the *custodian and wielder within the United States itself of the physical forces of the National Government.* The subject falls into the following four divisions: (1) his powers in the presence of domestic "war," as shown by the events of the Civil War; (2) his powers in the presence of conditions of violence, real or threatened, that are less than "war"; (3) his powers in the establishment of "martial law"; (4) his powers as the delegate of Congress when the country is involved in foreign war, as displayed during the war with Germany. Finally, the closing section of the chapter will treat briefly the President's organizational relations with the national forces.

LINCOLN AND THE WAR POWER—THE PRIZE CASES AND EX PARTE MILLIGAN

Our point of departure, naturally, is Lincoln's "dictatorship" during the Civil War. Then and there was achieved, although the development was not entirely unheralded, a mergence of the President's role as Commander-in-Chief with his role as Chief Executive, to the vast and permanent enhancement of each. Writing during the World War, Mr. Charles Warren sought to soothe, or perhaps to exasperate, critics of Woodrow Wilson by reminding them of some of the things that had been said of Lincoln two generations earlier. I quote his words:

"Who now recalls that on the floor of Congress Lincoln was termed again and again 'tyrant,' 'usurper,' 'despot'—as 'absolute as the Czar of Russia'? Senator after Senator charged that for much less arbitrary acts Kings of England and France had lost their heads. One of them termed Lincoln 'the most weak and imbecile man' he had ever met. Benjamin R. Curtis, a former Justice of the United States Supreme Court, described Lincoln's powers as 'a military despotism,' and Joel Parker, a former Chief Justice of the Supreme Court of New Hampshire, wrote, Nov. 1, 1862, that: 'The President is not only a monarch, but his is an absolute, irresponsible, uncontrollable Government; a perfect military despotism.'

"A foreign observer, Schleiden, wrote to Charles Sumner: 'One of the most interesting features of the present state of things is the illimited power exercised by the Government. Mr. Lincoln is, in that respect, the equal, if not the superior, of Louis Napoleon. The difference consists only in the fact that the President rests his authority on the unanimous consent of the people of the loyal States, the Emperor his on the army.' "[3]

Viewed from this distance, nothing in Lincoln's entire administration is more astonishing than something he did *not* do at the outset of it. I mean his failure to summon Congress into immediate session, and his further postponement of that event after the fall of Sumter for more than ten weeks. One possible explanation of this extraordinary course was suggested in an earlier chapter—the lamentable state in which prevalent theories of constitutional law had left national power when it came to dealing with States Rights.[4] From Lincoln's recognition of this the reflection must have followed that if the Union was to be saved, some as yet largely *untested,* and hence *unembarrassed,* source of national authority had to be tapped; and this he found in the powers of the President as Commander-in-Chief. But whatever its explanation, Lincoln's failure to bring Congress together for full four months after he took office involved inevitably a "gigantic exaltation of the executive power," an "amazing assumption of responsibility,"[5] from which our Constitutional System has never recovered.

In Ship Money Case, decided in 1637, Justice Vernon declared:

"The King *pro bono publico* may charge his subjects for the safety and defense of the kingdom, notwithstanding any act of Parliament, and a statute derogatory from the prerogative doth not bind the king, and the king may dispense with any law in cases of necessity."[6]

The actual course pursued by Lincoln in the days following the attack on Fort Sumter closely approximated this theory. Borrowing the phraseology of the Militia Act of 1795, he described the secession movement as comprising "combinations too powerful to be suppressed" by the ordinary processes of the courts and the powers of the marshals, and from this premise drew the conclusion that he was authorized to summon the total man power of the nation as a species of *posse comitatus* in order to overcome the illegal combinations, and to adopt such other measures as he deemed essential to success. Thus he embodied the militia into a volunteer army, added 23,000 men to the Regular Army and 18,000 to the Navy, pledged the credit of the United States for a quarter of a billion dollars, paid out two millions from unappropriated funds in the Treasury to persons unauthorized to receive it, closed the Post Office to "treasonable correspondence," proclaimed a blockade of the Southern ports, suspended the writ of habeas corpus in various places, caused the arrest and military detention of persons "who were represented to him" as being engaged in or contemplating "treasonable practices"—and all this either without one whit of statutory authority or with the merest figment thereof.[7]

Subsequently, in justifying certain of these measures in his message to Congress of July 4, Lincoln expressed the belief that he had done nothing "beyond the constitutional competency of Congress," nothing therefore which might not be regularized by congressional ratification. Even if Lincoln's apology had stopped at this point, it would not be without great significance for constitutional theory, since it claims for the President the right in an emergency to take measures which would otherwise be illegal, subject to the risk of having those measures subsequently disallowed by Congress. In point of fact, it went considerably beyond this. "The Executive," he says, "found the duty of employing the war power in defense of the Government forced upon him." "The war power," then, is the executive's. Again he says: "These measures, whether strictly legal or not, were ventured upon under what appeared to be a popular demand and a public necessity, trusting then, as now, that Congress would readily ratify them." "Popular demand," therefore, and "public necessity" may in some circumstances be invoked by the President in justification of otherwise illegal measures. Finally, referring specifically to his suspension of the habeas corpus privilege, he put his question: "Are all the laws *but one* to go unexecuted, and the Government itself to go to pieces lest that one be violated?"[8]

Already in his Inaugural Lincoln had argued that "the Union is much older than the Constitution," and to that contention he now added the assertion that the Union is older than the States;[9] and from these two positions emerges the assumption underlying both his course of action and his reasoning in support of it, the conception of a Nation standing back of and rising above the Constitution, a Nation whose inherent right of self-preservation is not confinable by legal prescriptions. Of this inherent right "the war power" of the executive was instrumental.

In the famous Prize Cases,[10] decided early in 1863, the Supreme Court endorsed for the time being the idea of presidential dictatorship, and even added measurably to it. The cases grew out of the seizure of certain foreign vessels and two of Southern ownership, under the President's blockade of the Southern ports, prior to the Validating Act of August 6, 1861. Blockade, it was argued on behalf of the claimants, was allowable under the Law of Nations only as an incident of "war," which signified a status created by "the sovereign power of the State." Under the Constitution of the United States this sovereign power was vested in Congress, which alone may "declare war." It followed that the President's blockade, until it had received the formal sanction of Congress, was without legal standing either under the Constitution or the Law of Nations. Indeed, the whole argument in support of the President's course was founded, claimants continued,

"upon a figure of speech which is repugnant to the genius of republican institutions, and, above all, to our written Constitution. It makes the President, in some sort, the impersonation of the country, and invokes for him the power and right to use all the forces he can command to *save the life of the nation.* The principle of self-defense is asserted, and all power is claimed for the President. This is to assert that the Constitution contemplated and tacitly provided that the President should be dictator, and all constitutional government be at an end whenever he should think that 'the life of the nation' is in danger. To suppose that this Court would desire argument against such a notion would be offensive."[11]

The Court nevertheless sustained in all essentials the argument thus arraigned, though by the narrow vote of five to four. Said Justice Grier, speaking for the majority:

"The greatest of civil wars was not gradually developed by popular commotion, tumultuous assemblies, or local unorganized insurrections. However long may have been its previous conception, it nevertheless sprung forth suddenly from the parent brain, a Minerva in full panoply of *war.* The President was bound to meet it in the shape it presented itself, without waiting for Congress to baptize it with a name; and no name given to it by him or them could change the fact. . . .

"Whether the President in fulfilling his duties as Commander-in-Chief, in suppressing an insurrection, has met with such armed resistance, and a civil war of such alarming proportions as will compel him to accord to them the character of belligerents, is a question to be decided *by him,* and this Court must be governed by the decisions and acts of the political department of the Government to which this power was entrusted . . . the proclamation of blockade is itself official and conclusive evidence to the Court that a state of war existed which demanded and authorized a recourse to such a measure under the circumstances peculiar to the case."[12]

And on these grounds the Court held that the legal result of the President's action had been to convert all the inhabitants of the Southern states, both the loyal and the disloyal, into "enemies" of the United States, with the effect of rendering their property, wherever situated, subject to confiscation by the United States.

In short, the Court held that the President, by virtue of his office as Commander-in-Chief and his duty in execution of the laws, had the power, in a situation judged by himself to make such a step necessary, to impress upon all the inhabitants of any section of the country generally known to be "in insurrection" against the United States *the status of enemies of the United States, and so to put them outside the protection of the Constitution;* nor had congressional ratification of his acts based on these premises been necessary, though had it been it would have been effective. The minority held, to the contrary, that only Congress, "the war-making power," could do all this, nor could Congress do it retroactively.

There are numerous indications that the decision in the Prize Cases was considered by Lincoln himself as definitely confirming the theory which he had offered only tentatively in his message of July 4, that "the war power" was vested in the President as Commander-in-Chief, and that "as President he had extraordinary legal resources which Congress lacked."[13] Throughout the remainder of the war he sanctioned innumerable arbitrary arrests and detentions, and repeated interferences by subordinates with freedom of speech and the press.[14] By his Proclamation of September 24, 1862, he declared subject to martial law and to trial and punishment by military commissions all "aiders and abettors" of rebellion in the United States, and "all persons discouraging voluntary enlistments, resisting militia drafts, or guilty of any disloyal practice," and pronounced the suspension of the writ of habeas corpus with respect to all such persons;[15] nor did he in his message the following December ask for congressional ratification of this drastic measure as he had for the much more restricted suspension of 1861. It is true that by the Act of March 3, 1863, Congress declared the President "authorized to suspend" the privilege of the writ in all cases deemed by him to require it, but it refrained from saying *how* or *whence* he was thus authorized.[16] Nor in fact did Lincoln issue a fresh proclamation invoking this ambiguous sanction until six months later; and the provisions of the act which were intended to secure for civilians arrested under military orders either a regular judicial trial or their early discharge he ignored at convenience to the very end of the war.

And meantime, in 1862, the President had set up a limited conscription several months before conscription was authorized by Congress, and had promulgated a code of "Laws of War" to regulate the conduct of the armies in the field, although under the Constitution this power is specifically vested in Congress.[17] Furthermore, in his veto of the Wade-Davis bill of 1864 Lincoln squarely challenged "the constitutional competency of Congress to abolish slavery in the states at a time when his own edict of emancipation had been in force eighteen months";[18] and, what is perhaps even more remarkable, he made in the final form of the Emancipation Proclamation not the least reference to the Confiscation Act of July 17, 1862,[19] although he might easily have treated it as furnishing complete legal justification for the Proclamation.[20]

Yet at no time did the doctrine of presidential dictatorship go unquestioned. From the viewpoint of private rights it met from the first with repeated and sharp challenge, and from that of the competing claims of Congress it was contradicted at least as early as 1862.[21] The latter phase of the controversy eventually became the politically more important one. As the problem of Reconstruction began to loom and divergences of opinion disclosed themselves regarding it between Lincoln and the Republican leaders in Congress, each side was driven more and more to assert its possession of constitutional prerogatives entitling it to the exclusive direction of this grave business. Yet not until the war was safely over, not until the famous Milligan Case,[22] which was decided at the end of 1866, were the exponents of presidential dictatorship forced to defend their thesis simultaneously against the partisans of Congress and the champions of private rights.

Milligan was arrested in Indiana in the autumn of 1864 upon charges of disloyal practices, tried by a military commission, and sentenced to be hanged. Sentence, however, not having been executed, Milligan, shortly following the surrender of Lee, petitioned the United States circuit court for Indiana for his release upon a writ of habeas corpus, alleging that, since he had never been in the military service of the United States and Indiana had never been in rebellion against the United States, his trial had been totally illegal and without jurisdiction. The circuit court, being divided in opinion, certified certain questions to the Supreme Court, among them being that of the jurisdiction of the military commission.

The argument for the government was based upon the President's proclamation of September 24, 1862, mentioned above, which in turn was rested upon his powers as Commander-in-Chief in wartime. "The proclamation," said counsel, "was an exercise of sovereignty in carrying on war, which is vested by the Constitution in the President." To be sure, Congress, by the specific terms of the Constitution, had the power to declare war, to raise and support armies, and "to reap the fruits of victory" (a singular trimming of sails in deference to issues then breezing up between President Johnson and Congress); but otherwise during war, the President's powers were "without limit, because, if defending, the means of defence may be nearly illimitable, or, if acting offensively, his resources must be proportionate to the end in view—to conquer peace." *"In the absence of all restraining legislation by Congress"* these propositions were "axiomatic."[23]

Milligan's counsel in answer repelled all such notions of presidential prerogative. "Much confusion of ideas," said they, "has been produced by mistaking executive power for kingly power. Because in monarchical countries the kingly office includes the executive, it seems to have been sometimes inferred that, conversely, the executive carries with it the kingly prerogative. Our executive is in no sense a king, even for four years." The question boiled down to this: What does the authority to command an army comprise, and that question was easily answered. "To command an army, whether in camp, or on the march, or in battle, requires the control of no other persons than the officers, soldiers, and camp followers." It could hardly be contended that if Congress neglected to find subsistence, the Commander-in-Chief could lawfully take it from our own citizens, nor could it be supposed that if Congress failed to provide the means of recruiting, the Commander-in-Chief could lawfully force citizens into the ranks. "What is called the war power of the President, if indeed there be any such thing, is nothing more than the power of commanding the armies and fleets which Congress causes to be raised. To command them is to direct their operations." And whatever the scope of the President's power, at least it was subject to the definite limitations of the Third, Fourth, Fifth, and Sixth Amendments, which "were made for a state of war as well as a state of peace," and "were aimed at the military authority as well as the civil." "This government of ours," counsel concluded, "has power to defend itself without violating our laws," and "a violation of law on pretence of saving such a government as ours is not self-preservation, but suicide."[24]

The Court unanimously held Milligan's trial to have been illegal, but divided five to four as to the grounds of their holding. The majority, adopting the restricted definition furnished by Milligan's counsel of the President's power as Commander-in-Chief, held that this did not extend to the creation of military commissions for the trial of civilians in regions outside the immediate theater of military operations and where the civil courts were open. Nor, they added, could Congress, consistently with the Fifth and Sixth Amendments, have authorized such trials, a dictum from which the minority, headed by Chief Justice Chase, dissented. The latter conceded that Milligan's trial had been illegal, because in contravention of a fair reading of the Act of March 3, 1863, which was controlling on the President outside the field of military operations. But Congress could, they insisted, had it found it expedient to do so, have authorized such trials so long as the war continued. For the war power was the power to wage war successfully, and hence was limited only by war necessity which, however, under the Constitution must be judged, when the constitutional rights of the citizen are concerned, by Congress, that is to say, the national legislative power. Five years later a new majority of the Court frankly invoked the emergency

which the Legal Tender Acts[25] were enacted to meet as affording
their justification.

While the Civil War has been to date our greatest national
emergency, it may be deemed as more or less typical of any
serious national emergency; and since then life has become definitely more dangerous, especially for popular governments.
What was done at that time may therefore be of prophetic as
well as historical interest, since it illustrates the great, the controlling, importance of presidential initiative in such a situation.
Ultimately to be sure, in a popular government such as ours, the
determining voice must be ascribed to the legislative power—to
that extent the minorities in the Prize Cases and *ex parte* Milligan
were unquestionably right. At the same time, candor compels
recognition of the fact that in emergencies the legislative power
has to stomach many a *fait accompli* with such cheerfulness as it
can muster, and that always under the Constitution a part of the
legislative power is the heavily weighted veto power of the usual
author of *faits accomplis*.

But what, it will be asked, of the decision in the Milligan Case?
It shows, to be sure, that two or three years after a grave emergency has been safely weathered and the country has reaped the
full benefit of the extraordinary measures which it evoked, a
judicial remedy may be forthcoming for some of the individual
grievances which these produced, and a few scoundrels like Milligan himself escape a deserved hangman's noose—but it shows
little more. And among judicial records it would be difficult to
uncover a more evident piece of arrant hypocrisy than the following passage—a favorite one with lawyers—from Justice Davis's
opinion for the majority on that occasion:

"No doctrine involving more pernicious consequences was ever invented by the wit of man than that any of its [the Constitution's]
provisions can be suspended during any of the great exigencies of

government. Such a doctrine leads directly to anarchy or despotism, but the theory of necessity on which it is based is false; for the government, within the Constitution, has all the powers granted to it, which are necessary to preserve its existence; as has been happily proved by the result of the great effort to throw off its just authority."[26]

Yet according to the decision then and there being handed down, the Constitution *had been "suspended" in this very case,* which was but one of many! To suppose that such fustian would be of greater influence in determining presidential procedure in a future great emergency than precedents backed by the monumental reputation of Lincoln would be merely childish.

MILITARY POWER IN LAW ENFORCEMENT— PRESIDENT VERSUS CONGRESS

We turn now to consider, on the one hand, the antecedents of Lincoln's "dictatorship"; on the other hand, its effect upon presidential power in the face of situations of violence less than "war." The discussion focuses upon the twofold question: What are the respective powers of the President and Congress in determining (1) the employment of the national forces in the enforcement within the United States of the national laws and treaties; (2) their employment in fulfillment of the guaranty of Article IV, section 4, to the several states against "domestic violence"?

The earliest piece of legislation that is relevant to the subject is the Act of May 2, 1792, under which "the Whiskey Rebellion" of 1792 was put down.[27] The act dealt only with the "calling forth" of the state militias, but this circumstance is probably without interpretative significance, inasmuch as the small Regular Army of that day was fully employed in manning the seacoast and frontier fortifications. The notable feature of the measure is its formulation of the contingency in which the powers it con-

[handwritten margin note: Calling out the militia / original act of 1792]

ferred were to be exercised: "Whenever the laws of the United
States shall be opposed or the execution thereof obstructed, in
any state by combinations too powerful to be suppressed by the
ordinary course of judicial proceedings or by the power vested in
the marshals." Upon such a situation being "notified" to him by
an associate Justice or district judge of the United States, it was
made "lawful for the President" to call forth the militia of the
state involved in the disturbance, and, if necessary, the militias
of other states; but before despatching them against "the insurgents" the President must first issue a proclamation commanding
the latter "to disperse and retire peaceably to their respective
abodes."

In the Act of February 28, 1795,[28] the above measure underwent
revision in two important respects. The requirement that a situation bringing its provisions into operation must be first judicially "notified to the President" was eliminated, with the result
of making him, in the language of the Court, "the sole and exclusive judge" of the facts justifying a use of his powers under the
act.[29] At the same time he was authorized to call forth the militia
to aid a state in suppressing "domestic violence," a provision
which evidently assumes a close identity between "domestic violence" and "insurrection," and in so doing enlarges the possible
realm of martial law.

Twelve years later, by the Act of March 8, 1807,[30] Congress
extended the provisions of the Act of 1795 to the national forces
in the following terms:

[handwritten margin note: insurrection clause]

"That in all cases of insurrection or obstruction to the laws, either of
the United States or of any individual State or Territory, where it is
lawful for the President of the United States to call forth the militia
for the purpose of suppressing such insurrection or of causing the laws
to be duly executed, it shall be lawful for him to employ, for the same

purposes, such part of the land or naval force of the United States as shall be judged necessary, having first observed all the prerequisites of the law in that respect."

Presumably this measure testifies to Jefferson's conception of the proper relation both of the legislative to the executive power and of the civil to the military power. All the more, therefore, ought it be observed that in availing himself of the resources which the act put at his disposal, Jefferson by no means confined himself to its precise terms. Thus in his proclamation of April 19, 1808, addressed to "sundry persons" in the region of Lake Champlain who were found to be "combining and confederating" against the enforcement of the Embargo Act, Jefferson supplemented the customary warning to "the insurgents" that they disperse, with a sweeping command to "all officers having authority, civil or military, and all other persons, civil or military, who shall be found in the vicinity" to aid and assist "by all means in their power, by force of arms and otherwise" the suppression of the unruly combinations.[31]

Manifestly, this comes very near asserting that all citizens of the United States whose services may be needed in that connection may be called upon by the President to act as a *posse comitatus* to aid in the enforcement of "the laws of the Union." The idea thus set going lay dormant until 1851, when it was revived by President Fillmore in an effort to overcome resistance in Boston to the Fugitive Slave Act. On the same occasion Fillmore urged Congress to modify the proclamation requirement of the Acts of 1795 and 1807 on the ground that it seriously diminished the availability of military aid to the civil authority by putting unruly elements on notice. Indeed, so far as the requirement purported to restrain the President's employment of the Army and Navy in enforcing "the laws of the Union," Fillmore challenged its constitutional validity. By the Constitution, said he, "The

Army and Navy are ... placed under the control of the Executive; and probably no legislation by Congress could add to or diminish the power thus given but by increasing or diminishing or abolishing altogether the Army and Navy."[32]

Though Congress did not amend the Act of 1807 to meet Fillmore's ideas, the virtual elimination of the proclamation requirement was accomplished three years later by an ingenious opinion of Pierce's Attorney General, Caleb Cushing, which attributed to *marshals* of the United States, when opposed in the execution of their duties by unlawful combinations, the authority to summon to their aid not only bystanders and citizens generally, but armed forces within their precincts, both state militia and United States officers, soldiers, sailors, and marines.[33] Then early in 1856 Pierce himself, pursuing the logic of this opinion a step farther, announced the doctrine, apropos of the civil war then raging in Kansas, that it lay within his obligation to "take care that the laws be faithfully executed" to place the forces of the United States in Kansas at the disposal of the marshal there, "to be used as a portion of the *posse comitatus*."[34] Lincoln's call of May 3, 1861, for volunteers was, on the other hand, a fresh invocation, though of course on a vastly magnified scale, of Jefferson's conception of a *posse comitatus* subject to presidential call; and the Act of July 29, 1861, ratified this conception so far as the state militias and the national forces were concerned. By this measure, still on the statute books, "whenever by reason of unlawful obstructions, combinations," etc., "it shall become impracticable, in the judgment of the President, to enforce, by the ordinary course of judicial proceedings, the laws of the United States," "it shall be lawful" for him "to call forth the militia of any or all the States, and to employ such parts of the land and naval forces of the United States as he may deem necessary to enforce the faithful execution of the laws of the United States...."[35] Nor is the earlier requirement of a preliminary proclamation repeated. Finally, in 1903 the President was authorized, when calling a state militia into the national service, to issue his orders for that purpose, via the governor, to the militia officers.[36] Previously the call had gone simply to the governor.

In short, the President's power to employ military force in the enforcement of the laws of the United States has undergone enlargement from the first, thanks in part to presidential initiative, in part to congressional legislation. How has it been with the discharge by the "United States" of its guaranty to the states against "domestic violence"? Although it is clearly assumed by the Acts of 1795 and 1807 that the term "United States" here means *Congress* primarily—a theory which Chief Justice Taney's opinion in *Luther v. Borden*[37] ratifies—yet in the great railway strikes of 1877, which came finally to involve some ten states, President Hayes broke through the trammels of these acts, as well as those of Article IV itself, again and again. Upon quite informal requests of governors, and without awaiting their assurance that the legislatures of their states could not be convened, Hayes repeatedly furnished the state authorities with arms from the national arsenals. Exercising, too, his indubitable right to dispose of the national forces, or professing the purpose of aiding in the enforcement of "the laws of the Union," and "to protect the property of the United States," he transferred troops from remote posts to posts adjacent to the scenes of trouble, where as he explained to Congress "the influence of their presence" contributed "to preserve the peace and restore order."[38]

And the tactics thus inaugurated by Hayes were utilized and extended by President Cleveland in the Pullman strike of 1894, when, in the face of the vehement protests of Governor Altgeld, the President despatched troops to Chicago to protect the property of the United States and to "remove obstructions to the United States mails."[39] What is more, in the Debs Case, decided a few months later, not only did the Supreme Court underwrite Cleveland's course, but it improved upon his plea in justification, in a dictum which enlarges indefinitely the basis for such action in the future. I refer to Justice Brewer's statement in his opinion for the unanimous Court that "the entire strength of the nation may be used to enforce in any part of the land the full and free exercise of all national powers and the security of all rights entrusted by the Constitution to its care."[40] Read in the context of the contemporaneous situation, these words appear to mean that the national forces are thus available, at least in the absence of restrictive legislation, at the President's discretion. They reverse, in other words, the assumption of the Act of 1807 that such employment of the national forces must first be authorized by Congress.

Nor, with the exception to be noted in a moment, has Congress ever enacted such restrictive legislation. On the contrary, by the Act of April 20, 1871, it imparted to presidential authority a new extension. This measure, passed in the presumed exercise by Congress of its power to enforce the opening section of the Fourteenth Amendment, makes it the right and the duty of the President, whenever unlawful combinations in a state hinder the execution of the laws, state or national, with the result that any class is denied the equal protection of its constitutional rights, or "the due course of justice" is obstructed,

"to take such measures, by the employment of the militia or the land and naval forces of the United States, or of either, or by other means, as he may deem necessary, for the suppression of such insurrection, domestic violence, or combinations."[41]

While no President since Reconstruction days has ever invoked the vague powers conferred by this measure, it still remains on the statute books a potential threat to lynchers and their ilk.

Finally, in the course of the years 1917-1922, we discover the most complete, sustained, and altogether deliberate neglect of the formalities required by Article IV and the supplementary acts of Congress that has thus far occurred. The controlling factor at the outset of this period was the circumstance that the National Guard had been drafted under the National Defense Act of 1916 into the national service, thus leaving the states practically stripped of armed forces. In view of this condition of affairs, Secretary of War Baker as early as May 29, 1917, requested General Bliss

"to direct the commanders of the several departments to maintain relations of cordial cooperation with the Governors of the several States in their respective departments, and to respond to any call for military assistance from such Governors for the purpose of maintaining the domestic peace within the State, by the use of any troops under the command of the department commander as are available for the duty."[42]

The following November 20 the extremely expeditious procedure here outlined was modified by the requirement that commanders of the national forces should, "except in cases of unforeseen emergency," refer all requests of the kind indicated above to the Adjutant General of the Army at Washington. And so matters stood until September 29, 1919, when, following President Wilson's collapse, a telegram was sent to all department commanders ordering them henceforth to furnish troops directly on the request of state authorities without consulting Washington. First and last, between 1917 and 1922 soldiers were sent into states under the procedures sketched above more than thirty times, the majority of the instances being occasioned by labor troubles.

Fifty years ago the Court proclaimed, in the Neagle Case, that "there is a peace of the United States." Today we have to go further and recognize that the line which Article IV impliedly draws between this general peace and the domestic peace of the individual states has become an extremely tenuous one. That is the moral to be drawn from the record of legislation and practice just reviewed, and it is confirmed by many other trends in our contemporary constitutional development.

However, there is another side to the story—not a vastly impressive one perhaps, yet one requiring passing notice. What it amounts to is for the most part simply this: that from time to time members of Congress have arisen in their places, and others have echoed them, to proclaim that Congress, and Congress alone, is entitled, by virtue of its creative powers over the national forces and its control of the purse, to say for what purposes these forces may be employed, whether at home or abroad; or, at least, is entitled to say for what purposes they shall *not* be employed.

Certainly this is an arguable position on both logical and historical grounds, and particularly as respects control of the purse. Throughout the centuries lying between the first convocation of the Mother of Parliaments down to the formation of the Constitution of the United States the right to withhold supplies was the unrestricted right which accompanies all largess. It has been urged, to be sure, that under the Constitution this unrestricted right becomes clipped to the dimensions of a constitutional right and must accommodate itself to the entire constitutional structure.[43] But, although the principle be conceded, the question still remains as to who possesses final authority in applying it; and the verdict of practice under the Constitution is that this authority lies with Congress itself except so far as its determinations may be upset by presidential veto.

Unfortunately, a power or control claimable in theory may be unavailable in fact, or at best be so only with considerable difficulty. When Congress appropriates hundreds of millions of dollars for the support of the Army it unavoidably leaves many loopholes to executive discretion in their expenditure. Indeed, under the Budget and Accounting Act of 1921 appropriation bills are virtually drawn by the executive in the first instance. Furthermore, a military or naval unit can often be maintained quite as inexpensively at one station as at another, and whether it is active in enforcing "the laws of the Union" or protecting American interests abroad, or is merely engaged in the daily routine of camp or ship life. Besides, even lack of funds will not necessarily deter a sufficiently enterprising President, who has been duly instructed by his Attorney General in his prerogatives as Commander-in-Chief, from an occasional dramatic and popular stroke, as when the first Roosevelt started the fleet off around the world and left it to Congress to provide the wherewithal to bring it back home.[44] The statutes, it is true, say:

"All sums appropriated for the various branches of expenditure in the public service shall be applied solely to the objects for which they are respectively made, and for no others."[45]

The principle, indeed, is axiomatic, and hardly required formal statement. The difficulty is to give "the objects" a definition which is capable of restricting presidential discretion without at the same time nullifying "the objects" for which an army or a fleet is maintained at all.

The one legislative result from the attempts which have been made in Congress on various occasions to restrict the power of the President in the use of the national forces is to be found in section 15 of the Army Appropriation Act of June 18, 1878, which was the meager result of a protracted struggle between a Republican President and a Democratic Congress over federal interference in elections in the South. The provision is still on the statute books, and reads as follows:

"From and after the passage of this act it shall not be lawful to employ any part of the Army of the United States, as a *posse comitatus* or

Statute now on books

otherwise, for the purpose of executing the laws, except in such cases and under such circumstances as such employment of said force may be expressly authorized by the Constitution or by act of Congress; and no money appropriated by this act shall be used to pay any of the expenses incurred in the employment of any troops in violation of this section; and any person wilfully violating the provisions of this section shall be deemed guilty of a misdemeanor, and on conviction thereof shall be punished by fine not exceeding $10,000 or imprisonment not exceeding two years, or by both such fine and imprisonment." [46]

This measure was hailed by its sponsors at the time as a tremendous victory for the cause of "government by the laws." Said one of these gentlemen:

"Thus have we this day secured to the people of this country the same great protection against a standing army which cost a struggle of two hundred years for the Commons of England to secure for the British people." [47]

Actually, what the provision does, and all that it does, is to repeal the Cushing-Pierce device for getting around the proclamation requirement. Nor does it necessarily operate beneficially for "government of the laws," since in minor emergencies it may easily provoke resort to martial law when, but for the restriction, the forces employed would have been put at the disposal of a federal court and marshal.

In fact, the comparative ineffectiveness of the measure led the year following to a further attempt in Congress to curtail presidential prerogative. In his veto of the main effort of this sort Hayes stated the issue as follows:

"[The] principle is [asserted] that the House of Representatives has the sole right to originate bills for raising revenue, and therefore has the right to withhold appropriations upon which the existence of the Government may depend unless the Senate and the President shall give their assent to any legislation which the House may see fit to attach to appropriation bills. To establish this principle is to make a radical, dangerous, and unconstitutional change in the character of our institutions. The various departments of the Government and the Army and Navy are established by the Constitution or by laws passed in pursuance thereof. Their duties are clearly defined and their support is carefully provided for by law. . . . It was not the intention of the framers of the Constitution that any single branch of the Government should have the power to dictate conditions upon which [the public funds] should be applied to the purpose for which [they were] collected. Any such intention, if it had been entertained, would have been plainly expressed in the Constitution."[48]

While the abstract merits of this argument are open to serious question on grounds already indicated, it prevailed at the time, and the appropriations were voted without the objectionable riders.[49]

In short, it still rests with the President, as it has ever since the Act of 1807, to say when the national forces shall be employed "against combinations too powerful to be dealt with in the ordinary course of judicial proceedings," and hence to say whether such combinations exist. The formula, vague as it is, yet lays a restraining hand upon the presidential conscience, or at least provides a plausible pretext for presidential inaction;[50] and when the use of force goes to the length of involving "martial law" it may at times afford basis for some measure of judicial review.[51]

MARTIAL LAW UNDER THE CONSTITUTION; HABEAS CORPUS

A regime of martial law may be compendiously, if not altogether accurately, defined as one in which the ordinary law, as administered by the ordinary courts, is superseded for the time being by the will of a military commander. It follows that, when martial law is instituted under national authority, it rests ultimately on the will of the President of the United States in his capacity as Commander-in-Chief. It should be added at once, nevertheless, that the subject is one in which the record of actual practice fails often to support the niceties of theory. Thus, the employment of the military arm in the enforcement of the civil law does not invariably, or even usually, involve martial law in the full sense, for, as was noted in the preceding section, soldiers are often placed simply at the disposal and direction of the civil authorities as a kind of supplementary police, or *posse comitatus;*[52] on the other hand, due to the discretion which the civil authorities themselves are apt to vest in the military in any emergency requiring its assistance, the line between such an employment of the military and a regime of martial law is frequently anything but a hard and fast one. And partly because of these ambiguities the conception itself of martial law today bifurcates into two conceptions, one of which shades off into *military government*[53] and the other into the situation just described, in which the civil authority remains theoretically in control although it is dependent on military aid. Finally, there is the situation which obtained throughout the North during the Civil War, when the privilege of the writ of habeas corpus was suspended as to certain classes of suspects, although other characteristics of martial law were generally absent.

The Petition of Right of 1628 forbade "commissions of martial law," which is perhaps the first use of the term. The immediate occasion for this provision was furnished by the fact that Charles I, following a bad example set by several of his predecessors, had haled certain of his subjects before military courts for offenses against the ordinary law. But, whether with design or not, the sweeping terms of the prohibition gave countenance to the claim, soon advanced by the King's enemies, that it forbade *courts-martial* even for the trial of soldiers charged with breaches of discipline. By this view a standing army became impossible, and James II's endeavor to maintain one in the face of it was a principal cause contributing to his forced abdication. From 1690 on a standing army was rendered possible in England only by the annual enactment by Parliament of the Mutiny Act, authorizing courts-martial for the maintenance of discipline in the army but for no other purpose. Meanwhile, out of the facts just recited arose the dogma that "the common law knows nothing of martial law." Numerous English authorities, reaching far down into the nineteenth century, ring the changes on this theme: martial law has "no place whatsoever in this realm"; it can never be resorted to without parliamentary authorization; since the time of the Stuarts it has been "a totally exploded thing"; "it is the most unconstitutional procedure conceivable"; "no authority for anything of the sort can be found"—a chorus which an American writer swells with the assertion that martial law "is a threat ... a mere bluff. There is under the Constitution [of the United States] no such thing."[54]

How seriously are these asseverations to be taken? Nowadays they are generally, I surmise, mere rhetoric; for that there is such a thing as "martial law" in some sense of the term is today recognized by the most conservative authorities. An outstanding illustration is Professor Albert Venn Dicey's *Introduction to the Law of the Constitution,* where martial law is depicted, like the British constitution itself, as an outgrowth of principles of the common law. More in detail, Dicey's conception sums up in the following propositions: (1) Aside from the Crown's right to put down breaches of the peace, martial law does not depend upon any official prerogative, but only on a right and duty shared by all. (2) Martial law is not *established* by the customary official declaration of its existence, but arises "from the nature of things"—it is, in fact, "the law of paramount necessity." (3) The necessity of martial law, therefore, as well as of whatever measures are resorted to in its name, is a matter to be "ultimately determined by a judge and jury." Lastly, the measures thus taken must be purely of a *"preventive"* nature—martial law cannot *punish*.[55]

"Martial law," in other words, is hardly anything more than a general term for the operation in situations of public emergency of certain well-known principles of the common law—the right of self-defense of the individual, his right, attended by the correlative liability, to abate a nuisance, his right and duty to arrest one whom he knows to have committed a felony or whom he observes in the act of committing a breach of the peace. But if the individual, official or otherwise, exceeds the rights of "self-help" just enumerated, then he himself becomes subject to the penalties of the law notwithstanding the excellence of his motives, and only an omnipotent Parliament can save him from the unpleasant consequences of his zeal by an act of indemnity.[56]

The judicial history of martial law under the Constitution opens with the case of *Luther v. Borden,* which grew out of Dorr's insurrection in Rhode Island in the year 1842. In meeting the situation caused by the insurrection, the *legislature* of Rhode Island, which in those days exercised at will any and all of the powers of government in that commonwealth, had declared martial law, and under the authority thereby created Luther's house had been invaded and Luther himself put under arrest. The majority of the Court held that the questions raised by the case were "political" and so not within the judicial province to decide; but Justice Woodbury, in a dissenting opinion, argued at length that in thus declaring martial law the Rhode Island legislature had exceeded its powers under the Constitution of the United States. "By it [martial law]," said he, "every citizen, instead of reposing under the shield of known and fixed laws as to liberty, property, and life, exists with a rope round his neck, subject to be hung up by a military despot at the next lamp-post under the sentence of some drum-head court-martial." Such a regime, he insisted, could exist under the Constitution only as an incident of the rights of war, which belonged only to the National Government; for not only could Congress alone declare war but the states were forbidden to engage in it without the consent of Congress. "All other conditions of violence," he continued, within the states "are regarded by the Constitution as but cases of private outrage, to be punished by prosecutions in the courts; or as insurrections, rebellions, or domestic violence to be put down by the civil authorities, aided by the militia; or, when these prove incompetent, by the general government, when appealed to by a state for aid"; and it was only in the last instance that, following a declaration of war by Congress, martial law might be resorted to.[57]

The majority of the Court, however, while conceding that "military government" unduly prolonged would not be "a republican form of government" in the sense of the Constitution, was of the opinion that the situation in Rhode Island had been "a state of war" and that the local government had been within its rights in resorting "to the rights and usages of war." It added, nevertheless, that in such a situation "no more force . . . can be used than is necessary to accomplish the object. And if power is exercised for purposes of oppression, or any injury wilfully done to person or property, the party by whom, or by whose order, it is committed would undoubtedly be answerable."[58] Just how this accountability was at that date supported by the Constitution of the United States, or whether it was so supported, the opinion does not indicate.

The President's powers in relation to martial law were first dealt with by the Court in the Prize Cases, and then only in implication. It was there held, as we saw above, that the President, by virtue of his power as chief executive and his power as Commander-in-Chief, was entitled to treat a region in insurrection as enemy country and thereby strip all of its inhabitants of their constitutional rights. The case thus attributes to the *President alone* the power which in *Luther v. Borden* is attributed to government as a whole; and it builds upon the proposition in *Luther v. Borden* that *an insurrection may be treated as constituting a state of war,* which it pursues to its logical conclusion. For if insurrection is war, then the scene of it is *a seat of war,* and the difference between *martial law* and *military government* becomes merely one of probable duration and objective. Such being the case, the possibility of a judicial remedy for acts performed by presidential authorization in the suppression of insurrection at the seat of it, except possibly in the extremest cases of outrage, becomes negligible.

The authority, however, of the Prize Cases as a definition of the President's power in the employment of martial law was soon subordinated, for the time being at least, to that of *ex parte* Milligan, in which the conception of martial law as resting on the war power and as measured by its rights was superseded by the British conception of it as a law of necessity to be determined ultimately by the ordinary courts. In the words of the Court:

"If, in foreign invasion or civil war, the courts are actually closed, and it is impossible to administer criminal justice according to law, then, on the theatre of active military operations, where war really prevails, there is a necessity to furnish a substitute for the civil authority, thus overthrown, to preserve the safety of the army and society; and as no power is left but the military, it is allowed to govern by martial rule until the laws can have their free course. As necessity creates the rule, so it limits its duration; for, if this government is continued after the courts are reinstated, it is a gross usurpation of power. Martial rule can never exist where the courts are open, and in

proper and unobstructed exercise of their jurisdiction. It is also confined to the locality of actual war."[59]

Obviously, this in all essentials anticipated Dicey's conception.
Indeed, Dicey cites the Milligan Case as embodying the correct
doctrine.

What, then, is the relative standing today of these two famous
cases as regards presidential power? In answer we are compelled,
for lack of more direct evidence, to turn to two cases which deal
with comparable powers of state governors, although this is not to
say that a doctrine which is valid for governors would necessarily
be valid—or at any rate, viable—in the case of the President.

In the earlier of these cases[60] Moyer, a labor leader, had brought
suit against Peabody, a former governor of Colorado, for ordering
his imprisonment in the course of a labor dispute which arose
during Peabody's incumbency. Speaking for the Court, Justice
Holmes conceded that the state courts were open at the time; also,
"as it must be, that the governor's declaration that a state of insurrection existed is conclusive on the courts"; and, lastly, "that the
governor, without sufficient reason but in good faith, in the course
of putting the insurrection down, held the plaintiff until he
thought that he safely could release him." In the face of these
admissions—or rather on the basis of them—the Court held that
Moyer had no action. Quoting the constitution and statutes of the
state to the effect that the governor was empowered to employ the
National Guard to suppress insurrection, the opinion proceeds:

"This means that he shall make the ordinary use of the soldiers to
that end; that he may kill persons who resist, and of course, that he
may use the milder measure of seizing the bodies of those whom
he considers to stand in the way of restoring peace.... So long as such
arrests are made in good faith and in the honest belief that they are
needed in order to head the insurrection off, the Governor is the final

judge and cannot be subjected to an action after he is out of office on the ground that he had not reasonable ground for his belief. .... When it comes to a decision by the head of the State upon a matter involving its life, the ordinary rights of individuals must yield to what he deems the necessities of the moment. Public danger warrants the substitution of executive process for judicial process."[61]

The opinion thus brushes aside as immaterial the fact which the majority opinion in the Milligan Case treats as absolutely crucial. In spite of that fact, the governor's finding that an insurrection existed and that the arrest and detention of Moyer was a necessary measure toward putting it down was accepted as conclusive because, although it was "without sufficient reason," it was "in good faith." The one handle, in short, which the case offers for judicial review of executive proceedings to put down private violence, in distinction to punishing it, is the question of the executive's "good faith."

And it is this handle which the Court seizes upon in the recent case of *Sterling v. Constantin*,[62] which grew out of an attempt by the governor of Texas to enforce the law of the state limiting the production of petroleum, by declaring martial law in certain counties. A federal three-judge court received testimony flatly contradicting the allegations of the governor's proclamation that the region involved was in "a state of insurrection, riot, and a breach of the peace." It found, on the contrary, that the evidence showed "no insurrection nor riot in fact . . . no closure of the courts, no failure of the civil authorities," and on this ground enjoined the governor from proceeding with his military measures; and on appeal it was sustained by the Supreme Court in so doing.

Should this result be interpreted as affecting the doctrine of *Moyer v. Peabody* as to the scope of judicial review in the field of martial law? Some words of Chief Justice Hughes's opinion seem to imply as much. Thus he remarks at one point:

"It does not follow from the fact that the Executive has this range of discretion, deemed to be a necessary incident of his power to suppress disorder, that every sort of action the Governor may take, no matter how unjustified by the exigency or subversive of private right and the jurisdiction of the courts, is conclusively supported by mere executive fiat. . . . What are the allowable limits of military discretion, and whether or not they have been overstepped in a particular case, are judicial questions."[63]

But if this means that the courts may *ordinarily* review an executive finding of facts in support of martial law, then his authorities do not bear him out; nor did the case before the Court call for any such statement. Furthermore, as was hinted before, in the realm of military action, the President and a governor are two different orders of being.

So coming back to our question, what is the relative standing of the Prize Cases and *ex parte* Milligan today? The truth seems to be that current doctrine respecting martial law embodies elements from both decisions. The Milligan Case is still sound doctrine in asserting that martial law is not a constitutionally permissible device for superseding civil with military government, except possibly when the United States is a party to a public war, and then only by the express allowance of Congress. The Prize Cases, on the other hand, are sound doctrine in claiming for the executive the right to use such force as he deems necessary to put down a condition of public disorder without, save in extreme cases of abuse of power, having to justify his measures before a judicial tribunal. Or more briefly, present doctrine concedes considerably less to judicial review than does *ex parte* Milligan, but rather more than do the Prize Cases.

And this brings us to consider the President's power in relation to that greatest of all muniments of Anglo-American liberty, the writ of habeas corpus, whereby is guaranteed, so long as it is available, prompt judicial inquiry into all cases of physical restraint and, where the restraint is found to be without legal justification, the release of the party. The relevant constitutional provision reads as follows: "The privilege of the writ of habeas corpus shall not be suspended, unless when in cases of rebellion or invasion the public safety may require it."[64] It is a significant fact that this is the only mention of the writ in the entire Constitution. Its existence as part and parcel of the law of the land is simply taken for granted.

The first question to confront us is that of the location of the above recognized power to suspend the privilege of the writ. In the once famous Merryman Case,[65] which arose early in the Civil War out of Lincoln's suspension of the writ as to "any military line" between New York and Washington, Chief Justice Taney, then on circuit, argued that only Congress possessed this power. The clause occurs, he pointed out, among the restraints on the powers of Congress, and in Article I which deals primarily with the legislative power. Furthermore, in England only Parliament may suspend the writ. Also, it was universally assumed at the time of the Burr Conspiracy that the power was Congress's, a view in which Story later concurred in his *Commentaries*.[66] The only power of the President where the rights of the citizen are concerned, said the Chief Justice, "is to take care that they [the laws] be faithfully carried into execution as they are expounded and adjudged by the co-ordinate branch of the government to which that duty is assigned by the Constitution," in other words, the judicial department.

Taney's views were sharply challenged from many quarters, and of course remained practically ineffective, their intended beneficiary continuing to languish in Fort McHenry. Attorney General Bates answered Chief Justice Taney's conception of executive power as subject to judicial guidance by reiterating the very different theory of Attorney General Taney. The executive was not subordinate to the judicial power, but one of three coördinate departments of government. It was, moreover, "the most active of all," "the most constantly in action"; and, while the other departments were sworn to support the Constitution, the President was sworn to "preserve, protect and defend it." Furthermore, under the legislation of Congress the President was explicitly empowered to use the military forces of the country to suppress insurrection, which meant that he must be free to judge what measures this exigency required. He had, therefore, the right to "arrest and imprison persons guilty of holding criminal intercourse" with the authors of insurrection, and of this right the power to suspend the writ of habeas corpus was a necessary and logical ingredient.[67]

The President's action was also endorsed by a number of publicists. One of these urged the ingenious argument that the constitutional clause itself stood "in the place of an act of Parliament," with the result that the President did not need congressional authorization. Others held that the President's power was an emergency power, and action under it was subject to congressional review. A third view was that "in case of invasion from abroad or rebellion at home, the President may declare, or exercise, or authorize, martial law at his discretion," and in so doing suspend the writ.[68]

Lincoln's own views, as we have seen, underwent a gradual stiffening. In his message of July 4, 1861, he had asked for congressional ratification, but fifteen months later he proclaimed a far more sweeping suspension of the privilege without apparent thought of Congress. And Congress was also uncertain of its

ground. Not until March 3, 1863, did it finally authorize a suspension of the habeas corpus privilege, and then in terms which
still left the constitutional issue open. Nor is the verdict of judicial opinion free from doubt. The controlling opinion in the Prize
Cases squints one way, that in *ex parte* Milligan the other. Indeed, even the minority in the latter case would apparently have
required congressional ratification for a suspension of the habeas
corpus privilege in areas not subject to martial law or to military
government.

Nowadays, the consensus of learned opinion seems to favor
Taney's doctrine that Congress has the *exclusive* suspending
power, though it is not clear whether those who take this view
would also accept what Taney himself undoubtedly regarded as
the corollary principle—that a presidential suspension was in any
circumstances mere usurpation which even ratification by Congress could not legalize. For my own part, I am inclined to think
that Professor Randall has the nub of the matter when he says:

"In a future crisis the Presidential power to suspend would probably
be just as much an open question as during the Civil War. As to the
actual precedent of that war, the outstanding fact is that the Chief
Executive 'suspended the writ,' and that, so far as legal consequences
were concerned, he was not restrained in so doing by Congress nor by
the Courts."[69]

The further question presents itself, whether, "when the writ
is suspended, the Executive is authorized to arrest as well as to
detain." The majority opinion in *ex parte* Milligan implies a negative answer to this question, to which the minority demurs; and
certainly the latter is the logical view. How can there be detention
if there is not an arrest in the first place; and if the arrest was not
for justifiable cause, how can the resulting detention be?

But conceding that a justifiable cause exists, does suspension of the writ relieve the executive from the necessity of complying with the requirements of the Fourth Amendment and the common law regarding arrests? As a matter of fact, summary arrests were frequent throughout the Civil War, and made without any pretense of complying with either the forms of the common law or the Fourth Amendment; and because of this Congress eventually passed an act to indemnify the authors of such arrests against "any action or prosecution, civil or criminal," which of course is tantamount to a claim of power to have authorized the questioned procedures in the first place.[70] So again, while the weight of authority is undoubtedly in favor of the more conservative view of executive power, the verdict of practice under a suspension of the writ is distinctly otherwise.

Lastly, the question arises whether a suspension of the writ is subject eventually to judicial review on the complaint that "the public safety" did not "require" it. Judicial dicta furnish materials for an argument either way; but the usual tests clearly make the question "political," inasmuch as no court would be in a position to answer it except *in abstracto* once the emergency had passed.[71]

But the paucity of judicial restraints upon presidential action which is based on the plea of necessity does not mean that such action is subject to *no* restraint. On the contrary, the final evaluation of such a plea would seem theoretically to rest with the national *legislative* authority under the "necessary and proper" clause. At the same time, the practical efficacy of even this limitation upon a resolute President who felt he had the backing of public opinion may well be questioned. A statutory rule definitive of occasions requiring martial law would have to be in such broad terms as to leave it at the mercy of interpretation. This, in fact, is proved, as we have seen, by the existing statutes which have to do with the employment by the President of the national forces and of the state militias. On the other hand, for Congress to interfere with an executive declaration of necessity would require, in the face of certain veto, a two-thirds vote in each house. In short, *we see illustrated once more the critical importance of that course of reasoning whereby the initiative has come to be attributed to the President in the presence of emergency conditions, whether at home or abroad.*

DELEGATED WAR POWER — THE WORLD WAR

Prior to the World War it was customary for writers on the subject to treat war as an affair of governments, not of populations, and to draw a hard and fast line between "combatants" and "non-combatants." Both conceptions hail from the eighteenth century and are reflected in the Constitution.[72] Even while insisting in *The Federalist* upon the unlimited character of the power of the proposed government for "the common defense," Hamilton described those powers as embracing simply "the formation, direction, and support of the National Forces."[73] Nor—unless the country was invaded—was any of these activities apt at that date to be of much concern to the great mass of citizens. Armies were still volunteer or mercenary. Supplies, when forthcoming from domestic sources, were usually purchased in the open market. Taxes were indirect. Some governmental propaganda there was no doubt, but not on a scale demanding a name; and morale was something which pertained only to the forces in the field. The contrast which the World War presents to this picture hardly requires elaboration. That was a struggle which came gradually to involve every energy, material and moral, of the populations concerned. It was accompanied by the most thoroughgoing social and industrial regimentation in each of the warring states; and in the endeavors put forth to this end small heed was paid to hitherto prevailing doctrines and principles concerning the powers of the State over the rights of the individual.

At the very outset of the War the British Defense of the Realm Act of November 27, 1914, gave startling proof that for the period of the war at least the conventional contrast between constitutional and autocratic governments had lost much of its validity. As one authority has put it, this measure, together with the Regulations of the King in Council which it authorized, "struck down with a single blow the personal liberties and rights of property which have been held as the most sacred tradition of the British Constitution."[74] This country was, of course, much more advantageously situated in relation to the war than our European associates. We were in the war only a little over a year and a half; we were more than three thousand miles from the scene of the major hostilities, and at no time was there the remotest likelihood of our being invaded. For all that, the strain on our national resources both of men and of materials was enormous, and in meeting it the daily life of the people was brought under the control of the government and their property put at its disposal on a previously unparalleled scale. And, in the main, this regimentation of the nation was accomplished by Congress through the simple device of transferring to the President its applicable powers.

As early as March 4, 1917, or more than a month prior to our declaration of war against Germany, Congress authorized the President, within the limits of existing appropriations, to order from private firms dealing therein such ships and materials of war as he found to be necessary; to compel preferential compliance with such orders; to modify or cancel any existing contracts for war supplies; to commandeer any factory or part thereof for operation by the government itself; and to fix, subject to an appeal to the Court of Claims, the compensation due private owners in all such cases.

Of the multitudinous delegations of power to the President which followed our declaration of war, the most striking were those effected by the Lever Food and Fuel Control Act of August 17, 1917. These embraced the power to regulate by license the importation, manufacture, storage, mining, or distribution of necessaries; the power to requisition foods, feeds, fuels, and other necessaries; the power to purchase, store, and sell certain foods; the power to take over factories, packing houses, pipe lines, mines, or other plants, and operate the same; the power to fix a minimum price for wheat; the power to limit, regulate, or prohibit the use of food materials in the production of alcoholic beverages; the power to fix the price of coal and coke and to regulate the production, sale, and distribution thereof. Similarly, the Selective Service Act vested the President with authority to raise an army by conscription; the Espionage Act with power to declare certain exports unlawful; the Priority Shipment Act with power to determine priority in car service; the Trading with the Enemy Act with power to license trade with the enemy and his allies, and to censor all communications by mail, cable, radio, or otherwise with foreign countries. Still other statutes clothed him with authority to regulate the foreign-language press of the country, to regulate the conduct of enemy aliens resident in the country and its possessions, to take over and operate the rail and water transportation systems of the country, to take over and operate the telegraph and telephone systems, and to redistribute functions among the executive agencies of the National Government.[75]

Ordinarily the President's first step in exercise of the powers thus conferred was to redelegate them in whole or in part to a designated agent or agents, while first and last their exercise involved the issuance in the name of the President, or with his implied sanction, of a vast mass of administrative regulations out-bulking many hundreds of times the statutory provisions upon which they were ultimately grounded. In its governmental aspect the war was fought by means of the administrative ordinance.

What attitude did the Supreme Court assume toward this altogether revolutionary legislation—revolutionary both as to substance and as to method? The fact is that the Court had the opportunity to pass upon very little of it except the Selective Service Act during the period of the war; the legislation had accomplished its purpose before the formalities of appeal could be got through—something that with a little contriving would happen in any war. Still, it is satisfactory to know that sooner or later the major features of the above legislation were endorsed by the Court as to their constitutionality.

In the War Prohibition Cases[76] it was recognized that war endows Congress with an indefinite legislative competence in the promotion of "war efficiency" which is closely comparable with the power of the states at all times in the promotion of public welfare. In the Espionage Act Cases[77] it was held that freedom of speech and press may be abridged in wartime substantially at the discretion of the national legislative power. In the Selective Draft Cases[78] the power to raise armies was given previously unheard of extension, when the government was conceded the power to conscript men for service abroad.[79] In the Emergency Rent Cases[80] the "just compensation" clause of Amendment V was held to be less restrictive of governmental power in "a public exigency" and to "tide over a passing trouble" than in normal times. Nor did the Court at any time hint that any of the war legislation was invalid as transgressing the maxim against delegation of legislative power.

In short, it is the lesson of these cases that in the war crucible the more general principles of constitutional law and theory, those which ordinarily govern the delegation of legislative power, the scope of national power over the ordinary life of the citizen, and the interpretation of the "due process" clause as a restraint on substantive legislative power, become highly malleable, and that even the more specific provisions of the Bill of Rights take on an unaccustomed flexibility.[81]

The contrast, therefore, between the Wilsonian "dictatorship" and the Lincolnian is not one of tenderness for customary constitutional restraints; it is one of method. The immediate basis of the latter was the "Commander-in-Chief" clause and insistence upon the separation of powers principle; the immediate basis of the former was the national legislative power and minimization of that principle. At the same time, Wilson did not by any means overlook his constitutional prerogative as Commander-in-Chief. His creation of the Committee on Public Information and of the War Industries Board rested exclusively on this basis, as did many of the vast powers exercised by these bodies in enforcing a so-called "voluntary censorship" of the press and in "coördinating" private industry.[82] And his action at the outbreak of the war in closing German wireless stations, and somewhat later with respect to German insurance companies and patent rights, invoked the same principle, as likewise did his subjection of all telephone, telegraph, and cable companies to regulation with respect to all messages received from or going abroad.[83] Indeed, the month before we entered the war Wilson ordered the arming of American merchantmen against German submarines in the teeth of Congress's failure, thanks to "a little group of willful men," to concede him the power.[84] Conversely, Lincoln's "dictatorship" had been amplified at many points by broad delegations of power from Congress.[85]

And so much for our first, and to date only, modern war. Our conduct of it indicates two rules of constitutional practice for such situations: (1) Congress is able to assert, practically unchecked by judicial review, any powers which under the stress and excitement of the times it succeeds in persuading itself are calculated to bring victory; (2) it exercises such powers by handing them over wholesale to the President, thereby merging them with his indeterminate prerogative as Commander-in-Chief.

But the less definite results of such a war effort may be even more serious in the long run. I mean its inevitable impairment of the resiliency of the constitutional structure and its disturbance of popular standards in judging of questions of power even in normal times. The former effect is illustrated by the fact that several of the delegations of power to President Wilson during the war with Germany still remain on the statute books.[86] The latter effect is seen in the numerous proposals in Congress within recent years which, if adopted, would virtually convert the United States the moment it entered a war—any war at all, apparently— into a totalitarian state. While such proposals may possibly have a certain value as deterrents from war, they seem to me otherwise nonsensical and vicious. Why on earth should we *plan* on making a holocaust of our liberties unless and until we have to? Let us see our war first![87]

THE PRESIDENT AS HEAD OF THE ARMY AND NAVY

Certain intra-organizational features of the Commander-in-Chiefship can be disposed of quite briefly. While the President usually delegates his power of supreme command over the national forces in active service, there is no constitutional reason why he should do so. At the time of the Whiskey Rebellion, Washington, a soldier, took the field, remaining at the seat of operations nearly a month.[88] The early days of 1862 were signalized by orders from the White House for a general advance of the Union armies, the motivating purpose of which was to get the dilatory McClellan under motion,[89] and in the ensuing months

Lincoln visited the Army of the Potomac repeatedly to advise with its commanders concerning plans of operation. When later Grant assumed the command before Richmond these usually ill-advised interferences ceased; nor did President Wilson—some three thousand miles from the battle front—seek to emulate them during the World War. As a matter of fact, Mr. Wilson finally agreed to the American forces in France being placed under a command which was not subject to his ultimate control, although no doubt he could at any time have revoked his consent.[90]

As against an enemy in the field the President possesses the powers which are conceded by international law to any supreme commander, though the final interpretation of these appears theoretically to rest with Congress.[91] Actually the latter has never adopted any legislation which would seriously cramp the style of a President who was attempting to break the resistance of an enemy.

Also, the President has the power of any supreme commander to terminate hostilities by arranging an armistice, a power which has at times blended into and merged with the theoretically distinct power of negotiating the final peace. Thus the protocol which President McKinley authorized on August 12, 1898, with the Spanish government largely foreshadowed the ensuing Peace of Paris. With a similar purpose in mind President Wilson obtained the incorporation of his "Fourteen Points" in the armistice which was imposed upon the Central Powers in November 1918; but this later endeavor to guide peace negotiations was rather less successful.[92]

Can the President as supreme military commander acquire territory for the United States? So far as international law is concerned the rule is generally stated to be that a conquest, to be valid, must be succeeded either by an act of cession on the part of the former sovereign of the conquered region or by continued occupancy on the part of the conquering nation, and this rule has been recognized by the Supreme Court.[93] So far as municipal law is concerned the final status of conquered territory is subject to determination by the treaty-making power or by Congress.[94] But whatever its status otherwise, recently acquired territory may be governed by the President until Congress steps in and provides a more permanent regime.[95] The Canal Zone was governed under presidential authorization for seven years, from 1905 to 1912.

Again, the President is, naturally, chief executive of the rules and regulations which Congress adopts for the government of the land and naval forces and for their safety and welfare. Also, in the absence of conflicting legislation he has powers of his own which he may exercise for the same ends. Prior to 1830 courts-martial were convoked solely on the authority of the President as Commander-in-Chief.[96] At the outset of the Civil War, Lieber's Instructions for the Government of the Armies in the Field were promulgated on the same authority.[97] During the World War legislative provisions for the health of the forces were supplemented by executive orders.[98]

The action of the first Roosevelt in summarily dismissing on November 5, 1906, three companies of Negro soldiers for alleged disorderly behavior at Brownsville, Texas, is a further illustration of the President's residual power over the forces, and also of its limits. In the debate which developed in the Senate on the subject Senator Spooner's contention "that where Congress has failed to make rules for the discipline of the Army the power of command lodged in the President carries with it authority in him to issue an order absolutely necessary to the discipline of the Army" was not challenged. The President's critics contended only that Congress had laid down rules for such situations and that the President had violated them. Ultimately Mr. Roosevelt asked Congress to give him authority to reinstate the discharged men.[99]

One power of supreme military command the President curiously lacks—that of choosing his subordinates. Not only does Congress determine the grades to which appointments may be made and lay down the qualifications of appointees, but it has always been assumed that the Senate shares the appointing power in the case of military as well as civil officers. Without doubt Congress could transfer the power to "the President alone," but has never done so.[100] Indeed, it has at times attempted to usurp the appointing power itself.[101]

Also, the President's power to dismiss an officer from the service, once unlimited, is today confined by statute in time of peace to dismissal "in pursuance of the sentence of a general court-martial or in mitigation thereof."[102] But the provision is not regarded by the Court as preventing the President from displacing an officer of the Army or Navy by appointing with the advice and consent of the Senate another person in his place.[103] The President's power of dismissal in time of war Congress has never attempted to limit and it remains absolute.

By way of summary: [Abstractly considered, there is no reason why more power should be attributed to the office of Commander-in-Chief in the hands of the President than if it had been conferred by the Constitution on somebody else. Actually, there was never any suggestion in 1787 or later that it should or could go to anybody except the Chief Executive. And once the Constitution was set going, the idea was quick to emerge—first in legislation, then in presidential action undertaken independently of legislative sanction—that the President's power of military command should be available to him as Chief Executive whenever the normal processes of law enforcement broke down. Then in 1849 the Supreme Court imparted a collateral impetus to this trend of constitutional development by its dictum in *Luther v. Borden,*

that insurrection is "war"—a proposition which received its cul-
minating expression in Lincoln's "dictatorship" and in the Supreme Court's opinion in the Prize Cases. Nor has the later
reaction from these extremes of doctrine and practice, which was
registered especially in the majority opinion in the Milligan Case,
proved more than partially corrective of them. Today, when there
is actual disorder it is within the discretion of the executive to
stamp it as insurrection and to use such force as he deems requisite to put it down, with only a dim possibility in the background
to temper his decisions that his subordinates will be later called
upon to justify his orders in court. And meantime Presidents have
repeatedly lent military aid to state executive authorities without
observance of the restrictions of Article IV, section 4, of the Constitution, or have employed troops in situations of local disorder
on the justification of protecting national interests, precedents of
practice to which the Court's decisions in the Neagle Case and
the Debs Case go far to furnish doctrinal sanction.

And so much for those situations in which the President's role
as Commander-in-Chief is instrumental, his role as Chief Executive is primary. When the country is involved in war—a first-class
war—the relationship is reversed, for then, as our war with Germany proved, *all* the applicable powers of the National Government—that is to say, all which its political branches deem to be
applicable—are focused upon the one objective of victory through
the person and office of the Commander-in-Chief.

CHAPTER VI

ORGAN OF FOREIGN RELATIONS

WHERE does the Constitution lodge the power to determine the foreign relations of the United States?[1] Before this question can be profitably considered a distinction or two must be noted. The most centralized government on earth is, simply from the nature of things, incapable of determining beforehand the actual conditions with which it will have to deal in its intercourse with other governments. The humblest subject of the most thorough-paced autocrat may plunge his sovereign into war, as did a Spanish *gardacosta* early in the eighteenth century, when he struck off the famous Jenkins' gory ear.[2] Nor is our Constitution at all superior in this respect to those of other governments—rather, owing especially to the large powers which it leaves with local authorities, it is sometimes inferior. Certainly it contains no guarantee that a mob, a petty magistrate, a city council, or a state legislature may not at any time do something calculated to cast a shadow upon our relations with a friendly power. Friendly relations with friendly governments have been jeopardized more than once in just these ways.[3]

Indeed, a nation's relations with another nation may be determined by the latter's decisions rather than by its own. The United States may proclaim its intention of rendering all possible aid falling "short of war" against "aggressor nations"; but if the latter choose to regard the aid rendered under this formula as amounting to war upon themselves and proceed accordingly, then such aid will not, in fact, have fallen short of war. Likewise, however, an announced policy of keeping out of war would not necessarily produce that outcome, but might lead to the exactly opposite result.

The question in which we are interested demands, therefore, a somewhat precise statement. It may be put thus: *Where does the Constitution vest authority to determine the course of the United States as a sovereign entity at international law with respect to matters in which other similar entities may choose to take an interest?* Many people are inclined to answer offhand, in the President; but they would be hard put, if challenged, to point out any definite statement to this effect in the Constitution itself. What the Constitution does, *and all that it does,* is to confer upon the President certain powers capable of affecting our foreign relations, and certain other powers of the same general nature upon the Senate, and still other such powers upon Congress; but which of these organs shall have the decisive and final voice in determining the course of the American nation is left for events to resolve.

All of which amounts to saying that the Constitution, considered only for its affirmative grants of powers which are capable of affecting the issue, is an invitation to struggle for the privilege of directing American foreign policy. In such a struggle the President has, it is true, certain great advantages, which are pointed out by Jay in *The Federalist;* the *unity* of the office, its capacity for *secrecy* and *despatch,* and its superior sources of *information;* to which should be added the fact that it is always on hand and ready for action, whereas the houses of Congress are in adjournment much of the time.[4] But despite all this, actual *practice* under the Constitution has shown that while the President is usually in a position to *propose,* the Senate and Congress are often in a position to *dispose.* The verdict of history, in short, is that the power to determine the substantive content of American foreign policy is a *divided* power, with the lion's share usually falling to the President, though by no means always.

It will be of referential value later if, before undertaking to describe the powers which the President exercises in the foreign field, and the relation of these powers to the impinging powers of the Senate and of Congress, I discuss briefly some of the principles which delimit the field itself, and so supply the setting in which presidential prerogative operates. The most important of these, indeed the controlling one, is that the power of the National Government in respect to external affairs is as broad, as complete as that of any other nation. Indeed, as Hamilton pointed out in *The Federalist,* it could not safely be otherwise;[5] and another member of the Convention, James Wilson, implied the same conclusion in his assertion that:

"When the United States declared their independence, they were bound to receive the Law of Nations in its modern state of purity and refinement."[6]

Whether from the angle of self-interest or that of international obligation the powers of the new government were assumed to match those of other civilized states.[7]

But whence comes this plenary power? Is it the summation of constitutionally delegated powers, or does it come from some source external to the Constitution? That the Constitution assigns to the President, to the Senate, and to Congress many powers in the exercise of which these bodies are respectively able to influence the conduct of the nation's foreign relations is unquestionable. To assume, however, that these powers are sufficient, either separately or together, to meet all the requirements of an expedient and just foreign policy would be entirely gratuitous; and, as a matter of fact, many powers have been asserted both by the President and by Congress in the field of foreign relations as to which the Constitution is completely silent.

It must follow, then, that the Constitution, instead of being the *immediate* source of the external powers of the National Government, is only their *mediate* source, and confers them simply in consequence of having established a nation which is truly sovereign in relation to other nations. Or in other words, the power of the National Government in the diplomatic sphere, while susceptible of limitation by the Constitution when the restrictions which it imposes upon all power apply, is an *inherent* power, one which owes its existence to the fact that the American People are a sovereign entity at international law.

And not only is this power of the National Government an *inherent* power, it is also an *inherited* power, though as to whence inherited there has always been some disagreement. In his opinion in the early case of *Penhallow v. Doane*,[8] Justice Iredell advanced the theory that sovereignty originally belonged to the states in the external as well as the internal field, but that upon the establishment of the Constitution their sovereignty in the former field passed to the National Government. Justice Patterson, on the other hand, took the position that external sovereignty never did belong to the states and that the sovereignty of the National Government as to foreign relations was an inheritance from the Continental Congress; and this latter theory is adopted by the Court in the recent case of *United States v. Curtiss-Wright Export Corporation*. Said Justice Sutherland on that occasion:

"As a result of the separation from Great Britain by the colonies, acting as a unit, the powers of external sovereignty passed from the

Crown not to the colonies severally, but to the colonies in their collective and corporate capacity as the United States of America. Even before the Declaration, the colonies were a unit in foreign affairs, acting through a common agency—namely the Continental Congress, composed of delegates from the thirteen colonies. That agency exercised the powers of war and peace, raised an army, created a navy, and finally adopted the Declaration of Independence. Rulers come and go; governments end and forms of government change; but sovereignty survives. A political society cannot endure without a supreme will somewhere. Sovereignty is never held in suspense. When, therefore, the external sovereignty of Great Britain in respect of the colonies ceased, it immediately passed to the Union."[9]

But the other theory, too, is perfectly adequate logically if we assume that the states are today devoid of capacity to sustain foreign relationship, inasmuch as, unless it has dropped entirely out of existence, their former sovereignty in this respect must have passed to the National Government, and hence be as complete in the latter as by hypothesis it originally was in the former.[10]

That national power is *exclusive* in the realm of foreign relations is, in fact, an obvious corollary of its being *plenary,* even though the deduction is not entirely sustained by the language of the Constitution itself. Thus section 10 of Article I quite clearly recognizes the states as retaining a certain rudimentary capacity in this field, upon the exercise of which it lays certain restraints. No state, the section reads, may enter into "any treaty, alliance or confederation," or grant "letters of marque and reprisal," nor, *"without the consent of Congress,"* enter "into any agreement or compact with a foreign state." The capacity thus inferred must, nevertheless, be today regarded as atrophied, no such consent having ever been sought or granted.

Curiously enough, the notion of the complete incapacity of the states for foreign relationship first achieved judicial recognition during the very period when States Rights were most dominant in the Court's thinking. I refer to the case of *Holmes v. Jennison*,[11] which was decided in 1841. The matter at issue was whether Jennison, governor of Vermont, was constitutionally entitled to surrender Holmes to the government of Lower Canada from whose justice the latter was alleged to be fugitive. On account of the equal division of the Justices respecting the Court's jurisdiction no judgment was handed down in the case, but the opinion of Chief Justice Taney for himself and three associates denied the power of the Vermont governor in unqualified terms. "All the powers which relate to our foreign intercourse," the Chief Justice asserted, "are confided to the general government." "The framers of the Constitution manifestly believed that any intercourse between a state and a foreign nation was dangerous to the Union"; and one of their main objects was "to make us, so far as regarded our foreign relations, one people and one nation; and to cut off all communications between foreign governments and the several state authorities."[12]

Later utterances of the Court unite assertion of the principle of the exclusiveness to that of the completeness and inherency of the national power. In the words of a recent opinion by Justice Sutherland:

"The investment of the Federal government with the powers of external sovereignty did not depend upon the affirmative grants of the Constitution. The powers to declare and wage war, to conclude peace, to make treaties, to maintain diplomatic relations with other sovereignties, if they had never been mentioned in the Constitution, would have vested in the Federal government as necessary concomitants of nationality."[13]

Lastly, the plenary character of national power in the foreign field involves the consequence that it is not affected by the principle of "dual federalism"; that is, is not limited by the so-called "reserved powers" of the states. This obvious corollary was first recognized and applied with regard to the treaty-making power in 1796, in the case of *Ware v. Hylton*,[14] and during Marshall's Chief Justiceship the same or equivalent doctrine was reiterated many times. During Chief Justice Taney's presidency of the Court, it is true, the theory was repeatedly broached, although it never became the basis of a decision, that the treaty-making power was restricted to some indefinite extent by state power; but the latest utterances of the Court go straight back to the original conception of the subject.[15] In sustaining in *Missouri v. Holland*[16] the right of the National Government to treat with another nation with regard to game which was seasonally migratory between them, the Court disparaged the idea that some "invisible radiation from the Tenth Amendment" limited the treaty-making power, and hinted that the fact that treaties do not have to be "in pursuance of the Constitution" but only "under the authority of the United States" was not without significance.[17] And more recently still, in sustaining the right of the National Government to levy customs duties upon apparatus imported by a state university, Chief Justice Hughes, speaking for the Court, remarked generally:

"In international relations and with respect to foreign intercourse and trade the people of the United States act through a single government with unified and adequate power . . . there is no encroachment [here] on the power of the state, as none exists with respect to the subject over which the federal power has been exerted."[18]

Such are the general contours of this field of national power; but there are also one or two matters of internal arrangement, as it were, which need to be mentioned at this point. The first of these—an aspect of the principle of departmental autonomy[19]—is the doctrine that neither Congress nor the Senate can be *constitu-*

tionally bound—however ineffective *practically* their freedom may be—by anything done previously by the President in his capacity as organ of foreign relations. Sometimes termed the doctrine of "concurrent" or "coördinate powers," this principle first assumed importance in the controversy over Congress's duty to appropriate certain monies needed to carry the highly unpopular Jay Treaty into effect. Spokesmen for the administration, notably Hamilton, argued that in making treaties "supreme law of the land" the Constitution converted the obligation of a treaty at international law into complete *constitutional* obligation, and hence left Congress no discretion in such a situation.[20] Madison and Gallatin answered that the very purpose of the Constitution in forbidding any money to be paid out of the Treasury except in consequence of "an appropriation made by law" was to leave Congress a free agent in voting such appropriations.[21] Although few if any treaty provisions have ever failed for lack of funds to carry them out, the latter view has in principle prevailed. Today it is well established that Congress may even repeal treaties in their quality as law of the land; and more generally, that whatever any department does in the exercise of its powers is frequently at the mercy of what another department may do—or refuse to do—in the exercise of its powers.[22] Thus the argument which was advanced in 1919, both in the Senate and elsewhere, against our entering the League of Nations, that to do so would deprive Congress "unconstitutionally" of its discretion in the matter of declaring war, was valid only in the loose general sense which enjoins Congress always to observe good faith toward other nations in the exercise of all its powers. Almost any treaty whatsoever would be open to the same criticism.[23]

The second matter of "internal arrangement" is the doctrine of Political Questions which was first formulated by Chief Justice Marshall in the early case of *Foster v. Neilson*.[24] The question at issue was the validity of a grant made by the Spanish government in 1804 of land lying to the east of the Mississippi River, but underlying this question was the broader one whether the region between the Perdido and Mississippi Rivers belonged in 1804 to Spain or to the United States; and on this point the Court held that its judgment was concluded by the action of "the political departments," the President and Congress, in claiming the land for the United States. The Chief Justice said:

"If those departments which are entrusted with the foreign intercourse of the nation, which assert and maintain its interests against foreign powers, have unequivocally asserted its rights of dominion over a country of which it is in possession, and which it claims under a treaty; if the legislature has acted on the construction thus asserted, it is not in its own courts that this construction is to be denied. A question like this respecting the boundaries of nations is, as has been truly said, more a political than a legal question, and in its discussion, the courts of every country must respect the pronounced will of the legislature."[25]

On the basis of this principle the Court has subsequently held at one time or another that it must accept as final and binding on itself the determinations of one or other, or both, of "the political departments," with respect to all such questions as, whether a certain newly constituted community was a qualified belligerent at international law; what was the correct boundary of a certain country; what country was the sovereign of a particular region; whether a certain community was entitled to be considered as a "belligerent" or as an independent state; who was the *de jure*, who was the *de facto* ruler of a certain country; whether a particular person was a duly accredited diplomatic agent to the United States; how long a military occupation of a certain region should continue in order to fulfill the terms of a treaty; whether a certain treaty was in effect; and so on.[26]

The reader will quickly perceive that it is the tendency of both the doctrines just considered to keep the powers of the National Government in the field of foreign relations continually fluid and easily available. By the same token, both doctrines also invite a constant struggle for power in this field on the part of the political branches of the government—President, Congress, and Senate.

"SOLE ORGAN OF EXTERNAL RELATIONS"— HAMILTON VERSUS MADISON

"The President is the sole organ of the nation in its external relations, and its sole representative with foreign nations." These words of John Marshall, spoken in 1799, state what has today become a commonplace, which is the reason perhaps why their precise significance has been so rarely considered. The fact is that the statement is susceptible of two widely divergent inter-pretations.

Marshall's remark was made in his capacity as a member of the House of Representatives to uphold President John Adams in having ordered the extradition under the Jay Treaty of one Jona-than Robbins, who was alleged to be a fugitive from British justice. The President's critics contended that the situation was one which required judicial action, an argument which Marshall answered by pointing out that "the case was in its nature a national demand made upon the nation." The parties were two nations. "They cannot come into court to litigate their claims, nor can a court decide them." Then follow the words quoted above, which conclude with the statement, "of consequence, the demand of a foreign nation can only be made on him."[27]

Clearly, what Marshall had foremost in mind was simply the President's role as *instrument of communication* with other gov-ernments. And the same is true of Jefferson when, some years before, he answered Genêt's request for an exequatur for a consul whose commission was addressed to "the Congress of the United States." Jefferson's reply was that:

"As the President is the only channel of communication between the United States and foreign nations, it is from him alone that foreign nations or their agents are to learn what is or has been the will of the nation, and whatever he communicates as such they have a right and are bound to consider as the expression of the nation, and no foreign agent can be allowed to question it."[28]

That is to say, while the President alone may address foreign governments and be addressed by them, yet in fulfilling these functions he is, or at least may be, the mouthpiece of a power of decision which resides elsewhere. Nor do statements made in Congress in 1789 in the course of the debate on the removal power—which, it will be remembered, dealt with the official relationship between the President and the Secretary of State— necessarily infer a broader conception of the President's diplomatic role save in connection with the negotiation of treaties, an exception which both Marshall and Jefferson would unquestionably have allowed.

Elaboration of the conception of the President's external role as essentially dynamic and positive was the work in the first instance of Alexander Hamilton. The opportunity was furnished by the issuance of Washington's so-called "Proclamation of Neutrality" upon the outbreak early in 1793 of war between France and Great Britain. This document declared the intention of the United States to "pursue a course friendly and impartial to both belligerent powers" and enjoined upon all citizens its observance under pain of prosecution. While its author, Attorney General Randolph,[29] had industriously avoided the word "neutrality," the proclamation was immediately challenged by French sympathizers as having been outside the President's constitutional competence. Its defense was thereupon undertaken by Hamilton, writing over the pseudonym "Pacificus,"[30] in a series of articles in *The Gazette of the United States,* the first of which deals with the constitutional issue. In brief, Hamilton's argument comprises the following contentions: first, that the opening clause of Article II is a grant of power; secondly, that the succeeding more specific grants of the article, except when "coupled with express restrictions or limitations," "specify the principal articles" implied in the general grant and hence serve to interpret it; thirdly —by inference—that the direction of foreign policy is inherently an *"executive"* function.[31]

By way of illustrating his position Hamilton cites certain powers which he regards as exercisable by the President in conjunction with or in the interstices of the specific grants of the Constitution. One of these is the power of "recognition" of new governments; another the power to judge for the United States "what rights the law of nature and nations gives"; another the power to determine "virtually upon the operation of national treaties," for while "treaties can only be made by the President and Senate jointly; . . . their activity may be continued or suspended by the President alone." He then adds:

"This serves as an example of the right of the executive, in certain cases, to determine the condition of the nation, though it may, in its consequences, affect the exercise of the power of the legislature to declare war. Nevertheless, the executive cannot thereby control the exercise of that power. The legislature is still free to perform its duties, according to its own sense of them; though the executive, in the exercise of its constitutional powers, may establish an antecedent state of things, which ought to weigh in the legislative decision.

"The division of the executive power in the Constitution creates a *concurrent* authority in the cases to which it relates."[32]

In short, the President has all powers which the facts of international intercourse may at any time make conveniently applicable and which the Constitution does not vest elsewhere in clear terms; ordinarily this means that the *initiative* in the foreign field rests with him. He is consequently free to confront the other departments, and Congress in particular, with *faits accomplis* at will; although on the other hand Congress is under no *constitutional* obligation to back up such *faits accomplis* or to support the policies giving rise to them.

Although he had approved of the proclamation Jefferson was so disturbed by Hamilton's constitutional views in support of it that he appealed to Madison to refute the latter. "Nobody," he wrote, "answers him and his doctrines are taken for confessed. For God's sake, my dear Sir, take up your pen, select the most striking heresies and cut him to pieces in face of the public."[33] Madison complied in the letters of "Helvidius," which also appeared in the *Gazette* and are devoted solely to the constitutional issue.[34] Endeavoring first to explain away his own argument four years before regarding the location of the removal power—an effort more adroit than convincing—he proceeds to charge Hamilton with seeking to annex to the Presidency the prerogative of the British Crown. His words are:

"Thus it appears that by whatever standard we try this doctrine, it must be condemned as no less vicious in theory than it would be dangerous in practice. It is countenanced neither by the writers on law; nor by the nature of the powers themselves; nor by any general arrangements, or particular expressions, or plausible analogies, to be found in the constitution.

"Whence then can the writer have borrowed it?

"There is but one answer to this question.

"The power of making treaties and the power of declaring war, are *royal prerogatives* in the *British government,* and are accordingly treated as *executive prerogatives* by British *commentators.* . . ."[35]

Madison's own theory is that the right to determine the foreign policy of the United States devolves upon Congress by virtue of its power to declare war, and that the powers of the President in the diplomatic sphere are *instrumental* only, or involve at most no greater range of discretion than the determination of "matters of fact." Nor has he any patience with Hamilton's doctrine of *concurrent* powers, although two years later, when the Jay Treaty was under discussion in the House of Representatives, a close approximation to this theory was to furnish his main reliance—a *volte-face* which was matched by one on Hamilton's part in the opposite direction. But in 1793 the duties of advocacy required of Madison that he show that, if a power was claimable for the President on sound constitutional grounds, Congress was constitutionally obligated by the President's exercise thereof, for it would then follow that, *if* the President's proclamation was valid, it took from Congress the power to decide as between war and peace, a conclusion manifestly at variance with Congress's possession of the war-declaring power. The proclamation, therefore, was not valid, nor the conception of presidential power on which it was based a constitutionally tenable one.

However the palm for argumentation be awarded in this famous disputation, the practical fruits of victory were divided between the parties to it. In 1794 Congress passed our first Neutrality Act, and ever since then the subject of neutrality has been conceded to lie within its jurisdiction whenever it chooses to exert itself—a matter to which I shall return.[36] But to make up for this—indeed, more than make up for it—were the two tendencies in constitutional interpretation to which Hamilton's argument gave rise: (1) that of regarding the "executive power" clause as an always available peg on which to hang any and all unassigned powers in respect to foreign intercourse; and (2) that of treating these and all other presidential powers in the diplomatic field as potentially *policy-forming powers,* and constitutionally independent of direction by Congress.

Both tendencies find ample illustration in the further proceedings of Washington's administration. Let us consider, for instance, what happened at this period to the President's power to "receive" ambassadors and other public ministers. As the above colloquy between Jefferson and Genêt suffices to show, this power was considered as embracing also the power to receive consuls; and sixty years later Attorney General Cushing was to assert sweepingly that it extended to "all possible diplomatic agents which any power may accredit to the United States"—doctrine which the record of practice amply confirms.[37]

Furthermore, the reception of Genêt himself involved consequences of the greatest moment. "Helvidius" had professed to consider exercise of the power of reception as a mere "ceremony," comprising only the examination and authentication of the credentials of the foreign representative, which "it would be highly improper to magnify . . . into an important prerogative." Such questions, he continued, "belong of necessity to the executive"; but they involve no cognizance of the question whether those exercising the government "which despatched the representative have the right along with the possession." That question could arise only on "great and extraordinary" occasions, "by no means submitted to so limited an organ of the national will as the executive of the United States."[38] Actually, the reception of Genêt involved this very issue, and yet it was decided by Washington without consulting Congress. Nor did Washington consult Congress when some months later he demanded Genêt's recall, thereby establishing a precedent which has been followed by later Presidents again and again, and more than once in the face of impending war.[39]

Another precedent of great significance from Washington's administration was the first President's refusal in 1796 to comply with a call from the House of Representatives for papers relative to the negotiation of the Jay Treaty. The demand was originally fathered by Madison, and presumably reflected the theory of "Helvidius" that the President's diplomatic role is chiefly instrumental of the national legislative power in the realm of foreign relationship. Washington's declination, nevertheless, he now conceded to be proper so far as it represented the President's deliberate judgment that the papers were "of a nature that did not permit of disclosure at this time."[40] The concession so broadened the force of the precedent that nowadays a President feels free by the same formula to decline information even to his constitutional partner in treaty making, whereas Washington's refusal rested primarily on his denial that the House was entitled to discuss the merits of a treaty. In 1906 a debate arose in the Senate over the adventurous foreign policy of the first Roosevelt, in the course of which the entire ground that had been covered by "Pacificus" and "Helvidius" more than a century before was retraveled, Senator Spooner assuming the Hamiltonian part, Senator Bacon the Madisonian. In the face of his general position Bacon conceded that "the question of the President's sending or refusing to send any communication to the Senate is not to be judged by legal right, but [is] . . . one of courtesy between the President and that body."[41] The record of practice amply bears out this statement.

Washington's success in foreshadowing "the shape of things to come" is seen also when we turn again to presidential monopolization of the right to communicate with foreign governments. The process envisaged is, it should be noted, a two-way process, depending on whether the President is its *terminus ad quem* or is its *terminus a quo*; or, in other words, is functioning as the nation's earpiece or its mouthpiece. The latter, obviously, is the vastly more important capacity since, as was pointed out earlier, it involves potentially *formation,* as well as *formulation,* of the policy communicated; while the role of being earpiece is an essentially passive one. Even so, a Secretary of State found it necessary as late as 1833 to apprise foreign chancelleries that when they wished to inform the United States of royal births, deaths, marriages, and the like, they should address their communications to "the President of the United States of America" and leave Congress out of the business. As to ordinary diplomatic intercourse, he added, it should be "carried on as usual" through the State Department.[42]

And meantime Congress had itself come to the aid and protection of the President's prerogative to speak for the nation. This occurred in 1799, when one Logan, a Philadelphia Quaker, thought to avert war between the United States and France by undertaking a private negotiation with the latter. Manifesting perhaps some lack of humor, Congress passed a law to penalize such enterprises, entitling the measure "an Act to Prevent Usurpation of Executive Functions."[43] In later years, although presidential spokesmen frequently assumed strange disguises which might easily have caused confusion, "the Logan Act," while still on the statute books, dropped out of common ken till the period of the World War. Then from 1920 on for several years excited patriots were constantly arising to demand that its penalties be visited, now upon ex-President Taft and his League to Enforce Peace, now upon Senator France for his philandering with "the Genoa Economic Conference," and at various times upon Senator Borah who, having become Chairman of the Foreign Relations Committee about that time, had set up as a sort of State Department of his own.[44]

Indeed, the War proved generally relaxing of the established etiquette of international intercourse, more or less permanently so. Early in 1920 Viscount Grey came to this country on an informal mission, but being unable to see the President, who was ill, held conversations with certain Senators respecting the League of Nations fight, following which he published a letter in the

London *Times* stating that the Lodge reservations were "satis-factory" to the Allies. President Wilson, apparently missing the subtle flattery of this imitation of his own prior exploit in taking the Fiume question to the Italian people over the heads of their government, professed to be greatly angered at this "grossest pos-sible breach of courtesy." Likewise, when Candidate Harding, who was then campaigning for the Presidency from his own front porch in Marion, Ohio, was quoted in the papers to the effect that a French representative had approached him "infor-mally" with the hope that he would "lead the way to a world fraternity," Mr. Wilson sharply questioned the Republican leader, who replied with elaborate irony, "Official France would never seek to go over your high office as our Chief Executive to appeal to the American people or any portion thereof." By way of contrast, President Hoover, following his defeat at the polls in November 1932, actually invited his successful rival to discuss with him certain proposals of the British Ambassador with regard to the war-debt situation; and while Mr. Roosevelt declined the suggestion, he later on his own initiative invited the Ambassador to come to Warm Springs for a conference, thereby, as Mr. Krock of *The New York Times* commented, virtually taking over "this function of the Presidency a month before his inauguration."[45]

All such episodes to the contrary notwithstanding, there is no more securely established principle of constitutional practice than the exclusive right of the President to be the nation's intermedi-ary in its dealing with other nations.[46]

CONGRESSIONAL COLLABORATION AND CONTROL—
RECOGNITION

Returning for a moment to the subject of recognition, we again encounter Congress—that is, the national legislative power—as a factor in the direction of American foreign policy. The breakup

of the Spanish Empire in America during the first quarter of
the nineteenth century raised questions which Washingtonian
precedents answered very imperfectly. When Louis XVI was
dethroned by the French people he was at the same time "liqui-
dated," so that recognition by our government that the French
people had an inherent right to determine their own forms of
government incurred slight if any risks. But when the South
Americans revolted from the Spanish monarchy the latter still
remained in existence with some power to resent and resist outside interference. The question whether the new governments
should be recognized by the United States involved therefore the
further question of the extent to which the danger of war should
be taken into account, and consequently the attitude of the war-
declaring organ.[47]

Moreover, this was the period when, as we saw in an earlier
chapter, Congress, and especially the House of Representatives,
was at the top of the governmental heap. This had been definitely
shown in 1812 when James Madison had as President enjoyed the
dubious satisfaction of seeing the theories of "Helvidius" realized,
through being forced by Henry Clay and his swashbuckling followers into war with Great Britain. And six years later, when
the South American issue first loomed on the horizon, though
Monroe was now President, the House of Representatives was
still dominant and Clay was still dominant in the House.

We learn from John Quincy Adams's Memoirs that as early as
December 1817 Clay had in hand "a motion to acknowledge the
Government of Buenos Ayres and perhaps Chile." The motion,
in fact, was never offered. Instead, on March 24, 1818, Clay proposed in committee of the whole, as an amendment to the then
pending appropriation bill, a motion to appropriate $18,000 for
the outfit and one year's salary of a minister to "the independent
provinces of the River Plata in South America." But this proposal,

too, proved abortive, being replaced the day following by one which omitted the word "independent" and was to go into effect only "whenever the President shall deem it expedient to send a minister," etc.[48]

But even in this attenuated form Clay's amendment stirred up much opposition as invading presidential prerogative. Recalling the Washington administration's recognition of the French Republic, Smith of Maryland queried: "Did Congress on that occasion direct the conduct of General Washington? ... No, sir; they left him to exercise the powers vested in him by the Constitution—to the exercise of his own judgment."[49] And Adams recorded in his *Memoirs* the fact that in a Cabinet meeting he urged a like objection against such proceedings in Congress:

"Instead of admitting the Senate or House of Representatives to any share in the act of recognition, I would expressly avoid that form of doing it which would require the concurrence of those bodies. It was, I had no doubt, by our Constitution an act of the Executive authority. General Washington had exercised it in recognizing the French Republic by the reception of Mr. Genest. Mr. Madison had exercised it by declining several years to receive, and by finally receiving, Mr. Onis; and in this instance I thought the Executive ought carefully to preserve entire the authority given him by the Constitution, and not weaken it by setting the precedent of making either House of Congress a party to an act which it was his exclusive right and duty to perform."[50]

Nor did Clay in defending his measure suggest that Congress had power to compel presidential action; rather, his object, he declared, was to aid executive deliberations, a thought which was further elaborated by Tucker of Virginia in the following words:

"But gentlemen seem to consider this an interference with the constitutional powers of the Executive. I do not think so. This House has at all times, and on all subjects, a right to declare its opinions, leaving it to the Executive to act upon them or not, according to its pleasure. Nay, it has often done more. Whenever the act to be done by the Executive has been intimately connected with the constitutional powers of this body, it has always deemed itself competent to act. Thus, before the treaty for the purchase of Louisiana was made, $2,000,000 were put at the disposal of the Government for the purchase of Southern territory. Here there was an act perfectly analogous. This body had no right to make a purchase, or to command the President to do so; but, as the purchase, if made, would have called upon the legislative body for an appropriation, it was thought advisable to make it beforehand, and thus indicate a correspondence of views on the subject, where correspondence was necessary. . . . It would appear to me indeed of the utmost importance, that this correspondence of views should be preserved between these two branches of the Government. How embarrassing to the Executive must it be, if, after a treaty has been made calling for a large appropriation this body should refuse to make it, and to sanction a contract entered into with a foreign State. How much more embarrassing if, in the exercise of its constitutional powers, the Executive should involve the nation in a war against the wishes of its Representatives. The jarring and confusion and inefficiency that would result might have the most fatal influence on the national success. No, sir, frankness and candor, and a free and unreserved communication of the feelings and opinions of each by the other, can never have any other than the happiest influence upon the National Councils."[51]

Clay's motion failed, nevertheless, and recognition was postponed some four years. Yet when it did come the course which was followed by the administration vindicated his and Tucker's theory of executive-congressional coöperation most strikingly. On January 30, 1822, the House requested the President to lay before it such documents bearing on the South American question "as it may be consistent with the public interest to communicate," to which the President responded on March 8 following with a message stating that the time had come to recognize the new republics and inviting Congress, if it concurred in that view, to make "the necessary appropriations for carrying it into effect," and in due course Congress appropriated $100,000 for "such missions to the independent nations of the American continent as the President of the United States may deem proper." [52]

This entire story seems to me highly instructive. It reaffirms the President's monopoly of the function of international intercourse and his constitutional independence in the performance of that function. Not even Clay seems to have supposed either that Congress could "recognize" the new republics without executive approval and collaboration or that these were constitutionally required. At the same time Monroe, while fully advised as to his constitutional rights, seems not to have resented Congress's efforts to get its "views" on record; indeed, in the end he carefully invited congressional coöperation. It is thus borne in upon one that the principle of departmental autonomy does not necessarily spell departmental conflict, but that mutual consultation and collaboration are quite as logical deductions from it. Nor should it be overlooked that throughout this episode it was Congress who forced the pace, not the President.

The lessons deducible from our recognition of Texan independence in 1837 are similar.[53] Cuban recognition sixty years later, on the other hand, is a somewhat different story.[54] In the spring of 1896, more than a year after the outbreak of revolution in the island, the two houses adopted a concurrent resolution expressing the opinion that the situation there called for the recognition of a state of belligerency. President Cleveland ignored the suggestion; but meantime congressional opinion of a more extreme brand was rapidly developing, with the result that early in 1897 two joint resolutions made their appearance in the Senate, one of which purported to acknowledge "the independence of the Republic of Cuba" and the other of which proffered "the friendly offices" of the United States "with the government of Spain to bring to a close the war between Spain and the Republic of Cuba." The two resolutions were referred to the Committee on Foreign Relations which, after an extensive survey of the precedents, rendered an adverse report on constitutional grounds. The tenor of the report is indicated in the following extracts from it:

"The executive branch is the sole mouthpiece of the nation in communication with foreign sovereignties. Foreign nations communicate only through their respective executive departments. Resolutions of their legislative departments upon diplomatic matters have no status in international law. In the department of international law, therefore, properly speaking, a Congressional recognition of belligerency or independence would be a nullity. . . .

"Congress can help the Cuban insurgents by legislation in many ways, but it can not help them legitimately by mere declarations, or by attempts to engage in diplomatic negotiations, if our interpretation of the Constitution is correct. That it is correct will be shown by the opinions of jurists and statesmen of the past."[55]

Notwithstanding the flavor of finality which attaches to this statement, a few months later when President McKinley proposed intervention in Cuba the whole question was reopened. The President was opposed to recognizing the Cuban insurgent government, as was also a strong majority of the Foreign Relations Committee. A minority of the committee on the other hand favored "the immediate recognition of the Republic of Cuba, as a free, independent and sovereign power"; and this view prevailed to the extent that the opening resolution of the measure which "authorized and directed" the President to employ the land and naval forces of the United States to expel Spain from Cuba declared that the "people of Cuba are and of right ought to be free and independent." So, by incorporating it in what was tantamount to a declaration of war, Congress contrived to perform an act of recognition of which a foreign government was entitled by international law to take direct notice.[56]

Throughout the entire course of our national history the President has performed dozens of acts of recognition of new *governments* without consulting, or being expected to consult, Congress. At times, indeed, this prerogative has proved a most potent instrument of foreign policy, a remark which applies as well to its nonuse as to its use. President Wilson encompassed the downfall of Huerta's regime in Mexico in 1915 by refusing to recognize it as even a government *de facto,* and the pivotal feature of our relations with both Mexico and Russia for some years was the refusal of successive administrations at Washington to recognize as *de jure* the governments of those countries.

The general subject of congressional power in relation to presidential prerogative has, however, many other phases besides recognition. The principle that the National Government is as to external affairs a completely sovereign government being conceded, it logically follows that Congress's legislative power in the same field is also plenary. Except indeed for its inability to require the President to exercise his concurrent powers in the same field, Congress has approximately as broad powers over such matters as has the British Parliament. And of course once Congress has legislated, the President becomes constitutionally obligated to take care that its laws be "faithfully executed." Where—how—is a line to be drawn between these logical incompatibles? The answer seems to be, "that depends." For example, section 34 of the Jones Merchant Marine Act of 1920 "authorized and directed" the President within ninety days to give notice to the other parties to certain treaties, which the act infracted, of the termination thereof. President Wilson refused to comply, asserting that he "did not deem the direction contained in section 34 . . . an exercise of any constitutional power possessed by Congress." His action was roundly denounced by Senator Harding from the front porch earlier mentioned, despite which one of the first things Mr. Harding did upon becoming President was to announce—presumably with the concurrence of his Secretary of State, Mr. Hughes—that he proposed to follow precisely the same course. And yet had Congress contented itself with enacting the material portions of the statute it would unquestionably have become the President's constitutional duty to enforce these, regardless of their operation upon existing treaties, and at least it would have been only common sense and common courtesy on his part, as the national organ of foreign relations, to have given the other parties to the treaties advance notice. In fact, Mr. Wilson did so proceed in 1915 in connection with the LaFollette Act—despite the fact that that act "requested and directed" him to do so![57]

Of course, when it comes to legislation which would be capable of tying his hands because of his constitutional obligation in respect to law enforcement, a President has usually an effective weapon of defense for his policies in his veto power. The trouble is that an act which was put on the statute books with the approval of a predecessor, or even with his own approval, may later turn out to be seriously cramping. Thus it was that President Wilson found it necessary early in 1914, when he was being subjected to strong pressure from Great Britain on account of his Mexican policy, to go before Congress and urge repeal of the Panama Tolls Act of 1911:

"I ask this of you in support of the foreign policy of the Administration. I shall not know how to deal with other matters of even greater delicacy and nearer consequence if you do not grant it to me in ungrudging measure."[58]

Some other measures which represent attempts by Congress to guide and control foreign policy warrant mention. Thus a rider to the Appropriation Act of March 4, 1913, forbids the President to "extend or accept any invitation to participate in any international congress, conference, or like event without specific authorization to do so."[59] This measure is so obviously in conflict with doctrines and precedents already reviewed that its successful defiance only awaits an adequate occasion. The Act of May 26, 1924, on the other hand, by which Japanese immigration to this country was brought to an abrupt halt, while it signalized a particularly wild romp of the congressional bull in the diplomatic porcelain shop, was a type of legislation which Congress for many years has had conceded power to enact.[60] Equally would it be impossible to challenge Congress's power to pass the act of April 13, 1934—the so-called "Johnson Act"—which forbids the sale or purchase within American jurisdiction of any securities of a government now in debt to the United States; and the same remark applies to the various neutrality acts of recent years. As was pointed out above, Congress turned its attention to the subject of neutrality as early as 1794. Earlier acts, to be sure, merely purported to declare and sanction the existing usages of international law, but there is certainly no constitutional reason why congressional legislation should be confined to so narrow a basis.[61]

[Congress has, in short, large powers to determine the bounds within which a President may be left to work out a foreign policy. Indeed, it may effectively block presidential policy by simply declining to pass implementing legislation—appropriations for instance.] Conflict and antagonism, nevertheless, are not inevitable; to the contrary, there may be mutual consultation, coöperation, collaboration as, for example, there was in the summer of 1931 between President Hoover and Congress, resulting in the Debt Moratorium of that year. In point of fact, congressional legislation operates to augment presidential powers in the foreign field much more frequently than it does to curtail them, and especially has this been so the last few years. I quote a recent writer:

"During the first term of the Roosevelt Administration, the Executive received extended power over foreign relations, often as a by-product of legislation dealing with domestic affairs. New discretionary authority over the currency is granted through the emergency Banking Act of 1933, which permits the President to regulate or prohibit transactions in foreign exchange, transfer of credit, and export or hoarding of gold and silver. By the Thomas amendment to the Agriculture Adjustment Act of 1933, the President was authorized to revalue silver and, by the Silver Purchase Act of 1934, to nationalize silver and regulate or prohibit its import and export. The Gold Reserve Act of 1934 empowered the President to revalue the dollar at 50 to 60 per cent of its existing gold content. By means of an exchange equalization fund, financed by the $2,000,000,000 profit on devaluation, the President is granted a new weapon in international affairs. Under the Tripartite Agreement of September 25, 1936, the United States collaborates, through Executive action, with Great Britain and France for the stabilization of currencies. The Trade Agreements Act of 1934 authorized the President to conclude reciprocal trade agreements with other countries, without approval by Congress. The Executive can raise or lower any duty up to 50 per cent or to bind any duty against increase, but is forbidden to transfer articles between the free and dutiable lists. Although these agreements must provide most-favored-nation treatment, the President can refuse to extend the benefits to any third countries that discriminate against American trade. Through the Export-Import Bank, established in 1934 and capitalized by the Reconstruction Finance Corporation, the Executive is empowered to finance trade with foreign countries."[62]

Such measures, of course, are constantly being repealed or rendered obsolete by events, but new ones of the same general character are as constantly being enacted.

Nor has President Roosevelt hesitated to use these powers in the furtherance of objectives in the foreign field which Congress probably did not have in view in conferring them. Thus in his message of January 4, 1939, he said: "There are methods short of war, but stronger and more effective than mere words, of bringing home to aggressor governments the aggregate sentiments of our own people"; and it was presumably in pursuance of this thought that, following Hitler's invasion of Czecho-Slovakia, he invoked the penalties of section 303 of the Tariff Act of 1930, to which Germany had already rendered herself technically liable, and that last December he granted a credit of $25,000,000 to finance the exportation to China of American agricultural and manufactured goods and the importation of wood oil from that country.[63] Besides, thanks to the fact that the maxim against delegation of legislative power is held not to apply in the diplomatic field, inasmuch as the powers delegated merge with "cognate" powers of the President, acts of Congress may validly leave the President substantially complete discretion whether he shall enforce them or not, and this freedom of action—or inaction—may be utilized to promote a specific diplomatic policy, as it was when the present administration declined to apply the Neutrality Act of 1937 to the conflict in China;[64] and when there is no legislation at all, inaction—or feeble action—may still be an instrument of policy, as it is when the administration fails to protest with convincing vigor against the violations by favored belligerents of our rights as a neutral.

But not only is Congress a legislative body, its houses are also forums of public opinion, and their right to act as such has been asserted by their members over and over again. In the debate in the House in 1826 on the proposed mission to the Panama Congress, a Kentucky member said:

"It is its duty upon all fit occasions to pronounce the judgment of the people upon measures perfected or contemplated touching the foreign relations of the United States."

A statement which Webster endorsed in the following words:

"It has expressed its opinions, when it deemed proper to express them at all, on great leading questions, by resolution, and in a general form. These general opinions being thus made known have, doubtless, always had and such expressions of opinion doubtless always will have, their effect. This is the practice of the Government. It is a salutary practice."[65]

Almost one hundred years later resolutions were introduced in the House expressing "its cordial approval" of the World Court and its "earnest desire that the United States give early adherence to the protocol establishing the same with the reservations recommended by President Harding and President Coolidge." The resolutions were referred to the Committee on Foreign Affairs, which in reporting them favorably listed more than thirty "precedents relating to action by the House of Representatives upon treaties and foreign affairs." Some of the actions mentioned were based upon exaggerated, or otherwise mistaken, notions as to the consequences that ought to be expected to flow from them, but considered solely as expressions of opinion, it is difficult to see what constitutional objection they were open to. Sometimes Presidents have found such resolutions embarrassing, and sometimes no doubt they were intended by their proponents to be precisely that. Yet even at such times Presidents would occasionally have done better to heed them for the indication they gave of the trend of public opinion. At any rate, there seems to be no constitutional way in which a President can stop Congress's mouth whether it is saying encouraging things or the reverse.[66]

Finally, the two houses, both separately and conjointly, are able to create committees and endow them with ample powers of investigation into matters of public interest.[67] In the realm of domestic legislation such bodies have frequently done work of great importance, and there is no *a priori* reason why they should not prove of similar value when questions affecting the conduct of foreign relations are the subject of investigation. Actually, they have accomplished very little in the latter field, for the reason principally that they are usually brought about at the insistence of a special group which is much more bent on publicizing a special point of view than it is on getting sound information. Well-planned, properly staffed inquiries should be very different affairs. The efficacy of the congressional investigating committee as a device for keeping presidential foreign policy open and above-board still remains to be adequately tested.[68]

PRESIDENT VERSUS SENATE—"PERSONAL AGENTS" AND "EXECUTIVE AGREEMENTS"

As we have seen, two factors have proved of chief importance to the President in his struggle for power with Congress in the sphere of foreign relations, the natural advantages of his office and the Hamiltonian conception of "executive power." In his similar struggle with the Senate these advantages have not deserted him. Indeed, the extent to which the two constitutional clauses which give the Senate its participation in foreign relations have become infused with the Hamiltonian doctrine is one of the most remarkable features of the development of the working Constitution of 1939 from the document of 1789.

"He [the President]," reads Article II, section 2, paragraph 2, "shall nominate, and, by and with the advice and consent of the Senate, shall appoint ambassadors, other public ministers and consuls. . . ." The earliest important controversy to arise on this language was provoked by Madison's action in appointing during a recess of the Senate the commission which negotiated for the United States the Treaty of Ghent.[69] The President's critics urged that the office to which the pretended appointment had been made, having never been authorized by Congress, did not exist, and that consequently no vacancy existed to which an appointment could be made during a recess of the Senate. The answer returned was that the office of ambassador or public minister exists by the Constitution itself whenever an international exigency arises which such office is calculated to serve, and that of such exigency the President is the sole judge; also that a vacancy *happens* during a recess of the Senate if for any reason it happens then to exist.

Subsequent developments have ratified the last of these propositions,[70] but have rejected the first though this too seems clearly to have the support of early practice and opinion under the Constitution. As I mentioned in another connection, early Congresses passed no act purporting to create any diplomatic office or rank, but merely appropriated lump sums "for the expenses of foreign intercourse" to be expended at the discretion of the President.[71] Not until March 1, 1855, in fact, was the practice that obtains today introduced. By this measure it was enacted that from a stated date the President should "by and with the advice and consent of the Senate" appoint representatives of specified grades to specified countries, which representatives must be citizens of the United States, etc.[72] Attorney General Cushing, with his accustomed zeal for executive power, endeavored to explain the act as merely a kind of notification by Congress as to the sort of diplomatic and consular representatives it would be willing to appropriate salaries for, and hence as recommendatory rather than mandatory;[73] but a series of enactments exemplified by that of August 18, 1924, are hardly susceptible of this mitigated construction. Today new posts of ministerial rank are dependent upon congressional authorization, and no new ambassadorships may be created for existing posts "unless the same shall be provided for by act of Congress"; while, in general, the entire regular diplomatic and consular establishment is organized in detail as to grades, salaries, appointments, promotions, and in part as to duties, by statute.[74]

But what the President has lost in one way he has more than made good in another. I refer to his long since conceded right to employ in the discharge of his diplomatic function so-called "special," "personal," or "secret" agents in whose designation the Senate has no voice.[75] Indeed, as was pointed out in the Senate itself in 1831, when Jackson without consulting that body sent a special commission to Turkey, a similar practice was "coeval with our existence as a nation." "All those great men," the same speaker continued,

"who have figured in the history of our diplomacy, began their career, and performed some of their most important services in the capacity of secret agents, with full powers. Franklin, Adams, Lee, were only commissioners; and in negotiating a treaty with the Emperor of Morocco, the selection of the secret agent was left to the Ministers appointed to make the treaty; and, accordingly, in the year 1785, Mr. Adams and Mr. Jefferson appointed Thomas Barclay, who went to Morocco and made a treaty, which was ratified by the Ministers at Paris."[76]

Under the Constitution the practice was resumed—or continued—by Washington. On February 14, 1791, the President informed the Senate that he had "employed Mr. Gouverneur Morris, who was on the spot," to confer with the British Government concerning their further carrying out of the Treaty of Peace, "considering that in the possible event of a refusal of justice" on their part "we shall stand less committed should it be made to a private rather than a public person"; and four days later he reported having sent his friend Colonel David Humphreys to Madrid and Lisbon on a similar mission.[77] These precedents have since been multiplied many times, a peculiarly extreme example being President Cleveland's despatch of J. H. Blount to Hawaii in 1893. Blount was appointed while the Senate was in session, was given "paramount authority" over the American resident minister at Honolulu, and was further empowered to employ the military and naval forces of the United States if it was necessary to do so in order to protect American lives and property. Nevertheless a special committee of the Senate which was created to canvass the constitutional issue gave the President a clean bill of health.[78] For recent decades the continued vitality of the practice is sufficiently attested by the mere mention of President Wilson's *éminence grise,* Colonel House, and Mr. Norman H. Davis, who has filled the role of ambassador at large for a succession of administrations, including the present.

The convenience of employing such agents as "unofficial observers" of conditions abroad or to effect contact with communities or groups devoid of standing at international law is manifest. Manifest too is the fact that the practice, considering the dimensions which it has attained, is to be reconciled with the Constitution only by invoking the Hamiltonian conception of residual executive power. Though such agents are sometimes termed "secret," yet neither their existence nor their mission is invariably such. While they are sometimes called "private" or "personal" agents of the President, they have at times been appointed under the great seal. They have been justified as organs of negotiation and so as springing from the executive's power in negotiating treaties, yet this is also a normal function of our regular representatives. They have been considered as agents appointed for special occasions, although the term "public ministers" of the Constitution is broad enough to include all categories of diplomatic agents.[79] Theoretically, perhaps, they could not claim full diplomatic privileges abroad, yet practically, if their identity were known, they would probably be accorded them.[80]

Frequently, in short, the only test which is available for distinguishing this kind of agents from the other kind is to be found in the method of their appointment and in the fact that they are usually paid out of the "contingent fund." In no other way has the notion of presidential prerogative in the field of foreign relations asserted itself more strikingly.

Paragraph 2 of section 2 of Article II further ordains that the President "shall have power, by and with the advice and consent of the Senate, to make treaties, provided two-thirds of the Senators present concur." This clause too has come in time to be thoroughly infiltrated with presidential prerogative, although again—thanks to a certain gyroscopic quality of the Constitution—the story is not entirely one-sided.

Taken literally, the word "make" associates the President and Senate throughout the entire process of making a treaty, from prior to the initiation of negotiations to the final ratification of the document; a reading which is confirmed by the phrase "by and with the advice and consent," that is to say, *by the advice and with the consent,* and the words of both Jay and Hamilton in *The Federalist* afford further evidence in the same behalf,[81] as likewise does Washington's practice at the outset of his administration. The story has been told many times of how the first President went before the Senate one day in August 1789 to get its "advice and consent" to the terms of a treaty "to be negotiated with the Southern Indians," and how when a motion was made to "commit" his proposals he "started up in a violent fret," declaring "this defeats every purpose of my coming here"; and though he "cooled down by degrees" and even consented to come back the following Monday for the Senate's answer, he did not repeat the experiment of oral consultation.[82] He did, nevertheless, still endeavor usually to keep the Senate in touch by written communications with the earlier stages of treaty making. Thus at times he apprised the Senate of the terms of a "proposed agreement, and expressly requested it to reply whether or not it could consent to the final draft of the treaty in the form presented," while at other times, "he submitted the names of the negotiators together with a statement of their instructions, and declared that he would accept the Senate's confirmation of his nominees as an indication of its intention to consent to the treaty formulated in pursuance of these instructions"—this, although nominations are approved by a simple majority while treaties require a two-thirds vote. But in the important case of the Jay Treaty he failed to take the Senate into his confidence even to this extent, merely outlining when submitting Jay's nomination the advantages to be anticipated from the negotiation.[83]

Such consultation of the Senate as takes place today respecting a treaty prior to its formal submission is usually informal and via selected members of the Senate, especially members of the Foreign Relations Committee, the creation of which in 1816 as a standing committee was tacit recognition that the preliminary processes of treaty making had come to be segregated to the President, as in fact the actual initiative had been from the first.[84] There have been, it is true, occasions when the President has sought to share a specially heavy responsibility with the Senate by reverting to the earlier practice, the most notable instance being Polk's successful effort in 1846 to obtain the Senate's promise in advance to ratify a convention with Great Britain for the settlement of the Oregon boundary question, thus enabling him to start his contemplated war with Mexico.[85] But such episodes only emphasize the general sway of the contrary rule. So far as practice and weight of opinion can settle the meaning of the Constitution, it is today established that the President alone has the power to negotiate treaties with foreign governments;[86] that he is free to ignore any advice tendered him by the Senate as to a negotiation; and that he is final judge of what information he shall entrust to the Senate as to our relations with other governments.

The Senate's role in treaty making, therefore, ordinarily comprises nowadays simply the power of saying whether a proposed treaty shall be ratified or not—the act of ratification being the President's. Its power, in other words, is that of *veto,* which may be exercised outright, or conditionally upon the nonacceptance by the President or the other government or governments concerned of such amendments or reservations as it chooses to stipulate, the difference between the two being that while an amendment alters the content of the treaty itself, a reservation merely qualifies the obligations assumed thereunder by the United States. The question has been frequently debated in recent years whether the Senate's exercise of its veto power has been so excessive as to amount to an "unconstitutional invasion of executive power." Considering the extensive role which the Framers obviously intended to assign it in this particular, the answer must undoubtedly be no. Nor do I, in saying this, overlook the statistics which have been adduced in this connection. Such evidence is at best highly inconclusive as to an issue of this nature, but so far as it goes it shows that the numerical proportion of treaties failing nowadays because of senatorial action on them is not significantly greater than during the first century under the Constitution. It may be argued, to be sure, that some of the treaties of recent years belonging in this category—the Treaty of Versailles, for instance—were of much greater intrinsic importance than were the earlier ones. Conceding the point, still it can hardly be assumed that the Framers of the Constitution intended that the Senate should proceed most indulgently in the most important cases.[87]

So, if the Senate's participation in treaty making was a mistake, that mistake must be chalked up against the Framers; nor is there the least likelihood in the world of its ever being corrected by the method indicated by the Framers for such cases—that of constitutional amendment. When two thirds of the Senate consent to relax any of that body's powers something like the millennium will have dawned. At the same time, such is the "infinite variety" of the Constitution that less formal means have been discovered for mitigating "the mistake"—means the full potentialities of which have not even yet been fully realized.

As we have just seen, the Senate has today lost any right to have a voice in the negotiation of treaties, this function having been totally absorbed into the presidential prerogative as the exclusive organ of external relations. But more than that, constitutional devices now exist by which even its unquestioned veto power over treaties can often be evaded. As early as 1792 Congress authorized the Postmaster General to enter into postal conventions;[88] as recently as 1934 it authorized the President to enter into foreign-trade agreements and to lower customs rates as much as fifty per cent on imports from the other contracting countries in return for equivalent concessions;[89] while between these two statutes stretches a long series of similar delegations of what is in effect treaty-making power. Nor is the validity of such agreements and compacts today open to serious question in view of repeated decisions of the Court.[90]

Meanwhile, the power thus illustrated, recruiting strength from doctrines which have been considered earlier in this chapter, has bifurcated into two powers: that of Congress to legislate generally concerning external affairs; and that of the President as organ of foreign relations and Commander-in-Chief to enter into agreements with foreign governments. Examples of use of the former power to circumvent the senatorial veto, while not numerous, are of great significance. The annexation of Texas in 1845 by joint resolution is the leading precedent. The example thus set was followed a half century later in the case of Hawaii; and of similar import are the Joint Resolution of July 2, 1921, by which war with the Central Powers was brought to a close, and the Joint Resolution of June 19, 1934, by which the President was authorized to accept membership for the United States in the International Labor Organization.[91] Such precedents make it difficult to state any limit to the power of the President and Congress, acting jointly, to implement effectively any foreign policy upon which they agree, however "the recalcitrant third plus one man" of the Senate may feel about it.

Instances of "treaty making" by the President without the aid or consent of either Congress or the Senate are still more numerous. One was the exchange of notes in 1817 between the British Minister Bagot and Secretary of State Rush for the limitation of naval forces on the Great Lakes. Not till a year later was it submitted to the Senate, which promptly ratified it. Of like character was the exchange of notes between the State Department and various European governments in 1899 and 1900 with reference to the "Open Door" in China; the exchange in 1908 of so-called "identic notes" with Japan concerning the maintenance of the integrity of China; the "gentlemen's agreement," first drawn in 1907, by which Japanese immigration to this country was long regulated; the *modus vivendi* by which after the termination of the Treaty of Washington in 1885 American fishing rights off the coast of Canada and Newfoundland were defined for more than a quarter of a century; the protocol for ending the Boxer Rebellion in 1901; the notorious Lansing-Ishii agreement of November 2, 1917, recognizing Japan to have "special rights" in China; the armistice of November 11, 1918— to say nothing of the entire complexus of conventions and understandings by which our relations with our "Associates" in the

World War were determined, nor yet of the considerable series of agreements under which Presidents have at times employed the Army and Navy in the supervision of elections in certain of the Caribbean countries.[92]

That such agreements are "treaties," in the sense at least that they might have been submitted to the Senate for it to pass upon, is clear. The Rush-Bagot Convention is a case directly in point, and a parallel to it is the agreement which the first Roosevelt entered into with Santo Domingo ninety years later for putting the customs houses of that bankrupt nation under American control, in order to forestall its European creditors attempting the same thing. The story is told by Mr. Roosevelt in his *Autobiography* as follows:

"The Constitution did not explicitly give me power to bring about the necessary agreement with Santo Domingo. But the Constitution did not forbid my doing what I did. I put the agreement into effect, and I continued its execution for two years before the Senate acted; and I would have continued it until the end of my term, if necessary, without any action by Congress. But it was far preferable that there should be action by Congress, so that we might be proceeding under a treaty which was the law of the land and not merely by a direction of the Chief Executive which would lapse when that particular Executive left office. I therefore did my best to get the Senate to ratify what I had done. There was a good deal of difficulty about it. . . . Enough Republicans were absent to prevent the securing of a two-thirds vote for the treaty, and the Senate adjourned without any action at all, and with the feeling of entire self-satisfaction at having left the country in the position of assuming a responsibility and then failing to fulfil it. Apparently the Senators in question felt that in some way they had upheld their dignity. All that they had really done was to shirk their duty. Somebody had to do that duty, and accordingly I did it. I went ahead and administered the proposed treaty anyhow, considering it as a simple agreement on the part of the Executive which would be converted into a treaty whenever the Senate acted. After a couple of years the Senate did act, having previously made some utterly unimportant changes which I ratified and persuaded Santo Domingo to ratify. In all its history Santo Domingo has had nothing happen to it as fortunate as this treaty, and the passing of it saved the United States from having to face serious difficulties with one or more foreign powers."[93]

In short, the only substantial difference between the President's "agreement" and the "treaty" which superseded it is to be found in the fact that the latter was ratified by the Senate.

It has, I know, been contended that such "executive agreements" bind only the administration entering into them, and that they are not "law of the land." The former contention is refuted by history, the latter by decisions of the Supreme Court. Of these *United States v. Belmont*,[94] decided in May 1937, is the most recent. Here the issue was whether a district court of the United States was free to dismiss an action by the United States as assignee of the Soviet government for certain moneys which were once the property of a Russian corporation whose assets had been appropriated by the Soviet government. The court, speaking by Justice Sutherland, held not. The President's act in recognizing the Soviet government, and the accompanying agreements, constituted, said the justice, an international compact which the President, "as the sole organ" of international relations for the United States, was authorized to enter upon without consulting the Senate.[95] Nor did state laws and policies make any difference in such a situation; for while the supremacy of treaties is established by the Constitution in express terms, yet the same rule holds "in the case of all international compacts and agreements from the very fact that complete power over international affairs is in the National Government and is not and cannot be subject to any curtailment or interference on the part of the several states."[96] Not only, therefore, may "executive agreements" have the force of law—they may have the force of "supreme law of the land."

Writing in 1908, Woodrow Wilson remarked with entire accuracy:

"There can be little doubt in the mind of any one who has carefully studied the plans and opinions of the Constitutional Convention of 1787 that the relations of the President and Senate were intended to be very much more intimate and confidential than they have been; that it was expected that the Senate would give the President its advice and consent in respect of appointments and treaties in the spirit of an executive council associated with him upon terms of confidential cooperation rather than in the spirit of an independent branch of the government, jealous lest he should in the least particular attempt to govern its judgment or infringe upon its prerogatives."[97]

He was of the opinion, moreover, that it was still "not only the privilege of the President," but "also his best policy and plain duty," to treat the Senate as "an executive council"; and he added:

"If he have character, modesty, devotion, and insight as well as force, he can bring the contending elements of the system together into a great and efficient body of common counsel."[98]

How little he himself realized this ideal in his own dealings with the Senate is a matter of familiar record. Yet it would be a rash and inconsiderate critic who would say that the blame lay all with him—or, on the other hand, all with the Senate—or, indeed, that there was so much "blame" in the usual sense of the word. For what happened at that time was the logical outcome of 130 years of institutional history. From the first the President and the Senate tended to draw apart, owing simply to the different make-up of the two organs and the diversity between the roles which this difference of make-up naturally assigned to each. Somebody had to take the initiative, and who but the President? By the same token, the Senate found its business to be primarily that of a critic of proposals; and with the rise of parties over the question of neutrality in 1793 criticism inevitably became edged with hostility. The fight over the Jay Treaty was as partisan a struggle as that over the Treaty of Versailles 124 years later. To be sure, the general preponderance of Congress after the turn of the century and until Jackson's accession restored for a time, in some measure, the original conception; but other things were happening meanwhile, especially the rise of the President's Cabinet and the growth in membership of the Senate. The effect of these was to undermine the institutional setup whereby, in the imagination of the Framers, the nation's external affairs were to be largely conducted.[99] The final upshot of the business is that the Senate today is the censor of presidential foreign policy, or it is negligible, a truth the popular implication of which it grasped perfectly when in 1919 it voted to consider the Treaty of Versailles in open session.

So, from being an unwilling and unwieldy collaborator in presidential policy-making, the Senate has become a "ventilating chamber," a critic, a check. At least, it is doing the work it can do best. Sometimes, no doubt, it gives dangerous signs of having developed a swelled head. When this happens a President who has the country with him is not helpless, thanks to the weapons which constitutional doctrine and practice, and the radio, put at his disposal. And, as Mr. Wilson contended, though he failed to live up to his own good counsel, there is even today nothing to forbid a President who has the requisite flexibility of mind and method from making the Senate a partner instead of a rival.[100]

EXECUTIVE OF THE LAW OF NATIONS—PRESIDENTIAL WAR MAKING

Finally, it devolves on the President, in the first instance at least, to assert American rights and discharge American duties under international law. In this connection not only is his pre-rogative as organ of international intercourse supplemented by his duty and correlative powers as Chief Executive and Com-mander-in-Chief, but he also enjoys a kind of international capacity—an inheritance from the days when kings were more plentiful than now—as enforcer of the Law of Nations.

In the famous Neagle Case, decided in 1890, Justice Miller, speaking for the Court, put the question with regard to the Presi-dent's duty to "take care that the laws be faithfully executed":

> "Is this duty limited to the enforcement of acts of Congress or of treaties of the United States according to their *express terms,* or does it include the rights, duties and obligations growing out of the Consti-tution itself, our international relations, and all the protection implied by the nature of the government under the Constitution?" [101]

The answer evidently intended is no. Indeed, nearly eighty years earlier Attorney General William Wirt had advanced precisely this answer. The "laws" to which the "faithfully executed" clause referred, said he, comprised not only the Constitution, statutes, and treaties, but also "those general laws of nations which govern the intercourse between the United States and foreign nations." The United States, having become a member of the Society of Nations, was obliged to respect the rights of other nations under that code of laws and the President, as the chief executive officer of the laws and the agency charged with the superintendence of the nation's foreign intercourse, was bound to rectify injury and preserve peace. [102]

And nearly thirty years before that "Pacificus" had written to like effect:

> "The President is the Constitutional EXECUTOR of the laws. Our treaties, and the laws of nations, form a part of the law of the land. He, who is to execute the laws, must first judge for himself of their

meaning. In order to the observance of that conduct which the laws of nations, combined with our treaties, prescribed to this country, in reference to the present war in Europe, it was necessary for the President to judge for himself, whether there was anything in our treaties, incompatible with an adherence to neutrality."[103]

With this duality of the executive role in mind, let us consider "Pacificus' " contention, mentioned earlier in this chapter, that the President has the "power of determining virtually upon the operation of national treaties." The question raised is a twofold one: that of the President's power in relation to treaties as "law of the land"; and that of his power in relation to treaties as international obligations.

Treaty provisions are sometimes addressed *exclusively* to the President, as for instance are certain articles of the treaties which resulted from the Washington Conference of 1921, and which provide for conference among the high contracting parties in named contingencies. The duty of communication thus cast upon the President is, obviously, well within his diplomatic prerogative. Other treaty provisions, however, are addressed primarily to Congress. Indeed, it is a strongly held view, and one that has usually prevailed in practice, that if a treaty provision would operate within the field of Congress's enumerated powers—as would, for instance, a commercial treaty—it can be put into effect as "law of the land" only by sanctioning legislation;[104] and, as we have seen, Congress is free in enacting such sanctioning legislation to vest the President with large discretionary powers. Lastly, the doctrine was early established that treaty provisions which reciprocally accord privileges to the nationals of each of the contracting states within the other's jurisdiction were susceptible in the United States of direct application and enforcement through the ordinary courts.[105] In relation to such provisions, which are regarded as being addressed primarily to the judiciary, the President's power is simply that of Chief Executive, constitutionally bound to carry out the decisions of the courts.

But now suppose that it becomes desirable for the United States to cast off a treaty—whether justly or unjustly by the standards of international law—what is the constitutional procedure for accomplishing this end? The cases are clear in establishing the power of Congress to strike down in its quality as "law of the land" any treaty or treaty provision to which the United States is party;[106] while as a matter of fact treaties of the United States have been terminated on several occasions by the President, now on his own authority, now in accordance with a resolution of Congress, at other times with the sanction simply of the Senate.[107] So, while there is only one way of getting a treaty in the full constitutional sense, there are three ways of getting rid of one. For I assume that when a treaty or treaty provision has been discarded in any one of the ways just mentioned, it ceases to be "law of the land" for any purpose whatsoever—*ceases, that is, to be a source of authority* either for supplementary legislation by Congress, for action by the President, or for adjudication by the courts.

The question remains whether the international obligation of a treaty continues after it has ceased to exist as "law of the land" and the performance of the duties of the United States under it has accordingly come to an end. In general, the answer must be that the United States is no more entitled to determine finally its duties toward other nations than are the latter to determine finally their duties toward the United States.[108] At the same time, in the absence of an international tribunal with authority to pass ultimately upon such questions, each sovereign government is an organ of the international society, and in the case of the United States government the immediate bearer of this capacity is, by Hamiltonian doctrine, the President.

But the President may also make himself the direct administrator of the international rights and duties of the United States, or of what are adjudged by him to be such, without awaiting action either by the treaty-making power or by Congress, or by the courts. Significant in this connection is the course laid down by various Presidents with regard to the landing of foreign submarine cables.[109] President Grant established the germinal precedent in 1869, when he was approached with a request from a French company which desired to connect Duxbury, Massachusetts, with Brest, France, via the Island of St. Pierre in the Gulf of St. Lawrence. "In the absence of legislation by Congress" the President conceded the request upon certain stipulated conditions, and in 1879 and again in 1884 his successors followed suit. In 1893, however, President Cleveland refused a request of this sort on the ground of lack of statutory authority, with the result that the company proceeded to make a landing anyway. In the subsequent proceedings which the administration—quite inconsistently—brought to enjoin the intruder, the federal court hinted its opinion that the President's legal scruples had been misconceived. The question was finally disposed of by an opinion of Solicitor General Richards in 1898. Citing the Neagle Case, Mr. Richards placed power to act on the twofold basis of "the fundamental rights which. . . grow out of the jurisdiction of this nation over its own territory" and the President's constitutional position as the organ of American foreign relations.[110]

And it was with these precedents back of him that President Wilson in August 1913 granted permission for the introduction of electrical current from Canada,[111] and thirteen months later closed the Marconi wireless station at Siasconset, when the company refused assurance that it would comply with naval censorship regulations. The former action was admittedly without statutory basis; and while the Act of August 19, 1912,[112] probably supported the later drastic invasion of private rights, justification for it was based by Attorney General Gregory largely on the President's powers as Commander-in-Chief and as organ of foreign relations:

"The President of the United States is at the head of one of the three great coordinate departments of the Government. He is Commander-in-Chief of the Army and Navy. . . . If the President is of the opinion that the relations of this country with foreign nations are, or are likely to be, endangered by action deemed by him inconsistent with a due neutrality, it is his right and duty to protect such relations; and in doing so, in the absence of any statutory restrictions, he may act through such executive office or department as appears best adapted to effectuate the desired end. . . . I do not hesitate, in view of the extraordinary conditions existing, to advise that the President, through the Secretary of the Navy, or any other appropriate department, close down or take charge of, and operate, the plant . . . should he deem it necessary to secure obedience to his proclamation of neutrality."[113]

And it was on comparable grounds that the President met the renewal by Germany of unrestricted submarine warfare by ordering on March 12, 1917, an armed guard to be placed on all American merchant vessels. As is mentioned in another connection, this action followed hard upon the heels of failure by Congress, owing to the opposition of "a little group of willful men" in the Senate, to authorize it.[114]

Nor is this more than the beginning of the story. Thanks to the same capacity to base action directly on his own reading of international law—a capacity which the Court recognized in terms in the Neagle Case—the President has been able to gather to himself powers with respect to war making which ill accord with the specific delegation in the Constitution of the war-declaring power to Congress.

The question early presented itself whether the President, in view of the constitutional clause just mentioned, may ever recognize "a state of war" and proceed accordingly, in consequence of the hostile acts of another power? Writing in 1801 as "Lucius Crassus," Hamilton heaped scorn upon Jefferson's view that unless and until Congress formally declared war American naval vessels had the rights only of self-defense against vessels of the Bey of Tripoli. The plain meaning of the Constitution, Hamilton asserted, was

"That it is the peculiar and exclusive province of Congress, *when the nation is at peace* to change that state into a state of war; whether from calculations of policy or from provocations, or injuries received; in other words, it belongs to Congress only, *to go to war*. But when a foreign nation declares, or openly and avowedly makes war upon the United States, they are then by the very fact *already at war,* and any declaration on the part of Congress is nugatory; it is at least unnecessary."[115]

More than sixty years later Hamilton's argument was renewed by Richard Henry Dana in the Prize Cases and was, as we have seen, ratified by the Court for situations involving insurrection and actual invasion.[116] As to foreign wars, on the other hand, congressional declarations of war have always taken the form of merely recognizing a state of war begun by the hostile acts of the other party, and so have never exceeded the power which Hamilton and Dana claimed for the President acting alone.

Far more important is the question whether the President may, without authorization by Congress, take measures which are technically acts of war in protection of American rights and interests abroad. The answer returned both by practice and by judicial doctrine is yes. The leading precedent was an outgrowth of the bombardment in 1854, by Lieutenant Hollins of the U.S.S. *Cyane,* of Greytown, Nicaragua, in default of reparation from the local authorities for an attack on the United States consul. Upon his return to the United States Hollins was sued in a federal court by one Durand for the value of certain property which was alleged to have been destroyed in the bombardment. His defense was based upon the orders of the President and Secretary of Navy, and was sustained by Justice Nelson in the following words:

"As the Executive head of the nation, the President is made the only legitimate organ of the General Government, to open and carry on correspondence or negotiations with foreign nations, in matters concerning the interests of the country or of its citizens. It is to him, also, that citizens abroad must look for protection of person and of property, and for the faithful execution of the laws existing and intended for their protection. For this purpose, the whole Executive power of the country is placed in his hands, under the Constitution, and the laws passed in pursuance thereof; and different Departments of government have been organized, through which this power may be most conveniently executed, whether by negotiation or by force—a Department of State and a Department of the Navy.

"Now, as respects the interposition of the Executive abroad, for the protection of the lives or property of the citizen, the duty must, of necessity, rest in the discretion of the President. Acts of lawless violence, or of threatened violence to the citizen or his property, cannot be anticipated and provided for; and the protection, to be effectual or of any avail, may, not unfrequently, require the most prompt and decided action. Under our system of Government, the citizen abroad is as much entitled to protection as the citizen at home. The great object and duty of Government is the protection of the lives, liberty, and property of the people composing it, whether abroad or at home; and any Government failing in the accomplishment of the object, or the performance of the duty, is not worth preserving."[117]

And further illustrative of the President's power and duty to protect American rights abroad was President McKinley's despatch of a naval force and an army of some five thousand men under General Chaffee to China in 1900, at the time of the Boxer Rebellion. In his annual message the President referred to his action thus:

"Our declared aims involved no war against the Chinese nation. We adhered to the legitimate office of rescuing the imperiled legation, obtaining redress for wrongs already suffered, securing wherever possible the safety of American life and property in China, and preventing a spread of the disorders or their recurrence."[118]

The expedition took place in coöperation with like expeditions of several European governments, whose plenipotentiaries were joined by the American minister to China in pressing the Protocol of September 7, 1901, upon the Chinese Imperial Government. This instrument detailed certain acts of reparation by the Chinese authorities for the injuries that foreign powers, their citizens and subjects, had suffered from the uprising, among these being the payment of an indemnity. The protocol was ratified for the United States by the President without reference to the Senate. President Wilson's despatch in 1916 of General Pershing to the Mexican border and the latter's invasion of Mexican territory in pursuit of Villa may possibly be justified under a broad interpretation of the power conferred on the President by the Act of 1807 to "repel invasion."

Passing then from "rights" to "interests," the leading precedent was furnished by Tyler's action in 1844 in so disposing the naval and military forces of the United States as to protect Texas against Mexican wrath on account of the then pending treaty for the annexation of Texas to the United States. In answer to a resolution of inquiry by the Senate, Tyler defended his course as follows:

"It is due to myself that I should declare it as my opinion that the United States, having by the treaty of annexation acquired a title to

Texas which requires only the action of the Senate to perfect it, no other power could be permitted to invade and by force of arms to possess itself of any portion of the territory of Texas pending your deliberations upon the treaty without placing itself in an hostile attitude to the United States and justifying the employment of any military means at our disposal to drive back the invasion."[119]

Tyler's efforts to annex Texas had their counterpart a quarter of a century later in Grant's efforts to annex Santo Domingo, and the same question arose on the latter occasion as to the right of the President to protect the so-called "inchoate interests" of the United States in Santo Domingo until the final disposition of the main question. Drawing a sharp distinction between such "interests" and "rights," Grant's critics endeavored to confine existing precedents to the latter. But, notwithstanding their triumph, later events in the Caribbean, especially after 1916, went far to discredit this distinction for that particular region, where American interests are peculiarly sensitive.[120]

Of course, it may be argued, and has in fact been argued many times, that the President is under constitutional obligation not to incur the risk of war in the prosecution of a diplomatic policy without first consulting Congress and getting its consent. In view, nevertheless, of what has been said already, the supposed principle is clearly a maxim of policy rather than a generalization from consistent practice. Sometimes it has been observed, as when Presidents Monroe and Jackson consulted with Congress prior to recognizing the South American republics and Texas, respectively; at other times Presidents have pursued policies which led to war, or might easily have done so, without previously confiding in Congress to any great extent. Such was Polk's course prior to the Mexican War, and it was Wilson's course immediately prior to our entry into the World War; while the first Roosevelt constantly skated the thin ice of international embroilment, consulting nothing but his own fondness for adventure. It is quite true that Congress by the principle of concurrent powers is free to refuse to back up a President in a warlike situation precipitated by him; but such refusal has never occurred, nor is it likely to in the presence of a first-class foe. Conversely, no President has so far refused to exercise his powers as Commander-in-Chief to fight a war foisted on the country by Congress, as were the War of 1812 and the war with Spain, although Mr. Cleveland is said to have threatened to do this very thing in 1897 when Congress was pressing him for intervention in Cuba.[121]

In short, the Constitution contains no guarantee against our being involved in war by either the President or Congress. It is now proposed, however, to remedy the defect by transferring the war-declaring power, with certain important exceptions, to a popular referendum. The proposal in its present incarnation is an outcome in part of popular revulsion from our participation in the World War, regarding which a considerable mythology has grown up in recent years; and, in part, of the conflict of views which had been developing from an earlier date over the issue of Isolation versus International Coöperation. Throughout the last forty years the inclination of successive Presidents has been, in however varying degrees, toward the latter alternative; and it is the hope of the champions of the War Referendum to curb this tendency, which they think invites to war. Furthermore, they argue that it will spike the guns of "pressure groups" which have an interest in promoting war. Opponents of the proposal answer, on the other hand, that it might actually increase the war danger by causing an antagonist to overestimate the strength of this country's passivism, and furthermore that the agitation which would presumably precede a referendum vote would be dangerously demoralizing in case war was finally voted by a narrow margin. Between such speculations *in vacuo,* proceeding from so widely divergent premises, or preferences, it is clearly impossible to strike an intelligent balance.[122]

The referendum proposal is probably no more radical for these days than the provision in the Constitution itself which vests the war-declaring power in Congress was for 1789; and, what is more to the point, it is not likely to prove more effective so long as the President retains the powers which have enabled him to seize the war-declaring power on two occasions. Yet, by and large, Presidents have not shown themselves to be more war-minded than Congress, nor the latter more so than the people at large. The assumption that war is the one thing respecting which the government as at present constituted is incapable of sensing and representing public opinion, therefore, seems extreme. Even the diplomatic adventuring of the first Roosevelt—so far as it was known—met the popular mood, and if a different mood prevails today there is no reason to believe that it will not find expression in governmental policy—*provided* it continues to prevail.[123]

Moreover, this question should be posed: what effect would the War Referendum be likely to have on existing institutions? On the face of it, the proposal takes power from Congress and transfers it to the people at large. Must not the long-run tendency of this be to weaken Congress and at the same time build up a more palpable and continuous connection between the Presidency and the electorate than has heretofore existed? That is to say, does it not point rather definitely to government by *plebiscite*? So, even though it be conceded that the President's initiative in the foreign field demands curbing, still it would seem only good sense to find out what can be made of existing institutions for this purpose before adding to their number a new one which may throw the whole mechanism more or less out of gear.[124] Indeed, the recent decision of Congress to remain in session in view of the international crisis, in spite of repeated hints from the White House that it would do better to adjourn, is a greater contribution toward securing the kind of check just mentioned than a half dozen War Referendum amendments would be.

By way of summary: The powers which under the Constitution are capable of determining the policy of the National Government toward other governments are divided. The states, to be sure, have no share in these powers—today there are no States Rights in the foreign field, and few private rights. The prime division is between the President—sometimes acting with the Senate, more often alone—and Congress, that is, the national legislative power; a secondary division is that between President and Senate.

Not only is a struggle for power in this field thus invited; in the absence of a coöperative disposition all around it is well-nigh inevitable. Nor do the applicable principles of constitutional law help much in resolving such a quarrel. By the doctrine of political questions the Court refrains from thrusting its oar into the troubled waters; by the principle of concurrent powers neither Congress nor the Senate is constitutionally concluded by anything done by the President, while he—because of his obligation to the law—*is* usually concluded by what Congress has done. Even so, if our diplomacy was to have a reasonable chance of success in the world at large it had to have unity of direction from an organ of government which was "always in session," which could act swiftly and secretly, and which commanded the widest information; and these requirements the Presidency met.

Definite clauses of the Constitution make the President the organ of communication with foreign governments; and since Hamilton's "Letters of Pacificus," written in 1793 in defense of Washington's Neutrality Proclamation, few have ever ventured to contend that when acting in this capacity the President is the mere mouthpiece of policies determined upon elsewhere. What is more, Hamilton's contention that the "executive power" clause of the Constitution embraces a prerogative in the diplomatic field which is plenary except as it is curtailed by more specific clauses of the Constitution has consistently prospered. The President to-day is not only the organ of communication of the United States with foreign governments—he is the *only* organ of communication therewith; and as such he is entitled to shape the foreign policies of the United States so far as he is actually able to do so within the conditions which are imposed by the acts of Congress; and more often than not Congress chooses to follow the leadership which his conspicuous advantages of position serve to confer upon him.

Moreover, it is necessary to remember that the President is not only the organ of foreign relations but also Chief Executive and Commander-in-Chief, since on the basis of these blended powers he has been able to lay claim successfully to a kind of international capacity as executive of the Law of Nations, especially when American interests abroad are menaced by other countries. He has thus come to exercise at times the war-making power without prior consultation of Congress, especially in the region of the Caribbean. What is of vastly greater importance, however, is the ability of the President simply by his day-to-day conduct of our foreign relations to create situations from which escape except by the route of war is difficult or impossible. Indeed, there are times when his power is most effective in shaping policy by not being exercised or by being exercised weakly; while because of its primitive organization, executive power has an ever available capacity for putting forth new methods, new instruments of policy, in a way not open to the more complex and cumbrous agencies of government, a fact well illustrated by the recently contrived "moral embargo," and other expedients for carrying out the policy of furnishing aid against aggressors "short of war."

And in the presence of such facts it is not easy to see how the War Referendum would afford much of a guarantee of peace if presidential prerogative is to be left otherwise untouched. At the same time presidential prerogative in the diplomatic field is not even today unlimited, either theoretically or practically. No President has a mandate from the Constitution to conduct our foreign relations according to his own sweet will. If his power in that field is indefinite, so is Congress's legislative power; and if he holds "the sword," so does Congress hold "the purse-strings." For the rest, the President's diplomatic powers are, and always have been, a function of our foreign policy, and if they seem dangerously great today it is partly because our position in the world has become, for one reason or another, dangerously great.

CHAPTER VII

POPULAR LEADER AND LEGISLATOR

THE revival of presidential leadership in legislation is one phase of the revival of legislation of a national scope. While Sir Henry Maine's assertion that "the energy of legislatures is the prime characteristic of modern societies" is now three quarters of a century old, it is only within the last thirty-five years that the activities of Congress have brought it notable confirmation. The Reconstruction Era was marked by an outpouring of legislation which was volcanic in volume and violence, as well as in the suddenness with which it came to an end. The succeeding period was dominated by the gospel of *laissez faire,* that, except when it has favors to confer, government had best refrain from meddling in the economic field—doctrine which was reinforced in the case of the National Government by a rigidly conceptualistic constitutional law.

But gradually a new point of view emerged, the increasing influence of which is registered by the history of congressional legislation touching interstate commerce. I quote from Professor Ribble's recent volume:

"Before 1887 there were but few statutes of material importance regulating the conduct of the inland commerce of the United States. Such statutes as existed dealt chiefly with bridges, the improvement of rivers and harbors, and general admiralty regulations. . . .

"This record is in sharp contrast with Congressional activity in succeeding years. To show an awakened Congress, it is sufficient to recite some of the more important statutes following the Interstate Commerce Act of 1887. Thus mention may be made of the following pieces of federal legislation dealing with commerce; Labor Arbitration Act of 1888; Sherman Anti-Trust Act of 1890; Federal Safety Appliance Acts, beginning with that of 1893; Erdman Act of 1898; Elkins Act of 1903; Federal Employers' Liability Law of 1906; Hepburn Act of 1906; Federal Hours of Labor Law of 1907; Federal Employers' Liability Act of 1908; Mann-Elkins Act of 1910; Panama Canal Act of 1912; Newlands Act of 1913; Cotton Futures Act of 1914; Federal Trade Commission Act of 1914; Clayton Act of 1914; Adamson Act of 1916; the Transportation Act of 1920; Packers and Stockyards Act of 1921; Grain Futures Act of 1922; Air Commerce Act of 1926; Railway Labor Act of 1926; Radio Act of 1927; Longshoremen's and Harbor Workers' Compensation Act of 1927; Hawes-Cooper Act, 1929; Perishable Agricultural Commodities Act of 1930; Emergency Railroad Transportation Act of 1933; Agricultural Adjustment Act of 1933; National Industrial Recovery Act, 1933; Communications Act of 1934; Cotton Marketing Act of 1934; Act of 1934, prohibiting the moving in interstate commerce after the commission of certain specified crimes; National Stolen Property Act of 1934; Securities Exchange Act of 1934; National Labor Relations Act of 1935; Interstate Transportation of Petroleum Act of 1935; the Guffey-Snyder Coal Act of 1935; the Railroad Reorganization Act of 1935."[1]

Does government exist primarily to supplement and reinforce other forces of social control—economic superiority, for instance? Or ought it attempt to correct and improve such forces, in the interest of certain ideals of justice—the notion of the Equality of Man, for instance? *Laissez faire*-ism held to the former view, but more recent trends in governmental policy in this country proceed from the latter view. And the theme of the present chapter is the effect of this altered outlook on the Presidency.

THE LITERARY SOURCES OF PRESIDENTIAL LEADERSHIP—
WOODROW WILSON

In Woodrow Wilson's *Congressional Government,* which appeared in 1885, we have the earliest attempt to give a nonlegalistic, factual description of the reciprocal roles of Congress and the President, and it is evident that Wilson regarded Congress as decidedly the dominant member in the partnership. I quote some characteristic passages from the "Introduction":

"The noble charter of fundamental law given us by the Convention of 1787 is still our Constitution; but it is now our *form of government* rather in name than in reality, the form of the Constitution being one of nicely adjusted, ideal balances, whilst the actual form of our present government is simply a scheme of congressional supremacy. . . .

"It is said that there is no single or central force in our federal scheme . . . but only a balance of powers and a nice adjustment of inter-active checks, as all the books say. How is it, however, in the practical conduct of the federal government? In that, unquestionably, the predominant and controlling force, the center and source of all motive and of all regulative power, is Congress. . . .

"Congress [is] the dominant, nay, the irresistible, power of the federal system, relegating some of the chief balances of the Constitution to an insignificant role in the 'literary theory' of our institutions. . . . "

And then by way of "Conclusion":

"Congress is fast becoming the governing body of the nation, and yet the only power which it possesses in perfection is the power which is but a part of government, the power of legislation."[2]

Contrast with this the picture which Wilson paints of the Presidency at this period:

"Independently of experience, however, it might reasonably have been expected that the prerogatives of the President would have been one of the most effectual restraints upon the power of Congress. He was constituted one of the three great coordinate branches of the government; his functions were made of the highest dignity; his privileges many and substantial—so great, indeed, that it has pleased the fancy of some writers to parade little doubt that, had the presidential chair always been filled by men of commanding character, of acknowledged ability, and of thorough political training, it would have continued to be a seat of the highest authority and consideration, the true center of the federal structure, the real throne of administration, and the frequent source of policies.

"But the prestige of the presidential office has declined with the character of the Presidents. And the character of the Presidents has declined as the perfection of selfish party tactics has advanced. . . .

"I am disposed to think, however, that the decline in the character of the Presidents is not the cause, but only the accompanying manifestation, of the declining prestige of the presidential office. That high office has fallen from its first estate of dignity because its power has waned; and its power has waned because the power of Congress has become predominant. . . ."[3]

Searching for an explanation for this outcome of the struggle for power between the President and Congress, Wilson finds one ready at hand in a passage of Bagehot's famous work on the *English Constitution,* which he paraphrases, substituting "Congress" for "Parliament":

"Congress is 'nothing less than a big meeting of more or less idle people. In proportion as you give it power it will inquire into everything, settle everything, meddle in everything. In an ordinary despotism the powers of the despot are limited by his bodily capacity, and by the calls of pleasure; he is but one man; there are but twelve hours in his day, and he is not disposed to employ more than a small part in dull business; he keeps the rest for the court, or the harem, or for society.' But Congress 'is a despot who has unlimited time,—who has unlimited vanity,—who has, or believes he has, unlimited comprehension, —whose pleasure is in action, whose life is work.' Accordingly it has entered more and more into the details of administration, until it has virtually taken into its own hands all the substantial powers of government. It does not domineer over the President himself, but it makes the Secretaries its humble servants. Not that it would hesitate, upon occasion, to deal directly with the chief magistrate himself; but it has few calls to do so, because our latter-day Presidents live by proxy; they are the executive in theory, but the Secretaries are the executive in fact."[4]

Wilson had an axe to grind—two axes to grind in fact. For himself he desired to emulate Bagehot's attack on "the literary theory" of the British Constitution; from a broader point of view he wished to see the British cabinet system adapted to the American Constitution; and this twofold bias led him to exaggerate the phenomenon which he recorded. Yet when James Bryce brought out his *American Commonwealth* some three years later, he did little more than retouch Wilson's picture. He wrote:

"In quiet times the power of the President is not great. He is hampered at every turn by the necessity of humouring his party. He is so much engrossed by the trivial and mechanical parts of his work as to have little leisure for framing large schemes of policy, while in carrying them out he needs the cooperation of Congress, which may be jealous, or indifferent, or hostile. He has less influence on legislation,— that is to say, his individual volition makes less difference to the course legislation takes, than the Speaker of the House of Representatives."[5]

The President was virtually without initiative in legislation, Bryce held; what strength he possessed in that field lay in his veto power. And why had the President lost ground? Bryce answered as follows:

"Men come and go, but an assembly goes on forever; it is immortal, because while the members change, the policy, the passion for extending its authority, the tenacity in clinging to what has once been gained, remain persistent. A weak magistrate comes after a strong magistrate, and yields what his predecessor had fought for; but an assembly holds all it has ever won. Its pressure is steady and continuous; it is always, by a sort of natural process, expanding its own powers and devising new methods for fettering its rival. Thus Congress, though it is no more respected or loved by the people now than it was seventy years ago, though it has developed no higher capacity for promoting the best interests of the State, has succeeded in occupying nearly all the ground which the Constitution left debatable between the President and itself; and would, did it possess a better internal organization, be even more plainly than it now is the supreme power in the government."[6]

Yet Bryce is not altogether satisfied with this disposition of the subject; and when at the very end of his work he recurs to it, he ventures a word of prophecy:

"One is sometimes inclined to think that Congress might lose its hold on the respect and confidence of the nation, and sink into a subordinate position, were there any other authority which could be substituted for it. There is, however, no such authority, for law-making cannot be given to a person or to a court, while the State legislatures have the same faults as Congress in a greater degree. We may accordingly surmise that Congress will retain its present place; but so far as can be gathered from present phenomena, it will retain this place in respect not of the satisfaction of the people with its services, but of their inability to provide a better servant.

"The weakness of Congress is the strength of the President. Though it cannot be said that his office has risen in power or dignity since 1789, there are reasons for believing that it may reach a higher point than it has occupied at any time since the Civil War. The tendency everywhere in America to concentrate power and responsibility in one man is unmistakable. There is no danger that the President should become a despot, that is, should attempt to make his will prevail against the will of the majority. But he may have a great part to play as the leader of the majority and the exponent of its will. He is in some respects better fitted both to represent and to influence public opinion than Congress is. . . .

"A vigorous personality attracts the multitude, and attracts it the more the huger it grows; while a chief magistrate's influence excites little alarm when exerted in leading a majority which acts through the constitutional organs of government. There may therefore be still undeveloped possibilities of greatness in store for the Presidents of the future. But as these possibilities depend, like the possibilities of the British and German Crowns, perhaps one may add of the Papacy, on the wholly unpredictable element of personal capacity in the men who may fill the office, we need speculate on them no further."[7]

Congressional Government and *The American Commonwealth* were written in a period of declension of the presidential office in all its phases. Henry Jones Ford, in his *Rise and Growth of American Politics,* which appeared in 1898, was encouraged by more recent developments, and especially the two Cleveland administrations, to spotlight the office in the tradition of its successes rather than its failures. In this volume—one of the most brilliant interpretations of American political history that we possess—one reads:

"The agency of the presidential office has been such a master force in shaping public policy that to give a detailed account of it would be equivalent to writing the political history of the United States. From Jackson's time to the present day it may be said that political issues have been decided by executive policy. . . .

"While all that a President can certainly accomplish is to force a submission of an issue to the people, yet such is the strength of the office that, if he makes a sincere and resolute use of its resources, at the same time cherishing his party connection, he can as a rule carry his party with him, because of the powerful interests which impel it to occupy ground taken for it by the administration. . . .

"On the other hand, unless a measure is made an administrative issue, Congress is unable to make it a party issue. . . .

"The rise of presidential authority cannot be accounted for by the intention of presidents; it is the product of political conditions which dominate all the departments of government, so that Congress itself shows an unconscious disposition to aggrandize the presidential office. . . .

"The truth is that in the presidential office, as it has been constituted since Jackson's time, American democracy has revived the oldest political institution of the race, the elective kingship. It is all there: the precognition of the notables and the tumultuous choice of the freemen, only conformed to modern conditions. That the people have been able to accomplish this with such defective apparatus, and have been able to make good a principle which no other people have been able to reconcile with the safety of the state, indicates the highest degree of constitutional morality yet attained by any race."[8]

That same year occurred the Spanish-American War, and the Presidency was, as is always the case, lifted by emergency into a new high relief. Contributing a new preface to the eighteenth impression of *Congressional Government*, Woodrow Wilson noted the fact in these words:

"Much the most important change to be noticed [*i.e.*, since 1885] is the result of the war with Spain upon the lodgment and exercise of power within our federal system: the greatly increased power and opportunity for constructive statesmanship given the President, by the plunge into international politics and into the administration of distant dependencies, which has been that war's most striking and momentous consequence. When foreign affairs play a prominent part in the politics and policy of a nation, its Executive must of necessity be its guide: must utter every initial judgment, take every first step of action, supply the information upon which it is to act, suggest and in large measure control its conduct. The President of the United States is now, as of course, at the front of affairs, as no president, except Lincoln, has been since the first quarter of the nineteenth century, when the foreign relations of the new nation had first to be adjusted. There is no trouble now about getting the President's speeches printed and read, every word. Upon his choice, his character, his experience hang some of the most weighty issues of the future. The government of dependencies must be largely in his hands. Interesting things may come out of the singular change."[9]

An assassin's bullet soon put this prophecy on the way to fulfillment. In his *Constitutional Government in the United States*, comprising lectures delivered at Columbia in 1908, Wilson re-assessed the Presidency in the light of the first Roosevelt's performance, and in words which offer a striking contrast to his disparaging evaluation twenty-three years earlier. Here are some sentences from the third chapter of the book:

"He cannot escape being the leader of his party except by incapacity and lack of personal force, because he is at once the choice of the party and of the nation."

"He can dominate his party by being spokesman for the real sentiment and purpose of the country, by giving direction to opinion, by giving the country at once the information and the statements of policy which will enable it to form its judgments alike of parties and of men."

"His is the only national voice in affairs. Let him once win the admiration and confidence of the country, and no other single force can withstand him, no combination of forces will easily overpower him. His position takes the imagination of the country. He is the representative of no constituency, but of the whole people."

"He may be both the leader of his party and the leader of the nation, or he may be one or the other. If he lead the nation, his party can hardly resist him. His office is anything he has the sagacity and force to make it."

"Some of our Presidents have deliberately held themselves off from using the full power they might legitimately have used, because of conscientious scruples, because they were more theorists than statesmen. . . . The President is at liberty, both in law and conscience, to be as big a man as he can."

"His is the vital place of action in the system, whether he accept it as such or not, and the office is the measure of the man,—of his wisdom as well as of his force."[10]

Four years later Wilson was himself given the opportunity to animate by his own practice the figure which he had wrought in the academic *atelier*. His success is sufficiently recorded for our immediate purpose in the opening words of H. C. Black's *The*

Relation of the Executive Power to Legislation, which appeared in 1919, while Wilson was still in office.

"The President of the United States has grown into a position of overmastering influence over the legislative department of the government. He presents and procures the enactment of such measures as he desires, and prevents the passage of those which he disapproves."

And again:

"The most portentous development in American political and constitutional history since 1865 is the change in the relations between the executive and legislative branches of government, the one making enormous gains in the direction of influence and actual power, the other suffering a corresponding decline in prestige and in its control over the processes of government. The President of the United States occupies today a position of leadership and of command over the government of the country so different from that which was intended by the framers of the Constitution that, if it were not the outcome of a natural process of evolution working through a long period of years, it would bear the stigmata of revolution, and if it had been achieved in a single presidential term, it would have been denounced as a *coup d'état.*"[11]

On a later page the same writer adds: "It is difficult to reverse an evolutionary process, and what we have been describing appears to be a true political evolution."[12] Subsequent events have verified these words—today things are blacker than ever—from the Black point of view.

THE CONSTITUTIONAL BASIS AND *MODUS OPERANDI* OF PRESIDENTIAL LEADERSHIP — FROM ROOSEVELT I TO ROOSEVELT II

The formal taking-off ground of presidential leadership in legislation is furnished by the opening clause of Article II, section 3, of the Constitution: "He shall from time to time give to the Congress information of the state of the Union, and recommend to their consideration such measures as he shall judge necessary and expedient. . . . "[13] Although this language imposes a *duty* rather than confers a *power,* Presidents are apt to be like other people who feel they have a duty to perform; they can make themselves extremely importunate at times. Is there any constitutional reason why they should not do so in the present instance? Many people have argued that there is a very good reason, namely, that the Constitution vests the legislative power in *Congress,* and that therefore performance by the President of the above duty ought to stop well short of invading that power, an argument which is usually bolstered by an invocation of the principle of the separation of powers.

The relations of the first President with Congress were, as I pointed out earlier,[14] modeled on contemporary British practice. While featured by considerable formality, they were otherwise rather more free from self-consciousness on either side than they were soon to become. One reason was that the great business of getting the new government started offered at first sufficient outlet for the best talents of everybody, there being at that date fewer than one hundred members of Congress. Another was that party divisions had not yet crystallized. Moreover, the principle of the separation of powers was at that date more or less under a cloud, having failed in the state constitutions to prevent all power from slipping into "the legislative vortex." Thus Madison, who was later to become a fearful pedant on this very point, had argued in *The Federalist* that the principle ought not to be interpreted as forbidding a reasonable amount of intermingling of powers, and particularly of the executive with the legislative power, and in that connection had cited the British Constitution, from which "the celebrated Montesquieu" had drawn his evangel of liberty.[15]

But the Age of Innocency soon came to an end. It was not long before the ever alert suspicion of Jefferson discovered that Hamilton's connection with Congress, whereby "the whole action of the Legislature was . . . under the direction of the Treasury," tended definitely to the overthrow of republican institutions. Indeed, it was on this fundamental ground, according to his later account in his famed *Anas,* that he erected against Hamilton's measures the opposition from which the Jeffersonian party in due course took its rise. In his own words:

"Its [the opposition's] object was to preserve the Legislature pure and independent of the Executive, to restrain the administration to republican forms and principles, and not permit the Constitution to be construed into a monarchy, and to be warped in practice into all the principles and pollutions of their [the Hamiltonian Federalists'] favorite English model."[16]

For all that, as was pointed out in Chapter I, no President ever dominated Congress more completely, or more successfully if legislative output be the test of success, than did Jefferson; and he managed it without conspicuous departure from his professed principles through the private exertion of his influence with his party associates and the party caucus. The clandestine aspect of Jefferson's contribution to presidential leadership long ago became secondary. Nowadays when a President approaches a Congress of the same political complexion as himself, he does not hesitate to invoke his role both as Chief Executive and as Party Leader; and, if Congress still remains insufficiently impressed, he falls back on a still more portentous claim, that of being *Representative of the People.*

This third person of the presidential trinity first achieved embodiment in Andrew Jackson. While Jefferson was never confronted with a politically hostile Congress or a Congress either house of which was hostile, Jackson was compelled virtually to create a new party out of a new electorate, and to the end of his Presidency was beset by a powerful and brilliant opposition in the

Senate. In this situation the undercover methods of Jefferson did not suffice. A new technique had to be devised, that of appealing to the people over the heads of Congress's leaders; and Jackson met this need. His triumph was climaxed in the Senate's adoption within a few weeks of his retirement of the famous "Expunging Resolution" by which it struck from its Journal its resolutions censuring three years earlier his financial policies. Never before and never since has the Senate so abased itself before a President.[17]

The present-day role of the President as policy determiner in the legislative field is largely the creation of the two Roosevelts and Woodrow Wilson, each of whom came to the Presidency following a notable and successful experience as governor of his home state. Discussing his governorship of New York, in his *Autobiography,* the first Roosevelt remarks:

"In theory the Executive has nothing to do with legislation. In practice as things now are, the Executive is or ought to be peculiarly representative of the people as a whole. As often as not the action of the Executive offers the only means by which the people can get the legislation they demand and ought to have. Therefore a good executive under the present conditions of American political life must take a very active interest in getting the right kind of legislation, in addition to performing his executive duties with an eye single to the public welfare."[18]

As these words indicate, Roosevelt I's approach to the problem of executive leadership was Jacksonian rather than Jeffersonian; but he enjoyed advantages which were not available to his predecessor, certainly not in the same measure. One of these was a quite personal gift. No more convinced preacher of the platitudes, none more adept at translating his preferences into moralistic axioms and attitudes, ever attained the Presidency. In his own words, "The White House is a bully pulpit"; and not only the White House, but the country-wide press as well. Not only had "T. R."

access to the news columns of those hundreds of papers which supported him editorially; but also of those other hundreds which opposed him editorially. In part this was the result of clever contriving. The Sunday news release, it was early found, was always sure of making the first page in Monday's otherwise usually drab issue.[19] More largely it was the general result of good all-round showmanship. What "T. R." did was always interesting, or at least the correspondents came to think it was.[20]

The difficulties which Roosevelt encountered in building up the legislative role of the President were, nevertheless, formidable. Foremost of these was the internal organization of the houses of Congress. The committee system was vastly more extended and more closely knit than in Jackson's time, and its governing principle was that of seniority. So, although Congress was in the hands of Roosevelt's own party, its immediate direction was in the hands of the older and more conservative members thereof, men who on the score of experience alone were disposed to regard the temporary occupant of the White House with a certain condescension. And aggravating this situation were the defects of "T. R.'s" personal qualities of combative assertiveness, impulsiveness, and habit of drastic criticism of any who opposed his purposes at the moment.[21] Commenting afterward in his *Autobiography* upon his relations with the principal congressional leaders of the period—Senators Aldrich and Hale and Speaker Cannon—Roosevelt wrote:

"I made a resolute effort to get on with all three and with their followers, and I have no question that they made an equally resolute effort to get on with me. We succeeded in working together, although with increasing friction, for some years, I pushing forward and they hanging back. Gradually, however, I was forced to abandon the effort to persuade them to come my way, and then I achieved results only by appealing over the heads of the Senate and House leaders to the people, who were the masters of both of us." [22]

These words are at once an avowal and a confession. For while resort to Jacksonian methods undoubtedly suited Roosevelt's boisterous temperament, yet the drawbacks from such methods are serious. As Dr. Small puts it:

"Unless an Executive be willing to jeopardize his chances of securing the adoption of his remaining recommendations, it is inadvisable to risk an appeal on a single issue; for though he may be successful in his attempt, his conduct is likely to rekindle even more intensely a spirit of resentment in Congress and to confirm it in its resolve to combat his leadership. Moreover, if the public fail to honor his petition . . . the President has thus by his own hand prematurely terminated his ascendancy. . . . An harmonious cooperation between Executive and Legislature in which the former aspires to the role of an uncompromising leader is unusually [usually ?] tenuous; and, when congressional leaders subsequently rebel against the abridgment of their freedom of discretion, the President has no alternative other than to revert to certain threats of coercion in order to achieve the acceptance of his program." [23]

While written with Wilson's abortive appeal in October 1918 for a Democratic Congress in mind, these words are more appropriately applicable to the closing chapter of "T. R.'s" dealings with Congress; and they have also considerable relevancy to more recent happenings. [24]

Although destined to be cast somewhat in the shade by subsequent achievements in the same field, the first Roosevelt's legislative performance was notable; while his contributions to the technique of presidential leadership were not only contemporaneously impressive but durable. Detailing the "arts of management" by which "Roosevelt, Taft and Wilson," Roosevelt leading the way, "pushed their suggestions to a legislative conclusion," Professor Finer writes:

"They sent messages to the Houses, and letters to party friends; held conferences and breakfasts in their room adjoining the Senate, and invited the Chairmen of Committees and the 'floor leaders' to the White House. Their most trusted and astute Cabinet officers were often sent to the Congressional lobbies to whip up support, and to exert the influence of personal representation of the President. Heads of departments attended caucus meetings; information was poured into Congress; party friends were provided with drafts of bills and the vindicating briefs."[25]

It is the last of these devices which is of special interest from the constitutional point of view. Bills were not yet sent openly from the White House to the Capitol in those days, but Mr. Roosevelt's congressional spokesmen nevertheless admitted the practice occasionally. Said Senator Dolliver of Iowa at the time when the Senate was debating the Hepburn bill for amending the Interstate Commerce Act: "There are at least five acts of legislation, all of them referring to this and similar questions, that were put through both Houses of Congress in the last five years practically without change, as they came from the office of the Attorney General of the United States"; and a few weeks later it was admitted on the floor of the House that the then pending Pure Food and Drug bill was of similar provenience.[26]

One trick "T. R." missed, probably to his considerable chagrin later. He retained the outworn and overgrown "annual message," even greatly distending it. It is true that he made the message a vehicle to Congress and the country of his legislative demands in a way not previously surpassed. Yet interlarded in a scissors and paste compilation from departmental reports which ran at times to nearly thirty thousand words, these naturally failed of full effectiveness. Woodrow Wilson was to demonstrate how much better the thing could be done.

Adding his observation of Roosevelt's successes and failures to his studies of British constitutional practice, Wilson had conceived the idea by 1908 that it was possible to remodel the Presidency somewhat after the pattern of the British Premiership.[27] For the first time in its history the United States had a President who knew something about the functioning of political institutions abroad, and who had the intellect and skill to apply his knowledge to the stimulation and enrichment of the political process in this country. A Jeffersonian in his acceptance of the legislative power as the supreme directing power in a popular government, Wilson rejected unconditionally Jefferson's conception of the separation of powers doctrine, and boldly proclaimed his constitutional right and duty as executive to guide the legislative process. The similar pretensions which Roosevelt had advanced were thus divested of their accidental association with the latter's picturesque traits of personality and endowed with the authority of constitutional principle.

Nor was this the only advantage which "the Schoolmaster President" enjoyed over his more "practical" forerunner. For one thing Wilson's party had been out of power for two decades. Consequently he was not compelled as Roosevelt had been to combat or else come to terms with an experienced and sophisticated leadership in the houses of Congress. On the contrary, Wilson's party associates were almost naïvely ready to concede his intellectual eminence, just as Jefferson's had been more than a century earlier. Finally, Wilson had the inspiration to dramatize his conception of legislative leadership in a fashion which henceforth put all potential critics of it on the defensive.

This noteworthy event in the history of American governmental usages occurred on April 8, 1913, when the new President appeared before a special session of the 63rd Congress to demand a new tariff act. A memorable passage of his address on this occasion reads:

"I am very glad indeed to have this opportunity to address the two houses directly, and to verify for myself the impression that the president of the United States is a person, not a mere department of the government hailing Congress from some isolated island of jealous power, sending messages, and not speaking naturally and with his own voice, that he is a human being trying to coöperate with other human beings in a common service. After this first experience I shall feel quite normal in all our dealings with one another."[28]

On June 23 Wilson appeared a second time before the special session to urge it to attack the problem of currency reform. The closing words of this address too are noteworthy for their statement of Wilson's President-Prime Minister conception: "I have come to you as the head of the government and the responsible leader of the party in power to urge action now, while there is time to serve the country deliberately, and as we should, in a clear air of common counsel." The measure which was finally passed in response to this call to duty, the Federal Reserve Act of December 23, 1913, was largely drafted in conferences at the White House between the President and representatives of all shades of opinion, some quite sharply antagonistic to Mr. Wilson's views.[29] It was then ratified by the Democratic caucus, and so made an obligatory party measure. Its later progress through Congress was greatly aided by Mr. Bryan, whom Mr. Wilson had made a member of his Cabinet, it may be surmised, with just such services in contemplation.

When the European war loomed on the horizon in the summer of 1914 Mr. Wilson is reported to have remarked that it would be "the irony of fate" if his energies as President were to be diverted to problems of foreign relationship, whereas his training had been intended for a very different purpose. In point of fact, not only did the legislative output of Congress during the ensuing two years continue to testify to his strong guidance of its activities, but our own entrance into war in 1917 enabled him to rivet the principle of presidential leadership to the working Constitution of the United States in a way that the demands of domestic reform could not have done at that date.

A sharp clash with the Senate shortly before our declaration of war against Germany gave the President the opportunity to display to Congress the advantage which he would enjoy over that body during a war emergency, and at the same time to reduce substantially the chief remaining barrier to executive leadership. Having failed on account of a Senate filibuster to get congressional sanction for supplying American merchant vessels with defensive arms, Mr. Wilson proceeded to do so without statutory authorization, in exercise of his "constitutional powers and duties." At the same time he denounced "the Senate of the United States" as "the only legislative body in the world which cannot act when the majority is ready for action." He continued:

"... A little group of willful men, representing no opinion but their own, have rendered the great Government of the United States helpless and contemptible.

"The remedy? There is but one remedy. The only remedy is that the rules of the Senate shall be so altered that it can act. The country can be relied upon to draw the moral. I believe that the Senate can be relied on to supply the means of action and save the country from disaster."[30]

Early in the first session of the 65th Congress the Senate for the first time in its history adopted a cloture rule—not a tremendously effective rule, but still a rule. Nor was there any further delay in the Senate merely for delay's sake till the end of the War.

Most, if not all, of the principal war statutes, from the Selective Service Act of June 5, 1917, to the Overman Act which, after being before the Senate eighty-three days, was finally passed by that body April 29, 1918, were drafted in the first instance—at times none too skillfully—in an executive department, and a head of department was generally told off to facilitate the passage of the bill through the purifying flames of the congressional purgatory.[31] From the very nature of the case, moreover, the houses were compelled to devote a goodly portion of their working hours and energies to the consideration of "administration measures," as they were termed. The situation was summed up at the time by a writer in the *New Republic* in these words:

"The private individual of Congress is dead, and it is surely important that there is none to sing his requiem. The traditional separation of powers has broken down for the simple reason that it results only in confounding them. Congress may delay presidential action; but there is evidence enough, even apart from the fact of war, that it is finding it increasingly difficult ultimately to thwart it. For congressional debate has largely ceased to influence the character of public opinion.... Nor is the individual member of Congress alone in his eclipse. The congressional committees have become less the moulders of legislation than the recipients who may alter its details. Even on the committees themselves the administration now has its avowed spokesmen. They seem to act very much as a British minister in charge of a measure in the House of Commons. They interpret the executive will; and we have seen recalcitrant members interviewed on policy by the President himself. The key to the whole, in fact, has come to lie in the President's hands. The pathway of decision is his own, influenced above all by his personal cast of mind and by the few who can obtain direct access to him. This is not, it is clear, the government envisaged by the Constitution. Equally certain it is not a government which meets with the approval of Congress. But outside of Washington, the old suspicion of executive power is dead, and popular sentiment has become so entirely uninterested in the processes of politics as to ask only for substantial results. In such an aspect, executive action is far more valuably dramatic than the action of Congress."[32]

The picture is doubtless exaggerated; but the thing itself was exaggerated by all previous standards, and the war being ended, some degree of reaction to earlier, conventional views of the relations of President and Congress was to be expected. The really surprising thing is that the reaction was so slight. Candidate Harding announced that while as President he would recommend a program, as the Constitution required him to do, legislation would be the work of Congress; but there is good reason to believe that he later regretted the promise thus implied. His ultimate failure to lead was apparently due much less to lack of willingness than of will. Although to Mr. Coolidge's ingrained conservatism legislation was in itself thoroughly distasteful, he nevertheless asserted it to be "the business of the President as party leader to do the best he can to see that the declared party platform purposes are translated into legislative and administrative action." Mr. Hoover was rather less articulate regarding his views on the subject, but according to Mr. Luce, an excellent authority, "he sent drafts of several important proposals to the Capitol to be introduced by leaders."[33] And thanks to his inaction at the time of framing the Hawley-Smoot Tariff, he has had in retrospect the doubtful satisfaction of being responsible for the supreme legislative monument to the futility of the gospel of hands-off.[34]

While President Franklin D. Roosevelt's accomplishment as legislator has surpassed all previous records, yet the story of it, so far as it is of interest to us, offers little of novelty. Old techniques have been sharpened and improved, sometimes with the aid of modern gadgets—radio, for instance—and there are certain lessons for the future which the record underlines. But for the most part the pleasure afforded by its study is that of recognition rather than of surprise.

First of all we perceive again the immense reinforcement which recognized "emergency" is capable of bringing to presidential leadership in this field of power as well as in others. For confronted with such a condition, Congress at once feels the necessity for action and its inability to plan the action needed. So it turns to the President. Contrariwise, once the pressure for action lessens, congressional docility speedily evaporates. Casting a backward glance in his first annual address to Congress upon the remarkable performance of the 73rd Congress in its first session, Mr. Roosevelt said:

"A final personal word. I know that each of you will appreciate that I am speaking no mere politeness when I assure you how much I value the fine relationship that we have shared during these months of hard and incessant work. Out of these friendly contacts we are, fortunately, building a strong and permanent tie between the legislative and executive branches of the Government. The letter of the Constitution wisely declared a separation, but the impulse of common purpose declares a union. In this spirit we join once more in serving the American people."[35]

In point of fact, the "strong and permanent tie" revealed even then to close observation several signs of fraying, and these rapidly became more generally evident.

Secondly, Mr. Roosevelt's experience also illustrates once more the aid which a President can derive from an active and widespread popular understanding of an announced program and from interest in his political good fortunes, a fact of which he has evinced constant awareness both in utterance and in practice. Within a few days of his first election Mr. Roosevelt took occasion to formulate his conception of the Presidency at some length. He said:

"The Presidency is not merely an administrative office. That is the least of it. It is pre-eminently a place of moral leadership.

"All of our great Presidents were leaders of thought at times when certain historic ideas in the life of the nation had to be clarified. Washington personified the idea of Federal Union. Jefferson practically originated the party system as we know it by opposing the democratic theory to the republicanism of Hamilton. This theory was reaffirmed by Jackson.

"Two great principles of our government were forever put beyond question by Lincoln. Cleveland, coming into office following an era of great political corruption, typified rugged honesty. Theodore Roosevelt and Wilson were both moral leaders, each in his own way and for his own time, who used the Presidency as a pulpit.

"That is what the office is—a superb opportunity for reapplying, applying to new conditions, the simple rules of human conduct to which we always go back. Without leadership alert and sensitive to change, we are bogged up or lose our way."[36]

There is little of originality here—indeed, except for the complimentary references to Jefferson and Wilson, one might easily parallel the passage from the writings of Roosevelt I. The President's assiduity in reducing his philosophy to practical form has, however, been unsurpassed. "T. R." traveled widely, yet not nearly so widely as his cousin, who by the time of his reëlection in November 1936 had journeyed nearly 83,000 miles by train, and undetermined thousands by automobile, and had visited all but three states of the Union.[37] "T. R.'s" relations with the press were excellent, but the press was not yet represented at Washington on its present scale, nor was the newspaper "columnist" the power in the land he has since become. By his liberal employment of "off the record" remarks, "F. D. R." flatters the newspaperman's sense of honor, while by handing out "background information" he guarantees the semiweekly "story" that spells for the latter his daily bread; and by both devices he assures publicity for an intelligent, if not always sympathetic, version of presidential policies.[38] Nor has Mr. Roosevelt's suavity, genial and impenetrable, often deserted him in his conferences with the press's representatives. Whereas "T. R.'s" famous "Ananias Club" came finally to be the best "covered" organization in the country, "F. D. R." has found it necessary to resort to the "short and ugly" but once.[39] And in the radio Mr. Roosevelt has an instrument that enables him to bring his views to the immediate attention of millions of voters under circumstances which rule out all danger of disconcerting interruption or challenge from anybody.[40]

In the third place, however, before the dispersed energies of popular support can generate legislative current they must, of course, be adjusted to the organization and procedures of Congress. In the endeavor to accomplish this Mr. Roosevelt has relied conspicuously on the well-timed special message.[41] To the 73rd Congress nearly thirty such communications went; to the 74th about half that number; to the 75th something like seventy. Some of these communications merely drew attention in general terms to the need for legislation on a particular subject; others contained specific recommendations as to the content of the needed legislation; a few were accompanied by draft bills to which Congress's attention was definitely directed; the "economy message" of March 9, 1933, the message of March 16 of the same year which led to the first AAA, the message of May 17 which led to the NRA, and—later—the Court Reform message of February 5, 1937, all belong to this category. But other outstanding measures of Mr. Roosevelt's first term were also the work in the first instance of administration draftsmen, and known to be such—the act establishing TVA, the hard-fought Holding Company Act, and the Social Security Act furnishing the principal illustrations. And more formal communications were frequently followed by letters to committee chairmen or even to private members, one of the former being the unfortunately worded communication in

which he expressed the hope, with reference to the pending Guffey-Snyder Coal bill, that "your committee will not permit doubt
as to its constitutionality, however reasonable, to block the suggested legislation." He could just as easily have invoked the
highly reasonable doubt as to the bill's *unconstitutionality* as an
argument *for* its passage.[42]

In the fourth place, Mr. Roosevelt's experience underscores a
lesson to be drawn also from that of the first Roosevelt and of
Woodrow Wilson, that presidential leadership is subject to a law
of ebb and flow. The remarkable achievement of the 73rd Congress bespoke almost continuous presidential stimulation and
direction and equally continuous congressional response. The
first session of the 74th Congress, on the other hand, convened
amid cries of "dictatorship" and some of the most raucous voices
were of Mr. Roosevelt's own party. The principal policy-making
legislation of the session comprised the Wagner National Labor
Relations Act and the Social Security Act. While the former,
named for its author, represented legislative initiative and presidential sponsorship, the latter was largely the handiwork of the
President's own Committee on Economic Security, consisting of
the Secretaries of the Treasury, Agriculture, and Labor, the Attorney General, and the Federal Emergency Relief Administrator. Although there were times in the course of the session when
it was predicted that the President's leadership had been broken,
the final outcome refuted the Cassandras.[43]

On its face the election of 1936 was a tremendous endorsement
of the New Deal and so of the methods of leadership by which it
had been set up. ("Who wishes the end wishes the means.") The
opening session of the 75th Congress witnessed nevertheless a
definite crisis in the President's relations with that body, one
which was largely of Mr. Roosevelt's own creation. For whatever
else may be said of his startling and practically unheralded Court

Reform message, it produced at a single stroke a serious cleavage in both his popular and his party support, and in so doing afforded his congressional critics a powerful handle for their accumulated discontents. Although special messages were never showered upon Congress more lavishly, the legislative product of the 75th Congress was chiefly by way of repairing the breaches which successive Supreme Court decisions had made in the New Deal; and final adjournment was followed by an attempt by the President, which proved unrewarding for the most part, to "purge" Congress of certain nonresponsive members of the Democratic party. The 76th Congress, with an increased representation of the Republican opposition, has disclosed a renewed initiative on its own part, which was evidenced in its first session by the enactment, despite many covert frowns from administration circles, of the Hatch Act for the political sterilization of federal office holders.

Fifth and finally, while all this is more or less according to pattern, one factor of Mr. Roosevelt's leadership, although by no means novel in itself, is in effect so in view of the dimensions which it has reached. I mean its consistent championship of the demands of certain groups, especially Agriculture and Labor. Congressional legislation meant to promote the general welfare via the welfare of particular groups is as old as Congress itself. The element of novelty presented by the New Deal legislation in this respect is furnished by the *size and voting strength of the groups served by it*. On the other hand, Mr. Roosevelt has with equal consistency, though considerably less success, opposed his influence to that of another widespread "pressure group," the American Legion, being skeptical, seemingly, of the Legion's capacity to translate its own prosperity into that of the public to any marked extent. Yet it is this encounter with the American Legion which may signalize for future Presidents their best opportunity for statesmanship in normal times—the mediation among and mitigation of the pretensions of clamant groups, rather than their stimulation. In that event we may expect to see the veto power emerge once more as one of the principal weapons in the presidential armory.

Thus, presidential leadership has usually been a function of two highly variable factors, *Crisis* and *Personality*. It is therefore sporadic and discontinuous. Its tactic has, to be sure, become fairly well stereotyped; but its availability cannot be counted on. Is there any way of overcoming this defect, of giving presidential leadership something of the solidity of a continuing institution of government? I shall return to this question on a later page.

The further question arises, whether the President's duty "from time to time [to] give to the Congress information of the state of the Union" infers the duty to give them such information as the houses, or either of them, may desire, provided he is in possession of it? The answer established by practice from the beginning is that the President is complete master of the situation and is entitled to select both the occasions of his communications and their content. Thus neither the President nor the Secretary of State is ever "directed" by the houses to furnish desired information or papers, but only "requested" to do so, and then only if it is "in the public interest" that they should comply—a question left to be determined by the President.[44] More than that, however, Presidents have sometimes intervened to exonerate other heads of departments than the Secretary of State, and even lesser administrative officials, from responding to congressional demands for information, either on the ground that the papers sought were "private," "unofficial," or "confidential," or that the demand amounted to an unconstitutional invasion of presidential discretion.[45]

Nevertheless, should a congressional investigating committee issue a *subpoena duces tecum* to a Cabinet officer ordering him to appear with certain adequately specified documents, and should he fail to do so, I see no reason why he might not be proceeded against for contempt of the house which sponsored the inquiry. And the President's power of pardon, if measured by that of the King of England, does not extend to contempts of the houses of Congress.[46]

ANCILLARY WEAPONS OF PRESIDENTIAL LEADERSHIP — THE VETO POWER

We recur to the constitutional document, and first of all to Article I, section 7, paragraphs 2 and 3, dealing with the "veto power." They read as follows:

"Every bill which shall have passed the House of Representatives and the Senate shall, before it become a law, be presented to the President of the United States; if he approve he shall sign it, but if not he shall return it, with his objections, to that house in which it shall have originated, who shall enter the objections at large on their journal and proceed to reconsider it. If after such reconsideration, two-thirds of that house shall agree to pass the bill, it shall be sent, together with the objections, to the other house, by which it shall likewise be reconsidered, and if approved by two-thirds of that house it shall become a law. But in all such cases the votes of both houses shall be determined by yeas and nays, and the names of the persons voting for and against the bill shall be entered on the journal of each house respectively. If any bill shall not be returned by the President within ten days (Sundays excepted) after it shall have been presented to him, the same shall be a law, in like manner as if he had signed it, unless the Congress by their adjournment prevent its return, in which case it shall not be a law.

"Every order, resolution or vote to which the concurrence of the Senate and House of Representatives may be necessary (except on a question of adjournment) shall be presented to the President of the United States; and before the same shall take effect, shall be approved by him, or being disapproved by him, shall be repassed by two-thirds of the Senate and House of Representatives, according to the rules and limitations prescribed in the case of a bill."

This ingredient of presidential prerogative is to be accounted
for in part by the mistaken belief, derived from Blackstone, that
the King's veto was a still vital element of the British constitution, although in fact it had not in 1787 been employed for almost
eighty years. Much more, however, is the President's veto traceable to the general conviction of the Framers that without some
such defense against the legislature the executive would soon be
"sunk into nonexistence." But what form was the veto to assume:
was it to be absolute or qualified; if the latter, by what vote ought
the houses of Congress be enabled to override it; and was the
President to exercise it alone or in association with a Council of
Revision, comprising also "a convenient number of the national
Judiciary"? While the first question was speedily answered, the
Convention vacillated almost to the date of its adjournment between requiring a two-thirds and a three-quarters vote in both
houses for overriding a veto; and only a little less pertinacious
were the champions of the Council of Revision proposal. The
final rejection of this idea, in leaving the President his own sole
master in this field of power, was a decision of first importance.[47]

Naturally, the veto power did not escape the early talent of
Americans for conjuring up constitutional limitations out of thin
air. The veto was solely a self-defensive weapon of the President;
it was the means furnished the President for carrying out his oath
to "preserve, protect and defend the Constitution" and was not
validly usable for any other purpose; it did not extend to revenue
bills, never having been so employed by the King of England; it
did not extend to "insignificant and trivial" matters like private
pension bills; it was never intended to give effect merely to presidential desires, but its use must rest on considerations of great
weight, and so on and so forth.[48] Although efforts of this nature
to forge shackles for the powers derived a certain specious plausi-
bility from the rarity of the veto's use in English history, they met

with failure from the first. Washington exercised the power twice, once on constitutional grounds, once on grounds of expediency. Neither Adams nor Jefferson exercised the power at all. Of Madison's six vetoes four urged constitutional objections to the measure involved, two objections of policy. Summing the matter up for the first century under the Constitution, the leading authority on the subject says: "From Jackson's administration to the Civil War vetoes on grounds of expediency became more frequent, but they were still in a decided minority. Since the [Civil] War constitutional arguments in a veto message have been almost unknown."[49] The latter statement applies moreover equally to the last fifty years, if exception be made for one or two vetoes by Presidents Taft and Coolidge, both of whom had a special penchant for constitutional niceties.[50]

Nor have attacks upon the veto via the amending process fared any better. In 1818 and once or twice later exasperated Congressmen have even proposed that the President be entirely stripped of the power, but their efforts were stalled at the first parliamentary hurdles. Proposals to supersede the requirement of a two-thirds vote in each house for overriding the veto with a simple majority vote have been more numerous but no more successful. On the other hand, some seventy amendments have been offered at various times since 1873 to give the President what is sometimes termed the "selective veto," which would enable him to veto parts of an enactment and approve the rest.[51] A recently suggested device for obtaining much the same end by ordinary legislation will be mentioned in a moment.

Finally, the Court has within recent years shown itself generally diligent to repel all constitutional sophistries whereby the practical availability of the power might have been curtailed. Bills which have been passed within ten days of the end of a session may be kept from becoming laws by the "pocket veto," that is, by the President's failing to return them till an adjournment of Congress has intervened; nor does it make any difference that the adjournment was not a final one for the Congress which passed the bill, but a merely *ad interim* one between sessions.[52] Also, he may return a bill with his objections to the house of its origin via a duly authorized officer thereof while it is in temporary recess in accordance with Article I, section 5, paragraph 4—a holding, however, which is not without its dangers, since it leaves it open for either house to fail to provide such duly authorized officer.[53] It would have been better perhaps to hold, as Justice Stone suggested, that neither house acting separately can adjourn so as to prevent a return by the President of his objections to a measure without thereby decapitating the measure.[54] Again, the Court has held that the President may effectively sign a bill at any time within ten calendar days of its presentation to him, Sundays excepted, even though Congress has meantime adjourned, and whether finally or for the session.[55] But here again a criticism should be noted, for the Court's assertion in the course of its opinion that the ten-day limitation applies to the President's power to *approve* as well as to his power to *disapprove* is not borne out by the words of the constitutional clause. The Court seems, indeed, to be going rather out of its way to supply an omission of the Constitution.[56]

And its further statement in this same opinion that "an incoming President, to whom a bill has not been presented by the Congress, cannot approve it" is also more or less of this nature.[57] Thus suppose that a new Congress meets, in accordance with the Twentieth Amendment, on January 3 and that a new President takes office on January 20, and suppose also that Congress passes a bill on, say, January 13 and presents it to the outgoing President, who fails to sign it before leaving office. His successor, by the above dictum, would not be entitled to sign the measure. Yet suppose that he was his own successor, what would be the rule then? Or suppose that a President died while still considering a bill, could the succeeding Vice-President sign effectively? Conceivably the former question should be answered, "yes"; the latter, "no."

But to turn again to the words of the Constitution—the fact that the President has ten days from their *presentation* rather than their passage in which to disapprove bills makes it possible for him to visit the remotest quarters of the globe without relaxing this control over Congress. Furthermore, by withholding their signatures from bills that have passed the houses, the presiding officers of those bodies can lengthen the period between the actual passage of a measure and its presentation to an absent President, so that on his return he will not be swamped with such measures.[58] Indeed, by an extraordinary collocation of events, helped out by some contriving, President Roosevelt was enabled, on July 13, 1936, to sign a bill no less than twenty-three days after the adjournment of Congress.[59]

As to the actual effectiveness of the President's veto as a check on Congress the testimony of statistics is conclusive. Between the first inauguration of George Washington and the second inauguration of Franklin D. Roosevelt 750 measures were vetoed, of which 483 were private bills. Of these 750 vetoes only 49 were overridden, six being vetoes of private bills. That is to say, 16 per cent of vetoes of public bills were overridden and 1 per cent plus of vetoes of private bills. Nor does this take account of the fact that 15 of the 43 overridden vetoes of public bills occurred during the vendetta between Andrew Johnson and Congress; nor yet of pocket vetoes, of which some 330 have been uncovered for the period from 1789 to 1936.[60] Altogether, it seems just to say that the President's veto is normally effective in nine cases out of ten.

Professor Finer appraises the veto with his accustomed perspicacity, as follows:

"Here is a power which costs no expenditure of effort, and which can be used with a fair prospect of success, and no punishment. A long and arduous legislative battle in the country and the legislature may be lost by any group of Congressmen in the time it takes to write 'No,' and a few phrases of explanation. It can only be overridden after reconsideration, and a two-thirds majority: and for these there is little chance, given the congested state of Congress, and the differences of party representation in the two Houses.

"It would be no wonder if the veto power were not only discriminatory among bills already passed, but if it became an ever-present, if unuttered, threat to promoters of bills (unless they were quite certain of a two-thirds majority in the ultimate resort), and tended to become an instrument of bargaining for other legislation—an instrument to be propitiated by timely and obvious surrenders. This, indeed, has happened."[61]

The President's veto is, in short, not a mere negative, it is a *positive* weapon of his legislative leadership.

All of which, however, does not signify that it might not be considerably improved for this purpose as well as others. I am thinking particularly of the item veto. As was mentioned a moment ago, proposals to amend the Constitution in this respect have been repeatedly offered in Congress, but have never got far along the legislative delivery belt. Recently it has been suggested that the desired result could be achieved by the simple device of incorporating in appropriation bills a provision modeled on that which appears today in the Reorganization Act of 1939. That is to say, the President would be authorized to eliminate or reduce specific items of appropriation, and his orders to that end would become effective unless the houses disallowed them within a stipulated period by concurrent resolution. Although accepted by the House as an amendment to the Independent Offices Appropriation bill of 1938, the proposal failed in the Senate. But the setback may be temporary; and once the general idea is accepted, the procedure for applying it can easily be expedited.[62]

But while the above idea is something of a novelty, it is not at all novel to give the sweeping mandate that "every order, resolution, or vote," etc., "shall be presented to the President," a qualified sense. Thus, in face of the phrase "every resolution," the proposals of the first Congress from which the Bill of Rights resulted were not presented to the President, nor have any similar proposals ever been presented to him since then; and in an early case one of the Justices remarked in an aside that this was not necessary, that "the negative of the President applies only to ordinary cases of legislation."[63] Certainly this has come to be the settled view, but at obvious cost to the literal sense of the constitutional clause, as well as at some cost to consistency. For it was held in the National Prohibition Cases[64] that the "houses" which propose an amendment to the Constitution are the same "houses" as legislate. Why then should not the procedure for proposing an amendment be the same throughout as that for enacting legislation except for the *specific* requirement of an initial two-thirds vote of the houses in the former instance? But I would not be misunderstood; I put the question merely for the benefit of those constitutional rigorists who are distressed at recent developments like the concurrent resolution feature of the Reorganization Act.[65]

Of the two remaining factors of the President's participation in legislation, so far as it has direct constitutional basis, his power in case of disagreement between the houses with respect to adjournment to "adjourn them to such time and place as he shall think proper" and his power to convene either or both houses on "extraordinary occasions" may be dealt with very briefly. The former meager remnant of the British monarch's power to prorogue Parliament has never been used, although Andrew Jackson once thought it worth while to pen a veto in its behalf; [66] nor is it easily imaginable that it ever will be used so far as "place" is concerned. The latter power, contrariwise, has been used so often that the word "extraordinary" in the constitutional clause has taken on a decidedly Pickwickian flavor. Today in common parlance "extraordinary" sessions are simply "extra" or "special" sessions. [67] On the other hand, there have been a few really extraordinary occasions when the President in power has disappointed expectations by not summoning Congress. Lincoln did this at the outset of his administration, to the vast aggrandizement of the presidential office for the time being at least, and Johnson followed his example four years later with the exactly opposite result. Under a majority of the state constitutions, when the governor calls the legislature together it may deal only with such matters as are specified in his call. However, once Congress has been convened by the President it is in full possession of its constitutional powers; and, of course, once in session, the houses are able by continuing so or by adjourning for only brief intervals to render this presidential prerogative altogether nugatory. Indeed, by legislation under Article I, section 4, paragraph 2, Congress could long since have rendered itself a practically perpetual body; and could still do the same under Amendment XX, section 2.

COLLATERAL FACTORS OF PRESIDENTIAL LEADERSHIP— PATRONAGE, FILIBUSTERS, JUDICIAL REVIEW

While by Article I, section 6, paragraph 2, it is put out of the President's power to "corrupt" the houses directly, he may still attain the same noxious end indirectly by bestowing offices upon the political henchmen of members in return for the latter's votes, or by getting rid of members who are willing to exchange their seats for more desirable posts; nor can there be any doubt that

Presidents have at times been able in this way to turn the scales in favor of desired legislation as, conspicuously, was President Cleveland in 1893 in his fight for the repeal of the discredited Sherman Silver Purchase Act. Indeed, it may be asserted generally that so long as the President possesses patronage to dispense, he will often be compelled to use it in order to obtain, or hold, support which ought to be forthcoming on other grounds—will, in brief, have to submit to political blackmail. Yet the question remains whether his possession of "the loaves and fishes" really strengthens the President in the long run. It cannot be doubted that the President's greatest weapon is always the power of a favoring public opinion. As Lincoln, than whom no President ever dispensed offices more lavishly, once put it, "With public opinion everything is possible; without public opinion nothing is possible." Pertinent too is Mr. Taft's considered verdict that every time he appointed any one to office he made "nine enemies and one ingrate." Furthermore, the elimination of federal patronage would undoubtedly tend to undermine the local party machines, and to that extent transform the parties into organs of opinion pure and simple, to the great advantage of the President as Party Leader. It is more than possible, therefore, that the anxiety of certain authorities to discover some mode of "compensating" the President for the loss of patronage which a professional civil service would mean is misconceived, and that the President would gain by the reform, in his legislative as well as in his executive capacity.[68]

Another collateral factor of presidential leadership is the power of the houses to shape their own rules of procedure, which may either help or hinder the enactment of measures desired by the President. The Senate's individualistic mode of doing business, which occasionally burgeons in the filibuster, must of course be set down as being of the "hinder" order, but it may pay for itself otherwise by the protection which it affords to "rights" of minorities, or for the maturing of a genuine public opinion on a presidential proposal. Nor is it easy to see how the freedom of debate which is so entirely lacking in the House can be preserved in the Senate except at the cost of an occasional stoppage in the business of turning out laws.

"It is a remarkable fact," says Professor Rogers in his excellent volume on the Senate, "that practically every proposal defeated by a filibuster has been unregretted by the country and rarely readvocated by its supporters"; but, he at once adds, "Such minority omniscience . . . must be more accidental than wise, and the danger is always present . . . that the interests of the country will be adversely affected."[69] Nor, unfortunately, is the question simply whether the filibuster has killed good measures, but also whether it has led to the enactment of bad ones. The indefensible concessions which a small bloc of so-called "Silver Senators" have been able to wrest from Congress from time to time during the past sixty years is conclusive testimony on that point.

But however its advantages and disadvantages be balanced against each other, this institution—altogether unique among the parliamentary devices of popular governments—has been losing ground now for some time. Filibustering Senators can no longer defend their endless trivialities and irrelevancies by arguing that they are "ambassadors of sovereign states"—as if ambassadors ever spouted nonsense! And in March 1917 a filibuster against a presidential proposal led to the Senate's adopting a cloture rule for the first time in its history. Finally, the Twentieth Amendment, by abolishing the "short session" which used to terminate the life of a Congress, has eliminated the situation in which the threat of a filibuster was most apt to prove effective in extorting special favors for its authors. Whenever a Senate filibuster today prevents the enactment of a measure which has the professed support of two thirds of that body's members—the Anti-Lynching bill for example—the sincerity of such support may well be questioned.[70]

The manner in which the two houses can facilitate executive participation in legislation is illustrated on a small scale by the steps they have taken to adjust their procedures in financial legislation to the Budget and Accounting Act of 1921. A provision of the act reads:

> "No estimate or request for an appropriation and no request for an increase in an item of any such estimate or request, and no recommendation as to how the revenue needs of the Government should be met, shall be submitted to Congress or any committee thereof by any officer or employee of any department or establishment, unless at the request of either House of Congress."[71]

To match this concentration of responsibility on the part of the executive branch the House has transferred the power of initiating appropriation bills, which had been shared theretofore by eight committees, to a single committee, and the Senate has taken similar action. This, however, is only a slight indication of what could be done to the same general end. Administration measures, which today have no status as such before either house, could be given preference over other bills to any extent deemed desirable. Imitating what was done during Reconstruction for a very different purpose, the houses could by concurrent resolution create a joint standing committee to maintain contact with the President for the purpose of discussing with him his legislative program and translating it into mutually satisfactory proposals. Indeed, a provision of the Reorganization Act of 1939 suggests that such arrangements may even be given the form of statute. Under this act, it will be recalled, the houses have the right by concurrent resolution to veto any presidential order issued under it, provided the disapproving resolution be passed within sixty days—otherwise the presidential order becomes effective. But suppose a Senate filibuster should develop in *support* of the order? In anticipation of this too obvious possibility the act itself provides that debate on a resolution of disapproval shall be limited in each house to ten hours, which shall be equally divided between opponents and advocates.[72] Of course, any restriction of this nature on the constitutional power of each house to "determine the rules of its proceedings" has only the force of an agreement between the houses; but for that very reason perhaps the more solemn form of statute may at times be preferable.[73]

Yet another collateral factor of presidential leadership is the Supreme Court's power of judicial review as it affects acts of Congress. It is a striking fact that of the Presidents who have made the Presidency what it is, all except two sooner or later crossed swords with the Court. The exceptions were Washington, who appointed the first Bench and, indeed, first and last, appointed no fewer than 13 Justices; and Woodrow Wilson who "insulted" the Court, as was asserted at the time by noted members of the Bar, by the appointment of Justice Brandeis, and who for the rest was able to appeal to tangible emergency, even before the war with Germany broke out, in justification of the Adamson Act, his most questionable piece of legislation on constitutional grounds.[74]

And from this fact have issued two others: first, the survival in face of the generally adverse opinion of the Bar of a potentially formidable challenge to the finality of the Supreme Court's conception of national legislative power; and, secondly, a series of measures whereby the Court has been subjected sometimes overtly, more often covertly, to political pressure.

Jefferson based his denial that the Court could establish the meaning of the Constitution for all time on the principle of the separation of powers. Jackson based his similar stand on the oath which every public officer takes to support the Constitution.

Lincoln argued that to identify the Court's version of the Constitution with the Constitution itself was incompatible with the idea of popular government.[75]

And each of these Presidents took a hand in legislation which altered the size of the Court. By the Judiciary Act of 1802, the Court, whose membership had been contingently decreased the year before from six Justices to five in order to prevent Jefferson from appointing a successor to the aged and ailing Cushing, was restored to six Justices for the diametrically opposed reason, and in 1807 a seventh Justice was added. One of Jackson's last acts was to sign a bill enlarging the Court to nine Justices, with the probably intended and certainly realized result of watering down the influence of the departed Marshall with his surviving brethren. During the Civil War the Court was temporarily enlarged to ten Justices after it had sustained the blockade of the Southern states by the narrow margin of one vote. And meantime by the Act of March 1, 1863, slavery had been prohibited in the territories, thus setting the Republican platform of 1861 above the Dred Scott decision as the effective Constitution of the country.[76]

Nor is this the whole story by any means. For both in 1866 and again in 1869 the size of the Court was changed by act of Congress. In the former year it was prospectively shrunk to a membership of seven Justices in order that Johnson should not be able to make any appointments; in the latter year—Grant now being President—it was restored to its ante-bellum membership of nine Justices. As we know today, Grant utilized his opportunity to nominate, the same day that *Hepburn v. Griswold* was decided, two Justices who, he believed, could be relied upon to bring about a reversal of that decision; and fifteen months later his confidence was rewarded by the event.[77]

"The traditional American way," it has been wittily remarked, "of being radical with the Supreme Court" is to alter its personnel rather than its structure and powers.[78] It should be added, nonetheless, that the procedure is expected to be accompanied by a certain amount of indirectness and disavowal of political motive. That President Roosevelt's proposal of February 5, 1937, was shaped by its authors to comply with the demands of the tradition appears at a glance. The serious justification of the proposal was, however, soon transferred to quite different grounds, and especially these two: the extension of judicial review in recent decades and the normal necessities of political leadership.

Since about 1895 three things had happened to the Court's constitutional supervision of acts of Congress: first, the Court had come to rely more and more upon doctrines of vague and variable content, such as the modern derived doctrine of due process of law and the doctrine of "dual federalism"; secondly, its invocation of these doctrines against acts of Congress had consequently taken on the appearance of an exercise of political judgment rather than the pronouncement of a legal doom; thirdly, it had come progressively to disregard the principle of *stare decisis* in the constitutional field. In brief, the Court had become more and more a kind of "super-legislature," and its constitutional decisions had come more and more to embody points of view of a controversial nature.

And *pari passu* with these developments recognition had dawned, though expression of it was sometimes timid and apologetic, that the probable point of view of a suggested appointee to the Supreme Court was a matter of legitimate concern to the appointing authority. Thus when Mr. Hughes's name was before the Senate in 1930, we find Senator Borah proclaiming: "I do not want to strengthen the view-point of the majority"; and during the debate on Judge Parker's name a few weeks later, Mr. Borah said:

"They [the Supreme Court] pass upon what we do; therefore, it is exceedingly important that we pass upon them before they decide upon these matters. I say this in all sincerity, we declare a national policy. They reject it. I feel I am well justified in inquiring of men on their way to the Supreme bench something of their views on these questions."

With all which even that great and good conservative William Howard Taft seems to have agreed in certain less guarded moments.[79]

The immediate instigation of the Roosevelt proposal came from the general election of 1936. The huge popular endorsement which this gave Mr. Roosevelt he not unreasonably interpreted as a mandate to establish certain legislation which by theories then dominant on the Court was clearly unconstitutional. The President was thus confronted with a difficult problem of political leadership: was he to postpone his program indefinitely while his political following dissolved, or was he to remove the principal obstacle to success within a comparatively brief time?[80]

In his address to Congress of January 6, 1937, Mr. Roosevelt said:

"With a better understanding of our purposes, and a more intelligent recognition of our needs as a nation, it is not to be assumed that there will be prolonged failure to bring legislative and judicial action into closer harmony. Means must be found to adapt our legal forms and our judicial interpretation to the actual present national needs of the largest progressive democracy in the modern world. . . .

"The judicial branch also is asked by the people to do its part in making democracy successful. We do not ask the courts to call nonexistent powers into being, but we have a right to expect that conceded powers or those legitimately implied shall be made effective instruments for the common good.

"The process of our democracy must not be imperiled by the denial of essential powers of free government."[81]

Unfortunately, the proposal of February 5 was not presented as a logical method of carrying out the message of January 6, but—in harmony with the evasive tradition mentioned above—

was directed to the largely, although certainly not altogether, irrelevant problem of superannuation on the Bench.[82] It was consequently much more extreme than a measure addressed to the main purpose need have been, and furthermore supplied only a partial guarantee against the recurrence of the situation most demanding remedy, a haphazard system of recruitment which entirely ignores the place of the Court in the lawmaking process.

While the proposal was defeated, this did not occur until the emergency which had challenged the President's leadership had been to a large extent removed by the Court itself by its decisions sustaining the Wagner Labor Relations Act and the Social Security Act.[83] But that the proposal had some influence, in conjunction with the election of 1936 and the C.I.O. strikes, in inducing the Court to restudy certain of its doctrines in the light of modern conditions, is not an extreme conjecture. At any rate, the time relationship between the proposal and the decisions just mentioned is something to take into account in estimating the future legislative role of the President. History does not regard very seriously the logician's criticism of the *post hoc ergo propter hoc*—to it the chronological *is* the logical.[84]

THE PROBLEM OF STABILIZING PRESIDENTIAL LEADERSHIP— THE CABINET

The expansion of the President's role as legislator has provoked a serious revival of the talk that the Presidency is a potential matrix of dictatorship. As we have seen, the dictatorship theme is a familiar one in the history of the Presidency—Jefferson was a dictator, Jackson was a dictator, Lincoln was a dictator—very much one—Theodore Roosevelt was a dictator, and so was Wilson. Nevertheless, it seems we still have rights and free institutions to be menaced.

That any one willing to "abandon his mind" to the enterprise can make a fairly strong case out for regarding the President as a potential despot has to be conceded. By *Mississippi v. Johnson,* which was decided shortly after the Civil War, though it only brought together the various strands of a good deal of earlier opinion and practice, the President has no judicially enforcible responsibility either for nonperformance of his duties or for exceeding his powers.[85] Impeachment is, as Jefferson discovered much earlier, a "scarecrow," and to galvanize this scarecrow into life would be to run the risk of reducing the Presidency to a nullity, as almost happened in 1868.[86] Congress has, to be sure, the power of the purse, and could not be deprived of it except by a *coup d'état;* but the President dominates Congress by the hold which fat relief rolls give him over millions of votes, and so a vicious circle is created whereby Congress pays for its own slow enslavement. Finally, within recent times propaganda, once the casual art of a gifted few, has been converted into a skilled technique, which is supplemented by the most ingenious gadgets of mechanical science. Today the President of the United States can at any time request that the nation's broadcasting channels be cleared that he may chat with the people, and the request will be granted *pronto,* for are not all the available frequencies allocated to companies on federal licenses which terminate every six months? Besides, any member of the administration is a propagandist and has access to the radio at will, although a first-class radio voice may not be the heaven-sent gift of all—and so on.

The picture is unquestionably overdrawn. If it is true that impeachment is no longer to be reckoned upon as an effective weapon in the arsenal of liberty, this is partly due to the fact that Presidents have in the past kept pretty clear of courses which might make people think of so extreme a discipline. Likewise, although there is no court which is entitled to order a President to perform his duties or to enjoin him from exceeding his powers, yet the subordinates through whom he must ordinarily act do not share his immunity in this respect; and his orders are at all times subject to judicial inquiry into their validity in any case in which anybody bases on them any claim or justification whatsoever.[87] Also, his subordinates are subject at any time to be summoned before a congressional investigating committee and—with due exceptions—forced to furnish required data bearing on their official conduct.[88]

Nor would it be at all easy to demonstrate that governmental largess aggrandizes presidential power in relation to that of Congress. Not only are such favors usually bestowed under rules which set up no distinction between "the just and the unjust," but facts under daily observation show that Congress is more inclined to "liberality" of spending than is the President. Nor has any one, so far as I am aware, yet suggested that the external forms of the Constitution are in immediate danger. All that is plainly asserted is that the President is in a position today to sway public opinion unduly. Perhaps so; but suppose a President sought to upset definite constitutional procedures—to put off an election, for instance—would he still sway public opinion? The defeat of Mr. Roosevelt's Court proposal, which did not transgress any such procedure, although some people claimed that it did, is at least one piece of evidence to the contrary.

The truth is that it is a somewhat contracted point of view from which presidential leadership appears as a menace to democratic institutions. Why, in the face of our democratic institutions, has presidential leadership attained its present proportions? Indeed, must not this development be considered as a fulfillment in a measure of those institutions, and as an answer to some demand from the public opinion on which, by hypothesis, they are grounded? Without doubt, such is the case; nor is it difficult to identify this demand—it is the demand that government assume an *active* role in matters of general concern, and especially in matters affecting the material welfare of the great masses of the people. This may eventually turn out to have been a demand impracticable of beneficial realization in the long run; but of its existence there can be no present question.

So we are not free to blame presidential leadership as such for those intrusions upon "liberty," as it has sometimes been understood, which present expanded theories of governmental function entail. We are free, on the other hand, to ask whether presidential leadership, as we know it, is as good an instrument of the demand which brought it into existence as it might conceivably be? Presidential leadership sets itself the task of guiding legislation; and the critics are numerous who say that it does the job badly. To make the indictment more specific, it is asserted that presidential leadership is discontinuous, not to say spasmodic; that it is too dependent on the personality of the President rather than on the authority of the office; that it is often insufficiently informed, especially as regards the all important matter of administrative feasibility; and, finally, that the contact between the President and Congress is most faulty, being, in fact, at the mercy of either's whim.[89] These contentions have too much obvious validity to make it worth while to attempt to refute them or even to qualify them nicely. The important question is, what remedy or remedies do existing constitutional arrangements admit?

A partial solution of the difficulties just mentioned is suggested by the provision of the Budget and Accounting Act for the clearance through the Bureau of the Budget, whose director is subject to presidential direction and removal, of all proposals originating in the Executive Department respecting governmental expenditure and revenue. The idea could easily be extended to nonfiscal proposals of the various departments and agencies of the government, the vast proportion of which grow out of their administrative experience. These at times are very numerous. Thus we are informed that "out of the total of 429 public acts exclusive of appropriation acts in the first session of the 74th Congress, 270 referred to the organization or functioning of administrative departments," and that "the great majority of these acts originated, directly or indirectly in the departments concerned."[90] That is to say, while administration is an outgrowth of legislation, so is legislation to a great extent nowadays an outgrowth of administration; and when it is, it should be initiated subject to a general control which is capable of evaluating the demands of the parts from the point of view of the whole.

But the stabilization of presidential leadership may be conceived on a broader scale, and as embracing, first, the minimization of its dependence on the accident of personality and the unevenness of performance which this involves; and, secondly, the provision of some kind of institutional link between the President and Congress. Relevant to the former of these objectives is an argument which has been advanced in support of the recommendation by the President's Committee on Administrative Management that the independent agencies be brought within the departments whose heads compose the President's Cabinet. It is upon these agencies, the argument proceeds, that the most novel, most controversial, most interesting activities of the National Government have been lodged in recent decades, with the result that the President has been constrained to look increasingly outside the Cabinet for advice in shaping his legislative program. But let the Committee's recommendation be adopted, the argument continues, and the President would be forced, or at any rate would have every incentive, to return to the bosom of his "official family" instead of consorting with this, that, and other anonymous adviser or dispenser of happy ideas. Thus, on the one hand the Cabinet would be revitalized, and on the other hand the President would be "the spokesman for the 'administration' in the real sense of the word, not merely the interpreter of his own fancies." He would be at all times what he has always been in times of his greatest power, the representative of the public.[91]

The argument overlooks certain facts, one of which is that "Kitchen Cabinets," far from being recent phenomena, on the contrary long antedate the first "independent agency." Nor is the reason far to seek. It is because the Cabinet seraglio has been recruited from an early date on principles which make it fairly certain that an active presidential imagination will frequently stray beyond its decorous precincts. And what are these principles? One of them—the one which is of chief importance for the present discussion—is the idea that the heads of the great majority of the departments ought to be administrative experts, or at least capable of quickly becoming such. Unfortunately, an expert in a particular area of governmental activity is not likely to possess the breadth of outlook which is most desirable in a political adviser, or the time or inclination to interest himself in the problems of other departments or of the country at large. And obviously the Committee's proposal to increase his departmental duties is badly calculated, if that was one of the ends in mind, to overcome these handicaps. In short, the argument overlooks the fundamental distinction between Politics and Administration, between determining *what* government ought to do and *how* it should do it, and the exigent need of a President for responsible counsel in relation to the former.

Two other plans for stabilizing presidential leadership, while also pivoting on the Cabinet, are directed primarily to the problem of creating a permanent link between the President and Congress. The less radical of these would give the Cabinet members the right to attend the houses in order to participate in debate on matters of official interest to them and impose on them the obligation of doing so in order to impart information desired by the houses. The proposal, far from raising any constitutional difficulties, has the countenance of early practice under the Constitution. The first volume of the *Annals of Congress* records that Secretary of State Jefferson "attended agreeably to order, and made the necessary explanations." This was on July 22, 1789. Secretary of War Knox later visited the Senate Chamber with the President on at least one occasion and by himself on two others. The Act of 1790, organizing the Treasury Department, provided that the head of the Department should digest plans for improving the revenue and public credit, and "make report and give information to either branch of the legislature, in person or in writing, as may be required," etc. That Hamilton, the first Secretary of the Treasury, was never asked to report in person was due to the opposition of the rising Jeffersonian party as voiced by Madison.[92]

And so matters rested till near the end of the Civil War when George H. Pendleton of Ohio began an agitation, the principal result of which was a report many years later by a distinguished Senate committee supporting the idea both on grounds of policy and of constitutionality;[93] and since then at least four future or past Presidents are on record as having expressed themselves in its favor.[94] Why then has the suggestion never produced tangible fruit? Chiefly because most of the legislative work of Congress is done by committees, and before such a body a head of department can always obtain a far more satisfactory hearing than would be conceivably possible before either of the houses in open session. Conversely, if it is Congress which is seeking information, it can do so through the investigatory process much more effectively and thoroughly than by the wasteful and pretentious methods of parliamentary interpellation.

We come now to the more radical proposal referred to above.

It is simply that the President shall construct his Cabinet, not as at present from the heads of the executive departments, but from such leading members of Congress as he may choose. Or, he might constitute a nuclear Cabinet, so to speak, out of those heads of departments whose activities are of general and constant political significance—say the Secretary of State, the Secretary of the Treasury, and the Attorney General—and the aforementioned leaders of the houses. Then to this central core of advisers could be added at times such other heads of departments, chairmen of independent agencies, and chairmen of congressional committees as the business forward at the moment might naturally indicate.

That the creation of such a body would not encounter constitutional difficulties was pointed out in an earlier chapter.[95] Nor would it amount to supplanting forthwith the "Presidential System" with the "Cabinet System." The President would not become a prime minister, bound to resign when outvoted in Congress, although circumstances might arise in which he felt it his duty to do so, as Mr. Wilson contemplated doing in 1916 in the event of Mr. Hughes's election. Nor yet would he be a figurehead like the King of Great Britain or the President of France, for he would still retain all his constitutional powers and prerogatives although, again, he might choose to use them at times less for pushing a program of his own than for the purpose of mediating between the programs of others, as did Washington at the beginning. The new Cabinet would, in other words, still be a body of advisers. But there are advisers *and* advisers. The proposed Cabinet would contain men whose daily political salt did not come from the presidential table, whose political fortunes were not involved with his, who could bring presidential whim under an independent scrutiny which today is lacking. It would capture and give durable form to the casual and fugitive arrangements by which Presidents have usually achieved their outstanding successes in the field of legislation.[96]

But it will be objected that such an arrangement could not long be adhered to, or if it was it must at times cut athwart the two-party system, and so weaken the political responsibility of the President. The objection has reference to the possibility that the President would belong to the party which was a minority in Congress. Actually, the supposed situation has obtained comparatively rarely—only twice, I believe, in the last seven administrations, or four years out of twenty-eight. What is more to the point, the objection considerably overvalues the importance of so-called "political responsibility," which operates in the main only *ex post facto,* that is, after the damage is done, whereas the problem is to prevent the damage being done in the first place. Nor does coöperation between the President and Congress under present arrangements invariably stop at the party line, or even generally do so when conditions of crisis arise; and why should it require a crisis to bring forth the best methods? Suppose one takes the position that government is normally a species of *nation-keeping;* then it is clear that much of the fuss and fury of politics is really factitious and a sheer waste to the community; that the chief objective to be sought in political discussion, whether carried on in Cabinet council, on the floors of Congress, or elsewhere, is *consensus*—in what light does the above proposal then appear?

Furthermore, it would seem that the principle of cycle holds in the matter of legislation as in so many other things mundane. The formal enactment of laws is only the first step toward incorporating them in the social order; following it ensues a process of gradual absorption into the general institutional setup and outlook of the community; and this process is apt to be hindered rather than helped if reforms are pressed forward too fast and furiously. As President Roosevelt has put it, "A social or economic gain in one Administration may . . . evaporate into thin air under the next one."[97] A wise legislative leadership will, therefore, reckon on a certain amount of reaction against its measures as inevitable and seek to forestall this. In such an endeavor the advice of potential political foes might conceivably be of more value than that of overenthusiastic supporters.

The power and prestige of the Presidency comprise the most valuable political asset of the American people; they are, moreover, in a very true sense the creation of the American people. But centering as they do in a single individual who is free to advise, or to refrain from advising, with whomsoever he chooses, this power and this prestige are apt to become unduly *personalized,* thus inviting two dangers: antagonism between President and Congress and autocracy. It is, therefore, an additional merit of the suggestion advanced above that it is calculated to meet, or at least abate, both these dangers. Presidential leadership is essential to the ready availability of the national law-making power; this ready availability reduces to a minimum the excuse for autocratic courses.

To sum up: Presidential leadership in legislation is the function of two highly variable factors—"Crisis" and "Personality." By "Crisis" is meant a condition requiring the enactment of new laws by Congress in order to end some condition of social or economic maladjustment or at least what an effective segment of the voters takes to be such. By "Personality" is meant the personal gifts, temperament, outlook, and political skill of individual Presidents. Consequently, presidential leadership is still, despite the success of practitioners of the art since 1900 in reducing its *modus operandi* to a more or less standardized pattern, a highly discontinuous feature of our constitutional system.

But what is more, this particular condition of affairs is accompanied by another which also is not without significance in a world dangerously inclined toward Totalitarianism and its expeditious ways of getting things done. I mean the fact that a President in office is—impeachment being left out of the reckoning—legally irresponsible; or, as Chief Justice Marshall early put it, is "accountable only to his country in his political character and to his own conscience," both of which may be very uncertain recourses.

It follows that what is sometimes termed the question of "presidential responsibility" is not a single problem, but presents two quite different, even opposed, aspects: (1) that of concern for the *responsiveness* of government, and particularly the legislative branch of it, to public opinion; (2) that of concern for the *accountability* of the executive branch to the existing constitutional structure, which also presumably embodies public opinion. Can it be possible that these two aspects admit of a common solution?

Practice under the Constitution clearly demonstrates that Congress responds most efficiently to public opinion when it submits itself to presidential guidance. But it shows too that no President can long shape policy without legislative support, *or*—as happened during the Civil War—an obvious breach of constitutional forms. The problem for which a constitutional solution is sought is, therefore, really the problem of equating easily, and without constant jar to society, the political forces which Congress at any time represents with those which the President represents at the same time, and of putting the relationship of the two on a durable and understood basis. And for this purpose a reconstruction of the Cabinet, which in its present form has proved but an indifferent success for more than a century, is at least a promising expedient, and one to which the Constitution interposes no obstacles.[98]

Such a solution would not, it is true, solve the problem of the alleged undue influence of the President on public opinion nowadays. For that, there is under our system no remedy except an unshackled public opinion itself. When the self-renewing stream of public opinion ceases to provide a cure for its own humors, free institutions fail of their main support and their main purpose.[99] For while Democracy implies leadership, it also implies criticism of that leadership, criticism outspoken and unremitting. Leadership without criticism is the very definition of Totalitarianism.

RÉSUMÉ

I T IS an axiom of American history that the Constitution came from the Framers "a bundle of compromises." Not so generally recognized is the confirmation which is lent this observation by those clauses of the Constitution most nearly affecting the office and powers of the President. The vagueness of the constitutional grants of power to the President has always furnished matter for comment, sometimes favorable, sometimes otherwise, depending on the commentator's bias.[1] "The executive power shall be vested in a President of the United States of America"; "the President shall be Commander-in-Chief of the Army and Navy"; with the advice and consent of the Senate he shall make treaties and appoint to office; he shall have power to "grant pardons for offenses against the United States," he shall "recommend ... such measures to Congress, as he shall judge necessary and expedient"; and so on and so forth. Yet, in order to exercise any of these powers—in order, indeed, to subsist—he must have money, and can get it only when and if Congress appropriates it. Likewise, he is dependent on Congress for the very agencies through which he must ordinarily exercise his powers, and Congress is the judge as to the necessity and propriety of such agencies. Again, he is bound to "take care that the laws" which Congress enacts are "faithfully executed"—for this purpose all his powers are in servitude; and Congress has the power to investigate his every official act, and can, by a special procedure, if it finds him guilty of "high crimes and misdemeanors," impeach him and throw him out of office. Moreover, by the standard set by the prerogative of the British monarch in 1787, his "executive power" and his power to protect that power were both seriously curtailed. The power to "declare war" was vested in Congress; the Senate was made a participant in his diplomatic powers; he was given a

---

The Notes to the Résumé begin on page four hundred forty-eight

veto upon all legislative acts, but one which the houses may override by a two-thirds vote.

In short, the Constitution reflects the struggle between two conceptions of executive power: the conception that it ought always to be subordinate to the supreme legislative power, and the conception that it ought to be, within generous limits, autonomous and self-directing; or, in other terms, the idea that the people are *re-presented* in the Legislature *versus* the idea that they are *embodied* in the Executive. Nor has this struggle ever entirely ceased, although on the whole it is the latter theory which has triumphed. To repeat what was said on an earlier page, "Taken by and large, the history of the Presidency has been a history of aggrandizement."

The office got off to a good start under a very great man. The principle of the separation of powers was not yet regarded as forbidding the executive to initiate legislation. In the act establishing the State Department Congress itself laid down a "practical construction" of the Constitution which, save for the interregnum of the Reconstruction Period, has left the President absolute master of his official family. A dangerous foreign situation in 1793 brought that family into existence, while it also enabled the President to translate his position as the organ of communication with other governments into a substantive, creative power. Finally, the Whiskey Rebellion provided the occasion for the first step in that course of legislation and of presidential action which has long since clothed the President in situations of widespread disorder, or threat thereof, with the powers of a dictator.

Under Jefferson and "the Virginia School of Presidents" a decided retrogression took place from the notion of presidential autonomy toward that of legislative supremacy. Under Jefferson himself the retreat was theoretical rather than actual. As the founder and leader of the first national party, Jefferson was able to dominate Congress by personal influence, and it was shown for the first time what accession of strength political skill can bring the Presidency. But Jefferson's successors, caught between the upper and nether millstones of their self-abasing conception of the Presidency and their lack of personal force, were reduced to official insignificance. The War of 1812 marked the near elimination for the time being of presidential prerogative in the field of foreign relations; the Monroe Doctrine announced to the world at large that opportunities for aggrandizing the Presidency from foreign adventuring were to be confined strictly to the Western Hemisphere.[2] Jefferson pronounced the dictum that no President could with safety to our democratic institutions be eligible for a third term, albeit he might nominate his successor; and the successors whom Jefferson himself nominated ratified the ban.

Jackson's Presidency was more than a revulsion to earlier ideas —it was a revolution. A new electorate was organized into a new party whose wide ramifications, focusing in the National Convention, rendered its continuance independent of accidents of personality. Guaranteed this powerful and persistent support among the people at large, Jackson extended the doctrine of the President's autonomy to embrace his obligation to the law; constitutional obligation was reduced—or exalted—to the level of *moral* obligation. At the same time the President's duty to "take care that the law be faithfully executed" was asserted to comprise the right to read the law for any and every member of the Executive Department; and through a vigorous and expanded use of his veto and removal powers, Jackson for the time being made this claim good.

Nevertheless, except for a few unfortunates like John C. Calhoun and Nicholas Biddle, the Jacksonian "dictatorship" was more bark than bite, more proclamation than performance. The

Monroe Doctrine, the taboo on a third term, and, what was even more important, the States Rights conception of national legislative power, all set conspicuous landmarks which Jackson himself had not the slightest inclination to disturb. His most outstanding assertions of power, and especially in the field of legislation, were negative and exercised by veto. Moreover, despite the permanency of the party organization which was reared by his henchmen in every quarter of the Union, the prominence of the office during his incumbency was predominantly a reflection of his own energetic personality. When he left office he left behind him a political vacuum which a resuscitated Congress promptly filled, and, thanks to the manipulations of the slavery interest, continued to fill—if exception be made for Slavery's tool, the sly, pious Polk— till the outbreak of the Civil War.

For all that, the Jacksonian conception of the Presidency was not forgotten. Indeed, its champions and its critics contributed about equally to render it more articulate than ever—a fact of the first magnitude when Lincoln became President and found himself confronted with a nation in dissolution. Lincoln's claim to "the war power" was derived from three sources: Jackson's doctrine that *all* the President's powers are autonomous; the Supreme Court's doctrine in *Luther v. Borden* (1849) that insurrection is "war"; and the measures which Pierce and Buchanan had taken in their efforts to put down civil war in Kansas, together with the budget of doctrine which the legal genius of Caleb Cushing had furnished them in justification thereof.

At first, as was pointed out on an earlier page, Lincoln laid claim only to an *ad interim* war power, one which was operative only until Congress could ratify and reinforce its measures; but the Supreme Court's sweeping language in the Prize Cases (1863) encouraged him to take a more forthright stand, and this, combined with his indisposition to coöperate with Congress, led him to break over constitutional bounds and become a dictator even exceeding the Roman model.[3] Nor was the constitutional corrective applied until after the war was comfortably over, by the Court's decision in *ex parte* Milligan and by the revolt of Congress under Johnson. The implication of Lincoln's course that the President has power to meet an emergency without awaiting action by Congress is accordant with the most ancient traditions of Anglo-American Law; but the further implication that this power does not have to submit itself to the laws which Congress is entitled, by an unforced reading of its own powers, to enact, lacks any such sanction and is the most excessive claim to power ever put forth by an American President. Yet Johnson, who asserted a like claim in an era of formal peace, escaped impeachment; and it was during his term that the Supreme Court virtually underwrote, in *Mississippi v. Johnson* (1867), Jackson's contention that the President's duty to the Constitution is solely the duty of conscience which his oath imposes.

But again the cyclical character of presidential power demonstrated itself. As from 1809 to 1829, so again from 1865 to 1885, the legislative power became the dominant element of the National Government. Indeed, except for the success of Presidents Hayes and Cleveland in using the Army to put down "domestic violence" within the states, the period of congressional preponderance reached to the death of McKinley. But meantime Congress had, by its own headiness, paved the way for the recrudescence of its constitutional rival, by forcing upon McKinley the war with Spain. By that act and the consequences which ensued from it, the restrictive effect of the Monroe Doctrine on presidential prerogative was seriously undermined. The United States was now a "World Power," and presently found itself involved in a World War.

The greatest accession to presidential power in recent decades has, however, taken place in the *internal* rather than the *external* field, and has been signalized by the breakdown of the two great structural principles of the American Constitutional System, the doctrine of dual federalism and the doctrine of the separation of powers; and along with this breakdown has gone a change of even more fundamental character in popular outlook regarding the purpose and scope of governmental power. I mean, of course, the replacement of the *laissez-faire* theory of government with the idea that government should make itself an *active, reforming force* in the field of economic enterprise, which has meant, necessarily, that the *National Government* should be active in this way, inasmuch as the field in question has long since come to transcend state lines.

And the result for the Presidency has been twofold. On the one hand, Presidents have made themselves spokesmen of the altered outlook, have converted their parties to it—a conversion not infrequently accompanied by backsliding—and, with the popular support thus obtained, have asserted a powerful legislative initiative. On the other hand, Congress, in responding to the President's leadership in its own peculiar field, has found it convenient to aggrandize his executive role enormously, by delegating to him the power to supplement its measures by a type of sublegislation called "administrative regulations." Not all this delegated power, it is true, has gone to the President, but a vast proportion of it has; and it constitutes a realm of presidential power of which the Framers had little prevision, although it began to appear in the field of foreign relations even as early as Washington's second administration.

The first exponent of the new Presidency was Theodore Roosevelt, but his achievement was to some extent negated by faults of method. Woodrow Wilson was enabled by the advantage of having critically observed his predecessor, by his knowledge of political methods abroad, by a taste for institution-building, which was later to divert him into an abortive effort at world organization, and finally by the opportunity afforded by our entrance into the World War, to illustrate on an unprecedented scale both the new roles of the President—that of legislative leader and that of recipient of delegated legislative power. Our war with Germany was prosecuted for the most part under laws which were drafted under the appraising eye of the President and which conferred upon him far greater powers than those which Lincoln had exercised as Commander-in-Chief.

And Wilson's achievement in a time of war emergency has been paralleled by President Roosevelt in peacetime, though not without important aid from the "emergency" concept. Beyond that, however, Mr. Roosevelt's methods raise no new questions of constitutional interpretation. His outstanding legislative product, comprising the so-called "New Deal," on the other hand, does this very thing, and especially in one respect. The Supreme Court's decisions sustaining the New Deal all turn on one essential idea, even when it is not distinctly stated, namely, that the reserved powers of the states do not afford a constitutional test of national legislation—in a word, the principle of dual federalism has been discarded.

The Presidency of this present year of grace, so far as it is explicable in terms of American constitutional law and theory, is the product of the following factors: (1) social acceptance of the idea that government should be active and reformist, rather than simply protective of the established order of things; (2) the breakdown of the principle of dual federalism in the field of Congress's legislative powers; (3) the breakdown of the principle of the separation of powers as defining the relation of President and Congress in lawmaking; (4) the breakdown of the corollary principle that the legislature may not delegate its powers; and

(5) the enlarged role of the United States in the international field.[4]

Does the Presidency, then, in the light of these facts, constitute a standing menace to popular government and to those conceptions of personal liberty to which popular government is, in part, traceable? So far as concerns popular government in the sense of majority rule, the exact contrary is the case—all the above developments are the direct consequence of Democracy's emergence from the constitutional chrysalis. That, on the other hand, these developments leave private and personal rights in the same strong position as they once enjoyed would be quite impossible to maintain. Nor is it feasible in this connection to distinguish too acutely between the property and other rights. Not only in the past, but even today, the property right is the right best capable of holding its own against political power. This is the principal lesson to be drawn from the history of Liberalism.

Finally, I return to the point that, as matters stand today, presidential power is dangerously *personalized,* and this in two senses: first, that the leadership which it affords is dependent altogether on the accident of personality, against which our haphazard method of selecting Presidents offers no guarantee; and, secondly, that there is no governmental body which can be relied upon to give the President independent advice and which he is nevertheless bound to consult. As a remedy calculated to meet both phases of the problem I have suggested a new type of Cabinet. At least, if a solution is to be sought in *institutional* terms, it must consist in stabilizing in some way or other the relationship between President and Congress. That, today, with the rapid relegation of judicial review to a secondary role, is the center of gravity of our Constitutional System.

NOTES TO CHAPTER I*

[1] *Myers v. United States*, 272 U. S. 52, 118 (1926). Construing the term "all cases" in Art. III, §2, par. 1, counsel in *Osborn v. The Bank,* remarked: "The pleonasm is here meant to perform its usual office, to be emphatic. It marks the intention, and affords a principle of construction." 9 Wheat. 738, 809 (1824). See also Hamilton's argument as "Pacificus," pp. 402–404 *infra. Cf.* note 46 *infra.*

[2] Constitution, Art. I, §8, cl. 18.

[3] *Ibid.,* Art. II, §3.

[4] 1 Cr. 137, 165–166.

[5] See Evarts B. Greene, *The Provincial Governor,* etc. (New York, 1898).

[6] Allan Nevins, *The American States During and After the Revolution* (New York, 1924), p. 166; also studies by W. C. Morey and W. C. Webster in *Annals of the American Academy of Political and Social Science* (1893).

[7] *Federalist* 48; Edward M. Earle (ed.), (Washington, 1938), p. 322. Cited hereafter as Earle.

[8] F. N. Thorpe (ed.), *American Charters, Constitutions,* etc., (Washington, 1909), VII, 3816–3817. A similar clause appeared also in the Maryland constitution of 1776. *Ibid.,* III, 1696.

[9] *Proceedings Leading to the Calling of the Conventions of 1776 and of 1790* (J. S. Wiestling, publ., Harrisburg, 1825), pp. 100–101. See also *ibid.,* p. 75; and Thorpe, *op. cit.,* III, 1708–1709.

[10] *Federalist* 69; Thorpe, V, 2632–2633.

[11] *Two Treatises of Government,* Bk. II, Ch. 14, §§159–166.

[12] *Ibid.,* Ch. 11, §134.

[13] *Politics* (Welldon, tr.), Bk. VI, Ch. 14. For Locke's contribution see *op. cit.,* Bk. II, Ch. 12.

[14] *Spirit of the Laws* (Nugent-Prichard, ed.) (London, 1905), Bk. XI, Ch. 3. For others who, besides Aristotle and Locke, are frequently set down as forerunners of Montesquieu, see John A. Fairlie, "The Separation of Powers," 21 *Michigan Law Review,* No. 3 (February 1923); and F. T. H. Fletcher, *Montesquieu and English Politics* (London, 1939), Ch. VIII. Most of the supposed forerunners, however, after Aristotle stopped short with pointing out the distinction between "legislative" and "executive" power. "Judicial power" does not reënter the picture to any great extent till after the British Act of Settlement of 1701, which guaranteed the judges security of tenure against the Crown. It is to be noted, too, that writers frequently confuse the notion of a balanced (or mixed) constitution, representing the three orders of society, with the principle of the separation of powers. Actually, Montesquieu is the first writer to bring the latter idea to the support of the former; and it is this fact which commended him so greatly to the founders of the American constitutional system, inasmuch as the social ingredients of a mixed constitution were absent in the United States. A work which should be of interest in this general connection to American students, although I have not been able to examine it, is H. Knust, *Montesquieu und die Verfassung der Vereinigten Staaten* (Munich, 1922).

[15] *Commentaries,* I, Intro., 49–51; Ch. 1, 154.

[16] *Ibid.,* Ch. 2, 161.

[17] *Ibid.,* Ch. 2, 154–155. Said George II to Walpole: "I will order my army as I see fit; for your scoundrels of the House of Commons, you may do as you please; you know I never interfere, or pretend to know anything about them." Quoted by Edgar Dawson in *The Sewanee Review,* July 1915, p. 264.

---

* *Chapter I (Conceptions of the Office) begins on page 1.*

[18] See generally C. C. Thach's excellent volume, *The Creation of the Presidency* (Johns Hopkins Press, 1922), especially Chs. 3–5.

[19] Max Farrand, *Records of the Federal Convention* (Yale University Press, 1911), I, 65. Cited hereafter as Farrand.

[20] *Ibid.*, 65, 68–69, 98. Two other important members of the "strong executive" party were Charles Pinckney, who probably deserves the credit for bringing the pertinent provisions of the New York constitution to the attention of the Committee of Detail, and also for proposing the title "President"; and Hamilton, who wished to see "the governor" chosen for life and vested with the power to appoint the governors of the states. Thach, *op. cit.*, pp. 92–94, 108–109, 116–117.

[21] Farrand, II, 181, 185–186.

[22] *Ibid.*, 541–542.

[23] *Ibid.*, 83, 132, 183, 185, 394, 498–499, 538–542, 547–550.

[24] *Ibid.*, 185.

[25] *Ibid.*, IV, General Index, 148–149.

[26] *Ibid.*, II, 52–54.

[27] Herman Finer, *Theory and Practice of Modern Government* (New York, 1932), II, 1009–1010 (quoted with the consent of the publisher, The Dial Press); Farrand, I, 56–57, 72, 80; II, 29–31; *Federalist* 68. Mason thought that a majority of the Electors would rarely agree on a President and that therefore the election would often fall to the Senate (later changed to the House). Gouverneur Morris thought otherwise, partly because a successful President would be reëlected. Farrand, II, 512.

[28] Art. I, §6, par. 2.

[29] Earle, pp. 436–437.

[30] *Ibid.*, pp. 454–455.

[31] *Ibid.*, p. 462.

[32] *Federalist*, Nos. 73–77. Necker, however, found it to his purpose to argue in 1792 that the President of the United States had more power than had the King of France in 1789. *An Essay on the True Principles of Executive Power in Great States* (London, 1792), II, Ch. 3.

[33] "In the Constitution are provisions in separate articles for the three great departments of government—legislative, executive and judicial. But there is this significant difference in the grants of powers to these departments: The first article, treating of legislative powers, does not make a general grant of legislative power. . . . By reason of the fact that there is no general grant of legislative power it has become our accepted constitutional rule that this is a government of enumerated powers. . . .

"On the other hand in Article III, which treats of the judicial department—and this is important for our present consideration—we find that Section I reads 'the judicial power of the United States, shall be vested,' etc. By this is granted the entire judicial power of the Nation." *Kansas v. Colorado*, 206 U. S. 46, 81, 82 (1906).

"The difference between the grant of legislative power under Article I to Congress which is limited to powers therein enumerated, and the more general grant of executive powers to the President under Article II is significant." Taft, C. J., in *Myers v. United States*, 272 U. S. 52, 128 (1926).

[34] See *Annals of Congress*, I, 462–463, 474, 481–482, 497, 515–519, *passim*; Edgar S. Maclay (ed.), *Journal of William Maclay* (New York, 1890), pp. 113–116; C. F. Adams, *Life and Works of John Adams* (New York, 1850–1856), III, 409.

[35] See *Works of Alexander Hamilton* (J. C. Hamilton, ed.), VII, 76 ff.; and *Writings of James Madison* (Hunt, ed., New York, 1900–1910), VI, 138 ff.

[36] It was Madison's contention precisely in 1793 that Hamilton was endeavoring to appropriate to the Presidency the royal prerogative of the King of England. *Ibid.,* 150. But in *Federalist* 69, Hamilton had disparaged all comparisons between the powers of the President and those of the British monarch; while in the Convention, Wilson, despite his belief in a strong executive, had remarked that "he did not consider the prerogatives of the British monarch as a proper guide in defining the Executive powers. Some of these prerogatives were of a Legislative nature." Farrand, I, 65. Most of the references by the Supreme Court to the British monarch's prerogative have been in elucidation of the President's pardoning power. *United States v. Wilson,* 7 Peters, 160; *ex parte* Wells, 18 How. 307, 311; *in re* Neagle, 135 U.S. 1; *ex parte* Grossman, 267 U.S. 109. Chief Justice Taft, however, endeavors to fortify his argument in the Myers Case by such a reference (272 U.S. 118); but seventy-five years earlier we find Chief Justice Taney writing: "In the distribution of political power between the great departments of government, there is such a wide difference between the power conferred on the President of the United States, and the authority and sovereignty which belong to the English crown, that it would be altogether unsafe to reason from any supposed resemblance between them, either as regards conquest in war, or any other subject where the rights and powers of the executive arm of the government are brought into question. Our own Constitution and form of government must be our only guide." *Fleming v. Page,* 9 How. 609, 618 (1851).

[37] When President Washington reached New York City to take the oath of office, he found Congress already in session, and his so-called Inaugural Address of April 30, 1789, was addressed not to the citizenry of the country at large, as Inaugural Addresses are nowadays, but to his "Fellow-Citizens of the Senate and House of Representatives." The address was followed by answering addresses of a congratulatory nature from the two houses, whose members proceeded by carriage to present them in person; and in due course the President sent brief, formal replies. The procedure thus initiated was followed throughout Washington's two administrations and that of Adams, at the opening of each succeeding session of Congress, though not for the Inaugural Address. This, in fact, seemed at one time likely to disappear altogether, for Washington's second effort of the kind, addressed to his "Fellow-Citizens" contained fewer than 150 words, in which the President announced that he was about to take the oath of office and expressed the wish that if he should be discovered violating "willingly or knowingly the injunctions thereof," he might "besides incurring constitutional punishment, be subject to the upbraidings of all who are now witnesses of the present solemn ceremony." The inadequacies of this performance, however, were later more than compensated for by the famous Farewell Address of September 17, 1796, which, addressed to "Friends and Fellow-Citizens," was not delivered orally but reached the country through the press.

And meanwhile the outbreak of the Wars of the French Revolution, by creating a serious cleavage in American public sentiment, had put the ceremonies attendant upon the President's address to Congress in an altered light. Sympathizers with France denounced the whole business as "monarchical" in character. From the same cause it became increasingly difficult for the houses to frame responses to the President without precipitating long-drawn-out and sometimes angry debate. So when the government moved to the new capital on the Potomac, and it was found that Pennsylvania Avenue was no better than a quagmire which it was dangerous to life and limb to traverse by carriage,

Jefferson, who was well aware that he wrote much better than he spoke, decided to replace "the speech from the Throne," as his partisans termed it, with a message sent by messenger. Though the change was bitterly criticized in the Federalist press, the precedent thus established continued in force until a follower of Jefferson upset it 113 years later. Charles Warren, "Jefferson and the Speech to Congress," *Proceedings of the Massachusetts Historical Society,* 1923, 123–172; James D. Richardson, *Messages and Papers of the President* (Washington, Government Printing Office, 1896–1899), I, 1–316, *passim.*

38 Albert J. Beveridge, *Life of John Marshall* (New York, 1916–1919), II, 537. "His whole system of administration," wrote J. Q. Adams later, "seems founded on the principle of carrying through the legislature measures by personal or official influence." *Memoirs,* I, 403; quoted in W. E. Binkley, *The Powers of the President* (New York, 1937), p. 52—a first class, though misnamed, volume.

39 Richardson, *Messages and Papers of the Presidents,* I, 331–332. Cited hereafter as Richardson.

40 See, e.g., his letter to Nicholson suggesting Chase's impeachment, Henry Adams, *History of the United States* (New York, 1889–1891), II, 150.

41 Binkley, *op. cit.,* p. 54; Ralph V. Harlow, *The History of Legislative Methods in the Period Before 1825* (Yale University Press, 1917), Ch. X; Norman J. Small, *Some Presidential Interpretations of the Presidency* (Johns Hopkins Press, 1932), pp. 164–167—another very competent and valuable study. It is interesting to note that Tocqueville, who visited the country at the beginning of the Jacksonian Era, but saw things governmental through the eyes of Webster and Story, records a very poor opinion of the Presidency and its potentialities, particularly in view of the nonparticipation of the United States in external affairs. "All his important acts are directly or indirectly submitted to the legislature; and where he is independent of it he can do but little." *Democracy in America* (New York, 1873), I, 126–132.

42 Small, *op. cit.,* p. 172 (quoted with the consent of the publisher, The Johns Hopkins Press).

43 See Binkley, *op. cit.,* Ch. III; Harlow and Small, *loc. cit.;* also H. J. Ford, *Rise and Growth of American Politics* (New York, 1898), pp. 165–167. Jefferson, writing in 1807, described his Cabinet as "my faithful and able fellow laborers in the Executive administration." *Writings* (Washington, ed.), VIII, 116. He also, the same year, set forth his theory of the Cabinet as follows: "All matters of importance or difficulty are submitted to all the heads of departments composing the Cabinet: sometimes by the President consulting them separately and successively, as they happen to call on him; but in the gravest cases, by calling them together, discussing the subject maturely, and finally taking the vote, in which the President counts himself but one. So that in all important cases the Executive is, in fact, a directory which certainly the President might control; but of this there was never an example, either in the first or the present administration" —that is, his own. *Writings* (Ford, ed.), IX, 69. See also *ibid.,* 273.

44 The literature on the National Convention is enormous. For a few leading references see H. R. Bruce, *American Politics and Parties* (rev. ed.) (New York, 1932), p. 379. Writing in 1859 Thomas H. Benton excoriated the National Convention:

"An irresponsible body (chiefly constituted, and mainly dominated by professional office-seekers and office-holders) have usurped the election of the President (for the nomination is the election, so far as the party is concerned); and always making it with a view to their own profit in the monopoly of office and plunder." He considered this method of choosing a President to be one of the two great "trials" confronting the capacity of the American people for self-government, the other being slavery. *Thirty Years View* (1859), II, p. 787.

In 1872 Charles Sumner, in urging a constitutional amendment to provide for direct election of the President, voiced a like judgment: "Whereas, the caucus or convention, after being the engine for the nomination of President, allowing the people a little more than to record its will, becomes the personal instrument of the President when elected, giving him dictatorial power, which he may employ in reducing the people to conformity with his purposes and promoting his re-election, all of which is hostile to good government, and of evil example. . . ." Quoted by Chambrun in work cited in note 61 *infra*, at p. 43.

I doubt if current developments would have caused either of these great men to alter materially his opinion on this subject.

[45] Richardson, II, 576, 582.

[46] Beveridge, *op. cit.*, IV, 535 n.; Binkley, *op. cit.*, pp. 80, 84. Webster, naturally, opposed the doctrine that the opening clause of Article II of the Constitution grants power. Speaking on the removal power in the Senate, February 16, 1835, he said:

"When they say it shall be vested in a President, they mean one magistrate, to be called a President, shall hold executive authority; but they mean, further, that he shall hold this authority according to the grants and limitations of the Constitution itself.

"They did not intend, certainly, a sweeping gift of prerogative. They did not intend to grant to the President whatever might be construed, or supposed, or imagined to be an executive power; and the proof that they meant no such thing is, that, immediately after using these general words, they proceed specifically to enumerate his several distinct and particular authorities; to fix and define them; to give the Senate an essential control over the exercise of some of them, and to leave others uncontrolled. By the executive power conferred on the President, the Constitution means no more than that portion which itself creates, and which it qualifies, limits and circumscribes." *Writings* (Constitutional ed., 1903), VII, 186–187; *Register of Debates in Congress,* XI, Pt. I, 462–463.

In the course of the same debate Calhoun confronted the idea of the equality of the three departments with that of legislative supremacy, in the following words:

"Permit each department to judge of the extent of its own powers, and to assume the right to exercise all powers which it may deem necessary and proper to execute the powers granted to it, and who does not see that, in fact, the Government would consist of three independent, separate, and conflicting departments, without any common point of union, instead of one united authority controlling the whole. . . . Under the opposite and true view of our system all these dangerous jars and conflicts would cease. It unites the whole into one, and the legislative becomes, as it ought to be, the center of the system; the stomach and the brain, into which all is taken, digested, and assimilated, and by which the action of the whole is regulated by a common intelligence. . . . Each [department] is left in possession of the powers expressly granted by the constitution, and which may be executed without the aid of the legislative department, and in the exercise of which there is no possibility of coming into conflict with the other departments; while all discretionary powers necessary to execute those granted, and in the exercise of which the separate departments would necessarily come into conflict are . . . transferred to Congress. . . ." *Ibid.,* 555–556.

This, in the main, was the position of the early Jeffersonians and of the later Whigs.

For further expressions of the same point of view, both earlier and later, see statements by Sedgwick and Sherman in the First Congress, *Annals of Congress*, I, 511, 541; speech by Tucker of Virginia in House of Representatives, August 15, 1876, *Congressional Record*, 44th Congress, 1st sess., 5699; dissenting opinion of Holmes, J., in *Myers v. United States*, 272 U. S. 52, 177; dissenting opinion of McReynolds, J., *ibid.*, 183.

47 *A Brief Inquiry into the True Nature and Character of Our Federal Government* (1840), pp. 116–117.

48 Charles Warren, "Presidential Declarations of Independence," 10 *Boston University Law Review* (1930), 1–35, at 17 and *passim*. My authority for the statement about the Swiss Constitution of 1848 is Professor Rappard. To the framers of the Weimar constitution the American Presidency appealed strongly—too strongly, it would seem. See Hajo Holborn in *The Constitution Reconsidered* (Conyers Read, ed.) (Columbia University Press, 1938), pp. 292–295.

49 A more positive assertion of power in the legislative field is, however, suggested by the Hon. Richard Fletcher's statement in a speech in Faneuil Hall in 1837 that "during Jackson's term of office the principal function" of the Ways and Means Committee, of which Fletcher had been a member, "was going through the form of approving the laws which Jackson prepared and handed down to them for acceptance." Speech of Representative Harlan of Ohio in the House, *Congressional Record*, February 27, 1935. Also Jackson gave as one of his reasons for vetoing Clay's Bank bill the failure of Congress to consult him prior to its passage. Richardson, II, 589. On the other hand, the first Harrison thought it worth while in his Inaugural to voice a very depreciatory construction of the President's power and duty to recommend measures to Congress. It was simply, he held, "a privilege which he holds in common with every other citizen." *Ibid.*, IV, 9. Similar views were later expressed by Polk, Taylor, and Fillmore. *Ibid.*, 517; V, 23 and 79.

50 Yet it is significant that even during this period the charge of "executive usurpation" was sometimes made. Warren, *loc. cit.*, pp. 17–20.

51 The following are characteristic laments of Mr. Welles on this point:

"There is really very little of a government here at this time, so far as most of the Cabinet are concerned; certainly but little consultation in this important period." "All this has been done without Cabinet consultation, or advice with any one, except Seward and the President." "Cabinet-meetings, which should, at that exciting and interesting period, have been daily, were infrequent, irregular, and without system." "But little was before the Cabinet, which of late can hardly be called a council. Each Department conducts and manages its own affairs, informing the President to the extent it pleases." "Stanton does not attend one half of the Cabinet-meetings. When he comes, he communicates little of importance. Not unfrequently he had a private conference with the President in the corner of the room, or with Seward in the library." "The President did not join us today in Cabinet. He was with the Secretary of War and General Halleck, and sent word there would be no meeting. That is wrong, but I know no remedy." "This is a specimen of the management of affairs. A majority of the members of the Cabinet are not permitted to know what is doing." "Chase spent an hour with me on various subjects. Says the Administration is merely departmental, which is true; that he considers himself responsible for no other branch of the Government than the Treasury, nor for any other than financial measures." "Chase . . . remarked that nothing could be expected where there were no Cabinet consultations and no concerted action." "Stanton has a cabinet and is a power in his own Department. He deceives the President and Seward, makes confidants of certain leading men, and is content to have matters move on without being compelled to show his exact position."

The Diary of Gideon Welles (New York, 1911) I, 131, 134, 136, 274, 320, 351, 391, 401–402, 526; II, 17, 58, 59, 62, 84, 86, 91, 98, 166, 203.

[52] Richardson, V, 626 ff.

[53] Message of July 4, 1861. *Ibid.*, VI, 20, 23–25, 31.

[54] James G. Randall, *Constitutional Problems Under Lincoln* (New York, 1926), p. 514. See also Ch. V *supra*.

[55] For new light on Lincoln's personal administrative habits in the White House see a letter of John Hay to Herndon in Emanuel Hertz, *The Hidden Lincoln* (New York, 1938), pp. 307–308. *Cf.* Fish, *The American Civil War* (New York, 1937), pp. 175–176, 356–362. Not only Lincoln's temperament, but his entire lack of previous administrative experience and the Western attitude that no elaborate bureaucratic machinery was needed must have contributed to this result.

[56] As a Whig member of Congress years before, Lincoln had written:

"Were I President, I should desire the legislation of the country to rest with Congress, uninfluenced in its origin or progress, and undisturbed by the veto unless in very special and clear cases." *Complete Works* (John G. Nicolay and John Hay, eds., New York, 1890), I, 134. And on his journey to Washington as President-elect, referring in his speech at Pittsburgh to certain "indirect" means by which a President may influence legislation, he said: "My political education strongly inclines me against a very free use of any of these means by the executive to control the legislation of the country. As a rule, I think it better that Congress should originate as well as perfect its measures without external bias." *Ibid.*, 679. Even in his message to Congress of July 4, 1861, he wrote, after remarking that he had performed his duty, "you will now, according to your own judgment, perform yours." *Richardson*, VI, 31. In view of the *faits accomplis* with which he confronted Congress, the statement sounds a bit ironical, to say the least; but Lincoln's acceptance of the principle of separation of powers saved it from insincerity. And in the main he undoubtedly adhered rather closely to his announced intention to avoid what he regarded as improper executive influence upon Congress. As Professor Randall points out, very little legislation was initiated or carried through by Lincoln, *op. cit.*, p. 387.

[57] Contemporary constitutional law was all with Congress in this dispute. Reciting Art. IV, §4, the Court had said in *Luther v. Borden:*

"Under this article of the Constitution it rests with Congress to decide what government is the established one in a State. For as the United States guarantee to each State a republican government, Congress must necessarily decide what government is established in the State before it can determine whether it is republican or not. And when the senators and representatives of a State are admitted into the councils of the Union, the authority of the government under which they are appointed, as well as its republican character, is recognized by the proper constitutional authority. And its decision is binding on every other department of the government, and could not be questioned in a judicial tribunal." 7 How. 1, 42 (1849).

And in *Texas v. White,* which was decided early in 1869, it endorsed this doctrine with direct reference to Reconstruction. Rehearsing the steps that Johnson had taken to restore civil government in Texas, Chief Justice Chase continued as follows:

"Whether the action then taken was, in all respects, warranted by the Constitution, it is not now necessary to determine. The power exercised by the President was supposed, doubtless, to be derived from his constitutional functions, as commander-in-chief; and, so long as the war continued, it cannot be denied that he might institute temporary government within insurgent districts, occupied by the National forces, or take measures, in any State, for the restoration of State government faithful to the Union, employing, however, in such efforts, only such means and agents as were authorized by constitutional laws.

"But, the power to carry into effect the clause of guaranty is primarily a legislative power, and resides in Congress. 'Under the fourth article of the Constitution, it rests with Congress to decide what government is the established one in a State. For, as the United States guarantee to each State a republican government, Congress must necessarily decide what government is established in the State, before it can determine whether it is republican or not.'

"This is the language of the late Chief Justice, speaking for the court, in a case from Rhode Island, arising from the organization of opposing governments in that State. And, we think that the principle sanctioned by it may be applied, with even more propriety, to the case of a State deprived of all rightful government, by revolutionary violence; though necessarily limited to cases where the rightful government is thus subverted, or in imminent danger of being overthrown by an opposing government, set up by force within the State.

"The action of the President must, therefore, be considered as provisional, and, in that light, it seems to have been regarded by Congress." 7 Wall. 700, 729–730 (1869).

[58] Edward McPherson, *History of the Rebellion* (2nd ed., 1865), p. 332. Cited hereafter as McPherson.

[59] *The New York Herald,* September 29, 1866; Binkley, p. 145, where "Andrew Jackson" is erroneously printed for "Andrew Johnson." *Cf.* James A. Woodburn, *Life of Thaddeus Stevens* (Indianapolis, 1913), p. 447.

[60] 4 Wall. 475 (1867).

[61] Lockwood, pp. 191–192.

"One of the most convincing evidences of the innate weakness of our form of Government is the fact that the people of this country are compelled, apparently, to turn to any one particular man in an emergency, for assistance and support. Woe to that country whose destinies are involved in the fortunes of any one man, however great and pure he may be!

"The true, logical, and efficient way to destroy imperialism in this country, is to abolish the system which makes it possible. With the destruction of presidential and the establishment of representative congressional government, we could, with impunity, place any man at the head of the executive branch, were he never so bad, ambitious, and inefficient, for it would then be known that at any moment he could be relieved from the cares of State." *Ibid.,* p. 195.

Note also the sweeping—much too sweeping—language in which John Norton Pomeroy describes the President's "affirmative powers" in relation to Congress's powers in his *Introduction to the Constitutional Law of the United States* (New York, 1877):

"The acts done by virtue of these powers are completely political. The subjects themselves, over which the powers extend, do not fall within the province of congressional legislation; and that body cannot by any laws enlarge or diminish the President's capacity; it can do nothing more than pass such laws, if it thinks proper, as shall aid the Chief Magistrate in the execution of these powers, nor may the Courts interfere and assume to regulate the President's conduct." *Ibid.,* pp. 420–421. This work was first published in 1868, the very year of Johnson's impeachment!

One other writing of this period should be mentioned briefly: *The Executive Power in the United States, A Study of Constitutional Law*, by Adolphe de Chambrun (Madeleine Vinton Dahlgren, tr.) (Lancaster, Pa., 1874). The writer, a grandson of Lafayette, was for many years Counselor of the French legation at Washington, and enjoyed the friendship of Caleb Cushing, Charles Sumner, and Carl Schurz, to all of whom he acknowledges indebtedness. The volume shows considerable discernment, and is notable for its discriminating choice of materials. It would, in fact, be unjust to term it out of date even today. Chambrun agrees, in effect, with Lockwood's evaluation of the Presidency. "If, then," he writes, "the exercise of popular sovereignty such as has been witnessed for more than eighty years, should cease, and the organization of the states lose its present strength, the powers of the central government, and especially the executive branch, would in a corresponding degree be enlarged. It is also quite true that a change of foreign policy and an undue territorial extension would, for different reasons, bring about an analogous transformation." *Op. cit.*, p. 286.

[62] Washington, Jefferson, Jackson, Polk, Lincoln, Hayes, Cleveland, Wilson, the two Roosevelts are my suggestions.

[63] See article cited in note 48 at pp. 9, 18–19; also Richardson, IV, 665.

NOTES TO CHAPTER II*

[1] Floyd R. Mechem, *A Treatise on the Law of Public Offices and Officers* (Chicago, 1890), §§89–94. See also 14 *Opins. A. G.* 406 (1874).

[2] David Hutchison, *The Foundations of the Constitution* (New York, 1928), p. 176. *Cf.* Calvin's Case, 4 Co. Rep. 1 (1608). On the source of the "natural-born citizen" clause, see Thach, *The Creation of the Presidency*, p. 137; *cf.* Farrand, III, 161.

[3] Act of March 26, 1790, 1 Stat. 415.

[4] Act of February 10, 1855, 10 Stat. 604; R. S., §1993; Act of March 2, 1907, 34 Stat. 1229; U. S. Code, tit. 8, §6.

[5] Art. I, §8, cl. 4.

[6] In *United States v. Wong Kim Ark,* 169 U.S. 649 (1898), Justice Gray, speaking for the Court, indicates quite clearly the opinion that the above legislation was passed under the "naturalization" clause, and that children born abroad of American parents are therefore *naturalized* citizens; that, in short, to be a natural-born citizen of the United States one has to be born "within the United States and subject to its jurisdiction." *Ibid.* 674, 702–703. The point, however, was not involved in the case; nor does Justice Gray explain why Congress in the Act of 1855 *"declares"* children born abroad of American parents *"to be* citizens of the United States."

[7] Mr. Hoover's eligibility was defended at length by Mr. Wickersham in an elaborate opinion late in 1927. One point much stressed was that, with all his absences abroad on business, Mr. Hoover had taken great pains to retain his legal domicile in the United States. *The New York Times*, December 20, 1927; see also editorial in the same issue, entitled "Residency and Presidency"; also C. K. Burdick, *ibid.*, February 2, 1920; and Farrand, II, 498, 536, 598.

When President Coolidge accepted membership of the Sioux tribe in August 1927, a correspondent of *The New York Times* expressed concern lest he might by so doing have lost his citizenship of the United States, and so his right to remain President. *The New York Times*, August 27, 1927.

---

* *Chapter II (Qualifications, Election, Tenure) begins on page 31.*

It should be noted that political considerations or accident have confined the Presidency to residents of twelve states, of which five—Virginia (5), New York (6), Ohio (6), Tennessee (3), and Massachusetts (3)—have supplied 23 of the 31. Of New York's 6 Presidents, 4 had been Vice-Presidents.

[8] U. S. Code, tit. 18, §§2, 4, 51, 192, 199, 203, 207, 235, 237, 238. Mr. Earl Browder's conviction recently was under such a section. *The New York Times,* June 25, 1940.

[9] Washington's announcement occurred at the outset of his Farewell Address. Richardson, I, 213. Jefferson's announcement was made December 10, 1807, in response to an address from the Vermont Legislature thirteen months earlier. It reads:

"I received in due season the address of the Legislature of Vermont, bearing date the 5th of November, 1806, in which, with their approbation of the general course of my Administration, they were so good as to express their desire that I would consent to be proposed again to the public voice on the expiration of my present term of office. Entertaining as I do for the Legislature of Vermont those sentiments of high respect which would have prompted an immediate answer, I was certain, nevertheless, they would approve a delay which had for its object to avoid a premature agitation of the public mind on a subject so interesting as the election of a Chief Magistrate.

"That I should lay down my charge at a proper period is as much a duty as to have borne it faithfully. If some termination to the services of the Chief Magistrate be not fixed by the Constitution, or supplied by practice, his office, nominally four years, will in fact become for life, and history shows how easily that degenerates into an inheritance. Believing that a representative Government responsible at short periods of election is that which produces the greatest sum of happiness to mankind, I feel it a duty to do no act which shall essentially impair that principle, and I should unwillingly be the person who, disregarding the sound precedent set by an illustrious predecessor [Washington], should furnish the first example of prolongation beyond the second term of office.

"Truth also requires me to add that I am sensible of that decline which advancing years bring on, and feeling their physical I ought not to doubt their mental effect. Happy if I am the first to perceive and to obey this admonition of nature, and to solicit a retreat from cares too great for the wearied faculties of age.

"For the approbation which the Legislature of Vermont has been pleased to express of the principles and measures pursued in the management of their affairs, I am sincerely thankful, and should I be so fortunate as to carry into retirement the equal approbation and good-will of my fellow-citizens, generally, it will be the comfort of my future days and will close a service of forty years with the only reward it ever wished." *Writings* (Memorial ed.), XVI, 293.

Similar addresses from seven other states at about the same time elicited like responses. Nearly two years earlier Jefferson had written his friend John Taylor of Caroline, under date of January 6, 1805, that he proposed to follow Washington's "example of voluntary retirement," hoping that "a few more precedents will oppose the obstacle of habit to anyone after a while who shall endeavor to extend his term" or even "beget a disposition to establish it by an amendment of the Constitution." Only "one circumstance," he continued, "could engage my acquiescence in another election; to wit, such a division about a successor, as might bring in a monarchist. But this circumstance is impossible." *Ibid.,* XI, 56–57. Indeed, even while the adoption of the Constitution was pending, he had expressed concern over the "perpetual reëligibility" of the President. Said he, in a letter to Washington, from Paris, which was dated May 2, 1788: "This, I fear, will make an office for life. I was much an enemy of monarchy before I came to Europe. I am ten thousand times more so since I have seen what they are. . . . I shall hope that before there is danger of this change taking place in the office of President the good sense and free spirit of our countrymen will make the change necessary to prevent it. Under this hope I look forward to the general adoption of the new Constitution with anxiety as necessary for us under our present circumstances." See *ibid.*, VI, 385, 447, 454.

Washington, however, deprecated these apprehensions. Writing Lafayette, April 28, 1788, from Mount Vernon, he said:

"There are other points in which opinions would be more likely to vary, as, for instance, on the eligibility of the same person for President, after he should have served a certain course of years. Guarded so effectively as the proposed Constitution is, in respect to the prevention of bribery and undue influence in the choice of President, I confess I differ widely myself from Mr. Jefferson and you, as to the necessity or expediency of rotation in that department. The matter was freely discussed in the convention and to my full conviction.

"Though I cannot have time or room to sum up the argument in this letter, there cannot, in my judgment, be the least danger that the President will by any practicable intrigue ever be able to continue himself one moment in office, much less perpetuate himself in it, but in the last stage of corrupt morals and political depravity, and even then there is as much danger that any species of domination would prevail. Though when a people have become incapable of governing themselves, and fit for a master, it is of little consequence from what quarter it comes. Under an extended view of this part of the subject I can see no propriety in precluding ourselves from the services of any man who in some great emergency shall be deemed universally most capable of serving the public." *Writings* (W. C. Ford, ed.), XI, 254, 257.

And Hamilton in *The Federalist* came out strongly for indefinite reëligibility:

"Nothing appears more plausible at first sight, nor more ill-founded upon close inspection than a scheme which in relation to the present point has had some respectable advocates,—I mean that of continuing the chief magistrate in office for a certain time and then excluding him from it, either for a limited period or forever after. This exclusion, whether temporary or perpetual, would have nearly the same effects, and these effects would be for the most part rather pernicious than salutary.

"One ill effect of the exclusion would be a diminution of the inducements to good behavior. There are few men who would not feel much less zeal in the discharge of a duty, when they were conscious that the advantages of the station with which it was connected must be relinquished at a determinate period, than when they were permitted to entertain a hope of *obtaining,* by *meriting,* a continuance of them. . . .

"Another ill effect of the exclusion would be the temptation to sordid views, to peculation, and, in some instances, to usurpation. An avaricious man, who might happen to fill the office, looking forward to a time when he must at all events yield up the emoluments he enjoyed, would feel a propensity, not easy to be resisted by such a man, to make the best use of the opportunity he enjoyed while it lasted. . . .

"An ambitious man, too, . . . in such a situation, would be much more violently tempted to embrace a favorable conjuncture for attempting the prolongation of his power, at every personal hazard, than if he had the probability of answering the same end by doing his duty.

"Would it promote the peace of the community, or the stability of the government to have half a dozen men who had had credit enough to be raised to the seat of the supreme magistracy, wandering among the people like discontented ghosts, and sighing for a place which they were destined never more to possess?

"A third ill effect of the exclusion would be, the depriving the community of the advantage of the experience gained by the chief magistrate in the exercise of his office. . . .

"A fourth ill effect of the exclusion would be the banishing men from stations in which, in certain emergencies of the state, their presence might be of the greatest moment to the public interest and safety. . . .

"A fifth ill effect of the exclusion would be, that it would operate as a constitutional interdiction of stability in the administration. By *necessitating* a change of men, in the first office of the nation, it would necessitate a mutability of measures. It is not generally to be expected, that men will vary and measures remain uniform. The contrary is the usual course of things. . . .

"There is an excess of refinement in the idea of disabling the people to continue in office men who had entitled themselves, in their opinion, to approbation and confidence; the advantages of which are at best speculative and equivocal, and are overbalanced by disadvantages far more certain and decisive." Earle, pp. 470–472.

With President Roosevelt deciding to run for a third term this year, we shall have the interesting spectacle of Democrats quoting Washington and Hamilton in defense of his course and Republicans quoting Jefferson in condemnation of it.

[10] The evidence relating to President Wilson's desire for a third term comprises some notes which were made at the time by the Hon. Carter Glass, a friend and supporter of Wilson, and which are reprinted in Mr. Rixey Smith's recent *Carter Glass, a Biography* (New York, 1939) (I quote the passage with the consent of the publisher, Longmans, Green and Company, Inc.):

"June 10, 1920. Grayson [Wilson's physician] told me President seriously contemplates permitting himself to be named for third term and said it would kill him. Later in the day Burleson [Postmaster General] told me he believed President wanted third term, saying he had told President latter or McAdoo would be nominated, to which President made no answer.

"June 16, 1920. Grayson at Executive Office expressed to me greatest anxiety about President's third term thoughts, saying he literally impossible to measure up to exactions of campaign. Would probably kill him. Said President's sole idea was to lead fight for covenant; he was totally indifferent to all other considerations. Would resign after covenant was adopted. I told Grayson I did not think convention could be induced to nominate man in President's disabled condition, and if President was in robust health, 'twas barely possible Democratic party and American people might submerge third-term antipathies in their desire for permanent guaranty against war; but not in present circumstances. Grayson begged me to do all possible to guard against such an untoward development in San Francisco. Tumulty also today expressed concern about this third-term manifestation." *Op. cit.,* pp. 205–206.

[11] The Democratic Platform of 1912 had contained a single term pledge for the party's nominee, which Wilson repudiated in his letter to A. Mitchell Palmer, February 5, 1913:

"As things stand now, the people might more likely be cheated than served by further limitations on the President's eligibility. His fighting power in their behalf would be immensely weakened. No one will fear a President except those whom he can make fear the elections. . . . If we want our Presidents to fight our battles for us we should give them the means, the legitimate means, the means their opponents will always have. Strip them of everything else but the right to appeal to the people, but leave them that. Suffer them to be leaders."

Cleveland, in his first Inaugural Address, announced that eligibility to reëlection constituted a grave danger to democracy; in fact, he served two terms and is the one President in our history who three times received a popular plurality.

[12] Irwin Hood Hoover, *Forty-Two Years in the White House* (New York, 1934), pp. 166–180, a circumstantial account which leaves little doubt in the reader's mind that Coolidge expected to be "drafted" and was chagrined to the point of positive illness when he wasn't. H. L. Stoddard's attempted refutation in *It Costs To Be President* (New York, 1938), pp. 91 and 124, and Chs. 13 and 14, is quite unconvincing. Coolidge issued his statement at Rapid City, South Dakota, August 2, 1927. Neither former Secretary of the Treasury Shaw nor ex-President Taft thought that the third-term tradition barred Coolidge from running in 1928. *The New York Times,* February 9, 1927; H. F. Pringle, *Taft* (New York, 1939), II, 1062–1063.

[13] Of the 85 proposals, 63 favored a single term of six years, and one of these was adopted by the Senate February 1, 1913, by a vote of 47 to 23, a bare constitutional majority. In the House it never got out of committee. M. A. Musmanno, *Proposed Amendments to the Constitution* (70th Cong., 2nd sess.; H. D. No. 551; Government Printing Office, 1929), pp. 51–60. Between 1789 and 1889 over 25 proposals to restrict presidential reëligibility were brought forward in Congress without result. *Ibid.,* pp. 51–52.

[14] Neither Willis Thornton's *The Third Term Issue* (New York, 1939) nor Fred Rodell's *Democracy and the Third Term* (New York, 1940) came out in time to be of much assistance in the preparation of the present work.

"History . . . has shown that the strong man who is good may very readily subvert free institutions if he and the people at large grow to accept his continued possession of vast power as being necessary to good government." T. Roosevelt to Sir George Otto Trevelyan, June 19, 1908. Joseph B. Bishop, *Theodore Roosevelt and His Time* (New York, 1920), II, 93.

[15] Art II, § 1, par. 2.

[16] 146 U. S. 1.

[17] *Ibid.,* 29.

[18] James Wilson made the suggestion. Farrand, II, 97.

[19] *McPherson v. Blacker* grew out of this legislation.

[20] Everett S. Brown, ed., *The Missouri Compromise and Presidential Politics* (Missouri, 1926), pp. 53–62; C. O. Paullin, *American Historical Review,* XXI, 318–319 and *cf.* note 22 *infra.*

[21] George H. Haynes, *The Election of Senators* (New York, 1906), p. 132.

[22] Benjamin Harrison, *This Country of Ours* (New York, 1898), p. 77; quoted in H. W. Horwill, *Usages of the American Constitution* (Oxford University Press, 1925), p. 38. For other statements to the same general effect, see *ibid.,* pp. 40–41. Horwill's account of what happened in 1872 and 1912 when one of the candidates—fortunately of the minority party—died between the November election and the meeting of the Electors affords a further demonstration of the present status of the Electoral College:

"Is there any possibility of the Electors regaining their forfeited independence? A situation is conceivable which would put the matter to the test.

" 'Should accident so shape events,' writes Dr. Von Holst, 'that the Presidential candidate of the victorious party should die immediately before the meeting of the Electoral College, then the United States would again have a President who was, not only in form but in truth, elected by the Electors. The effects that such an accident might produce are incalculable.'

"Such a case has never yet occurred. The nearest approach to it was in 1872, but with the important difference that the man who died was the candidate not of the victorious but of the defeated party. Horace Greeley, who had been defeated as Democratic candidate at the popular election on November 5, died on November 29. The Electors met a week later, on the very day on which he was carried to his grave. Out of a total of 366 Electoral votes there were sixty-six that would have come to him if he had lived. These sixty-six votes belonged to Democratic Electors in six States. The three Democratic Electors in Georgia evaded the difficulty by voting for the dead man. They felt themselves under a sacred obligation to vote for Greeley, and vote for him they did, although at the time he was in his coffin. The other Democratic votes were divided among four candidates, T. A. Hendricks receiving forty-two, B. Gratz Brown (the official party candidate for the Vice-Presidency) eighteen, C. J. Jenkins, two, and D. Davis one. As there was not the remotest chance of the election of a Democrat, what the Democratic Electors did with their votes did not really matter in the least.

"Another interesting incident occurred in 1912. In that year also the popular election was held on November 5. The Electors were to meet on January 13, 1913. The Vice-President, James S. Sherman, who had been nominated for re-election on the Republican ticket, died on October 30. It so happened that in this instance provision had been made for meeting such a situation. In its closing hours the Republican convention in June had passed a resolution authorizing the national committee to fill any vacancy on the ticket that might be caused by the death or disability of Mr. Taft (who was the party's candidate for re-election to the Presidency) or Mr. Sherman. This was done in such a way that it attracted no attention at the time. It was due to the fact that the managers of the convention were aware that Mr. Sherman's death was expected in the near future. The Republican national committee met hurriedly after Mr. Sherman's death, and decided that, as it was a question not of the Presidency but of the Vice-Presidency, it would not be worth while to complete the ticket until after the popular election. So that year the Republicans throughout the country cast their votes for Electors without knowing who would be Vice-President if their party was successful. The polling on November 5 showed that here, again, the choice of a substitute would be a mere formality. The committee, however, solemnly conferred together on November 12 and decided on a distinguished University President as the person for whom the Republican Electors should vote. With equal solemnity four Republican Electors in Vermont and four in Utah met on the appointed day in their respective State capitals, and cast for this gentleman the eight votes which were all that had been saved, out of a total Electoral vote of 531, from the wreck of orthodox Republicanism." Horwill, *op. cit.,* pp. 51–52.

When, nevertheless, in 1924 it appeared not unlikely that the late Senator LaFollette, who was running on a third party ticket, would capture enough electoral votes to prevent either of the major party candidates from getting a majority in the College, the suggestion was advanced that Mr. LaFollette might throw his strength in the college to the Democratic candidate, Mr. Davis, or to a compromise candidate to be selected by himself and the Democratic party management. *The New York Times,* October 12, 1924.

[23] An informed writer has expressed the opinion that popular election of the President

in 1860 would have postponed the Civil War and perhaps have prevented it. Arthur C. Cole, "Lincoln's Election," 36 *American Historical Review* (July 1931), 740 ff.

[24] For an interesting account of the first three presidential elections, and the gradual emergence of party lines, see an Associated Press despatch from Washington to *The New York Times* of July 12, 1936. Speaking of the third election the despatch says, among other things:

"In spite of his [Hamilton's] manoeuvring, when the votes were counted in the Electoral College, Adams had been elected by three votes. And Jefferson was the runner-up, thus giving the Federalist President a Republican Vice President.

"Pinckney had 59 votes and Aaron Burr had 30. The remainder were strewn among nine other candidates. Washington got two votes, one North Carolinian and one Virginian refusing to take his farewell message seriously.

"Curiously enough four of the votes were of questionable legality. And they were the four that decided the Presidency. Vermont had not enacted a law specifying how the electors should be chosen. But the Legislature had named four electors and sent them down to vote.

"They voted for Adams, thus giving him three more votes than Jefferson. Adams, presiding over the electoral colleges as President of the Senate, stated the result and then sat down to await a protest against the Vermont vote. Hearing none, he then declared himself elected President of the United States.

"And thus ended a campaign which had been so heated in spots that one orator had proclaimed:

" 'Damn John Jay. Damn every one who won't damn John Jay. Damn every one who won't put lights in his windows and sit up all night damning John Jay.' "

[25] See on this subject P. L. Haworth, *The Hayes-Tilden Disputed Election* (New York, 1906); W. A. Dunning, *Reconstruction Political and Economic* (New York, 1907), Chs. XIX–XXI; Henry L. Stoddard, *It Costs To Be President* (1938); Charles Bradley, *Miscellaneous Writings of the Late Honorable Joseph P. Bradley* (Newark, 1902), pp. 165–223.

[26] The constitutional question had been raised several times before this, in 1821, 1837, 1857, 1865, 1869, and 1873, but in circumstances which permitted its evasion. Stoddard, p. 262.

[27] The bill was passed January 26, 1877. In the total 186 Democrats and 52 Republicans voted for it, while 18 Democrats and 85 Republicans opposed it. Having the President *pro tem* of the Senate and being assured of the support of the army, the vast majority of the Republicans were opposed to compromise, or at least pretended to be. Stoddard, p. 264.

[28] *Miscellaneous Writings,* pp. 193–194.

[29] *Ibid.,* p. 195.

[30] It should be noted that even after the Electoral Commission had completed its work, the Democrats of the House were in a position by filibustering to prevent the count of electoral votes by the houses from being completed. That they did not was due to the assurance which the Southern leaders of the party received that Hayes, once seated, would withdraw the federal troops from the Southern states whose electoral votes had been in dispute. Thus, although the South lost that particular election, it became master of its own household for future elections. See Stoddard, *op. cit.,* p. 263.

[31] In the main the act ratifies and enacts into law the decision on the constitutional question of the Electoral Commission.

32 For existing legislation governing Presidential elections, including the Act of February 3, 1887, see U. S. Code, tit. 3, Ch. 1.

33 *Ex parte* Yarbrough, 110 U.S. 651 (1884).

34 289 U.S. 159 (1933).

35 The argument advanced by Justice Pitney in his partially concurring opinion in *Newberry v. United States,* in support of the power of Congress to control prenomination expenditures of candidates for Congress, is equally applicable to this question:

"It seems to me too clear for discussion that primary elections and nominating conventions are so closely related to the final election, and their proper regulation so essential to effective regulation of the latter, so vital to representative government, that power to regulate them is within the general authority of Congress. It is matter of common knowledge that the great mass of the American electorate is grouped into political parties, to one or the other of which voters adhere with tenacity, due to their divergent views on questions of public policy, their interests, their environment, and various other influences, sentimental and historical. So strong with the great majority of voters are party associations, so potent the party slogan, so effective the party organization, that the likelihood of a candidate succeeding in an election without a party nomination is practically negligible. As a result, every voter comes to the polls on the day of the general election confined in his choice to those few candidates who have received party nominations, and constrained to consider their eligibility, in point of personal fitness, as affected by their party associations and their obligation to pursue more or less definite lines of policy, with which the voter may or may not agree. As a practical matter, the ultimate choice of the mass of voters is predetermined when the nominations have been made. Hence, the authority of Congress to regulate the primary elections and nomination conventions arises, of necessity, not from any indefinite or implied grant of power, but from one clearly expressed in the Constitution itself (Art. I, §8, cl. 18)—'To make all Laws which shall be necessary and proper for carrying into Execution the foregoing Powers, and all other Powers vested by this Constitution in the Government of the United States, or in any Department or Officer thereof.' This is the power preservative of all others, and essential for adding vitality to the framework of the Government. Among the primary powers to be carried into effect is the power to legislate through a Congress consisting of a Senate and House of Representatives chosen by the people—in short, the power to maintain a law-making body representative in its character. . . .

"The passage of the act under consideration amounts to a determination by the law-making body that the regulation of primary elections and nominating conventions is necessary if the Senate and House of Representatives are to be, in a full and proper sense, representatives of the people. Not only is this true of those cases referred to in the report of the Senate Committee (*Senate Reports,* No. 78, 62nd Cong., 1st sess., p. 2) where the parties are so unequally divided that a nomination by the majority party is equivalent to election; but it is true in every case to the extent that the nominating processes virtually eliminate from consideration by the electors all eligible candidates except the few—two or three, perhaps—who succeed in receiving party nominations. Sinister influences exerted upon the primaries inevitably have their effect upon the ultimate election—are employed for no other reason. To safeguard the final elections while leaving the proceedings for proposing candidates unregulated, is to postpone regulation until it is comparatively futile. And Congress might well conclude that, if the nominating procedure were to be left open to fraud, bribery, and corruption, or subject to the more insidious but (in the opinion of Congress) nevertheless harmful influences resulting from an unlimited expenditure of money in paid propaganda and other purchased campaign activities, representative government would be endangered." 256 U. S. 285–286, 287–288.

The principal suggestions for legislation thus far have revolved about "the Presidential Primary," a sort of nine-days wonder, which has today lost most of its popular appeal. On the institution at its heyday, see Miss Louise Overacker's volume *The Presidential Primary* (New York, 1926). Woodrow Wilson, in his first annual message to Congress, urged "the prompt enactment of legislation which will provide for primary elections throughout the country at which the voters of the several parties may choose nominees for the Presidency without the intervention of nominating conventions." *Congressional Record*, 63rd Cong., 2nd sess., p. 44; Overacker, p. 188 n. Ten years later Professor P. Orman Ray suggested legislation providing for a presidential primary which should follow the national conventions, and at which the voters would choose the party candidates for President and Vice-President from five or six names submitted by the Convention for President. The person getting the highest popular vote of the party would be the party candidate for President and the second highest would be the party candidate for Vice-President. 106 *Annals of the Academy of Political and Social Science*, 62–71 (March 1923). Neither proposal has to date led to anything.

[36] No. 68; Earle, p. 441.

[37] On the discussion growing out of Garfield's fatal illness see especially the symposium of views in 133 *North American Review*, 417–446 (November 1881), the participants in which were Senator Lyman Trumbull, General Benjamin F. Butler, Judge T. M. Cooley, and Professor Theodore Dwight of Yale; also Urban A. Lavery's article on "Presidential 'Inability,' " in 8 *American Bar Association Journal*, 13–17. For President Arthur's repeated and ineffectual efforts to get Congress to legislate on the whole subject of presidential succession, see Richardson, VIII, 65, 147, 187. Not until 1886 did Congress respond, and then it did not touch the question of "inability."

Mr. Wilson's illness produced several legislative proposals in Congress, none of which was debated in either house, although evoking some discussion in committee. Their purport is sufficiently indicated in the following excerpt from a despatch to the *New York Evening Post* of March 1, 1920:

"Out of this discussion has come a quartet of bills on which hearings are now being held, designed to settle a question for which a satisfactory answer has long been awaited, namely, What constitutes the inability of a President within the meaning of the Constitution, and who shall decide when this disability arises?

"Representatives Fess of Ohio, Rogers of Massachusetts, Madden of Illinois and McArthur of Oregon, all Republicans, have introduced bills or joint resolutions which they believe will furnish the answer, and which are now receiving consideration at the hands of the House Judiciary Committee.

"All of the measures except that of Mr. Fess are based on the assumption that the power to prescribe a method of determining a President's disability is already vested in Congress by the Constitution. Representative Fess, on the other hand, believes that an amendment to the Constitution is necessary.

"The Rogers bill provides that on the request of either House the Supreme Court shall determine whether the President is unable to discharge his duties, and that the court may on its own initiative or on the request of either House determine whether the inability has been removed. If so, the President shall resume his official duties. In discussing this measure Chairman Volstead of the Judiciary Committee raised the point that it confers original jurisdiction upon the Supreme Court, whereas under the Constitution it has only appellate jurisdiction, except in certain cases specifically enumerated. He gave it as his view that if the fact of disability is to be judicially determined, this must be done by some other body than the Supreme Court.   .

"The bills of Representatives Madden and McArthur place the determination of the question in the hands of the Cabinet. In their view this body, being in political harmony with the President, will not be suspected of ulterior motives if it decides that a President is incapacitated. Moreover, their close contact with the Chief Executive will enable the Cabinet officers readily to ascertain the facts and render a quick decision. The McArthur bill defines inability as illness for a period of thirty days or absence from the continental United States for a similar period.

"Representative Fess, assuming that a constitutional amendment is necessary, has introduced a joint resolution proposing an amendment that empowers the Supreme Court to determine the question of disability when requested by a concurrent resolution of Congress. If Congress should not be in session, the Vice President is authorized to call a special session for this purpose upon the recommendation of the Cabinet.

"In opposition to all these measures another view has developed, namely, that these questions are already settled by the Constitution itself, and that no further legislation or amendment is necessary. It is held that the very act of a Vice President in calling Congress into session would establish the fact that a Presidential disability exists. Further machinery for passing on this question would therefore be superfluous. The fact of disability being thus established, the Constitution already provides that the duties of the Presidential office shall devolve upon the Vice President, and nothing further is required.

"This opinion has been enunciated by Henry E. Davis, a Washington lawyer, who has given considerable study to the subject and has prepared a monograph which the Senate sometime ago had printed as a public document. A number of Congressmen accepted this view. Mr. Davis contends that the wording of the Constitution concerning the disability of the President was not the result of carelessness on the part of the framers, but that it was drafted with the same care as the other provisions and was regarded as 'self-explanatory, self-operative and self-sufficient.' He maintains that the Vice President alone is the person to decide when this disability has arisen. 'No Vice President would assume to insist to a President against his judgment that he was under a disability,' says Mr. Davis, 'and so long as a President would resist such an intimation there would be no inability.'

"It has been brought out at the committee hearings that the problem involves much more than merely a definition of a President's inability. Some of the questions raised were: Who shall say when the inability ceases—the President himself, the Vice President or some other officer or officers? During the period of inability is the Vice President merely acting President for the time being or does he succeed to the full status of President?" See also The New York Times, February 19, 20, and 27, 1920; and 59 Congressional Record, 3106, 3158, 3217 (February 18, 19, 20, 1920).

The question of "inability" is not discussed by either Story or Hare, and is dealt with by Willoughby in his famous work only briefly. He considers the primary responsibility to rest with the Vice-President, but adds:

"It is to be assumed, however, that he would not take this serious step without previous consultation with, and approval by, the members of the President's cabinet and members of Congress. Having taken this step, its constitutionality could be tested in the courts by bringing before them the validity of his official acts, or of the acts of lower executive officials committed in reliance upon his orders. Thus, in last resort, the Supreme Court of the United States might be called upon to determine whether, in fact, there had existed an inability of the President which would constitutionally justify the exercise of presidential powers by the Vice-President. Similarly, should it happen that the disability of the President should prove to be temporary, and he should again claim the right to exercise the powers of his office, and the acting President should refuse, upon any ground to yield to this claim, the question as to who is to be recognized as legally entitled to exercise the powers of the President could be determined by the courts in cases involving the validity of the acts of either or both of the two claimants to the office." *Willoughby on the Constitution* (2nd ed., New York, 1929), III, 1470–1471. See also *Tucker on the Constitution* (Chicago, 1899), II, 713; and J. W. Burgess, *Political Science and Comparative Constitutional Law* (Boston, 1890–1891), II, 241.

[38] "Mr. Wilson's serious illness befell September 26, 1919, while he was on tour in the West in behalf of the Treaty of Versailles, which was then pending in the Senate. Three days later he returned to Washington. On October 4th he had a stroke of paralysis and was unconscious for nearly a week and semiconscious for over a month. His partial recovery was very slow and for three months he saw no one but Mrs. Wilson, his doctors and his nurses. During that period all state papers were given to Mrs. Wilson first. If she was in doubt as to the possible effect they would have on the President she submitted them to Dr. Grayson. If he thought that Mr. Wilson was strong enough to pass judgment on them without excitement, they were shown to him. If not, they were passed upon by Secretary of the Treasury Houston and one or two others in whom Mrs. Wilson had confidence." Letter by "Pollio," editorial page of *The New York Times,* March 29, 1921.

This brief narrative is much amplified by George Sylvester Viereck's articles in *Liberty* for February 20 and 27, 1932, entitled "When a Woman was President of the United States." Though written in a somewhat sensational strain, the articles are borne out as to their most important assertions of fact by Messrs. Tumulty, Houston, and others, as well as by press dispatches of the period. See especially Mr. Tumulty's communication to *The New York Times* of December 3, 1921, and his *Woodrow Wilson as I Know Him* (New York, 1921), pp. 435–456; also David J. Houston, *Eight Years with Wilson's Cabinet* (New York, 1926), II, 36–70. Mrs. Wilson's *My Memoir* (New York, 1939) adds certain personal details which are of no interest in the present connection. See *ibid.,* pp. 283–302.

As late as December 3, 1919, the *Times* recorded that Senator Hitchcock of Nebraska, who was conducting the fight for the Treaty in the Senate, was unable to see the President. Two days later, however, it was stated that the President had seen Hitchcock three times; also that he had received Attorney-General Palmer, William G. McAdoo, Dr. Axson, the King of Belgium, and the Prince of Wales. The day previous (December 4), the Senate Foreign Relations Committee created a subcommittee consisting of Senators Hitchcock and Fall to interview Mr. Wilson ostensibly in regard to our Mexican relations, really to find out if possible the extent of the President's incapacity. The request was granted after Admiral Grayson, the President's physician, had consulted Mrs. Wilson, who was present throughout the ensuing forty-minute interview. The Senators came away, the *Times* of December 5 records, "convinced that his [Mr. Wilson's] mind is vigorous and active."

Nevertheless, it was not until April 13, 1920, that the President was able to convene his Cabinet, which had meantime been meeting at intervals at the call of Secretary of

State Lansing. Word of this proceeding having reached the President, the latter, on February 7, wrote Lansing to learn if such was the case, for, if it was, he professed to believe, a most serious breach of "the Constitutional system" had occurred. Mr. Lansing's reply, dated February 9, 1920, follows:

The Secretary of State,
Washington, Feb. 9, 1920.

My Dear Mr. President:

It is true that frequently during your illness I requested the heads of the executive departments of the Government to meet for informal conference.

Shortly after you were taken ill in October, certain members of the Cabinet, of which I was one, felt that, in view of the fact that we were denied communication with you, it was wise for us to confer informally together on interdepartmental matters and on matters as to which action could not be postponed until your medical advisers permitted you to pass upon them. Accordingly, I, as the ranking member, requested the members of the Cabinet to assemble for such informal conference, and in view of the mutual benefit derived the practice was continued.

I can assure you that it never for a moment entered my mind that I was acting unconstitutionally or contrary to your wishes, and there certainly was no intention on my part to assume powers and exercise functions which under the Constitution are exclusively confided to the President.

During these troublous times, when many difficult and vexatious questions have arisen and when in the circumstances I have been deprived of your guidance and direction, it has been my constant endeavor to carry out your policies as I understood them and to act in all matters as I believed you would wish me to act. If, however, you think that I have failed in my loyalty to you and if you no longer have confidence in me and prefer to have another conduct our foreign affairs, I am of course ready, Mr. President, to relieve you of any embarrassment by placing my resignation in your hands.

I am, as always,

Faithfully yours,

ROBERT LANSING.

Upon receipt of this letter, finding "nothing in your [Lansing's] letter which justifies your assumption of Presidential authority in such a matter," Mr. Wilson on February 11 asked for the Secretary's resignation, a request which Mr. Lansing met the following day.

As a matter of fact, Lansing had not merely called the Cabinet together at times, but he had at the outset of the President's illness endeavored to induce the President's secretary, Mr. Tumulty, to join with him in calling on Vice-President Marshall to take over the President's "power and duties." The story is told by Mr. Tumulty with considerable indignation in his *Woodrow Wilson as I Know Him*, pp. 443–444.

That inability definitely existed early in Mr. Wilson's illness is clear. In addition to the evidence already presented, the following statistics compiled by Professor Lindsay Rogers at the time are pertinent:

"To mention only one evidence, twenty-eight bills became law during the special session of Congress owing to the failure of the Executive to act within ten days (exclusive of Sundays) after their receipt at the White House; and when full disclosures are made as to the nature and times of the President's complete inability to act, it will be interesting to check them up with the dates on which bills were signed. For example, the President was able to veto the Prohibition Enforcement act on October 27, but he did not approve two statutes which became law on October 22 and 25, and he failed to sign Public Laws

Numbers 67 and 82 inclusive (October 28 to November 18), with the exception of Number 73, the first General Deficiency Law for 1920, which was signed on November 4. After November 18 practically all of the bills became law with the signature of the President." *The Review,* May 20, 1920.

Public opinion as reflected by the press was substantially universal in its condemnation of the principal ground which Mr. Wilson advanced for dismissing Secretary Lansing. The following extract from the editorial column of *The New York Times* is sufficiently typical to warrant quotation:

"Of all men in the United States, President Wilson should have been most wary of raising that question. It was known early in October that he could not attend Cabinet meetings. If Congress had then accepted the theory which Mr. Wilson now propounds, that the Cabinet could do nothing without his presence, and consequently that Government business was at a standstill, Congress might have felt it to be its duty to ascertain whether in respect to the President the condition described by Article II., Section 5, of the Constitution as 'inability to discharge the powers and duties of the said office' actually existed. Had constitutional inability been ascertained and declared, the powers and duties of the President's office would at once have been devolved on the Vice President. That eventuality, we are very sure, would have been much more distasteful to President Wilson than Secretary Lansing's temporary and, as it seems to us and to the people of the country, absolutely necessary assumption of the power to bring the Cabinet members together in informal conferences." *Ibid.,* February 15, 1920.

See also Secretary of Commerce Redfield's astonished comment on the President's action. *Ibid.,* February 17, 1920.

The question remains whether Mr. Lansing's action amounts to a usurpation of presidential function. The precedents are few and of uncertain bearing. Secretary Blaine called Cabinet meetings during Garfield's illness, and Secretary Knox during an absence of President Taft from Washington; also, the Cabinet met during the Boxer troubles at a time when President McKinley was absent from the Capital. But it does not appear that on any of these occasions presidential approval was lacking. Nor is it to the point, as some of Mr. Wilson's critics seemed to think it was, that members of the Cabinet are sometimes required by statute to consult with one another. Thus, the Grain Futures Act of 1922 is administered in part by a commission consisting of the Secretaries of Agriculture and Commerce and the Attorney General, and the Council of National Defense is made up of the Secretaries of War, Navy, Interior, Agriculture, Commerce, and Labor. In short, Lansing acted without the backing of substantial precedent in a situation that was also without precedent.

The question of Mr. Wilson's "inability" was once raised in court. This was when the government attorneys, in the suit to upset the Alien Property Custodian's sale of German dye and chemical patents to the Chemical Foundation, asked the United States district court at Wilmington to take notice of the fact that when President Wilson signed the order approving the sale, he was a sick man. *The New York Times,* October 30, 1923. The sale was upheld.

[39] The story of Tyler's succession is graphically told in Henry W. Horwill's *Usages of the American Constitution* (Oxford, 1925), pp. 69–74.

[40] *Ibid.,* p. 75.

[41] The Hon. Leslie M. Shaw, as quoted in *The New York Times,* February 9, 1927.

[42] Horwill, pp. 58–66.

[43] Mr. Horwill also urges the fact that in the states of the Australian Commonwealth,

when a governor leaves his state temporarily or becomes ill, the lieutenant-governor administers the government in the interval, but does not become governor. *Ibid.*, p. 67. He might have added that a like practice prevails in the states of the United States. By way of illustration see a decision of the Oklahoma Supreme Court on the point which is mentioned in *The New York Times*, February 20, 1927. It is possible too that Mr. Horwill might have bolstered his grammatical argument by stressing the verb "devolve" in the constitutional clause. At least, it is the opinion of Mr. John Brook Leavitt that an "office" *passes,* but that "powers and duties" *devolve. Ibid.,* August 11, 1923. See also Fessenden's *Fessenden* (New York, 1907), II, 246–247.

44 Nevertheless, it was the opinion of Webster that there could be no temporary succession by the Vice-President, but that even though the President recovered from his "inability," the Vice-President, having once assumed the powers and duties of the presidential office, would continue to the end of the term for which both were elected. This, of course, was before the Twentieth Amendment, but it serves to strengthen the argument that the Vice-President was originally expected to succeed to the "office" and not merely its "powers and duties." See Thomas Ewing in *The New York Times,* December 10, 1921.

45 Stressing those powers and duties of the President which can be best performed at the seat of government, former Attorney General Wickersham was strongly of the opinion that Mr. Wilson's absence abroad would amount to "inability" in the constitutional sense, and suggested that the Vice-President could be compelled by mandamus to exercise the powers and duties of the presidential office while the "inability" continued. In the latter connection he cited *Attorney General v. Taggart,* 66 N. H. 362, a state case. At the same time he admitted that this would be "rather an unsatisfactory remedy." Mr. Wickersham was answered by Mr. Samuel Untermeyer and Mr. Louis Marshall, who pointed out that the President had powers and duties which might well take him abroad, namely, as Commander-in-Chief and as treaty maker, and that therefore the Constitution must have contemplated his occasional absence from the seat of government. *The New York Times, supra.* Nor did Vice-President Marshall agree with Mr. Wickersham, as the following despatch in *The Sun* of December 10, 1918, indicates:

"The first Cabinet meeting directed to a certain extent by wireless from mid-ocean was held in the White House today, with Vice President Marshall officiating in the President's absence. It lasted one hour and a half and by all reports had many novel features, though the business of the nation was transacted in the usual way. So far as the records go no other Vice-President ever has presided at a Cabinet meeting.

"A wireless message from the George Washington asked Vice-President Marshall if he would preside and the latter assumed his temporary duty as acting President. At the outset of the meeting the Vice President said:

" 'Gentlemen: In assuming the chair and presiding over what is known as a meeting of the Cabinet, I deem it proper to make a brief statement so that my conduct may not be misunderstood or misinterpreted. I am here and am acting in obedience to a request preferred by the President upon the eve of his departure and also at your request. But I am here informally. I am not undertaking to exercise any official duty or function. I shall preside in an unofficial and informal way over your meetings out of deference to your desires and those of the President.'

"Mr. Marshall astonished his audience by saying he had been much interested and concerned over the various opinions offered by constitutional lawyers as to whether he was or was not rightfully entitled to Mr. Wilson's job. Not knowing just where he stood, he said, he had written to Newt Plum, a constable in Indiana, to ask his advice. In reply he had received a message saying: 'The President by leaving the country loses his office but retains his salary.'

" 'Under these conditions,' the Vice-President said, 'I don't want to have anything to do with the office.'

"A report of the day's proceedings will be sent to the President either by wireless or cable after he reaches France."

On Washington's refusal to enter Rhode Island before she entered the Union, see Jared Sparks, *Life of Washington* (Boston, 1839), pp. 421, 429; and see generally David Hunter Miller's article on "Some Legal Aspects of the Visit of President Wilson to Paris," 36 *Harvard Law Review*, 51–78 (November, 1921). While it seems not to have occurred to Washington, in connection with any of his numerous tours, to ask Adams to act for him during his absence, an unwritten rule later developed that when the President was on an extended jaunt, the Vice-President should hover in the neighborhood of the Capitol. But even this rule was violated in October 1935 when both President and Vice-President were out of the country. *The New York Times,* October 17, 1935.

[46] Richardson, VII, 364–366.

[47] U. S. Code, tit. 3, §21. For an excellent discussion of the act against its historical and constitutional background, see Charles S. Hamlin, "The Presidential Succession Act of 1886," 18 *Harvard Law Review,* 182–195 (1905).

[48] Although no President has ever resigned, Mr. Wilson contemplated doing so if Mr. Hughes was elected in 1916. Says Mr. Lansing, in a "most confidential" communication, "the President . . . suggested the following plan: In the event of his defeat he would ask me to resign as Secretary of State and then he would name Mr. Hughes as my successor; as soon as the latter had assumed office, Mr. Wilson himself would resign as President, and Mr. Marshall, the Vice-President, would also resign; thus Mr. Hughes would succeed to the Presidency by reason of his holding the office of Secretary of State." R. S. Baker, *Woodrow Wilson,* VI, 292–293.

Later, during the fight over the Treaty of Versailles, the suggestion was made in certain quarters that both Mr. Wilson and Mr. Marshall should resign, thus bringing Secretary of State Lansing into the succession, whereupon Mr. Lansing would summon Congress into session, in accordance with the provisions of the Act of 1886, and it would proceed to call a special election, which would amount to a popular referendum on the Treaty of Versailles. Indeed, after the election of 1920, which Mr. Wilson asserted would be just such a referendum, and "a great and solemn" one, Mr. Bryan called upon Mr. Wilson to resign, after first making Mr. Harding Secretary of State. *New York Tribune,* November 5, 1920.

The possibility of a President's resigning is dealt with in a provision of the Act of March 1, 1792, which in substance still remains on the statute books:

"Resignation or refusal of office. The only evidence of a refusal to accept, or of a resignation of the office of President or Vice President, shall be an instrument in writing, declaring the same and subscribed by the person refusing to accept, or resigning, as the case may be, and delivered into the office of the Secretary of State." U. S. Code, tit. 3, §23.

On Calhoun's resignation from the Vice-Presidency December 28, 1832, see an interesting note by Professor Everett S. Brown in 22 *American Political Science Review,* 732–733 (August, 1928).

[49] Professor Brown points out still another possible situation under the Twentieth

Amendment for which legislative provision is desirable. He says:

"The Twentieth Amendment to the Constitution brought an end to 'lame duck' Congresses, but, paradoxically, it made possible 'lame duck' Presidents. Although attention was called to this contingency when the proposed amendment was under discussion in Congress, little has been said about it since.

"Let us suppose that a Republican President is elected in the forthcoming election, as well as a Republican House of Representatives. According to the provisions of the amendment just quoted, the new Congress would meet at noon on Jan. 3, 1937, while President Roosevelt would remain in office until noon of Jan. 20. During the period of two weeks between Jan. 3 and Jan. 20 the President would be a 'lame duck' President. It is likely that he would merely mark time, awaiting the inauguration of his successor.

"However, the difficulty is not thus easily averted. The Budget and Accounting Act of 1921 provides that the President shall transmit the budget to Congress on the first day of each regular session. If the law were carried into effect, the budget would be presented on Jan. 3 by the lame duck President, whose term would not expire until Jan. 20. Most assuredly this arrangement would not be satisfactory. . . .

"Formerly, when the President took office on March 4 and Congress did not meet in regular session until December, there was ample time in which to prepare the budget. Under the law the heads of departments must submit their departmental estimates to the Bureau of the Budget on or before Sept. 15.

"All of this is changed by the Twentieth Amendment. Unless the incoming President accepts the estimates of the outgoing one, he must be allowed sufficient time for the organization of his administration prior to the preparation of the budget." *The New York Times,* December 29, 1935.

In a letter dated February 20, 1940, Professor Brown informs me that the House the previous day passed and sent to the Senate a bill providing that in inauguration years when a President does not succeed himself the budget shall not be submitted earlier than January 21 or later than February 20.

In view of some of the things just said in the text it is pertinent to recall certain principles of the common law respecting public office. I quote another communication to the *Times:* "The United States is a corporation in a legal sense, as are all the individual States (*United States v. Maurice,* 2 Brock, 96, 109, by Chief Justice Marshall; *Respublica v. Sweers,* 1 Dall. 41; *Dugan v. U. S.,* 3 Wheat. 172; *State of Indiana v. Woram,* 6 Hill (N. Y.) 33, 38). It is, of course, the general rule as to all corporations that, in the absence of some positive law, charter or by-law to the contrary, the president continues in office until his successor is elected and qualifies (7 *Ruling Case Law* 427; 14a *Corpus Juris* 72). It is also the general rule that public officers, in the absence of any constitutional or statutory prohibition, hold over after the conclusion of their terms until their successors are elected and qualify (22 *Ruling Case Law* 554; *Jones v. Roberts County,* 27 So. Dak. 519). In particular, such is the rule with regard to the governor of a state (*Carr v. Wilson,* 32 W. Va. 419). The supreme court of appeals of West Virginia, in the case cited, decided, in 1889, that the provisions of the constitution of West Virginia expressly limiting the term of governor to four years and making him ineligible to re-election did not prevent him from continuing to discharge the duties of his office after his term and pending the decision of a contested election of a successor. It is particularly significant that the constitution in question expressly made the governor ineligible for a second term of four years, yet the court held that such clause did not operate to create a vacancy in the office of governor at the expiration of the term. The Constitution of the United States merely provides affirmatively that the President, 'shall hold office during the term of four years,' and nowhere therein can language be found expressly negativing a term of longer duration than four years or making the President ineligible for a second or third or greater term of office." John Edmund Hewitt, *loc. cit.*, December 14, 1924.

50 See Percy Ernst Schramm, *History of the English Coronation* (Legg, tr.; Oxford, 1937), pp. 179–227. Coke's remark in Sutton's Hospital Case, 10 Rep. 23a (1615) is also good indirect evidence: "A thing which is not *in esse* but in apparent expectancy is regarded in law; as a Bishop who is elected before he is consecrated; an infant in his mother's womb before birth." Had he regarded an uncrowned king as falling in the same class, Coke could not have failed to mention the fact.

The Hon. David R. Atchison's claim, therefore, that as President *pro tem* of the Senate he was "President *de jure* of the United States" a single day, namely Sunday, March 4, 1849, in consequence of General Taylor's refusal to take the oath of office on the Sabbath, must be disallowed.

The taking of the presidential oath once at least occurred in highly picturesque circumstances. The following despatch to *The New York Times* of August 3, 1923, tells the story:

"Plymouth, Vt., Aug. 3.—Facing his father and with his wife at his side, Calvin Coolidge was sworn in as the thirtieth President of the United States at 2:43 this morning, standard time, in the parlor of the Coolidge homestead, directly across the road from the house in which he was born.

"The President's father, John Calvin Coolidge, 78 years old, like his son, of stalwart New England stock, administered the oath of office. It was the first time in the history of the Republic that a father installed his son as the Chief Executive of the nation.

"The ceremony took place in a typical New England parlor or sitting room, a comfortably furnished, livable room in the father's farm house at Plymouth Notch, in the southern part of the Green Mountains, nearly 2,000 feet above the level of the sea.

"The faint light of an old-fashioned kerosene lamp, with a fluted top chimney and etched sides, was sufficient to throw the faces of the President and his father into bold relief. The rest of the small group that witnessed the simple ceremony were in a half light, almost a shadow. Back of the President was a large framed portrait of himself, which occupies the position of honor in his father's home.

"The President's father, sturdy and active despite his years, stood at the south side of a small centre table that held the lamp, the family bible and a number of other books. . . .

"It was an impressive sight when Mr. Coolidge took his place opposite his father. The President's face was pale. His bearing was marked by the simple dignity and poise which has characterized him all through the difficult period of President Harding's illness.

"The elder Coolidge, who bears a marked resemblance to his son and has the same immobility of features, asked the President to raise his right hand. The President did so, and his father then read him the following oath, prescribed by the Constitution of the United States, the form of which had been received by telegraph and telephone only a few minutes before from Washington.

" 'I do solemnly swear that I will faithfully execute the office of President of the United States and I will to the best of my ability preserve, protect and defend the Constitution of the United States.'

"The President repeated the oath after his father. There was a tense moment as he paused, with hand still uplifted, and added in a voice deep with feeling: 'So help me God.' "

On his return to Washington, however, Mr. Coolidge took the precaution to be sworn in a second time, the oath on this occasion being administered by Justice Hoehling of the supreme court of the District of Columbia, in a room of the New Willard Hotel, and a Gideon Bible was used. Attorney-General Daugherty pledged the justice to secrecy, and the transaction was not divulged till more than eight years later. *The New York Times,* December 3, 1932. No doubt Mr. Coolidge sensed the superior popular appeal of the original oath, whatever might be its constitutional deficiencies. See also H. B. Learned, "The Vice-President's Oath of Office," *The Nation,* March 1, 1917.

51 As a matter of fact the President enjoys many more "emoluments" from the United States than the "compensation" which he receives "at stated times"—at least, what most people would reckon to be emoluments. See B. Sparkes, "The President's Salary and Other Perquisites," *The Saturday Evening Post,* November 7, 1936.

The above provision is supplemented by Art. I, sec. 9, par. 8, which reads as follows: "No title of nobility shall be granted by the United States; and no person holding any office of profit or trust under them, shall, without the consent of the Congress, accept of any present, emolument, office or title of any kind whatever from any king, prince, or foreign state." But, of course, there are always other members of the family who do not hold "any office of profit or trust" under the United States.

Public taste has not invariably been quite as rigid as it is today as to what favors a President may properly accept from private givers. The following paragraphs from Mr. George Fort Milton's interesting volume, *The Age of Hate* (New York, 1930), are quoted with the consent of the publishers, Coward-McCann, Inc.:

"Early in the summer of 1865 a group of New York bankers and merchants opened a subscription to buy the President a span of horses, a handsome carriage and the requisite accoutrements. Johnson declined the gift in firm though courteous words which met with great approval through the whole country. 'Nothing has given more satisfaction to all patriots and thinking men than your refusal to accept the present,' Senator Dixon wrote from Hartford.

"It seems, however, that Johnson did accept a free insurance policy tendered by the Phoenix Mutual Life Insurance Company. At that time it was the custom of this company to vote policies free of cost to the President, the Vice-President, and Speaker of the National House of Representatives. On January 9, 1865, according to the minute book of the Board of Directors of the Phoenix, 'it was voted that the premiums on policies issued to President Lincoln, Vice President Hamlin, and Speaker Colfax, be tendered them as a gratuity.' On April 17, the minute book records that 'the policy of Andrew Johnson was made free for one year.' According to the legends of the company, Lincoln refused, while Johnson accepted the free policies." *Op. cit.,* p. 232.

52 *Evans v. Gore,* 253 U. S. 245; *Miles v. Graham,* 268 U. S. 501.

53 *O'Malley v. Woodrough,* 307 U. S. 277 (1939).

54 See generally L. C. Hatch and E. L. Shoup, *History of the Vice-Presidency of the United States* (New York, 1934), especially Chs. III–V; also Oliver P. Field, "The Vice-Presidency of the United States," 56 *American Law Review* (1922), 365–400. There have been thirty-two Vice-Presidents, six of whom (Adams, Clinton, Tompkins, Calhoun, Marshall, and Garner) were chosen for a second term, and six of whom (Tyler, Fillmore, Johnson, Arthur, T. Roosevelt, and Coolidge) succeeded to the Presidency in consequence of the death in office of the President. Of the latter group two (T. Roosevelt and Coolidge)

succeeded themselves in the Presidency. Of the remaining Vice-Presidents only three were elected to the Presidency (Adams, Jefferson, and Van Buren), and this occurred in the first half century of the government.

55 Adams was of a bilious and jealous disposition. Jefferson's attitude toward the office was very different. He professed to regard its "tranquil and unoffending" character as a recommendation, as assuring him "philosophical evenings in winter and rural days in summer."

56 It is further characteristic of Adams that the first time he became Vice-President he delivered an Inaugural Address. The custom—perhaps fortunately—died "a-bornin'."

57 Farrand, II, 536–537. A word further concerning Mr. Garner's success in exemplifying the possibilities of the office.

"It is difficult to recall a vice-president since the first 50 years of the republic who has been recognized as so active and influential a leader as Mr. Garner has been, especially during the second term of Mr. Roosevelt and himself. That this state of affairs has been due largely to the widening division in the administration party may be granted. The anti-new deal senators and representatives among the Democrats have found in the vice-president a conservative sympathizer whose long experience in Congress made him most valuable as an adviser and parliamentary strategist.

"Mr. Garner, however, has had the disciplined nerve to assume the extraconstitutional function of an undercover leader in the Senate, although the constitution gives him no seat in that body carrying with it a vote such as the senators themselves are privileged to cast. At the same time, he has continued to sit in at the President's cabinet meetings. So to speak, he has sat on both sides of the table. No other vice-president in our history has managed to do that and get away with it so successfully. Touchy old President Andrew Jackson broke angrily with Vice-President Calhoun. President Roosevelt has never said a cross word to Vice-President Garner, so far as the public knows." *Springfield Republican*, December 16, 1939.

NOTES TO CHAPTER III*

1 In the words of Hamilton in *Federalist* No. 69: "He [the King of Great Britain] not only appoints to all offices, but can create offices." Earle, 451. See further Alpheus Todd, *Parliamentary Government in England* (2nd ed.) (London, 1887), p. 609; *Encyclopaedia Britannica* (11th ed., 1913), XXII, 280; William R. Anson, *Law and Custom of the Constitution* (London, 1892), II, 405–406, 449–450.

2 *United States v. Maurice*, 2 Brock. 96; 26 Fed. Cas. No. 15,747 (1823); 5 *Opins. A. G.* 88 (1849); 10 *ibid.*, 11 (1861); 18 *ibid.*, 171 (1890).

3 *Ex parte* Robinson, 19 Wall. 505, 511 (1873); Chief Justice Taney's opinion in *Gordon v. United States*, 117 U. S. 697, 699 (Appendix). The date of the opinion is 1864.

4 7 *Opins. A. G.* 193–194 (1855).

5 *Infra*, Ch. V.

6 "An office is a public station, or employment, conferred by the appointment of government. The term embraces the idea of tenure, duration, emolument and duties." *United States v. Hartwell*, 6 Wall. 385, 393 (1868). The term is often used, nevertheless, to comprehend any public employment even of the most transitory nature, as in the fol-

---

* Chapter III (*Administrative Chief*) begins on page 64.

lowing dictum of a state court: "The essence of it is the duty of performing an agency, that is, of doing some act or acts, or series of acts for the State." See generally Floyd R. Mechem, *The Law of Public Offices and Officers*, pp. 1–3; also *People v. Tremaine*, 252 N. Y. 27 (1929) and cases there cited. It should be noted that the weight of congressional opinion seems to condemn acceptance by a Senator or Representative of any post which has been created by act of Congress, however lacking in other respects such post is in the tests of an office as set forth in the above quotation from the Hartwell Case. See Willoughby, I, 606; *Senate Reports* No. 563, 67th Cong., 2nd sess., March, 1922.

7 *Theodore Roosevelt, An Autobiography* (New York, 1913), pp. 365–369. Cited hereafter as *Autobiography*. The original inventor of this practice, however, seems to have been President Tyler, who in 1841 appointed a nonstatutory commission to conduct an investigation of the New York Customs House. His action led to a demand by the House of Representatives that he inform it under what authority the commission "was raised." Tyler answered by citing his duty to "take care that the laws be faithfully executed." Richardson, V, 99–100.

8 27 *Opins. A. G.* 309, 310 (1910).

9 *Autobiography*, pp. 416–417.

10 34 *Current History*, 491 (1931).

11 U. S. Code, tit. 40, §401; Resolution of June 21, 1938, c. 554; 52 Stat. 817. The idea was borrowed from the Lever Food and Fuel Control Act, passed during the war with Germany.

12 Clarence A. Berdahl, *War Powers of the Executive of the United States* (1921), pp. 197–200, 211–212. President F. D. Roosevelt's recent action (see Washington despatches of October 17, 1939) in designating Lieut. Col. Philip B. Fleming of the Engineer Corps to be "assistant to the acting Wages and Hours Administrator" in succession to Administrator Elmer Andrews is not so readily explicable. The Fair Labor Standards Act of 1938 provides only for an Administrator, not for an "acting Administrator" (U. S. Code, tit. 29, §§201 ff.). Perhaps the President's reliance was upon his power as Commander-in-Chief, since it was explained at the time that Colonel Fleming was "to remain on the active army list," and that there would consequently be no nomination to the Senate. It is true that Congress has from time to time authorized the President or the Secretary of War to detail officers, or even enlisted men, to special duties; but these were almost always duties closely connected with the military establishment in some way or other, such as to receive instruction in technical schools or industrial laboratories; to give instruction to R.O.T.C. units or to the National Guard; to aid the American Red Cross, or—on their request—the Republics of North, South, and Central America; to render engineering services to the Federal Power Commission or the Mississippi River Commission, and so on. U. S. Code, tit. 10, §§105, 106, 291b, 292c, 386, 535, 540, 541, 1063, 1067, 1072–1076, 1171–1181, 1454; tit. 16, §793; tit. 25, §§27, 273; tit. 32, §§649, 183; tit. 33, §647; tit. 36, §121; tit. 43, §33.

Not only, however, was Colonel Fleming's assignment without statutory warrant of any kind—wherein it differed from that of Colonel F. C. Harrington as WPA Administrator (see Washington despatches of December 24, 1938)—but it was to duties lacking any relationship with his military position and training. In short, the President appears by one and the same act: (1) to have created a new office out of hand; (2) to have filled it without recourse to the Senate; (3) to have set a precedent that would enable his successors gradually to replace the whole civil establishment with army officers. Perhaps it is fortunate that he seems subsequently to have reconsidered his position. For Washington despatches of December 1, 1939, state that he has extended an *ad interim* appointment to Mr. Harold D. Jacobs, a civilian, to the post of Wages and Hours Administrator, "with the idea that he will serve until Congress removes a statutory ban preventing the nomination [to the Senate?] of Lieut. Col. Philip B. Fleming, an army officer." *The New York Times,* December 2, 1939. As a matter of fact, no such *ban* exists upon the appointment of Colonel Fleming to the vacant post, the statute referred to in the despatch having to do only with the assignment of "retired officers" to duty (U. S. Code, tit. 10, §990). The ban on Colonel Fleming's assignment arose from the fact (1) that the nature of his new duties made the assignment as to him a new office; and (2) that Congress had not authorized any such assignment. But anyway, the President seems to have retired from a totally untenable position.

Since the above was written Colonel Fleming has been appointed Wages and Hours Administrator under legislation permitting him to assume a civilian post. Associated Press despatch, February 19, 1940.

¹³ In *Marbury v. Madison* Marshall concedes that in the case of officers appointed by the President with the consent of the Senate, appointment and commissioning are practically indistinguishable and declines to say whether the latter completes the former or is merely evidence of it. 1 Cr. 137, 156–157. It is not surprising, therefore, that cases have occurred in which the President, by withholding the commission, refused to complete an appointment to which the Senate had consented. 12 *Opins. A. G.* 41 (1866); *ibid.,* 306 (1867). In the case, on the other hand, of officers whose appointment is vested by act of Congress in the heads of departments, appointment and commissioning are distinct, since the latter has, by the requirement of the Constitution, to be by the President. Yet even such officers are covered by the legislative provision that their commissions shall not have the seal of the department affixed to them "before the same shall have been signed by the President of the United States" (U. S. Code, tit. 5, § 11), which seems well designed to leave with the President the final say whether the appointment shall be consummated.

¹⁴ On this and other constitutional questions raised by Justice Black's appointment, see Dudley O. McGovney, "Is Hugo L. Black a Supreme Court Justice De Jure?" 26 *California Law Review* 1–32 (1937). For a recent decision of the Supreme Court of Washington sustaining the thesis of eligibility in a case closely paralleling Justice Black's, see *State ex rel. Todd v. Reeves,* 196 Wash. 175 (1938).

¹⁵ Willoughby, *op. cit.,* I, 607.

¹⁶ See in this connection Madison's message of July 6, 1813, to the Senate, rejecting a suggestion that he confer with a committee of the Senate respecting a nomination. "The Executive and the Senate," said he, "in the cases of appointments and of treaties, are to be considered as independent of and coordinate with each other," and the appointment of a committee by the latter to confer with the former lost sight of the nature of this relationship. Richardson, I, 531. On the other hand, Mr. Roosevelt, in the controversy referred to in note 18, below, took occasion to state that all Presidents had recognized "that the constitutional procedure is for the President to receive advice, i.e., recommendations from Senators." *The New York Times,* February 8, 1939. In writing this the President conceded considerably more than he need have. At least, I know of no other authority for according the "recommendations" of individual Senators any higher status than those of Representatives, or indeed of private citizens. Besides, Senators generally make their recommendations prior to nomination, a stage in the procedure of appointment with which the Constitution does not associate them. *Vd.* note 31 *infra.*

¹⁷ Richardson, I, 58.

18 Earle, 494; Farrand, II, 523. "Senatorial courtesy"—in part an outgrowth of the secrecy of senatorial proceedings in executive session—was one of the early indications that the effort of the Constitution to make the Senate an executive council was not going to jell. See on the whole subject Professor George H. Haynes's admirable *The Senate of the United States* (New York, 1938), I, 54; II, 736–749; also 33 *Illinois Law Review,* 809–819 (1939).

In the case of nominees to Cabinet posts the operation of "senatorial courtesy" is almost but not quite automatic. Taney was rejected for Secretary of the Treasury in 1834; three Tyler nominees were rejected in 1843 and 1844; and one Johnson nominee in 1868. The latest victim of senatorial wrath was Charles B. Warren, whose nomination by President Coolidge to the Attorney Generalship was rejected in March, 1925.

A passing word should be given the recent controversy between President Roosevelt and Senators Glass and Byrd of Virginia, growing out of the Senate's rejection of the President's nominee, Judge Floyd H. Roberts, for a Federal judgeship in that state. The President, in a letter to Judge Roberts, charged the Senators who invoked "senatorial courtesy" on this occasion with "usurping" the presidential power of nominating to office. Actually, it would seem that what happened—as in all such cases—was a temporary abdication by the *Senate* to one or two of its members of its participation in the appointing power. On the other hand, Senator Glass, in his answer to the President, was able to adduce facts which went some way to show that the President, in an effort to "purge" the Virginia Senators, had for the time being abdicated his nominating power to Governor Price and other political foes of Senators Glass and Byrd. *The New York Times,* February 8 and 9, 1939.

19 On this point, examine the vast mass of data brought together in Justice Brandeis's dissenting opinion in *Myers v. United States* and accompanying notes. 272 U. S., 52, 264–274. Hundreds of statutory provisions are cited. "Thus," the opinion summarizes, "Congress has, from time to time, restricted the president's selection by the requirement of citizenship [some thirty distinct acts of Congress]. It has limited the power of nomination by providing that the office may be held only by a resident of the United States [Act of Mar. 1, 1855, c. 133, dealing with ministers and their subordinates]; of a state [one act]; of a particular state [five acts]; of a particular district [two acts]; of a particular territory [three acts]; of the District of Columbia [Act of May 3, 1802, and four other acts]; of a particular foreign country [one act]. It has limited the power of nomination further by prescribing professional attainments [some fifty-six acts and joint resolutions], or occupational experience [eighteen acts and joint resolutions]. It has, in other cases, prescribed the test of examinations [seven acts, including the Civil Service Act of Jan. 16, 1883, c. 27, sec. 2, and the Foreign Service Act of May 24, 1924, c. 182, sec. 5]. It has imposed the requirement of age [three acts]; of sex [two acts]; of race [one act]; of property [Act of Mar. 26, 1804, c. 38, sec. 4, legislative council of Louisiana, to be selected from holders of realty]; and of habitual temperance in the use of intoxicating liquors [one act—repeated, perchance, by the Eighteenth Amendment]. Congress has imposed like restrictions on the power of nomination by requiring political representation [eighteen acts, including those organizing the interstate commerce and federal trade commissions]; or that the selection be made on a nonpartisan basis [twenty-three acts]. It has required, in some cases, that the representation be industrial [six acts]; in others that it be geographic [seventeen acts and joint resolutions]. It has at times required that the President's nominees be taken from, or include representatives from, particular branches or departments

of the government [twenty-six acts and joint resolutions]. By still other statutes, congress has confined the president's selection to a small number of persons to be named by others [five acts, including act of February 23, 1920, c. 91, sec. 304, requiring that the railroad labor board consist of three to be appointed from six nominees by employees, and three to be appointed from six nominees by carriers]."

Cf. an opinion by Attorney General Sargent advising against a similar feature of the McNary-Haugen bill, *The New York Times,* February 26, 1927; also a protest by President Harding against a proposal to require that one member of the Federal Reserve Board be "a farmer." *Ibid.,* February 6, 1922.

[20] The following item from *The New York Times* of May 20, 1916, affords an illustration:

"Another joker in the Army Reorganization bill is very interesting to those who know of the circumstances connected with it. This joker, slipped into the bill behind the closed doors of the Conference Committee, as jokers frequently are, is contained in a paragraph providing for the appointment of Judge Advocates in the reorganized regular army. Probably there never was more peculiar language employed to frame a joker than that which reads this way: 'Provided further, That of the vacancies created in the Judge Advocate's Department by this act, one such vacancy, not below the rank of Major, shall be filled by the appointment of a person from civil life, not less than forty-five nor more than fifty years of age, who shall have been for ten years a Judge of the Supreme Court of the Philippine Islands, shall have served for two years as a Captain in the regular or volunteer army, and shall be proficient in the Spanish language and laws.'

"The one man in the world that this description seems to fit is Judge Adam C. Carson of the Supreme Court of the Philippine Islands. Judge Carson is now in the United States on leave of absence. His home is at Riverton, Va., in the Congressional district of Representative James Hay, Chairman of the House Committee on Military Affairs, and Chairman of the House conferees on the Army Organization bill. Judge Carson went to Cuba after the Spanish war as an officer of one of the immune regiments. Afterwards he was an officer in the Philippine army which supplemented the work of the regular troops in suppressing the Aguinaldo insurrection. President Taft, while Governor General of the Philippines, appointed him a judge of the Court of First Instance and later he was appointed a judge of the Philippine Supreme Court." Judge Carson got the job.

With this episode should be compared President Arthur's veto, July 2, 1884, of "an act for the relief of Fitz John Porter," the enacting clause of which read as follows:

"That the President be, and he is hereby, authorized to nominate and, by and with the advice and consent of the Senate, to appoint Fitz John Porter, late a major-general of the United States Volunteers and a brevet brigadier-general and colonel of the Army, to the position of colonel in the Army of the United States, of the same grade and rank held by him at the time of his dismissal from the Army by sentence of court-martial promulgated January 27, 1863. . . . " Richardson, VIII, 221.

To this the President objected:

"It is apparent that should this bill become a law it will create a new office which can be filled by the appointment of the particular individual whom it specifies, and cannot be filled otherwise; or it may be said with perhaps greater precision of statement that it will create a new office upon condition that the particular person designated shall be chosen to fill it. Such an act, as it seems to me, is either unnecessary and ineffective or it involves an encroachment by the legislative branch of the Government upon the authority of the Executive. As the Congress has no power under the Constitution to nominate or appoint an officer and cannot lawfully impose upon the President the duty of nominating or appointing to office any particular individual of its own selection, this bill, if it can fairly be construed as requiring the President to make the nomination and, by and with the advice and consent of the Senate, the appointment which it authorizes, is in manifest violation of the Constitution. If such be not its just interpretation, it must be regarded as a mere enactment of advice and counsel, which lacks in the very nature of things the force of a positive law and can serve no useful purpose upon the statute books." *Ibid.*

The veto prevailed. Congress has, nevertheless, repeatedly designated individuals, sometimes by name, more frequently by reference to a particular office, for the performance of specified acts or for posts of a nongovernmental character; e.g., to paint a picture (Jonathan Trumbull), to lay out a town, to act as Regents of Smithsonian Institution (note 40 *infra*), to be managers of Howard Institute, to select a site for a post office or a prison, to restore the manuscript of the Declaration of Independence, to erect a monument at Yorktown, to erect a statue of Hamilton, and so on and so forth. 42 *Harvard Law Review* 426, 430–431.

[21] The above note; also 13 *Opins. A. G.* 516 (1871). In his message of April 13, 1822, President Monroe stated the thesis that, as "a general principle," "Congress have no right under the Constitution to impose any restraint by law on the power granted to the President so as to prevent his making a free selection of proper persons for these [newly created] offices from the whole body of his fellow citizens." Richardson, II, 129, 132. The statement is ambiguous, but its apparent intention is to claim for the President unrestricted power in determining who are "proper persons" to fill newly created offices.

[22] U. S. Code, tit. 5, § 633 (2).

[23] *Ibid.*, tit. 22, §§ 4, 5.

[24] By the Act of June 25, 1938, first-, second-, and third-class postmasters are also brought under the Civil Service Act and Rules, although their original appointment continues to be by the President and Senate. U. S. Code, tit. 39, §§ 31a and b.

[25] *Shoemaker v. United States,* 147 U. S. 283, 301 (1893).

[26] *Ibid.; United States v. Ferreira,* 13 How. 40 (1851); *ex parte* Siebold, 100 U. S. 371 (1879). *Cf.,* however, note 20 *supra.*

[27] *United States v. Germaine,* 99 U. S. 508 (1878) is the leading case. For further citations see *Auffmordt v. Hedden,* 137 U. S. 310 at 327 (1890). The Court will, nevertheless, be astute to ascribe to a head of department an appointment made by an inferior of such head. *Ekiu v. United States,* 142 U. S. 651, 663 (1892). For the view that there is an intrinsic difference between a "public office" and a "public employment," see Mechem, *op. cit.,* pp. 3–5.

[28] On this subject see an extensive correspondence in *The New York Times* for February 12, 19, 21, and 26, and March 12, 1939, which was precipitated by Mr. Carr Van Anda's contention that "inferior officers" comprise all civil officers of the National Government except "ambassadors, other public ministers and consuls," and "judges of the Supreme Court," and that Congress could therefore at any time deprive the President of his appointing power except as to these. Mr. Van Anda relies chiefly on the following statement from the Court's opinion in the Germaine case, cited in the previous note:

"The Constitution for purposes of appointment very clearly divides all its officers into two classes. The primary class requires a nomination by the President and confirmation by the Senate. But foreseeing that when offices became numerous, and sudden removals necessary, this mode might be inconvenient, it was provided that, in regard to officers inferior to those specially mentioned, Congress might by law vest their appointment in the President alone, in the courts of law, or in the heads of departments." 99 U. S. at 509.

The statement is purely *obiter* and is furthermore ambiguous; "the President alone," "the courts of law," and "the heads of departments," are also "specially mentioned." The view adopted in the text is stated by the Court of Claims in the case of *Collins v. United States,* in the following words:

"The word inferior is not here used in that vague, indefinite, and quite inaccurate sense which has been suggested—the sense of petty or unimportant; but it means subordinate or inferior to those officers in whom respectively the power of appointment may be vested—the President, the courts of law, and the heads of departments." 14 Ct. Cls. 568 (1878).

Mr. Van Anda's suggestion that Congress divest the President of a large part of his appointing power is, of course, quite academic so far as officers appointed by him with the Senate's concurrence are concerned, inasmuch as it would at the same time divest the Senate of its part in such appointments. Besides, where could it lodge the appointment of "heads of departments" except with "the President alone"?

However, a question remains—why does the Constitution make specific mention of "ambassadors," etc., and of "judges of the Supreme Court"? Possibly as reflecting the theory mentioned on p. 66; more probably because the original intention of the Framers was to leave the appointment of ambassadors and judges of the Supreme Court to the Senate alone and they were accordingly listed specially for this purpose in the report of the Committee of Detail. Farrand, II, 183.

[29] 286 U. S. 6 (1932); *cf. United States v. Le Baron,* 19 How. 73 (1856).

[30] *The New York Times,* January 11, 1931.

[31] *Writings of James Madison,* IX, 112–113; Earle, 493–494; Adams, *Life and Works of John Adams,* III, 575–576. "The Senate cannot originate an appointment. Its constitutional action is confined to the simple affirmation or rejection of the President's nominations, and such nominations fail when it rejects them. The Senate may suggest conditions and limitations to the President, but it cannot vary those submitted by him, for no appointment can be made except on his nomination, agreed to without qualification or alteration." 3 *Opins. A. G.* 188 (1837). The opinion cites two unsuccessful attempts by the Senate, one in J. Q. Adams's administration, one in Jackson's, to reshape a nomination to a military grade to the advantage of the nominee.

[32] U. S. Code, tit. 4, § 6; *Marbury v. Madison,* 1 Cr. 137 (1803).

[33] 1 *Opins. A. G.* 631 (1823); 2 *ibid.,* 222 (1830); 3 *ibid.,* 673 (1841); 4 *ibid.,* 523 (1846); 10 *ibid.,* 356 (1862); 11 *ibid.,* 179 (1865); 12 *ibid.,* 32 (1866); 12 *ibid.,* 455 (1868); 14 *ibid.,* 563 (1875); 15 *ibid.,* 207 (1877); 16 *ibid.,* 523 (1880); 18 *ibid.,* 28 (1884); 19 *ibid.,* 261 (1889); 26 *ibid.,* 234 (1907); 30 *ibid.,* 314 (1914); 33 *ibid.,* 20 (1921).

In 4 *Opins. A. G.* 361, 363 (1845), the general doctrine was held not to apply to a yet unfilled office which was created during the previous session of Congress, but this distinction is rejected in 12 *ibid.,* 455 (1868); 18 *ibid.,* 28; and 19 *ibid.,* 261.

There have been no fewer than twelve recess appointments to the Supreme Court, and only one of the appointees, John Rutledge, whom Washington appointed as Chief Justice in 1795, was later rejected by the Senate. *The New York Times,* July 29, 1937.

[34] 23 *Opins. A. G.* 599 (1901); 22 *ibid.,* 20 (1898). A "recess" may, however, be

merely "constructive," as when a regular session succeeds immediately upon a special session. It was this kind of situation that gave rise to the once famous Crum incident. See Willoughby, III, 1508–1509.

35 U. S. Code, tit. 5, § 56.

36 The following extracts from a Washington press despatch of December 18, 1914, tell how President Wilson once violated the understanding:

"The Bloom case is unprecedented so far as Senators can recall. John H. Bloom was nominated for postmaster. Five hundred citizens of Devils Lake protested. The charges against Bloom were serious and involved his personal character. The Senate Committee rejected it in August.

"The President then sent to the Senate the nomination of Mrs. Marjorie Bloom, wife of the man whose nomination had been rejected. This nomination was in turn rejected. The President then conferred a recess nomination on Mrs. Bloom as soon as Congress adjourned and she took the office under a commission. Today her name was again sent to the Senate.

"It is probable that when the Senate comes to deal with the case at Devils Lake it may go even further than a formal rejection and refer the nomination of Mrs. Bloom back to the President with a direction to the Secretary of the Senate to call his attention to the fact that the nomination was rejected by the Senate in October and citing the Constitution of the United States, which provides that such nominations shall be made 'by and with the advice and consent of the Senate.' "

What the final dénouement of this episode was, I have not discovered. The Senate has occasionally confirmed nominees whom it originally rejected, upon the nomination being renewed. Willoughby, III, 1508.

37 6 Opins. A. G. 358 (1854); 12 ibid., 41 (1866); 25 ibid., 259 (1904); 28 ibid., 95 (1909). Probably the most extreme case on record of the assignment of a person—and one apparently without official status at the time—to the duties of an absent official, occurred in Jefferson's second term. Henry Adams tells the story in his History as follows:

"When Congress met, Dec. 2, 1805, Breckenridge was attorney-general under a temporary commission, and Robert Smith who had ceased to be Secretary of the Navy on the confirmation of his successor, March 3, was acting as secretary under no apparent authority. Dec. 20, 1805, the President sent a message to the Senate making nominations for vacancies which had occurred during the recess, for which commissions had been granted 'to the persons herein respectively named.' One of these persons was John Breckenridge of Kentucky to be Attorney-General of the United States, and the nomination was duly confirmed. Breckenridge's permanent commission bore date Jan. 17, 1806.

"These dates and facts are curious for the reason that Robert Smith, who had ceased to be Secretary of the Navy, March 3, 1805, ceased necessarily to be attorney-general on the confirmation of Breckenridge, and continued to act as Secretary of the Navy without authority of law. The President did not send his name to the Senate, or issue to him a new commission either permanent or temporary. On the official records of the Department of State, not Robert Smith, but Jacob Crowninshield, was Secretary of the Navy from March 3, 1805, till March 7, 1809, when his successor was appointed, although Jacob Crowninshield died April 15, 1808, and Robert Smith never ceased to act as Secretary of the Navy from his appointment in 1801 to his appointment as Secretary of State in 1809. During the whole period of Jefferson's second administration, his Secretary of the Navy acted by no known authority except the verbal request or permission of the

President." *History of the United States* (New York, 1893), III, 11–12. Adams might have added that from March 4, 1803, till his death in 1808, Crowninshield was a member of Congress. I must say, the story seems to me rather fishy. For legislation governing this matter today, see U. S. Code, tit. 5, §§ 4–8.

38 The outstanding cases of the President exercising his prerogatives directly are Washington's commanding in the field at the time of the "Whiskey Rebellion" (see p. 194 *supra*), and Wilson's attendance at the Versailles Peace Conference.

39 7 Opins. A. G. 453, 464–465 (1855).

40 *Williams v. United States,* 1 How. 290, 297 (1843). By the Act of August 19, 1846 (9 Stat. 102), as amended, the President, Vice-President, the Chief Justice, and the heads of the executive departments are constituted the Smithsonian Institution, over whose meetings "the President, and in his absence the Vice-President, shall preside." U. S. Code, tit. 20, §§ 41 and 45. This is doubtless a personal duty, but not a very arduous one. Earlier, expenditures from the secret-service fund had to be vouched for by the President personally (2 Stat. 78), but this provision has long since dropped out of the statute book.

The New York Times of March 12, 1923, contained the following item:

"A little less than two years ago Judson C. Welliver, executive clerk at the White House, stepped across the corridor which separates his office from that of President Harding to place some papers on the President's desk. To his surprise, for it was but a few minutes after 8 o'clock in the morning, he found the President already seated and busily signing papers from a two-foot stack.

" 'Good morning, Mr. President,' Mr. Welliver said. 'I didn't know you had come to the office.'

" 'Yes, I came in just now,' the President replied. 'I had a lot of papers to sign, and thought I might as well get them out of the way.'

" 'Anything important?'

" 'Yes and no,' said the President. 'I am beginning to find out something about being President and the amount of time it demands. You can hardly imagine what I am doing now. This stack of papers is just so much routine. They are the wills of Indians. The President has to countersign the will of every Indian with whom the Government has dealings. If the will is not so countersigned it is null and void. And so I expect to put in the next hour or so countersigning these wills.'

" 'But can't someone else sign them for you?' Mr. Welliver inquired.

" 'No; not under the law. There are only two—possibly three—persons in the United States authorized to sign the President's name. They are employees of the General Land Office and they sign the President's name, under certain safeguards and precautions, to the patents granted by that office. But there is no one else who may do so.'

" 'I am beginning to find out,' Mr. Harding went on, 'that this job of being President is one that makes almost inordinate demands upon a man's time.' "

I can find no justification in the U. S. Code for the statement that the President is required to sign the wills of Indians; that seems to be the duty of the Secretary of the Interior. *Ibid.,* tit. 25, §373. The statement, however, that the President's name is affixed to land patents by authorized clerks of the General Land Office is correct. *Ibid.,* tit. 43, §§ 8, 9. Originally it had to be affixed by the President himself. 1 Stat. 109 (April 10, 1790).

41 *Runkle v. United States,* 122 U. S. (1887). By the theory of the case the President was in this instance exercising a judicial, and hence nondelegable function; from which

it followed that his approval of the decree "must be authenticated in a way to show" that it was "the result of his own judgment." *Cf. in re Chapman*, 166 U.S. 661 (1897), and other cases there cited as establishing that "the presumptions in favor of official action . . . preclude collateral attack on the sentences of courts-martial." Confirmation by the President of sentences of courts-martial is still required in several instances. U.S.Code, tit. 10, § 1519. How this may be shown, however, still remains a question, in view of the Chapman Case.

42 *Wilcox v. Jackson,* 13 Pet. 498 (1839); *United States v. Eliason,* 16 Pet. 291 (1842); *Williams v. United States,* 1 How. 290 (1843); The Confiscation Cases, 20 Wall. 92 (1874); *Wolsey v. Chapman,* 101 U.S. 755 (1879); 7 *Opins. A. G.* 479 (1855).

43 *Ibid.,* 470.

44 *Writings of James Madison,* V, 392; also 398, 401, 402, etc., where he insists upon the *unity* of the Executive Department; although in other passages (*ibid.,* 362, 364, 399– 400), he seems to regard the power of removal as primarily a power to get rid of malfeasant subordinates. Hamilton's position in *The Federalist* is not entirely clear of doubt either. In No. 70 (Earle, p. 455), he insists upon the value of *unity* in the Executive, and in No. 72 he writes as follows:

"The administration of government, in its largest sense, comprehends all the operations of the body politic, whether legislative, executive, or judiciary; but in its most usual and perhaps in its most precise signification, it is limited to execuive details, and falls peculiarly within the province of the executive department. The actual conduct of foreign negotiations, the preparatory plans of finance, the application and disbursement of the public moneys in conformity to the general appropriations of the legislature, the arrangement of the army and navy, the direction of the operations of war,—these, and other matters of a like nature, constitute what seems to be most properly understood by the administration of government. The persons, therefore, to whose immediate management these different matters are committed, ought to be considered as the assistants or deputies of the chief magistrate, and on this account, they ought to derive their offices from his appointment, at least from his nomination, and ought to be subject to his superintendence." Earle, pp. 468–469.

The removal power, on the other hand, he divided between the President and the Senate. *Ibid.,* 497. Later, as Secretary of the Treasury, Hamilton regarded himself as standing in a very immediate relation to Congress. Says H. C. Lodge: "He could not rid himself of the idea that he was really the prime minister, a notion encouraged by the way in which Congress had thrown all sorts of questions into his hands for decision." *Alexander Hamilton* (Boston, 1898), p. 156.

45 Act of September 2, 1789, c. 12, § 2; U.S. Code, tit. 5, § 242.

46 *Cf.* U.S. Code, tit. 5, §§ 156, 190, 361, 412, 481, 485.

47 1 Cr. 137, 165–166 (1803).

48 1 *Opins. A. G.* 624 (1828). Wirt continued: "To interpret this [the "take care"] clause so as to throw upon the President the duty of personal interference in every specific case of an alleged or defective execution of the laws, and to call upon him to perform such duties himself, would not only be to require him to perform an impossibility himself, but to take upon himself the responsibility of all the subordinate executive officers of the government—a construction too absurd to be seriously contended for." See also 4 *ibid.,* 515 (1846); 5 *ibid.,* 287 (1851) and 630 (1852); 11 *ibid.,* 109 (1864); 15 *ibid.,* 94 (1876); etc. "The President has, under the Constitution and laws, certain duties

to perform, among these being to take care that the laws be faithfully executed; that is, that the other executive and administrative officers of the government faithfully perform their duties; but the statutes regulate and prescribe these duties, and he has no more power to add to, or subtract from, the duties imposed upon subordinate executive and administrative officers by the law, than those officers have to add to or subtract from his duties." 19 *ibid.*, 686 (1890). The decision of a United States consular officer refusing a visa to an alien may not be overruled by a Cabinet officer. *United States ex rel. Ulrich v. Kellogg,* 30 F. (2nd) 984 (1929). See further note 58 *infra;* also note 90.

49 See generally Mary L. Hinsdale, *A History of the President's Cabinet* (Ann Arbor, 1911); and Henry B. Learned, *The President's Cabinet* (New Haven, 1912).

For firsthand Cabinet interiors see the *Memoirs of John Quincy Adams* (Philadelphia, 1874–1877); *Diary of James K. Polk During His Presidency* (Chicago, 1910); *The Diary of Gideon Welles* (Chicago, 1911); and other similar works listed by William E. Binkley in his *The Powers of the President*, pp. 311–324.

50 Art. 1, § 2, par. 1. This clause is the modest residuum of numerous efforts in the Convention of 1787 to load the President with a "Council of State." H. B. Learned, *op. cit.*, ch. III. An "exclusive" construction of Art. 1, § 2, par. 1, such as was applied in *Marbury v. Madison* to the opening clause of Art. III, § 2, par. 1, defining the Supreme Court's original jurisdiction, would render the Cabinet "unconstitutional."

51 Learned, p. 127. Even at this time, however, written opinions of the heads of departments—and especially those of Hamilton and Jefferson—were of great importance in illuminating the presidential mind. See Marshall, *Life of Washington* (1807), V, 403 ff.

52 For a reliable although rather caustic narrative of the episode, see W. G. Sumner, *Andrew Jackson* (Boston, 1899).

53 Wyman, Willoughby, Fairlie, Finley, and Sanderson all seem to take this general position. Wyman's language is as follows: "This account of this event is worth a hundred cases from the law reports. The President, it appears, has the power in all matters whatsoever to force any officer whatsoever to do any act which the officer has the power to do. He can dictate in all matters because of his power of instant dismissal, without giving reasons therefor, and thereupon the right to immediate appointment without limitation therein. . . . Might makes Right. *Whatever the superior commands will be done by the inferior.* Because of this sanction, an administration which is centralized in its organization will always prove to be centralized in action." Bruce Wyman, *Principles of the Administrative Law* (St. Paul, 1903), p. 233.

54 Richardson, III, 79–80.

55 12 Pet. 524 (1838).

56 *Ibid.*, 539–540.

57 The following extract from the argument for Kendall is worth quoting:

"The argument of the postmaster general, and of the attorney general, assumes that the post office department is an essential part of the executive department of the government; and from this position infers the want of the jurisdiction claimed. The assumption has been shown to be inaccurate; but even if true, it is not easy to perceive the connection between the premises and the conclusion.

"We are referred to the debates in the convention, to show the anxiety of that body to preserve separate and distinct the three great departments. I will, in return, refer to the 47th and to the succeeding numbers of the Federalist, for a correct exposition of this maxim of political philosophy, and its practical adoption in our constitution.

"Starting from this basis, the constitution is appealed to; and by the aid of some interpolation and some extravagant interpretation, we are told substantially, if not in terms:

"1. That the clause in the constitution which provides that the executive power shall be vested in the President, actually confers upon him all that power which, in any age of the world and under any form of government, has been vested in the chief executive functionary; whether king or czar, emperor or dictator.

"2. That the clause which imposes upon the executive the duty of seeing that the laws are faithfully executed, contains another large grant of power.

"3. That, as a means to the performance of this duty, he is invested with the power of appointment to and removal from office.

"4. That the power of appointment and removal carried with it the power to direct, instruct, and control every officer over whom it may be exercised, as to the manner in which he shall perform the duties of his office.

"My observations upon these points shall be few and brief:

"The first proposition was, perhaps, for the first time distinctly advanced by General Hamilton, in his Letters of Pacificus, No. 1, p. 535. A great and revered authority, but subject to occasional error. It was fully answered by Mr. Madison in the Letters of Helvidius, p. 594, etc., and has since remained dormant. The second is now for the first time broadly asserted. Its dangerous tendencies—its hostility to every principle of our institutions, cannot be exaggerated. The true signification of this part of the constitution, I take to be simply this, that the President is authorized to employ those powers which are expressly entrusted to him to execute those laws which he is empowered to administer; or, in the language of the late Chief Justice, he is at liberty to employ any means which the constitution and laws place under his control. 2 Brockenb. 101.

"The third proposition is a palpable and unwarrantable interpolation of the constitution. The fourth, if the power claimed is derived from the power of appointment, would make the judges dependent upon executive dictation; if from that power and that of removal, conjointly, would make it the true theory of the English constitution, that the king might instruct, direct, and control the lord chancellor in the performance of his judicial duties. It would make him the keeper of the chancellor's conscience.

"The right to command, direct and control, involves the correlative duty of obedience. No officer can be criminally or civilly punished for obedience to the lawful command of a superior, which he is bound to obey. This doctrine, then, asserts the entire irresponsibility of all officers, except to this one superior.

"One of the practical inferences from these premises is, that the judiciary department cannot execute its own judgments; a proposition distinctly avowed by the postmaster general in his return, p. 127–8–9, and asserted, in terms equally distinct, by the attorney general, in p. 152." *Ibid.*, 571–572.

[58] *Ibid.*, 610. Further along the Court adds: "It is urged at the bar, that the postmaster general was alone subject to the direction and control of the President, with respect to the execution of the duty imposed upon him by this law; and this right of the President is claimed, as growing out of the obligation imposed upon him by the constitution, to take care that the laws be faithfully executed. This is a doctrine that cannot receive the sanction of this court. It would be vesting in the President a dispensing power, which has no countenance for its support in any part of the constitution; and is asserting a principle, which, if carried out in its results, to all cases falling within it, would be clothing the President with a power entirely to control the legislation of Congress, and paralyze the administration of justice.

"To contend that the obligation imposed on the President to see the laws faithfully executed, implied a power to forbid their execution, is a novel construction of the constitution, and entirely inadmissible." *Ibid.*, 612–613.

Although Stokes got his mandamus, it seems to have netted him little, and his later attempt to recover damages from Kendall was thrown out of Court on the ground that he had already exhausted his right to a remedy. *Kendall v. Stokes et al.*, 3 How. 87 (1845).

[59] Art. I, § 4.

[60] 272 U. S. 52. Much of my discussion here of the Myers Case is taken from my *Removal Power of the President* (New York, 1927).

[61] In *Wallace v. United States*, 257 U. S. 541 (1922) it was held that the limitations imposed on the President's power to remove an army officer (119 Art. of War, 39 Stat. 699) do not apply when the removal is approved by the Senate through its consent to a new appointment to the post. Chief Justice Taft's opinion contains a suggestion that when the removal power is thus exercised it is illimitable—which is bad logic, but at any rate indicates the Court's perception of the special risks likely to attend judicial intervention in such a case.

[62] 19 Stat. 80, 91. To this day the Postmaster General and the Assistant Postmaster Generals are appointed and removable "by and with the advice and consent of the Senate." U. S. Code, tit. 5, §§ 361, 363.

[63] *Annals of Congress,* I, 368 ff., or 383 ff., according to the printing used.

[64] *Federalist* 77; Earle, p. 497. Earlier, however, in No. 72 Hamilton had indicated the opinion that the heads of departments ought always to be the choice of the incumbent President; Earle, 469. "In the Federalist, he, Hamilton, had so explained the removal from office as to deny the power to the President. In an edition of the work at New York, there is a marginal note to the passage that 'Mr. Hamilton had changed his view of the Constitution on that point.' " Madison to Rives, January 10, 1829. *Letters and Other Writings* (Philadelphia, 1865), IV, 5.

[65] My *Removal Power of the President* (note 60 *supra*), pp. 26–31. Webster's position, as set forth in his answer to Jackson's Protest Message, was as follows:

"The regulation of the tenure of office is a common exercise of legislative authority, and the power of congress in this particular is not at all restrained or limited by anything in the constitution, except in regard to judicial officers. All the rest is left to the ordinary discretion of the legislature. Congress may give to offices which it creates (except those of judges) what duration it pleases. When the office is created and is to be filled, the President is to nominate the candidate to fill it; but when he comes into office, he comes into it upon the conditions and restrictions which the law may have attached to it."

"If Congress," he continued, "were to declare by law that the Attorney General, or the Secretary of State should hold office during good behavior," its action might be unwise, but it would not be unconstitutional. *Writings and Speeches of Daniel Webster* (National ed.; Boston, 1903), VII, 196–199.

[66] 13 Pet. 225, 230 (two cases). The argument of counsel on both sides affords an exposition of the common law theory of office. Jones, who appeared against Hennen's application for a mandamus, set forth the theory adopted by the Court, as follows:

"The right to remove is an incident to the power of appointment. It is essential to the exercise of the power to appoint; and the power which is given by the law cannot exist without this incident.

"If the common law has any bearing on this question, it is very remote. The Constitution of the United States, and the laws made in conformity with the provisions of the

Constitution, are essentially different from the common law, as to appointments to offices, and as to the tenure by which they are held. 2 Black. Commentaries, 36, 37. The law of the tenure of office in England is regulated not by any principles of ethics, or express provision, but by immemorial usage. Office is there an incorporeal hereditament, as a right of way. There is, under the common law, an estate in an office.

"But in the United States this is not so. There is in this country no estate in any office. No property in an office. Offices are held for the benefit of the community in which their functions are exercised. As to the tenure and nature of office in England: cited Coke Litt. 378a. 4 Institute, 117. Coke Litt. 233b. 2 Institute, 388.

"The position in England is, that unless the statute which creates the office limits its tenure, at the time of the creation; it is an office for life, as at the common law. But here no such principles prevail. The common law does not apply to offices, which are all created by the Constitution, or by express statute." *Ibid.*, 253–254.

[67] P. 82 *supra*.

[68] *Removal Power*, 36–41.

[69] P. 65 *supra*.

[70] 272 U. S. at 134.

[71] All these provisions can be easily traced through the index to the U. S. Code.

[72] *Ibid.*, tit. 31, § 43.

[73] 295 U. S. 602 (also styled *Rathbun, Executor v. United States*).

[74] These facts are given at the outset of Justice Sutherland's opinion for the Court. See also *The New York Times*, October 8, 1933. The Federal Trade Commission at once recognized "the validity of said Executive order removing Mr. Humphrey"; and declined "to further recognize" him as a member of the commission. *Ibid.*, October 10, 1933. Also, in due course, Comptroller General McCarl ruled that Humphrey was no longer entitled to the salary of the post from which he had been ousted. *Ibid.*, November 12, 1933. Both actions were doubtless based upon the decision in the Myers Case.

But suppose a like situation should arise today, what attitude would the Trade Commission, or other similar body, and the Comptroller General be apt to take? Or suppose the Senate to have joined in a removal contrary to statute, would the Court itself interpose? Theoretically it ought to; but it would unquestionably be very astute to obviate such a situation. *Cf. Blake v. United States*, 103 U. S. 227 (1880) and *Wallace v. United States*, 257 U. S. 541 (1922).

[75] 295 U. S., 627–629.

[76] *Ibid.*, 631.

[77] But this interpretation of the decision still leaves doubtful the constitutionality of the Act of August 24, 1912, c. 389, 36, 37 Stat. 555, which provides that "no person in the classified civil service of the United States shall be removed therefrom except for such cause as will promote the efficiency of said service and for reason given in writing, and the person whose removal is sought shall have notice of the same and of any charges preferred against him, and be furnished with a copy of the same, and also be allowed a reasonable time for personally answering the same in writing; and affidavits in support thereof; but no examination of witnesses nor any trial or hearing shall be required except in the discretion of the officer making the removal. . . ." U. S. Code, tit. 5, §652.

Even if this be considered as restrictive of the President's removal power, it seems to me to be entirely constitutional so far as it protects officers with merely ministerial duties vested in them by statute. The distinction in the Humphrey Case between such an officer and those protected by that decision is not logical. For there is no reason why Congress should not have power to protect against *arbitrary* removal even the humblest agents of its delegated powers, a conclusion to which *Shurtleff v. United States,* 189 U. S. 311, lends aid and comfort. On the other hand, once Congress designates any officer or agency of the government as an instrument of the President's constitutional or statutory powers, it thereby automatically renders such officer or agency, whatever may be its other powers or duties, removable by the President at will. *Cf.* opening paragraph of note 57 *supra.*

[78] 277 U. S. 189, 202 (1928).

[79] The Comptroller's office is, of course, a direct descendant of the British Comptroller and Auditor, "who holds his office during good behavior, with a salary paid by statute out of the Consolidated Fund and who considers himself in no sense a servant of the Treasury but an officer responsible to the House of Commons." A. Lawrence Lowell, *The Government of England* (1908), I, 289. For an excellent discussion of the Comptroller General's powers under present legislation, see Harvey C. Mansfield, *The Comptroller General* (Yale University Press, 1939).

[80] That Justice Sutherland probably did not appreciate the logical bearing of his dictum is indicated by the following anecdote by Professor Cushman:

"In 1937 Mr. Justice Sutherland was on the bench during the oral argument in the *Shipping Board* cases. One who was present in Court at this time reported the following interesting colloquy which took place. Mr. James W. Ryan, counsel for the shipping company, was urging upon the Court the argument, earlier summarized, that the United States Shipping Board could not constitutionally be put by executive order or by act of Congress *'in'* the executive branch. The Shipping Board, he argued, was not an 'executive agency' and could not be an 'executive agency' because it was not *in* the executive branch of the government.

"Justice Sutherland, who had been sitting back in his chair and asking occasional questions during the course of the argument, leaned forward quickly when he heard this.

" 'Did you say that the Shipping Board was not *in* the executive branch of the government?' he said—as though he did not believe he had heard correctly. Several other Justices smiled condescendingly at counsel as though he were making a farfetched proposition.'

" 'Yes, your Honor,' Mr. Ryan replied.

" 'What makes you think that? Where do you find any legal basis for such a conclusion?' the Justice wished to know.

" 'Why in your Honor's opinion in the Humphrey case, this Court held that the Federal Trade Commission and similar regulatory agencies were not in the executive branch of the government. The Shipping Board fell within the same general category as the Federal Trade Commission and the Interstate Commerce Commission.' Mr. Ryan then proceeded to read certain portions of that opinion.

" 'What branch of the Government do you think the Shipping Board was in, if it was not in the executive branch?' the Justice wanted to know.

" 'In the legislative branch, your Honor.'

"Justice Sutherland shook his head, as though he disagreed, and seemed to be thinking the question over as the discussion went on to other points." 24 *Cornell Law Quarterly,* 13–53 and 163–197, at pp. 52–53.

[81] U. S. Code, tit. 16, §§831c and e.

[82] The President stated his own case very satisfactorily. *The New York Times,* March 19, 22, and 24, 1938; see also note 48 *supra;* and *Morgan v. T. V. A.,* 28 Fed. Supp. 732

(August, 1939). For the view that the President had no power to remove Morgan, see Arthur Larson, "Has the President an Inherent Power of Removal of His Non-Executive Appointees?" reprinted from the *Tennessee Law Review* for March 1940. Professor Larson's major premise is indicated in his title; it is that TVA lies outside the Executive Department. He accordingly gives the provisions of the TVA Act which makes members of the Authority removable by concurrent resolution of the houses an exclusive interpretation. Granting this premise, the conclusion follows logically enough, but I reject the premise. As appears from what I say in the text, I regard all nonjudicial agencies for carrying out the law as being "executive" in the sense of the Constitution, and think that the vast body of practice and doctrine under the Constitution sustains this view.

[83] See note 77 *supra*.

[84] President Coolidge attempted at least once, although unsuccessfully, to evade statutory restraints upon his removal power by demanding a blank resignation beforehand from the person whom he contemplated appointing. The story is told in the following memorandum of a conversation between the President and Hon. William F. Culbertson, Vice-Chairman of the Tariff Commission at the time, and a letter from Culbertson to the late Senator Costigan of Colorado:

"Contemporary memorandum of the interview with the President, Sept. 8, 1924:

"Shortly after I reached my office this morning, about 9:30, I received a request over the telephone to come to the White House to see the President. I went over immediately. The President was reasonably cordial. He began by saying that the subject of the interview was Mr. David J. Lewis's reappointment. Mr. Lewis's term as a member of the Tariff Commission expired yesterday. The President stated that he intended to reappoint Mr. Lewis, but that he desired that Mr. Lewis prepare and give to him a letter of resignation as a member of the Tariff Commission. At first I did not fully comprehend the nature of this request.

"I spoke of Mr. Lewis's term having already expired. Then the President explained that he wanted Mr. Lewis to submit his resignation under the new commission, to be effective in case he (the President) desired at any time in the future to accept it.

"The President at this point called in Mr. Forster, one of his secretaries, and instructed him to make out Mr. Lewis's commission of reappointment as a member of the Tariff Commission, effective today.

"The President then handed me a sheet of White House paper so that I could take down the tenor of the letter which he wished Mr. Lewis to write. I wrote down the following words: 'I hereby resign as a member of the Tariff Commission, to take effect upon your acceptance.'

"I raised the objection at this point that an unqualified resignation of this kind would imply on the record that Mr. Lewis did not desire to continue as a member of the Tariff Commission.

"The President replied that this was a matter for Mr. Lewis to decide. In explanation of his request, the President said he desired to be free after the election concerning the position filled by Mr. Lewis. He said that if he were not elected, the Democrats might undertake to hold up other appointments which he made during the next session of the Senate, and he implied that he desired to use the appointment of Mr. Lewis for trading purposes in case of necessity.

"I thereupon asked the President whether I could have his assurance that if he were re-elected Mr. Lewis could be continued as a member of the Tariff Commission. He said that he could not at this time make any commitments.

"We then talked of other matters, and at the end the President asked me to have Mr. Lewis see him during the afternoon, when he said he would give him his commission."

Mr. Lewis declined to sign the letter, but Mr. Coolidge, though greatly annoyed to see his little scheme thwarted, gave him his commission just the same. *The New York Times,* January 17, 1926. See also *Congressional Record,* January 13 and 16, 1926. Of course, a really successful enterprise of this sort, in evasion of the laws, would not be apt to leak out.

85 The Committee was created by the President March 20, 1936, in accordance with Public Law No. 739, 74th Congress, 2nd Sess. Its membership was distinguished, comprising Messrs. Louis Brownlow, Chairman, Charles E. Merriam, and Luther Gulick. It was aided by a highly competent research staff, including among others Professors Joseph P. Harris, Director, Robert E. Cushman, William Y. Elliott, James Hart, Arthur N. Holcombe, Arthur W. MacMahon, Harvey C. Mansfield, Schuyler C. Wallace, and Edwin E. Witte. It transmitted its Report to the President January 8, 1937, and he in turn forwarded it to Congress on January 12, with a covering message.

86 The quotations in the text can be readily found in the *Report of the Committee with Studies of Administrative Management in the Federal Government* (U. S. Government Printing Office, 1937), pp. iii–v, 1–53.

87 Dean Landis regards this feature of the Committee's Report as especially ill-founded. He says:

"Only a year ago a distinguished group of scholars, reporting to the President of the United States—in language hardly indicative of academic restraint—described the independent administrative agencies of the federal government as constituting 'a headless "fourth branch" of the Government, a haphazard deposit of irresponsible agencies and uncoordinated powers,' whose institution did 'violence to the basic theory of the American Constitution that there should be three major branches of the Government and only three.'

"Such apotheosizing obscures rather than clarifies thought. Despite this chorus of abuse and tirade, the growth of the administrative process shows little sign of being halted. Instead, it still exhibits the vigor that attends lusty youth, and, if we have defined our subject rightly, it is a youth with which we are concerned. For here is an institution that has existed for less than a century and which, with a few exceptions, has been of public moment for only a little more than half that time. Yet, its extraordinary growth in recent years, the increasing frequency with which government has come to resort to it, the extent to which it is creating new relationships between the individual, the body economic, and the state, already have given it great stature." *The Administrative Process* (Yale University Press, 1938), pp. 4–5 (quoted by permission of the publisher).

Commissioner Eastman had expressed similar views as far back as 1927: "The commissions are not irresponsible. Their members are appointed by the President, their decisions are subject to judicial review, and Congress, which establishes them, determines their policy and can change it at will. Quasi-legislative work through quasi-judicial procedure—that is the secret of the independent regulatory commissions.

". . . The place of the independent commissions in the Federal Government in my judgment is the place which they now occupy. I would not increase their dependence on any branch of the Government. . . . They are the evolutionary product of experience in meeting very genuine public needs and I know of no other way in which such needs can be met. . . ."

In his testimony before the Senate Select Committee on Government Reorganization,

August 9, 1937, he further developed these views. His testimony was largely repeated by representatives of the other commissions before the same committee in oral testimony, reënforced by letters and written transcripts.

[88] In this connection the following passages from Robert MacGregor Dawson's volume on *The Principle of Official Independence* (London and Toronto, 1922) seem extremely well worth quotation:

"Independence is not a mystical formula that will solve all the problems which confront a modern government; but it does give scope for the development of the positive side of the official's character. Instead of the physical threat of loss of office, independence supplies the moral inducement to do well; in place of distrust, it gives confidence; it calls forth a host of qualities that otherwise might have remained dormant—the official's vanity, his conscience, his desire for applause, his zeal for the public good, his feeling of special fitness for his post, his craftsman's delight in his skill—any one or all of these are given freer play."

Elsewhere, referring to certain remarks of Carlyle, Mr. Dawson adds:

"Carlyle thought that he was pointing out the absurdity of democracy; instead of that he was merely showing, what modern experience has confirmed, that the use of skilled officials is an essential condition of a democracy's existence. It is clear that to ascertain the will of the people is not sufficient; there must also be the means to ensure that what they desire will be carried out in the best possible manner. The real democracy demands a subtle combination of election and appointment, of non-expert minds and expert minds, of control and trust, of responsibility and independence. The size of the modern state and the complexity of our civilization may make it extremely difficult to attain this combination; but the survival of democratic government nevertheless depends on its attainment."

Again quoting Mr. Dawson:

"Removal may vary from a mere formality and simple dismissal in some cases to a long and weary procedure in others, as necessitated by statute, constitutional custom or both. Its effect on independence is obvious and may be expressed almost algebraically: the more involved and numerous are the formalities of removal, the greater are the opportunities for independence, and in proportion as the process becomes more simple the independence tends to diminish."

[89] The most thoroughgoing criticism of the committee's proposals from a "pluralistic" point of view is that to be gathered from the pages of Lewis Meriam and Laurence F. Schmeckebier's *Reorganization of the National Government—What Does It Involve?* (The Brookings Institution, 1939). See also note 87 *supra*.

[90] Furthermore, Presidents have more than once virtually ordered independent agencies to exercise their powers. President Wilson was reported in Washington despatches of June 23, 1920, to have "urgently requested" the Railroad Labor Board "to expedite" a then pending wage decision; and only recently President Roosevelt instructed the Federal Power Commission, through its chairman, to coöperate with the National Power Policy Committee and the Advisory Commission to the Council of National Defense for certain purposes in connection with the national defense. *The New York Times,* June 16, 1940. I know of no direct statutory warrant for either of these interventions, which must therefore be justified by reference to some kind of executive prerogative.

[91] See George A. Graham, "Reorganization—A Question of Executive Institutions," 32 *American Political Science Review,* 708–718. The article is an enthusiastic brief for the Committee's proposals, which it regards as well devised to revitalize the Cabinet and improve the quality of presidential leadership in legislation. See *infra.*

92 In general, the terminology here employed is sustained, I believe, by F. F. Blachly and M. E. Oatman, in their recent work on *Federal Regulatory Action and Control* (The Brookings Institution, 1940). See especially Chs. IV and V.

93 304 U. S. 1 (1938); preceded by *Morgan v. United States,* 298 U. S. 468 (1936).

94 304 U. S. at 19–20.

95 *Cf.* 298 U. S. at 479 and 304 U. S. at 14–15. I am assuming here—safely, I think— that the Committee's term "sublegislative" and the Court's term "quasi-legislative" mean the same thing.

96 The leading case asserting the right-to-a-hearing doctrine in connection with rate-making is *Chicago, Milwaukee and St. Paul R. Co. v. Minn.,* 134 U. S. 418 (1890). Also to the same effect is 227 U. S. 88 (1912). Five years earlier, however, in *Home Tel. and Tel. Co. v. Los Angeles,* 211 U. S. 265, Justice Moody, speaking for the Court, had said: "Rate regulation is legislative, and not a judicial function, and *quaere* whether notice and hearing are necessary to constitute due process of law in fixing rates." Head note and p. 278.

97 See further *Pacific States Box and Basket Co. v. White,* 296 U. S. 176 (1935). The pending Logan-Walter Bill would apparently affix the "notice-hearing" requirement to all administrative lawmaking.

98 U. S. Code, tit. 15, §§ 78K and S.

99 See note 79 *supra.*

NOTES TO CHAPTER IV*

1 The basis was laid for this doctrine by the protests of the judges leading up to Hayburn's Case, 2 Dall. 409 (1792). See also Chief Justice Taney's opinion, with note, in *United States v. Ferreira,* 13 How. 40 (1851); and the same Justice's posthumous opinion in *Gordon v. United States,* 117 U. S. 697 (1864). Interesting cases illustrating judicial review of executive interpretation of the law are *Morrill v. Jones,* 106 U. S. 466; *United States v. Symonds,* 120 U. S. 46; *United States v. George,* 228 U. S. 14; *Waite et al. v. Macy et al.,* 246 U. S. 606; *International Railway Co. v. Davidson,* 257 U. S. 506; the decisions sustaining in 1927, the cancellation of the notorious Fall leases of oil reserves of the United States to the Doheny and Sinclair interests, *Pan American Petroleum . . . Co. v. United States,* 273 U. S. 456; and *Mammoth Oil Co. v. United States,* 275 U. S. 13. The decision of the United States court of appeals for the District of Columbia in *Lukens Steel Corp. et al. v. Frances Perkins et al.* (October 3, 1939), setting aside the Secretary of Labor's very extreme interpretation of the word "locality" as used in the Public Contracts Act of June 30, 1936 (U. S. Code, tit. 41, §35b), was itself overruled by the Supreme Court in *Perkins v. Lukens Steel Co.* (April 20, 1940). The Court, speaking by Justice Black, held in effect that prospective bidders for government contracts cannot challenge judicially an executive interpretation of statutes applicable to such contracts—in that field the executive, so long as it has a statute to work behind, is endowed with the absolute power of the National Government to determine whom it will deal with and on what terms!

2 The principle was early stated as follows: "In the construction of a doubtful and ambiguous law, the contemporaneous construction of those who are called upon to operate under the law and were appointed to carry it into effect is entitled to very great

* *Chapter IV (Chief Executive) begins on page 111.*

respect"; *Edwards' Lessee v. Darby,* 12 Wh. 206, 210 (1827). See also *Stuart v. Laird,* 1 Cr. 299, 309 (1803). The doctrine holds especially in regard to public land and pension legislation, in which the government appears in the role of distributor of gratuities. See *United States v. Midwest Oil Co.,* 236 U. S. 459; and *Decatur v. Paulding,* 14 Pet. 497 (1840). In the latter case executive construction of statutes is put on a peculiarly exalted plane, showing the contemporary influence of the Jacksonian doctrine of the equality of the three departments.

3 *Autobiography,* Ch. XI.

4 U. S. Code, tit. 43, §141.

5 See note 2.

6 *Grisar v. McDowell,* 6 Wall. 364, 381 (1867).

7 2 *Opins. A. G.,* 482. The episode occurred in 1831, and so anticipated by two years the removal of the deposits, which Taney justified by substantially the same argument.

8 U. S. Code, tit. 5, §317; *ibid.,* tit. 28, §765.

9 During the war with Germany the government sought from the Supreme Court postponement of argument in certain pending prosecutions under the Sherman Act on grounds solely of public policy.

" 'In order that the Government in this time of stress may not meet with competition from private enterprises in its financial operations,' said the Government's brief filed in connection with the motion, 'and the flotation of its loans, the Treasury Department has been constrained to urge that all private financing on a large scale shall be avoided as far as is at all possible.

" 'It is quite clear that the dissolutions which are sought in the pending cases will require financial operations on a large scale if they are to be genuine and effective. Important as the remedy sought in these cases is believed to be, it must give place for the moment to the paramount needs of the hour.' "

Against the strong protest of some of the defendant companies the Court granted the motion. *The New York Times,* January 3, 1918.

The extent to which executive interpretation may often make or break a statute is well illustrated by the proceedings in Johnson's Cabinet over the Reconstruction Acts of 1867, when Attorney General Stanbery's hostile interpretation of these measures was confronted with Secretary Stanton's sympathetic interpretation. *The Diary of Gideon Welles,* III, 59, 60, 63, 64, 93, 96–99, 105, 109–117. The rule of sympathetic interpretation is stated by Justice McKenna for the Court, in the following words: "If it fulfills the purpose of the law it cannot be said to be an addition to the law. . . . The purpose of the law is the ever insistent consideration in its interpretation." *United States v. Antikamnia Chemical Co.,* 231 U. S. 654, 667. See also the same Justice's opinion for the Court in *United States v. Janowitz et al.,* 257 U. S. 42.

Instructive, too, of the problems of interpretation which the President has frequently to face without any possibility of assistance from or review by the courts is Mr. Roosevelt's recent action in discouraging the transfer of certain American vessels to Panama registry, on the vague ground that it would not be right "for the United States to put any other American nation in a position which he does not think proper for the United States." *The New York Times,* November 22, 1939.

"Note that the expected storm of protest over WPA's new wage scales has failed to materialize. Behind this is a story of practical coöperation by Sen. James Byrnes. Byrnes was one of the leaders responsible for the new WPA law requiring that WPA pay levels in various localities should differ no more than the cost of living differs. However, Byrnes and other figures behind the legislation belatedly realized this would bring shouts of anguish from WPA workers in Northern cities (where pay would be cut sharply) and from private employers in the rural South (where WPA pay would be raised above some private wages). So Byrnes and WPA officials quietly agreed that the new law should be given an extremely flexible interpretation. This was possible because there are no thoroughly accurate figures on cost of living. The result is that extreme pay changes were avoided and squawks kept to a minimum." *Newsweek,* November 6, 1939.

Nor was the protest recently raised by some people against certain questions to be put by the national census enumerators without basis. The newly inserted questions represented an entirely novel interpretation of the Census Act.

Presidential enforcement of the law has sometimes been directly stimulated by Congress. By the Joint Resolution of February 8, 1924, which he signed and promptly acted upon, President Coolidge was directed "immediately to cause suit to be instituted and prosecuted for the annulment and cancellation" of the notorious Fall oil leases; also, to "appoint special counsel who shall have charge and control of such litigation"—a provision which took the matter out of the hands of a suspect Attorney General.

[10] Presidential *proclamations* may be simply announcements by the President over the seal of the United States, his own signature, and the countersignature of the Secretary of State, of the construction put by the executive department upon specified acts of Congress, or they may represent, like proclamations of amnesty, the exercise by the President of one of his constitutional prerogatives. See the interesting collection of proclamations issued by President Wilson during the war with Germany. *Statutes of the U. S. A.* 2nd sess., 65th Cong., Pt. II (Government Printing Office, 1918). The diplomatic characteristics of a presidential proclamation are apparently a matter of precedent merely, although by an act of Congress passed in 1794 the seal of the United States may not be affixed to "any other instrument" than official commissions "without the special warrant of the President therefor"; U. S. Code, tit. 4, §4.

In the famous *Case of the Proclamations,* 12 Co. Rep. 74 (1611), Chief Justice Coke and three of his brother judges answered certain queries regarding the legality of royal proclamations with the following propositions: "1. The King by his proclamation cannot create any offence which was not one before. . . . 2. But the King, for the prevention of offences, may by proclamation admonish his subjects that they keep the law. . . . the neglect of such proclamations aggravates the offence. 3. . . . " In the main these principles undoubtedly govern the legality of presidential proclamations. The President cannot add to his constitutional or legal powers by proclamation, but it is possible that the issuance of a proclamation may sometimes impart to an authorized act of the President, particularly a pardon, a public character that it would not otherwise have had. See pp. 137–138 *supra* for comment on *Burdick v. United States,* 236 U. S. 79.

Some presidential proclamations can hardly be said to be official at all; they are the social acts of the highest official of government, the best known example being the Thanksgiving Proclamation. The first such proclamation under the Constitution was "authorized" by Congress, though not without certain constitutional scruples finding expression. *The New York Times,* November 24, 1932. The resolution was passed nevertheless, and a proclamation thereupon issued by President Washington. Richardson, I, 64. The first Adams and Madison issued several proclamations, on special occasions and at the instigation of Congress, calling for days of prayer, fasting, or thanksgiving, as the case might be. See Richardson, Index, under "Thanksgiving Proclamations." The first, however, of the since uninterrupted series of annual Thanksgiving Proclamations was issued by Lincoln in 1863, and without suggestion from Congress. It was dated October 3, the same date as Washington's proclamation in 1789, and set the last Thursday of the ensuing November as the festive day, November 26, 1789, the date of the Thanksgiving proclaimed by Washington having fallen on that day. Two Presidents at least refused to act upon suggestions that they should proclaim days of feast or fast, on account of constitutional scruples, Jackson and Taylor. *The New York Times,* November 26, 1931. For the recent only partially successful effort of Mr. Roosevelt to promote Christmas buying by moving Thanksgiving up a week, see the *Times* for August 15 and 16, 1939.

Executive *"laws"* fall into two categories: first, those which concern primarily the internal organization of the administration, and so are of interest chiefly to the members, or would-be members, thereof; secondly, those which supplement the general law. As to the former, each head of department is authorized by act of Congress "to prescribe regulations, not inconsistent with law, for the government of his department, the conduct of its officers and clerks, the distribution and performance of its business," etc. U. S. Code, tit. 5, §22. "Codes" of this character, determining the internal organization of administration, are those which govern the postal service, the Patent, Pension, and Land Offices, the Indian service, the customs, internal revenue, and consular services, the rules governing civil service examinations, and so on. Most such regulations stand in the name of some departmental head; but some, like those governing the consular service and civil service examinations, appear in the name of the President. Many rest on the explicit statutory basis just mentioned; but others arise simply from the discretion impliedly allowed by the statutes, and this is ordinarily so with those less formal orders, rules, and instructions which are issued to members of the administration as necessity arises.

Such regulations may not, of course, transgress the constitutional acts of Congress; and from this it follows that they are subject to judicial review in a case properly before the Court, and this even though the rights alleged to be infringed are those of a member of the administration as such. In *United States v. Symonds,* 120 U. S. 46, the question at issue was whether appellee, a lieutenant in the Navy, had performed certain services "at sea" within the meaning of §1556 R. S. Under an order of the Secretary of the Navy the services in question, which were performed aboard a training ship, were designated "shore services." But the Court held that it was not for the Secretary of the Navy to "fix by order and conclusively what was and what was not sea service"; that the facts of the case made appellee's service "sea service." See also *United States v. Hill,* 120 U. S. 169.

On the other hand, when such a regulation is within the law, it is endowed as against state authority with the supremacy of national law in general. Thus, in *Boske v. Comingore* a United States collector of revenue had been adjudged by a Kentucky court to be in contempt because he had refused, while giving a deposition in a case pending before the court, to file copies of certain reports made by distillers, basing his refusal upon a regulation of the Treasury Department which forbade the use of such reports for any other purpose than the collection of the revenues of the United States. The Supreme Court sustained the regulation in question as "a wise and proper one," and on this basis confirmed the order of the district court of the United States for Kentucky discharging the collector from the custody of the Kentucky court. 177 U. S. 459. For an executive order, on the other hand, which was designed to aid the enforcement of state criminal law, see *Ponzi v. Fessenden,* 258 U. S. 254 (1922).

Illustrations of the second category of executive "laws" are given in the ensuing text.

¹¹ The maxim that the legislature cannot delegate its power is commonly traced to the more general maxim which is discussed in the learned article by Patrick Duff and H. E. Whiteside, entitled "Delegata Potestas non Potest Delegari: A Maxim of American Constitutional Law," 14 *Cornell Law Quarterly,* 168. This form of the maxim, we here learn, is from Branch's *Maxims,* a work which was published in 1753. Coke, 2 *Inst., 597* (which Branch cites) gives a variant; while the phrase *"delegatus non potest delegare"* occurs as a gloss on certain texts of the Digest, "restricting subdelegation of delegated jurisdiction." In the Digest itself the same restriction is expressed as follows: *"Mandatam sibi jurisdictionem mandare alteri non posse manifestum est,"* D. 1.21.5. (See also D. 2.1.5, and Code 3.1.5.) Bracton's *De Legibus,* f. 55b, also contains the maxim, though his precise wording of it is a matter of dispute. All earlier printings give it thus: ". . . *sicut jurisdictio delegata non delegari poterit, quin ordinaria remaneat cum ipso rege,"* which Sir Travers Twiss translates, ". . . as delegated power cannot be delegated, but ordinary jurisdiction remains with the king." The most recent editor of Bracton, however, gives the passage as follows: ". . . *sicut jurisdictio delegata, nec delegari poterit, quin ordinaria remaneat cum ipso rege"* (Woodbine, ed., II, p. 167), which Messrs. Duff and Whiteside translate "[unless it be given from above] like delegated jurisdiction; nor can it be so delegated that the primary [or regulating] power does not remain with the king himself." The older reading seems to me the authentic one, both on account of its close similarity in sense to the text from the Digest, and also because of its obvious bearing upon the problem, pressing in Bracton's day, of subinfeudation.

Locke's application of the maxim to forbid a transference "of the power of making laws to any other hands" occurs in his *Second Treatise on Civil Government* (Ch. XI). It has played a twofold role in American constitutional law: (1) as restrictive or prohibitive of legislative efforts to condition the going into effect of statutes upon approval by popular vote—referendum measures, in other words; and (2) as restrictive or prohibitive of legislative delegation of conditional or discretionary powers to the executive. The latter role, in relation to the National Government, is, of course, the one in which we are interested. For the former role, which it is not pertinent to treat here, see the above mentioned article, and more extensively Ellis P. Oberholtzer, *The Referendum in America* (2nd ed., New York, 1911).

Two competent, but today partially out-of-date works, dealing with presidential legislative power, are James Hart, *The Ordinance Making Powers of the President* (Baltimore, 1925); and John Preston Comer, *Legislative Functions of National Administrative Authorities* (Columbia University Press, 1927).

¹² See also Ch. I, at pp. 2–3 *supra.*

¹³ Thomas M. Cooley, *Constitutional Limitations* (2nd ed., Boston, 1927), p. 191* and cases there cited.

¹⁴ Indeed, the first and second category are merged in the justification which has been sometimes offered for laws to go into effect upon the favorable vote of the locality affected. *Ibid.*

¹⁵ 7 Cr. 382 (1812). A few years later the case of *Wayman v. Southard,* 10 Wheat. 1 (1825), arose, involving a provision of the Judiciary Act of 1789, which authorized the courts of the United States "to make and establish all necessary rules" for the conduct of business in the said courts. Sustaining this measure, Chief Justice Marshall hinted a distinction between those powers which are "strictly and exclusively legislative" and those which are not so, although Congress is constitutionally empowered to exercise them. Although anticipated on the floor of the Philadelphia Convention (see Farrand, I, 67),

this doctrine has produced little fruitage. Another and frequently recurrent formula in the cases is that which distinguishes between the making of "general rules" and the filling in of "details," or between discretion as to what the "law"—that is, as it comes from the legislature—"shall be" and discretion as to its "execution"—"an observation which derives its importance from the applications thereof." See, e.g., *Interstate Com. Commission v. Goodrich Transit Co.,* 224 U. S. at 214.

One of the most sweeping delegations of power ever made by Congress was to the Supreme Court itself, by the Act of June 19, 1934, to regulate civil proceedings in the district courts of the United States. U. S. Code, tit. 28, §723 b and c.

[16] 143 U. S. 649.

[17] *Ibid.,* at 692–693.

[18] 276 U. S. 394.

[19] "All in all, if the President exercised every power delegated to him in section 315 of the Tariff Act of 1922, he could rewrite the entire tariff bill as soon as the Congress had finished it." John Day Larkin, *The President's Control of the Tariff* (Harvard University Press, 1936), p. 2.

[20] The leading case is *State ex rel. R. R. and Warehouse Commission v. C. M. and St. P. R. Co.,* 38 Minn. 281, at 298–302 (1889); 37 N. W. 782 (1889).

[21] 192 U. S. 471; 220 U. S. 506; 242 U. S. 311.

[22] 192 U. S. at 494.

[23] 216 U. S. 614.

[24] 220 U. S. at 516. Note also Justice McKenna's words as quoted on p. 362 *supra*.

[25] 242 U. S. at 326. For a general account of such congressional delegations to the states, and of resulting cases, see my *Court Over Constitution* (Princeton University Press, 1938), pp. 148–157.

[26] In this connection should be noted Story's remark that the principle of the separation of powers means "that the whole power of one of these departments should not be exercised by the same hands which possess the whole power of either of the other departments." *Commentaries,* §525. To the same effect are Madison's words in *Federalist* 47.

[27] *Panama Refining Co. v. Ryan,* 293 U. S. 388 (1934); *Schechter Bros. v. United States,* 295 U. S. 495 (1935); *United States v. Curtiss-Wright Export Corp.,* 299 U. S. 304 (1936).

[28] Passing on this very question in the early case of *Martin v. Mott,* the Court, speaking by Justice Story, said:

"But it is now contended, as it was contended in that case, that notwithstanding the judgment of the President is conclusive as to the existence of the exigency, and may be given in evidence as conclusive proof thereof, yet that the avowry is fatally defective, because it omits to aver that the fact did exist. The argument is, that the power confided to the President is a limited power, and can be exercised only in the cases pointed out in the statute, and therefore it is necessary to aver the facts which bring the exercise within the purview of the statute. In short, the same principles are sought to be applied to the delegation and exercise of this power intrusted to the Executive of the nation for great political purposes, as might be applied to the humblest officer in the government, acting upon the most narrow and special authority. It is the opinion of the Court, that this objection cannot be maintained. When the President exercises an authority confided to him by law, the presumption is, that it is exercised in pursuance of law. Every public officer is presumed to act in obedience to his duty, until the contrary is shown; and *a fortiori,* this presumption ought to be favorably applied to the chief magistrate of the Union. It is not necessary to aver, that the act which he may rightfully do, was so done. If the fact of the existence of the exigency were averred, it would be traversable, and of course might be passed upon by a jury; and thus the legality of the orders of the President would depend, not on his own judgment of the facts, but upon the finding of those facts upon the proofs submitted to a jury. This view of the objection is precisely the same which was acted upon by the Supreme Court of New York, in the case already referred to, and, in the opinion of this Court, with entire legal correctness." 12 Wheat. 19, 32–33 (1827).

Here, however, the President was exercising a power, as the Court pointed out, which was entrusted to him for "great political purposes." Where his power derives exclusively from an exercise by Congress of one of its delegated powers the rule may be different. In the previous chapter, indeed, I have proceeded on the assumption that a presidential order of removal for cause would be subject to judicial review at least to the extent of determining whether a fair hearing was had.

[29] In the course of the argument Mr. Fischer, one of counsel opposing the government, complained that his client "Smith was arrested, indicted and held in jail for several days and then had to put up bond for violating a law that did not exist, but nobody knew it." Thereupon ensued an interesting fifteen minutes in Court, albeit "a bad quarter of an hour" for Mr. Stephens, the government counsel.

In reply to a question, Mr. Fischer said he had not been able to obtain a true copy of the petroleum code or regulations. He said the only copy he had ever seen was in "the hip pocket of an agent sent down to Texas from Washington."

"Are the facts recited in connection with this code applicable in general to the other codes?" asked Justice Louis D. Brandeis.

"You'll have to ask the Attorney General," replied the Texan.

Mr. Stephens, who had completed his argument, arose and Justice Brandeis asked him the question.

"I think that is so," Mr. Stephens replied.

"Who promulgates these orders and codes that have the force of laws?" asked the Justice.

"They are promulgated by the President and I assume they are on record at the State Department," he replied.

"Is there any official or general publication of these executive orders?" Justice Brandeis continued.

"Not that I know of," replied Mr. Stephens.

"Well, is there any way by which one can find out what is in these executive orders when they are issued?"

"I think it would be rather difficult, but it is possible to get certified copies of the executive orders and codes from the NRA," Mr. Stephens explained.

"And that advantage is open to the staff of the Justice Department?" asked Justice Willis Van Devanter.

"Yes, sir," Mr. Stephens replied as a titter swept the room.

"How many of these orders and codes have been issued in the last fifteen months— several thousand?" asked Justice James Clark McReynolds, who earlier had quizzed Mr. Stephens about the omitted provision of the code.

"I am not certain, Your Honor, but I should say several hundred," the attorney replied. *Washington Post,* December 11, 1934.

One result, it may be surmised, of the above colloquy was the establishment of the *Federal Register,* the first number of which appeared March 14, 1936. About the size of the *Congressional Record,* the *Register* "is issued on almost every working day of the year, and in the first year it ran to over 3,000 pages. It includes (a) proclamations by the President of various holidays and of actions by the government, (b) executive orders issued by the President, usually of a legislative nature, (c) proclamations, notices of hearings, etc., by the executive departments and other agencies of the government, (d) general and special orders issued by departments and other agencies in particular cases, including decisions, and (e) rules and regulations of a legislative nature issued by the departments and other agencies. This publication, if continued, as it undoubtedly will be, will constitute one of the most important repositories of information about the government." William Anderson, *American Government* (New York, 1938), p. 662 (quoted by permission of the publishers, Henry Holt and Company).

In connection with the above, it is only fair to remember that there was no official publication of United States Supreme Court decisions until 1875.

[30] 295 U. S. at 537 and 553.

[31] See note 27 *supra.*

[32] 299 U. S. at 327. The word "cognate" is taken from the Chief Justice's opinion in the "Hot Oil" Cases. See 293 U. S. at 421–422.

[33] U. S. Code, tit. 7, §§601, 608c, 674. The act is now merged into the amended Agricultural Adjustment Act of August 24, 1935.

[34] 307 U. S. 533, especially at 574–580. It is impossible not to sympathize with Justice Roberts's dissenting opinion on this point:

"I am of opinion that the Act unconstitutionally delegates legislative power to the Secretary of Agriculture. Valid delegation is limited to the execution of a law. If power is delegated to make a law, or to refrain from making it, or to determine what the law shall command or prohibit, the delegation ignores and transgresses the Constitutional division of power between the legislative and the executive branches of the government.

"In my view the Act vests in the Secretary authority to determine, first, what of a number of enumerated commodities shall be regulated; second, in what areas the commodity shall be regulated; third, the period of regulation, and fourth, the character of regulation to be imposed and, for these reasons, cannot be sustained.

"The statute is an attempted delegation to an executive officer of authority to impose regulations within supposed limits and according to supposed standards so vague as in effect to invest him with uncontrolled power of legislation. Congress has not directed that the marketing of milk shall be regulated. Congress has not directed that regulation shall be imposed throughout the United States or in any specified portion thereof. It has left the choice of both locations and areas to the Secretary. Congress has not provided that regulation anywhere shall become effective at any specified date, or remain effective for any specified period. Congress has permitted such a variety of forms of regulation as to invest the Secretary with a choice of discrete systems each having the characteristics of an independent and complete statute." *Ibid.,* 603–604.

[35] Art. I, §9, par. 7. See my article "Constitutional Aspects of Federal Housing," 84 *University of Pennsylvania Law Review* (December, 1935), 131–156.

[36] 1 Stat. 95, 104–106, 190.

[37] 5 Stat. 17–31.

[38] 7 *Opins. A. G.* 186, 201 (1855), citing 2 Stat. 188 (1802), 214 (1803), 269 (1804), 321 (1805), 388 (1806), 436 (1807), 466 (1808), 524 (1809).

39 U. S. Code, tit. 31, §1; 42 Stat. 20.

40 *Encyclopedia of the Social Sciences,* III, 38, 42 (1930). But "his plan of operations" can be easily upset, in consequence of the theory that appropriations are mandatory. A threat by President Harding early in 1923 that he would order the War Department to keep expenditures on rivers and harbors within the amount fixed by the Budget Bureau and ignore an additional appropriation by Congress (*The New York Times,* February 11, 1923) led to the following protest by the late Senator Caraway of Arkansas:

"I hope that this report is not true. The President is the Chief Executive and it is his duty to see that the law is enforced. If it shall transpire that the President, instead of enforcing the laws, shall himself issue an executive order, forbidding the officers of this Government to obey the law, it will certainly be a very unfortunate circumstance. . . .

"The situation which will develop if the President makes good that threat will be one he will certainly regret. The time has not yet come when the people will tamely submit to executive domination, no matter who the President happens to be." *Ibid.,* February 13, 1923.

41 Because of its own almost unlimited power in the premises, Congress is not governed by the maxim when legislating for unincorporated territory of the United States. From the time of the purchase of Louisiana to the acquisition of the Panama Canal Zone, the first step taken by Congress in the case of recently acquired territory has invariably been to delegate unlimited power to the President to establish a government in such territory. Of course, the government so established has usually been quite temporary, but during its existence it has rested on power delegated to the President by Congress—that is to say, has represented a *twofold* delegation of legislative power. The vast range of delegated powers which President Wilson exercised during the war with Germany is dealt with in the following chapter. See also *Cincinnati Soap Co. v. United States,* 301 U. S. 308, 323 (1937).

42 *Congressional Record,* March 20, 1939 (Vol. 82, part 3, pp. 2946, 2958–2969); *Currin v. Wallace,* 306 U. S. 1 (1938); *United States v. Rock Royal Co-operative,* 307 U. S. 533 (1939).

43 The following digest of discretionary powers of the President, compiled for the National Committee to Uphold Constitutional Government, is substantially accurate as of January 1, 1940:

A. UNREPEALED DISCRETIONARY POWERS

Power to Seize Ships

1. Act of March 4, 1909 (35 Stat. 1090; U.S. Code 18:26). President authorized to employ land or naval forces of the United States, or militia, for taking possession of and detaining, in order to enforce execution of prescribed prohibitions and penalties, vessels which are fitted out and armed etc. contrary to the provisions of said act.

Power to Detain Ships

2. Act of March 4, 1909 (35 Stat. 1091 as amended; U.S. Code 18:37). President authorized to employ such part of land or naval forces of the United States, or militia, as he may deem necessary to compel any foreign vessel to depart from the United States or any of its possessions in all cases, by the law of nations or treaties of the United States, it ought not to remain, and to detain or prevent any vessel from so departing in all cases in which, by the law of nations or the treaties of the United States, it is not entitled to depart.

Power over Cargo

3. Act of March 4, 1909 (35 Stat. 1091; U. S. Code 18:29). Collectors of customs shall detain any vessel manifestly built for war-like purposes, and about to depart from the United States, the cargo of which

principally consists of arms and munitions of war, when it appears probable that such vessel is intended to be employed by the owners to cruise or commit hostilities upon subjects or properties of foreign countries with which the United States is at peace, until decision of the President is had thereon etc.

Power to Inspect

4. Act of Aug. 18, 1914 (38 Stat. 699, c. 256; U.S. Code 46:83.236). President is authorized to suspend citizenship requirements for inspection of certain foreign built vessels.

Power over Navigation

5. Act of March 4, 1915 (38 Stat. 1053, Sec. 7; U.S. Code 33:471). Secretary of War authorized to establish and make regulations for navigation of anchorage grounds etc.

6. Act of July 9, 1918 (c. 143 XIX; U.S. Code 33:3). Secretary of War is authorized to make regulations for use of navigable waters near Army proving grounds etc.

Power to Manufacture

7. Act of June 10, 1920 (41 Stat. 1072; U.S. Code 16:809). The United States may take over certain power houses, dams etc. for purpose of manufacturing nitrates, explosives, or munitions of war, or for any other purpose involving the safety of the United States "when in the opinion of the President . . . the safety of the United States demands it," paying just compensation for use.

Power over Exports

8. Act of January 31, 1922 (42 Stat. 361; U.S. Code 22:236). Whenever the President finds that in any American country etc., conditions of domestic violence exist, which may be promoted by use of arms or ammunition procured from the United States, and makes proclamation thereof, it shall be unlawful to export, except under such limitations and exceptions as the President prescribes, any arms or ammunition of war from any place in the United States to such country until otherwise ordered by the President or Congress.

B. Discretionary Powers Since 1933

1. Act of May 12, 1933 (48 Stat. 37 (c); F.C.A. 7:610). Regulations by Secretary of Agriculture to carry out Agricultural Adjustment Act. (With President's approval.)

Power to Revise Rates

2. TVA Act of May 18, 1933 (48 Stat. 66 #13,14); F.C.A. 16:8316–831m). Revision of TVA Board percentages of gross receipts from sale of power, paid to Alabama and Tennessee; findings of board as to value of Dam No. 2 etc. (With President's approval.)

Power to Fix Gold Content of Dollar

3. Act of January 30, 1934 (48 Stat. 340–343; F.C.A. 31:821–822b). President has power to approve orders etc. to be promulgated by Secretary of Treasury for regulating the gold content of the dollar and stabilization of exchange value of the dollar. (This power extended through June 30, 1939 subject to earlier termination by the President by Act of Jan. 23, 1937 (50 Stat. 4 c 5). Again extended July 5, 1939.)

Power over Silver

4. Act of January 30, 1934 (48 Stat. 342–343; F.C.A. 31:823). President may issue silver certificates, reduce the weight of standard silver dollar etc.

Power over Trading

5. Act of June 6, 1934 (48 Stat. 898 #19 (4); F.C.A. 15:785 (4)). Summary suspension by Securities and Exchange Commission of trading on national securities exchanges for not exceeding ninety days. (With President's approval.)

Power over Silver Mining

6. Silver Purchase Act of June 19, 1934 (48 Stat. 1179 #7; F.C.A. 31:316a). Presi-

dent may require delivery of all silver to United States mints.

Power to Make Loans

7. Act of January 31, 1935 (49 Stat. 3 #5; F.C.A. 15:606i). Loans by the Reconstruction Finance Corporation to national mortgage associations. (With President's approval.)

Power over Oil

8. Act of Feb. 22, 1935 (49 Stat. 31 #4; F.C.A. 15:715c). President may suspend provisions prohibiting interstate shipment of contraband oil.

Power on High Seas

9. Act of August 5, 1935 (49 Stat. 517 c. 438; F.C.A. 19: 1701a–b). President may establish customs-enforcement areas on the high seas to prevent unlawful introduction or removal of merchandise etc. (Anti-smuggling Act.)

Power over Property

10. Act of August 31, 1935 (49 Stat. 1076 #3; F.C.A. 16.831c (k)). Disposal by Tennessee Valley Board of real property no longer needed. (With President's approval.)

Power over Tin-Plate

11. Act of February 15, 1936 (49 Stat. 1140 c. 74; F.C.A. 50:86–87). President may grant licenses for export of tinplate scrap.

Power to Bar Photographs

12. Act of January 12, 1938 (52 Stat. 3 #1; Pub. No. 418; F.C.A. 50:45). President may define vital military and naval defensive installations which are not to be photographed.

Power to Recruit

13. Act of April 25, 1938 (52 Stat. 221, c. 171; Pub. No. 491; F.C.A. 10:343). President may prescribe regulations for the organization etc. of Regular Army Reserve as a part of the Regular Army.

Power over Munitions

14. Act of June 16, 1938 (52 Stat. c. 707–458; Pub. No. 639; F.C.A. 50:91). Contracts entered into by Sec. of War to familiarize concerns with manufacture etc. of munitions of war. (With President's approval.)

Power over Air Transport

15. Act of June 23, 1938 (52 Stat. 1014 #801; Pub. No. 706; F.C.A. 49:601). Certificates issued by Civil Aeronautics Authority authorizing air carriers to engage in overseas or foreign air transportation under Civil Aeronautics Act of 1938. (With approval of President.)

Power to Lease Oil Land

16. Act of June 30, 1938 (52 Stat. 1253; Pub. No. 786; F.C.A. 34:524). Lease by Secretary of the Navy of portion of naval petroleum reserves, contracts to alienate use etc., acquisition of privately owned lands for conservation of naval petroleum; direct expenditure of sums authorized to be appropriated for carrying out act.

C. Unrepealed Emergency Powers

Power to Suspend 8-Hour Law

1. Act of March 4, 1917 (39 Stat. 1192; U.S. Code 40:326). President authorized to suspend eight-hour law in emergencies.

Power over Ports

2. Act of June 15, 1917 (40 Stat. 220; U.S. Code 50; 191–194). Secretary of the Treasury authorized to make, subject to the approval of the President, regulations governing vessels in ports of the United States during emergencies.

Power to Seize Plants

3. U.S. Code, Title 50, Sec. 80. President authorized to take possession of any manufacturing plant refusing to give preference to government contracts or manufacture for a fair price arms and ammunition or other necessary material in time of war or when war is imminent.

Power to Alter Appropriations

4. Act of July 12, 1870 (16 Stat. 251 (R.S. Sec. 3679) as amended; U.S. Code 31:665). Authorized the waiver or modification of monthly apportionments of appropriations for governmental departments and agencies for expenses during the fiscal year, "upon the happening of some extraordinary emergency or other unusual circumstance which could not be anticipated at the time of making such apportionment."

Power to Give Preference

5. Act of February 28, 1920 (41 Stat. 476–477; U.S. Code 49:1 (15)). Interstate Commerce Commission authorized to direct preferences and priorities upon certification by the President that such preferences and priorities are essential to the national defense and security "in time of war or threatened war."

Power to Erect Forts

6. Act of April 11, 1898 (30 Stat. 737; U.S. Code 50:178). President authorized to order the erection of any temporary fort or fortification upon the written consent of the owner of the land upon which such work is to be placed "in case of emergency."

D. EMERGENCY POWERS SINCE 1933

Power to Govern Gold Export

1. Act of March 9, 1933 (48 Stat. 1 #2; F.C.A. 12:95a, 95b). The President may regulate foreign exchange export etc. of gold during a national emergency.

Power to Suspend Wage Law

2. Act of August 30, 1935 (49 Stat. 1013 #6; F.C.A. 40:276a–4). The President may suspend, in time of emergency, provisions of act relating to rate of wages for laborers and mechanics employed on public buildings.

Power over Alien Officers

3. Act of June 29, 1936 (49 Stat. 1993 (h); F.C.A. 46:1132h). The President may, at his discretion, suspend provisions relating to citizenship requirements of licensed officers of documented vessels during a national emergency.

Power over Sugar

4. Act of Sept. 1, 1937 (50 Stat. 916 #509; F.C.A. 7:1179). The President may suspend operation of quota provisions and conditional-payment provisions of the Sugar Act of 1937, in time of emergency.

Power over Ship Charter

5. Act of June 29, 1936 (49 Stat. 2010; U.S. Code 46:1202). Maritime Commission vessels' charters may be terminated "in any national emergency as proclaimed by the President."

Power to Requisition

6. Act of June 29, 1936 (49 Stat. 2015; U.S. Code 46:1242). Maritime Commission may requisition any vessel documented under laws of the United States "during any national emergency declared by proclamation of the President."

E. UNREPEALED WAR AND EMERGENCY POWERS

Power over Nationals

1. Act of July 6, 1798 (R.S. Sec. 4067) as amended by act of April 16, 1918 (40 Stat. 531; U.S. Code 50:21). "Whenever there is a declared war between the United States and any foreign nation or government, . . . and the President makes proclamation of the event, "all nationals of hostile nations of the ages of fourteen years and upward, within the United States and not naturalized, shall be liable to be apprehended, restrained etc. as alien enemies." The President is authorized by proclamation to direct the conduct to be observed by and toward such aliens etc.

Power to Acquire Land

2. Act of July 2, 1917 (40 Stat. 241 as amended; U.S. Code 50:171). Provides for acquisition of land for military purposes "in time of war or the imminence thereof."

Power over Metals

3. Act of July 1, 1918 (40 Stat. 671; U.S. Code 50:144). Director of the Bureau of Mines authorized, under regulations of the Secretary of the Interior, to limit sale, possession and use of platinum, iridium, palladium and their compounds.

Power to Restrict Travel

4. Act of May 22, 1918 (40 Stat. 559; U.S. Code 22:223–226). President authorized to restrict travel between the United States and foreign countries.

F. CERTAIN WARTIME EMERGENCY ECONOMIC POWERS

Power over Communications

1. Act of June 19, 1934 (48 Stat. 1104 #606). The President may direct that pref-erence be given certain communications in time of war; employ armed forces to prevent obstruction of communications; suspend, during war etc. regulations prescribed by the Federal Communications Commission.

Power over Electric Plants

2. Act of June 10, 1920 as amended by Sec. 213, Act of August 26, 1935 (49 Stat. 848). Federal Power Commission author-ized to require such temporary facilities and such generation etc. of electric energy as in its judgment will best meet the emer-gency and serve the public interest "during the continuance of any war in which the United States is engaged, or whenever the Commission determines that an emergency exists by reason of sudden increase in de-mand for electric energy" etc.

A more extensive, but incomplete list of similar powers of all administrative agencies of the National Government, as the statutes stood on May 10, 1937, is given in the *United States News* for that date. *Vid.* also *Congressional Record,* May 28, 1941, pp. 4605 *et seq.*

[44] See Ch. I, pp. 6–8 *supra.*

[45] 135 U.S. 1.

[46] *Ibid.,* 64.

[47] *Ibid.,* 69; U.S. Code, tit. 28, §504 (R.S., §788).

[48] *Dugan's Executors v. United States,* 3 Wheat. 172.

[49] *United States v. Tingy,* 5 Pet. 115 (1831).

[50] *Ibid.,* 122.

[51] See also *United States v. Bradley,* 10 Pet. 343; *United States v. Linn,* 15 Pet. 290. As early as *Chisholm v. Georgia,* 2 Dall. 419 (1792), it was held that the process of the United States courts would run in the name of the President until Congress otherwise provided—which it has never done.

[52] 6 *Opins. A. G.* 28; also to same effect is 4 *ibid.,* 248 (1843).

[53] 6 *Ibid.,* 220.

[54] *Ibid.,* 466.

[55] Richardson, VI, 13. See further *United States v. Hughes,* 11 How. 552; *Wells v. Nickles,* 104 U.S. 444; *United States v. San Jacinto Tin Co.,* 125 U.S. 273—all of which are mentioned by Justice Miller in his opinion. *Cf.* 28 *Opins. A. G.* 143 and 511; and 33 *ibid.,* 436, 438.

[56] 158 U.S. 564 (1895).

[57] *Ibid.,* 586. See also 128 U.S. 315, 367; and 224 U.S. 413, 438–442. Out of the Debs Case, in the main, has grown "government by injunction," a danger which was early recognized. See *Senate Reports.* No. 827, 54th Congress, 1st sess., p. 166.

[58] 2 Dall. 409 (1792).

[59] *Autobiography,* pp. 388–389. In June, 1908, and so some months before leaving the Presidency, Roosevelt wrote Sir George Otto Trevelyan as follows:

"While President I have *been* President, emphatically; I have used *every ounce* of power there was in the office and I have not cared a rap for the criticisms of those who spoke of my 'usurpation of power'; for I know that the talk has been all nonsense and that there had been no usurpation. I believe that the efficiency of this Government depends upon its possessing a strong central executive, and wherever I could establish a precedent for strength in the executive, as I did for instance as regards external affairs in the case of sending the fleet around the world, taking Panama, settling affairs of Santo Domingo, and Cuba; or as I did in internal affairs in settling the anthracite coal strike, in keeping order in Nevada . . . or as I have done in bringing the big corporations to book . . . in all these cases I have felt not merely that my action was right in itself, but that in showing the strength of, or in giving strength to, the executive, I was establishing a precedent of value. I believe in a strong executive; I believe in power; but I believe that responsibility should go with power, and that it is not well that the strong executive should be a perpetual executive." Joseph B. Bishop, *Roosevelt and His Time*, II, 94.

⁶⁰ *Autobiography*, pp. 474–476; see also Henry F. Pringle, *Theodore Roosevelt* (New York, 1931), pp. 268–274. Apparently President Wilson contemplated a similar step at the time of the Colorado coal strike in 1916. *The New York Times*, October 29 and 30, 1916.

Roosevelt's plans for the protection of the treaty rights of Japanese in the United States in 1906, at the time of the San Francisco School controversy, also contemplated the possible use of troops, and on very doubtful legal warrant. See Thomas A. Bailey, *Theodore Roosevelt and the Japanese-American Crises* (Stanford University Press, 1934), pp. 28–29, 45, 80–84; 100–101.

⁶¹ Taft, *Our Chief Magistrate*, pp. 139–140. The same issue had been thrashed out earlier in the famous Ballinger-Pinchot quarrel in 1910, in the course of which Mr. James R. Garfield, who had been Mr. Roosevelt's Secretary of the Interior, advanced the theory of a residual executive power and Ballinger's defenders took the other end of the argument. See, e.g., Senate debate in *Congressional Record* for May 11, 1910; also Rose M. Stahl, *The Ballinger-Pinchot Controversy* (Smith College, 1926). A statement of the residual power theory which attracted considerable attention at the time was that made by Senator Works of California in the Senate, January 5, 1917; see *Congressional Record* for that date.

⁶² See the chapter on "Executive Power" in that excellent old book, *The Trial of the Constitution*, by Sidney George Fisher (Philadelphia, 1862).

⁶³ The crisis of 1932–1933 evoked several suggestions of dictatorship in the United States. Mr. Ralph Adams Cram wanted President Hoover to suspend the Constitution, abolish the income tax and prohibition, dissolve Congress, and so on. *Boston Globe*, July 16, 1932. The Hon. Alfred E. Smith was for laying the Constitution "on the shelf." This was in February 1933; and at the same time *Pacific Banker*, a San Francisco publication, was urging a "National Manager," who was to be "of commanding ability" and was to be selected by "the business leaders of the country"—this although the country had just elected a President! *The New York Times*, February 5, 1933. Abroad there were predictions that the President would be presently vested with dictatorial powers. *Ibid.*, January 25, 1933.

Speaking of the Roman dictatorship, which was a "temporary concentration of powers for emergency purposes," and with which the Framers of the Constitution had a literary acquaintance, Professor Friedrich makes the following interesting observations:

"The Roman example is significant, because for several centuries dictatorship there remained a bulwark for the Republican government, and did not lead to any usurpation of powers. The conditions of this state of affairs seem to have been essentially four. In the first place the appointment of the dictator took place according to precise constitutional forms. Secondly, the dictator himself could not at his discretion declare the state of emergency. The dictatorship occurred, thirdly, always in defense of the existing constitutional order, never with a view to changing it (as under Caesar). And a fourth condition of great importance was a strict time limit imposed upon the dictator for the fulfillment of his task, never to exceed six months. Obviously, all these conditions are themselves dependent upon the constitutional order, and can therefore be properly called constitutional limitations." *Constitutional Government and Politics* (New York, 1937), p. 211.

Applying then these four features of the Roman dictatorship as criteria to the provision usually made under modern liberal constitutions for emergency situations, he points out that under our Constitution, as well as under the British and French, dictators—in the above sense—are "really self-appointed," in consequence of the influence which they can bring to bear upon the legislature in such situations. "This is no less true," he continues, "of Franklin D. Roosevelt than it was of Poincaré. And although parliamentary majorities may and do disintegrate—in which case genuine checks result—from the viewpoint of power analysis the disquieting feature of these arrangements is that the parliamentary majority initiating the dictatorship actually derives increased powers therefrom, at the expense of the minority whom they may be combating. The American Civil War situation is a doleful illustration of this interrelation. To make the point more practically applicable to present-day controversies: if the second Roosevelt had had to abdicate his presidential powers in asking Congress to appoint a temporary dictator to deal with the emergency which he claimed to exist, he would possibly have been more doubtful about it. And if it had been his function to determine the end of the crisis for the purpose of resuming his presidential powers, the end of the crisis might have come sooner. Such statements as these may sound partisan and biased, but they are not meant to be so; the same thing would hold true for any other man occupying the presidential office with a solid majority of partisans in Congress. What is, in this respect, true of the United States, is of course, *a fortiori* true of England and France, not to speak of Republican Germany. We must, therefore, conclude that the present systems of constitutional dictatorship in the leading countries do not accord with our second criterion. Whether their constitutional orders will, therefore, be perverted into governments with concentrated powers, as happened in Germany, would seem to depend upon the extent to which recurrent crises will entail the employment of presumably temporary emergency powers." *Ibid.*, p. 217. (The above passages are quoted from Professor Friedrich's work by permission of the publishers, Harper and Brothers.) *Cf. Federalist* No. 70; Earle, 454.

As to more permanent trends, independent of emergency, toward the exaltation of executive power in the states and municipalities, as well as the National Government, see the summary of the Report of the President's Committee on Social Trends, *The New York Times*, January 2, 1933.

[64] See Attorney General Murphy's letter of October 4, 1939, to the President of the Senate, where the appropriate citations to the Code are given. *Senate Documents,* No. 133, 76th Congress, 2nd sess.; also note 43 *supra*.

[65] *The New York Times*, September 9, 1939.

[66] Washington despatches of November 15, 1939, stated that the deficit spending in

question would run to nearly 272 millions, most of it going to the Army and Navy. That the President experienced some legal qualms about his course is disclosed by a despatch to *The New York Times* of October 4, 1939. It read in part:

"President Roosevelt disclosed today that he had ordered the War and Navy Departments to ignore statutory prohibitions against budgetary deficits growing out of unauthorized expenditures for army and navy housing, hospitalization and the reconditioning of obsolete vessels.

"After discussing the matter, involving an apparent conflict of laws, with two Supreme Court justices, and the Controller General, the President said that he had decided to anticipate Congressional approval of expenditures necessitated by the limited emergency program calling for 100,000 more soldiers, sailors and marines and the recommissioning of a hundred World War destroyers for patrol duty.

"Although admittedly aware of the statutory barrier, the President argued that if he had the clear authority to increase the enlisted strength of the army, navy and Marine Corps above the normal of recent years, he had also the implied authority to direct expenditures incident to such increases for housing, hospitalization and the reconditioning of the destroyers flotilla.

"Mr. Roosevelt did not disclose whether Associate Justices Harlan Stone and Felix Frankfurter had expressed any opinion on the wisdom of his course when he discussed the legal conflict with them on a week-end cruise down the Potomac River. He did claim support for his action in an informal opinion he said was given to him by Controller General Fred H. Brown, with whom he discussed the question just before his press conference today."

The statutory provision giving rise to the difficulties above referred to reads as follows:

"No executive department or other government establishment of the United States shall expend . . . or involve the government in any contract or other obligation for the future payment of money in excess of such appropriations unless such contract or obligation is authorized by law." U. S. Code, tit. 11, §665, c. 11.

The essential question is, when is an expenditure "authorized by law"? As I indicated in the text, it seems to me that the President was well within his rights in ordering the expenditure just mentioned, his "emergency" premise being conceded. If Congress does not like such expenditures it should revise the statutes. It is true, nevertheless, that Mr. Roosevelt is rather prone to place an "emergency" construction on events. See a compilation by Mr. Bruce Barton, in the *Times* of March 17, 1939, of some 39 uses by him of this or equivalent terms.

[67] 4 *Commentaries,* 397–398.

[68] Art. II, §2, par. 1. "It is declared in parliament, by statute 27 Hen. VIII. c. 24, that no other person hath power to pardon or remit any treason or felonies whatsoever; but that the king hath the whole and sole power thereof, united and knit to the imperial crown of this realm." Preceding note.

[69] Farrand, II, 426, 526–527. Sherman characteristically wanted pardons conditioned on the consent of the Senate, a suggestion which received the support of only his own state. *Ibid.,* 419.

[70] Earle, p. 484.

[71] 7 Pet. 150 (1833).

[72] The argument for the United States was made by Taney as Attorney General and was based exclusively upon British authorities. Marshall invoked British practice as fur-

nishing the proper rule of constitutional interpretation for the "reprieves and pardons" clause thus:

"As this power had been exercised from time immemorial by the executive of that nation whose language is our language, and to whose judicial institutions ours bear a close resemblance; we adopt their principles respecting the operation and effect of a pardon, and look into their books for the rules prescribing the manner in which it is to be used by the person who would avail himself of it." *Ibid.,* 160.

The rule was reiterated in *ex parte* Wells, 18 How. 307, 310–311 (1855), but met with strenuous protest in a dissenting opinion by Justice McLean: "The executive office in England and that in this country is [sic] so widely different that doubts may be entertained whether it would be safe for a republican chief magistrate, who is the creature of the laws, to be influenced by the exercise of any leading power of the British sovereign." *Ibid.,* 318. This was certainly good Jeffersonian doctrine. To the contrary effect, however, see 4 *Opins. A. G.* 456 (1843) and 5 *ibid.,* 536 (1852); also the Grossman Case, which is discussed below. But the McLean dissent may be said to have come into its own in the Perovich Case. Today, as is indicated in the text, the Court follows the Marshall rule at discretion—it has, in short, a choice.

[73] *Armstrong v. United States,* 13 Wall. 154, 156. For presidential proclamations of amnesty, see Richardson, I, 181 (Washington), 303 (Adams), 512, 514, 543 (Madison); VI, 213–216 (Lincoln), 310, 547, 655, 708 (Johnson); X, 496 (Roosevelt). This power was the pivot of "Presidential Reconstruction," just as the power of the houses of Congress to determine the qualifications of their respective members was the pivot of "Congressional Reconstruction." By a clause of the Confiscation Act of July 17, 1862 (12 Stat. 592), Congress purported to authorize the President to extend to participants "in the existing rebellion" "pardon and amnesty," with such exceptions and on such conditions as he deemed expedient. Lincoln, in his Proclamation of December 8, 1863, refers to this provision merely as "according with well-established judicial exposition of the pardoning power." He based his action on the Constitution. In consequence of the quarrel between Johnson and Congress over Reconstruction, Congress repealed the above provision of the Confiscation Act January 21, 1867; and in its Report of December 25, 1868, the Senate Committee on the Judiciary directly challenged the title of the President to the power of amnesty, which it claimed for Congress alone. *Senate Reports* 239, 40th Congress, 3rd sess. Royal amnesties, the committee argued, were always by virtue of parliamentary authorization. The contentions of the committee were, however, pretty well met and refuted by one "L.C.K.," writing in 7 *University of Pennsylvania Law Review* and *American Law Register* (New Series), 523–532 (September, 1869). In point of fact, Hamilton seems clearly to assume in the passage in *The Federalist* already referred to that the power to pardon includes amnesty. In *United States v. Padelford,* 9 Wall. 542 (1870), which involved Lincoln's amnesty, the Court said: "This proclamation, if it needed legislative sanction, was fully warranted by the Act of July 17, 1862." Three years later, in *United States v. Klein,* it is stated flatly "Pardon includes amnesty," a proposition which the dissenting minority does not challenge. 13 Wall. 128, 147; also to the same effect are *Armstrong v. United States, supra,* and *Jenkins v. Collard,* 145 U. S. 560.

[74] 236 U. S. 79 (1915).

[75] *Ibid.,* 90–91.

[76] Equally surprising is the Court's failure to take account of its own words in *Brown v. Walker,* 161 U. S. 591 (1896): "It is almost a necessary corollary of the above proposi-

tions that, if the witness has already received a pardon, he cannot longer set up his privilege, since he stands with respect to such offense as if it had never been committed." *Ibid.,* 599, citing British cases. To the same effect was a suggestion by the late Justice Cardozo, when he was Chief Judge of the New York Court of Appeals, that "the quickest and easiest way" to get the testimony of one Doyle, who was pleading his constitutional privilege, would be for the governor to pardon him. *The New York Times,* July 28, 1931.

77 For a most absurd tempest in the teapot, which first and last involved, besides President Coolidge and Craig, the United States Supreme Court, Attorney General Daugherty, Judge Mayer, Senator Copeland, Representative La Guardia, several labor organizations, and still others, see *The New York Times,* November 20 to December 11, 1923.

78 *Chapman v. Scott,* 10 F (2nd.) 156, 161 (December 14, 1925).

79 *Biddle v. Perovich,* 274 U. S. 480.

80 *Ibid.,* 486.

81 267 U. S. 87.

82 *The New York Times,* May 16, 1924. See also Story, 2 *Commentaries,* §1503.

83 Especially difficult to meet was the proposition that an "offense against the United States" must be violative of a statute of the United States (*United States v. Hudson,* 7 Cr. 32); nor can it be said that the Chief Justice's opinion entirely disposes of the question. 267 U. S. 114–115.

84 *Ibid.,* 110.

85 *Ibid.,* 118–119, citing 3 *Opins. A. G.* 622; 4 *ibid.,* 317 and 458, and 19 *ibid.,* 476.

86 *Ibid.,* 121.

87 *Ibid.,* 122. It may be remarked in passing that in classifying "criminal" contempts as "offenses against the United States," the Grossman Case would seem to throw down every barrier in the way of requiring that "contempts fully completed" be tried by jury, thus rendering obsolete the halfway doctrine of the slightly earlier Michaelson Case (266 U. S. 18). For being offenses against the United States, it is the public interest which is primarily involved in the punishment of "criminal" contempts, and only secondarily the dignity of the offended court. Indeed, as Chief Justice Taft takes pains to note in his opinion, such acts were triable in England at the time of the framing of the Constitution in both ways, that is, by the Court alone or by a court and jury, following indictment of the offender (267 U. S. at 110). See also J. Holmes on the same point in the Gompers Case, 233 U. S. 604; and compare the Court's ignorant denial of this in the Eilenbecker Case, 134 U. S. 3.

Instructive cases which are illustrative of the judicial power to punish "criminal contempts" are *ex parte* Robinson, 19 Wall. 505; *ex parte* Wall, 107 U. S. 265; *ex parte* Terry, 128 U. S. 289; *Gompers v. United States, supra; Toledo Newspaper Co. v. United States,* 247 U. S. 402.

88 The passage in Blackstone alluded to is to the effect that coercive measures of a court in support of the rights of a suitor, "being properly the civil remedy of individuals for a private injury, are not released or affected by a general pardon." 4 *Commentaries,* 285. But as general pardons, according to Blackstone, are by act of Parliament, what he here has in mind is apparently a rule of statutory construction rather than of constitutional limitation binding on the King. It may be granted, nevertheless, that the rule of restriction stated in the Grossman Case is a fairly logical application of the ancient maxim that the "King may not use his grace to the injury or detriment of others [*non poterit rex gratiam facere cum injuria et damno aliorum*]." Brac., lib. iii, f. 132; 3 *Inst.,* 236; 4

Commentaries, 398. See, however, *Young v. Chamberlain,* Tothill, 41, for a late use of the power to pardon what we should today term a civil contempt; *cf. ex parte* White-church, 1 Atk. 37 (1749).

89 The case referred to is *Besette v. McConkey Co.,* 194 U. S. 324, in which the Court, speaking by Justice Brewer, takes the distinction from Judge Sanborn's opinion in *in re* Nevitt, 54 C. C. A. 622, 632; 117 Fed. Rep. 448, 458 (1902). Justice Miller, speaking for the Court in *in re* Chiles, 22 Wall. 157 (1874), recognizes the twofold use of contempt proceedings, the punitive and the coercive, but does not distinguish "criminal" from "civil" contempts. Nor does the Act of 1831 (§725 R.S.) recognize such a distinction; nor yet does Story in his *Commentaries* (see §1503). In his article, however, in 21 *Harvard Law Review,* 161–174, on "Contempt of Court, Civil and Criminal," Professor Beale is able to supply a very different ancestry for each of the two types. *Criminal* contempts he traces to insults to the royal authority, and terms them "active contempts," while *civil* contempts he traces to disobedience of the Lord Chancellor's orders. "Punishment" in such cases, he explains, is not punitive in intention, but coercive and therefore is indefinite—that is, it continues until the order is performed by the recalcitrant party, or until he has restored the *status quo ante.* The comparatively recent formulation of the distinction is probably due to the tendency of the two concepts to merge.

The question is naturally suggested by the Grossman Case whether the President could pardon contempts of the houses of Congress. The general argument against the suggestion on the ground of the principle of separation of powers is logically invalidated by the holding; but the silence of precedent is a strong counter-consideration, and precedent is the basis of the decision. Moreover, the Chief Justice mentions specifically an opinion by Rawle about 1830 that the pardoning power did not extend to "contempts of a House of Congress." 267 U. S. 118.

90 Another interesting aspect of the case is its manipulation of the separation of powers principle, wherein it presents a striking contrast to the same Justice's opinion in the Myers Case. *Ibid.,* 119–121.

91 4 Wall. 333.

92 *Ibid.,* 380.

93 *Ibid.,* 396–397.

94 See especially Professor Williston's article, "Does a Pardon Blot Out Guilt?" in 28 *Harvard Law Review,* 647–663; and Mr. Henry Weihofen's article "The Effect of Pardon" in 88 *University of Pennsylvania Law Review,* 177–193.

95 142 U. S. 450 (1892).

96 See Professor Everett S. Brown's valuable article, "The Restoration of Civil and Political Rights by Presidential Pardon," 34 *American Political Science Review,* 295–300. On the question whether a presidential pardon is capable of relieving a federal convict of legal or political disabilities imposed by state laws, doctrine has varied somewhat. Attorney General Cushing's opinion in 7 *Opins. A. G.* 760–761 (1856), which is cited by Professor Brown as negativing the proposition, applied only to "a supplemental or special pardon," but apparently recognized that "a general pardon" would have been efficacious for the purpose. And four years later Attorney General Black ruled in unqualified terms that a person disfranchised as a citizen by conviction for crime under the laws of the United States could be restored to his rights by a pardon issued either before or after he had suffered the other penalties incident to his conviction. 9 *Ibid.,* 478 (1860). See also 21 *ibid.,* 242–243 (1893).

97 233 U. S. 51.

[98] The provisions of the Act of February 5, 1917, for the deportation of aliens convicted of certain offenses involving "moral turpitude" do not apply "to one who has been pardoned" (U. S. Code, tit. 8, §155); and on this ground the Attorney General has occasionally advised the President to pardon alien offenders against United States statutes upon completion of sentence.

Nor is the efficacy of this provision confined to presidential pardons for federal offenses, in which connection the following item from the *Boston Transcript* of December 24, 1938, is of interest:

"Pasquale Vallarelli, 30 year-old Boston alien, walked out of the East Boston Immigration Station today a free man after Washington authorities ruled that the pardon granted him by Governor Hurley and the Executive Council automatically canceled a deportation warrant for his detention.

"Vallarelli was pardoned by the Council Thursday night after serving more than nine years of a 21 to 24-year sentence for robbery. He was released from State Prison yesterday afternoon and was immediately taken into custody by immigration authorities.

"James H. Brennan, attorney for Vallarelli, contacted officials of the Labor Department in Washington last night and today word was received here by Immigration Commissioner Mary A. Ward that the pardon dismissed the deportation warrant."

[99] *Ex parte* Wells, 18 How. 307 (1855), the leading case, relies principally on British authority. Some early Attorneys General were reluctant to admit the propriety of conditional pardons or of pardons prior to the trial of the applicant. 1 *Opins. A. G.* 342 (1820); 2 *ibid.*, 275 (1829); 5 *ibid.*, 687 (1795). The broader view is based in 4 *ibid.*, 433 on the maxim *"quod omne majus continet minus"* (1845). See also *Senate Documents*, No. 123, 26th Congress, 2nd sess. For an interesting case growing out of a conditional pardon, see 21 *Harvard Law Review*, 541. On the royal dispensing power prior to the Revolution of 1688, see Frederic W. Maitland, *The Constitutional History of England* (Cambridge University Press, 1908), pp. 302–306.

[100] Art. I, §9, par. 7; *Knote v. United States*, 95 U.S. 149 (1877); *The Laura*, 114 U.S. 411 (1885); 5 *Opins. A. G.* 580 (1852); 6 *ibid.*, 393 (1853); 16 *ibid.*, 1 (1878).

[101] *The Laura, supra; Brown v. Walker*, 161 U.S. 591 (1896); *ex parte* United States, 242 U.S. 27 (1913).

[102] *Ex parte* United States, preceding note.

[103] Farrand, II, 185; Cf. 4 *Bl. Commentaries*, 399–400.

[104] Art. I, §3, par. 7.

[105] Maitland, *Constitutional History*, p. 99.

[106] Richardson, II, 576. For an anticipation of Jackson's position, however, see a portentously pompous passage which Jefferson had originally intended to include in his first message to Congress, and where, citing his oath, he declared the Sedition Act "to be a palpable and unqualified contradiction to the Constitution," and announced his intention on that ground of pardoning convicted offenders under it. Inasmuch as the President is free to exercise the pardoning power for good reasons, bad reasons, or no reason at all, the argument was quite superfluous, and so Jefferson evidently decided finally. Beveridge, *Life of John Marshall*, III, 605–606.

[107] Charles Warren, *The Supreme Court in United States History* (New York, 1926), II, 223–224.

[108] The oft-repeated story that Jackson remarked of the Supreme Court's decision in *Worcester v. Georgia*, "Well, John Marshall has made his decision, now let him enforce it!" has no better literary source than Greeley's *American Conflict*, I, 106, where Greeley credits it to "the late Governor George N. Briggs, of Massachusetts, who was in Wash-

ington as a member of Congress when the decision was rendered." Mr. Warren thinks the tale a myth, but Mr. Marquis James holds otherwise, quoting the following from the *National Journal* of April 7, 1832: "The prerogatives of nullifying laws and political decisions by denying their conformity to the court makes . . . [the President] supreme— the final arbiter—the very Celestial Majesty." *Andrew Jackson, Portrait of a President* (Indianapolis, 1937), pp. 304–305. The word "court" in the above quotation ought to be, I suspect, "constitution."

[109] Richardson, VI, 25.

[110] Evart's words were:

"Much has been said about the duty of the people to obey and of officers to execute unconstitutional laws. I claim for the President no greater right in respect to a law that operates upon him in his public duty, and upon him exclusively, to raise a question under the Constitution to determine what his right and what his duty is, than I claim for every citizen in his private capacity when a law infringes upon his constitutional and civil and personal rights. . . . And are we such bad citizens when we advise that the Constitution of the United States may be upheld, and that anybody, without a breach of the peace and in an honest purpose, may make a case that the instance may be given whereby the judgment of the court may be had and the Constitution safe from violation?" *Trial of Andrew Johnson* (Washington, 1868), II, 293, 296.

[111] *Ibid.,* 200.

[112] *Ibid.,* 71. Boutwell was the speaker.

[113] *Ibid.,* 256.

[114] See Willoughby, III, 1502–1504, for substantially this view. In *United States v. Lee,* Justice Miller, speaking for a divided Court, said:

"No man in this country is so high that he is above the law. No officer of the law may set that law at defiance with impunity. All the officers of the government, from the highest to the lowest, are creatures of the law, and are bound to obey it.

"It is the only supreme power in our system of government, and every man who by accepting office participates in its functions is only the more strongly bound to submit to that supremacy, and to observe the limitations which it imposes upon the exercise of the authority which it gives." 106 U. S. 196, 220.

While these words state the general theory of the President's duty as Chief Executive to the law as it comes from the courts, yet in the light of the Court's earlier ruling in *Mississippi v. Johnson* that duty must be held to be *moral* rather than *legal* in character —one the final forum of which is the President's own conscience, not a court of law. 4 Wall. 475 (1867). *Vd.* p. 27 *supra.*

NOTES TO CHAPTER V*

[1] *Commentaries,* 257, 262.

[2] No. 69; Earle, p. 448.

[3] *The New York Times,* May 12, 1918. As a further illustration of the extremes to which Senators, and others, occasionally went, Mr. Warren quotes an attack by Senator Richardson of Illinois on the employment of sentinels around the White House and War Department: "These emblems of regal power, placed there to familiarize our people with them, filled me with sorrow and sadness. For the first time in our history these things

---

* *Chapter V (Commander-in-Chief) begins on page 154.*

have occurred. . . . The ruins of this Republic will be scattered along the highway of nations where lie the ruins of all the republics that have gone before us." The date of this gloomy vaticination was February 28, 1863.

4 For example, according to Attorney General Black's opinion of November 10, 1860, the only "insurrections" which the National Government was authorized to suppress were "insurrections against the States"! McPherson, *History of the Rebellion* (1865), pp. 51–52.

5 Carl R. Fish, *The American Civil War* (New York, 1937), pp. 303–305.

6 F. W. Maitland, *op. cit.*, p. 299.

7 See proclamations of April 15 and May 3, 1861, Richardson, VI, 13–16; message of July 4, 1861, *ibid.*, 20–31; special message of May 26, 1862, in which the facts regarding the "advance" the year previous of $2,000,000 to Messrs. Dix, Opdyke, and Blatchford for confidential services were divulged for the first time, *ibid.*, 77–79; special message of February 14, 1862, giving other details, *ibid.*, 102–104. The loan referred to, a temporary one, was offered July 1, 1861, three days before Congress convened.

8 *Ibid.*, 23–25, 31.

9 *Ibid.*, 7, 27.

10 2 Bl. 635 (March 10, 1863).

11 *Ibid.*, 648.

12 *Ibid.*, 668–670.

13 These are Professor Randall's words, in his discerning *Constitutional Problems under Lincoln*, p. 514. Lincoln himself told Senator Chandler, in discussing his disapproval of the Wade-Davis Reconstruction bill (1864): "I conceive that I may in an emergency do things on military grounds which can not constitutionally be done by Congress." Nathaniel W. Stephenson, *Abraham Lincoln and the Union* (Yale University Press, 1921), p. 353.

14 The details are readily available in Randall's and Rhodes's volumes. See the following passages in the latter: III, 441–442, 553, 556n, 557–558; IV, 169–172, 234–235, 248, 250, 254–255, 423; V, 470.

15 McPherson, p. 177.

16 *Ibid.*, pp. 183–184.

17 Richardson, VI, 120: General Orders, No. 100, *Official Records, War of Rebellion,* ser. III, vol. III. It is interesting to contrast President John Adams's doubts regarding his powers, as reflected in a memorandum which was addressed January 29, 1799, by the Secretary of the Navy to other Cabinet members:

"Sir, The President requested me to consult the Heads of Departments, whether the President, in whom is vested the Executive Power of the Nation, possesses the Constitutional power of regulating the exchange of Prisoners, & all matters belonging to that subject." *Naval Documents—Quasi-War with France* (Washington, 1938). It should be noticed that no mention is made of the President's role as Commander-in-Chief.

18 Randall, *op. cit.*, p. 514.

19 McPherson, pp. 196–197, 227–229.

20 The extent to which Lincoln's thinking was influenced by William Whiting's *War Powers under the Constitution* is impossible to say; but it is not improbable that Whiting's views were frequently brought to his attention through Stanton. The first edition of this work appeared in 1862, the forty-third—the one cited here—in 1870. It was Whiting's task as Solicitor of the War Department to provide legal and constitutional justifications

for the policies and acts of that department, and especially for its policy in the matter of military arrests. Whiting's central proposition is the maxim that "amidst arms the laws are silent" (p. 52), which applied especially, he held, to the Bill of Rights of the Constitution. This was made for peacetime, not for wartime (p. 176). "The sovereign and almost dictatorial military powers" he wrote, "existing only in actual war, ending when war ends, to be used in self-defense, to be laid down when no longer necessary, are, while they last, as lawful, as constitutional, as sacred, as the administration of justice by judicial courts in time of peace" (p. 52). And again: "It [the Constitution] does not prescribe any territorial limits, within the United States to which his [the President's] military operations shall be restricted. . . . It does not exempt any person making war upon the country, or aiding and comforting the enemy, from being *captured,* or arrested wherever he may be found. . . . It requires the President, as Chief Executive Magistrate in time of peace to see that the laws existing in time of peace are faithfully executed—and as commander-in-chief, in time of war, to see that the laws of war are executed." *Op. cit.,* pp. 89, 165–166.

In short, Whiting contends that in time of war, the President's powers range over the entire country, and are subject to no constitutional limitations whatsoever. And, furthermore, Congress's auxiliary powers under the "necessary and proper" clause have equal scope, *provided* they be employed to *aid* and not to *hinder* "the war-making power."

One or two items may be added which bear upon the evolution of Lincoln's final position. In a confidential letter dated exactly a year before his Emancipation Proclamation, Lincoln wrote, with reference to Frémont's proclamation of martial law in Missouri, that he saw no difference between slaves and other forms of property:

"If the general needs them, he can seize and use them; but when the need is past, it is not for him to fix their permanent future condition. That must be settled according to laws made by law-makers, and not by military proclamations. The proclamation on the point in question is simply 'dictatorship.' . . . Can it be pretended that it is any longer the Government of the United States—any government of constitution and laws—wherein a general or a president may make permanent rules of property by proclamation? I do not say Congress might not pass a law on the point. . . . What I object to is, that I, as President, shall expressly or impliedly seize and exercise the permanent legislative functions of the government." Nicolay and Hay, *Complete Works,* II, 80–82.

Yet when he publicly revoked a similar proclamation of General Hunter in May 1862, he said:

"Whether it be competent for me, as commander in chief of the army and navy, to declare the slaves of any State or States free, and whether, at any time, in any case, it shall have become a necessity indispensable to the maintenance of the government to exercise such supposed power, are questions which, under my responsibility, I reserve to myself. . . . " Richardson, VI, 91.

The final Emancipation Proclamation simply spoke of the action "as a fit and necessary war measure for suppressing said rebellion . . . sincerely believed to be an act of justice, warranted by the Constitution upon military necessity. . . ." *Ibid.,* pp. 157–159.

It is also interesting to recall that as a Whig member of Congress years before, Lincoln had been one of Polk's severest critics and had voted for the Ashmun resolution of censure which declared that the President had "unconstitutionally" begun war with Mexico. Justifying his conduct in a letter to Herndon at the time, Lincoln said:

"Let me first state what I understand to be your position. It is that if it shall become necessary to repel invasion, the President may, without violation of the Constitution, cross the line and invade the territory of another country, and that whether such necessity exists in any given case the President is the sole judge. . . . Allow the President to invade a neighboring nation whenever he shall deem it necessary to repel an invasion and you allow him to do so whenever he may choose to say he deems it necessary for such purpose, and you allow him to make war at pleasure. Study to see if you can fix any limit to his power in this respect, after having given him so much as you propose. . . . The provision of the Constitution giving the *war-making* power to Congress was dictated, as I understand it, by the following reasons: Kings had always been involving and impoverishing their people in wars, pretending generally, if not always, that the good of the people was the object. This our convention understood to be the most oppressive of all kingly oppressions, and they resolved to so frame the Constitution that no one man should hold the power of bringing this oppression upon us. But your view destroys the whole matter, and places our President where kings have always stood." Nicolay and Hay, I, 111–112.

[21] The question of the location of the "war power" was the subject of a notable debate in the Senate between Sumner and Lincoln's friend Browning, June 27, 1862. Sumner's position is adequately stated in the following passage:

"There are Senators who claim these vast War Powers for the President, and deny them to Congress. The President, it is said, as commander-in-chief, may seize, confiscate, and liberate under the Rights of War, but Congress cannot direct these things to be done. Pray, Sir, where is the limitation upon Congress? Read the text of the Constitution, and you will find its powers vast as all the requirements of war. There is nothing that may be done anywhere under the Rights of War, which may not be done by Congress. I do not mean to question the powers of the President in his sphere, or of any military commander within his department; but I claim for Congress all that belongs to any Government in the exercise of the Rights of War. And when I speak of Congress, let it be understood that I mean an *Act of Congress,* passed, according to the requirements of the Constitution, by both Houses, and approved by the President. It seems strange to claim for the President alone, in the exercise of his single will, War Powers alleged to be denied to the President in association with Congress. If he can wield these powers alone, surely he can wield them in association with Congress; nor will their efficacy be impaired, when it is known that they proceed from this associate will, rather than from his single will alone. The government of the United States appears most completely in an Act of Congress. Therefore war is declared, armies are raised, rules concerning captures are made, and all articles of war regulating the conduct of war are established by Act of Congress. It is by Act of Congress that the War Powers are all put in motion. When once put in motion, the President must execute them. But he is only the instrument of Congress, under the Constitution.

"It is true, the President is commander-in-chief; but it is for Congress to make all laws necessary and proper for carrying into execution his powers, so that, according to the very words of the Constitution, his powers depend upon Congress, which may limit or enlarge them at its own pleasure. Thus, whether you regard Congress or regard the President, you will find that Congress is the arbiter and regulator of the War Powers.

"Of the pretension that all these enormous powers belong to the President, and not to Congress, I try to speak calmly and within bounds. I mean always to be parliamentary. But a pretension so irrational and unconstitutional, so absurd and tyrannical, is not entitled to respect. The Senator from Ohio [Mr. Wade], in indignant words worthy of the Senate, has branded it as slavish, and handed it over to judgment. Born in ignorance, and pernicious in consequences, it ought to be received most sternly, and, just in proportion as it obtains acceptance, with execration. Such a pretension would change the National Government from a government of law to that of a military dictator. It would degrade our proud Constitutional Republic, where each department has its appointed place, to one of those short-lived, vulgar despotisms appearing occasionally as a warning to mankind. That this pretension should be put forward in the name of the Constitution is only another illustration of the effrontery with which the Constitution is made responsible for the ignorance, the conceit, and the passions of men. Sir, in the name of the Constitution, which I have sworn to support, and which, according to my ability, I mean to maintain, I protest against this new-fangled effort to foist into it a pretension abhorrent to liberty, reason, and common sense." *Works of Charles Sumner* (Boston, 1872), VII, 138–140; *Congressional Globe,* 37th Congress., 2nd Sess., 2188–2196.

Browning, in answer, denied "that Congress may decide upon the measures demanded by military necessities and order them to be enforced. . . . However great the apparent necessity for such measures now, the events of an hour may so change the face of affairs that the necessity will be found in leniency, forbearance, and protection. . . . These necessities may be determined by the military commander, and to him the Constitution has entrusted the prerogative of judging of them. When the Constitution made the President 'Commander in Chief of the Army and Navy of the United States' it clothed him with all the incidental powers necessary to a full, faithful and efficient performance of the duties of that high office; and to decide what are military necessities, and to devise and execute the requisite measures to meet them, is one of these incidents. It is not a legislative, but an executive function, and Congress has nothing to do with it. . . . And whenever Congress assumes the control of the Army in the field, it usurps the powers of a coordinate department of the Government, destroys the checks and balances provided for the safety of the people, and subverts the Constitution." *Ibid.,* 2919.

However, the President was not irresponsible. Indeed, he was more responsible than Congress:

"If these extreme war powers be prostituted to the purposes of tyranny and oppression by the President, to whom the Constitution has intrusted them, when peace returns he is answerable to the civil power for that abuse. If Congress usurps and prostitutes them, the liberty of the citizen is overthrown, and he is hopelessly without remedy for his grievances . . . there is absolutely no remedy to be found anywhere." *Ibid.,* 1136.

This was said, of course, some years before *Mississippi v. Johnson.* See p. 27 *supra.*

The position of Sidney George Fisher in his still valuable work, *The Trial of the Constitution* (Philadelphia, 1862), was substantially the same as Sumner's. Writing with Lincoln's suspension of the writ of habeas corpus in mind, he said:

"What, then, is the whole law of England in reference to the two vital points of personal liberty and the public safety? Is it not that both are placed under the care of the whole Government, each branch acting in its appropriate sphere and manner; that the Executive is subordinate to the Legislature, and cannot act without its consent, expressly given before or after action; that the Executive represents the whole Government in the absence of the Legislature, and may, to protect the public safety, arrest and detain individuals at its discretion, subject to the subsequent approval of Parliament?" *Op. cit.,* p. 216.

And English law on this point had, he contended, been incorporated in the Constitution: "By that law Executive power, even in its primary and essential attributes, is subjected to legislative power. By our Constitution the subordination of Executive authority to the Legislature, is made even more complete than in the English model which was before the minds of the Convention. It is, therefore, reasonable to suppose, that in a matter so vital as personal liberty, and about which the American people were so sensitive, the founders of our Government would not intentionally depart from the English system, which, in other respects they copied so closely, or that if they meant to depart from it, they would have expressly said so. It cannot be implied that they intended to confer upon the Executive Magistrate a power so dangerous, so liable to abuse, as that of arbitrary and secret imprisonment, to be exercised without the knowledge or consent, or even against the will and protest of the Legislature, a power which it had cost the English people five centuries of effort to take from their kings. To this extent is authority now claimed for the President, not by himself, but by eminent jurists, whose names have just influence on public opinion. But not in the language of the Constitution, in reference to the writ of Habeas Corpus, nor in the provisions that confer and limit Executive power, nor in the analogy between the British Constitution and our own, is such a claim to be found. Neither is it supported by judicial or other authority, subsequent or contemporaneous." *Ibid.,* pp. 220–221.

Presidential war power was, in short, an *ad interim* power, operative when Congress was not in session, but subject to congressional review and supervision when Congress came together.

[22] 4 Wall. 2.

[23] *Ibid.,* 16–19.

[24] *Ibid.,* 31–34, 81.

[25] 12 Wall. 457 (1871).

[26] 4 Wall. 120–121. The befogging, or benumbing, influence of this dictum upon the mind is illustrated by the similar one in Chief Justice Hughes's opinion in the now largely discredited Poultry Case. "We are told," the Chief Justice there recites, "that the provision of the statute authorizing the adoption of codes must be viewed in the light of the grave national crisis with which Congress was confronted." He then continues:

"Undoubtedly, the conditions to which power is addressed are always to be considered when the exercise of power is challenged. Extraordinary conditions may call for extraordinary remedies. But the argument necessarily stops short of an attempt to justify action which lies outside the sphere of constitutional authority. Extraordinary conditions do not create or enlarge constitutional power. The Constitution established a national government with powers deemed to be adequate, as they have proved to be both in war and peace, but these powers of the national government are limited by the constitutional grants. Those who act under these grants are not at liberty to transcend the imposed limits because they believe that more or different power is necessary. Such assertions of extraconstitutional authority were anticipated and precluded by the explicit terms of the Tenth Amendment—'The powers not delegated to the United States by the Constitution, nor prohibited by it to the States, are reserved to the States, respectively, or to the people.'" 295 U. S. 495, 528–529.

The answer is the same as that just given—by the tests applied by the Court the National Government has frequently transcended its powers in order to accomplish what in fact it has accomplished.

[27] 1 Stat. 264.

[28] *Ibid.,* 424.

[29] 12 Wheat. 19, 31–32 (1827).

[30] 2 Stat. 443.

[31] "Federal Aid in Domestic Disturbances," *Senate Documents,* 209, 59th Congress, 2nd sess., p. 51.

[32] Richardson, V, 104–105.

[33] 6 *Opins. A. G.* 466 (May 27, 1854).

[34] Richardson, V, 358.

[35] 12 Stat. 282; U. S. Code, tit. 50, §202.

[36] 32 Stat. 776; U. S. Code, tit. 32, §81a.

[37] 7 How. 1. (1849).

[38] *Op. cit.,* in note 31, at pp. 188–205, and see generally *Senate Documents,* 263, 67th Congress, 2nd sess.

[39] On the whole episode, see Cleveland, *Presidential Problems* (New York, 1904).

[40] 158 U. S. 564, 582.

[41] 17 Stat. 14; U. S. Code, tit. 50, §203.

[42] This and the documents mentioned in the next paragraph are from the files of the War Department.

[43] Richardson, VII, 530–531.

[44] This seems a fair interpretation. See *Autobiography,* pp. 552–553.

[45] Act of March 3, 1809, 2 Stat. 535; U. S. Code, tit. 31, §628.

[46] 20 Stat. 152; U. S. Code, tit. 10, §15.

[47] Richardson, VII, 526.

[48] Note 43 *supra.*

[49] Some other discussions of "the power of the purse" may be mentioned briefly. In 1796 the House formally declared itself free in principle to refuse the legislation needed —including an appropriation—to carry the Jay Treaty into effect, but then voted the required legislation. The year following Nicholas of Virginia expressed himself in the House on the general issue to the following effect:

"The power of this house to control appropriations has been settled. It was indeed an absurdity to call a body a legislature, and at the same time deny them a control over the public purse; if it were not so, where would be the use of going through the forms of that house with a money bill? The executive might as well draw upon the treasury at once for whatever sums he might stand in need of. A doctrine like this would be scouted even in despotic countries." Elliot, *Debates* (1836), IV, 451.

Gallatin avowed a like opinion. Yet a year later Bayard of Delaware contended that Congress was constitutionally obliged to vote a sum asked for by the President for the conduct of foreign relations:

"It had been supposed by gentlemen, that he might appoint an indefinite number of ministers, and were the house, in that case, he asked, blindly to appropriate for them? This question was predicated upon an abuse of power, whilst the constitution supposed it would be executed with fidelity. Suppose he were to state the question in an opposite light. Let it be imagined that this country has a misunderstanding with a foreign power, and that the executive should appoint a minister, but the house, in the plenitude of its power, should refuse an appropriation. What might be the consequence? Would not the house have contravened the constitution by taking from the president the power which, by it, is placed in him? It certainly would. So that this supposition of the abuse of power, would go to the destruction of all authority. The legislature was bound to appropriate for the salary of the Chief Justice of the United States, and though the president might appoint a *chimney sweeper* to the office, they would still be bound. The constitution had trusted the president, as well as it had trusted that house. Indeed it was not conceivable that the house could act upon the subject of foreign ministers. Our interests with foreign countries came wholly under the jurisdiction of the executive. The duties of that house related to the internal affairs of the country, but what related to foreign countries and foreign agents, was vested in the executive. The president was responsible for the manner in which this business was conducted. He was bound to communicate from time to time, our situation with foreign powers, and if plans were carried on abroad for dividing or subjugating us, if he were not to make due communication of the design, he would be answerable for the neglect." *Ibid.*, 452–453.

And in 1826, when the opponents of the Panama Congress sought to attach certain conditions to the appropriation for the mission, Webster took a similar position, saying:

"He would recapitulate only his objections to this amendment. It was unprecedented, nothing of the kind having been attempted before. It was, in his opinion, unconstitutional; as it was taking the proper responsibility from the Executive and exercising, ourselves, a power which, from its nature, belongs to the Executive, and not to us. It was prescribing, by the House, the instructions for a Minister abroad. It was nugatory, as it attached conditions which might be complied with, or might not. And lastly, if gentlemen thought it important to express the sense of the House on these subjects, or any of them, the regular and customary way was by resolution. At present, it seemed to him that we must make the appropriation without conditions, or refuse it. The President had laid the case before us. If our opinion of the character of the meeting, or its objects, led us to withhold the appropriation, we had the power to do so. If we had not so much confidence in the Executive, as to render us willing to trust to the constitutional exercise of the Executive power, we have power to refuse the money. It is a direct question of aye or no. If the Ministers to be sent to Panama may not be trusted to act, like other Ministers, under the instructions of the Executive, they ought not to go at all." Benton, *Abridgment,* IX, 91.

Congress, in 1860, in appropriating money for the completion of the Washington Aqueduct, provided that it should be expended under the superintendence of one Captain Meigs of the Army. This provision evoked from President Buchanan the following protest:

"The first aspect in which this clause presented itself to my mind was that it interfered with the right of the President to be 'Commander in Chief of the Army and Navy of the United States.' If this had really been the case, there would have been an end to the question. Upon further examination I deemed it impossible that Congress could have intended to interfere with the clear right of the President to command the Army and to order its officers to any duty he might deem most expedient for the public interest. If they could withdraw an officer from the command of the President and select him for the performance of an executive duty, they might upon the same principle annex to an appropriation to carry on a war a condition requiring it not to be used for the defense of the country unless a particular person of its own selection should command the Army. It was impossible that Congress could have had such an intention, and therefore, according to my construction of the clause in question, it merely designated Captain Meigs as its preference for the work, without intending to deprive the President of the power to order him to any other army duty for the performance of which he might consider him better adapted." Richardson, V, 598.

In 1912 Senator Bacon of Georgia proposed an amendment to the Army Appropriation bill of that year, that "except as herein provided, or specifically otherwise provided by statute," none of the monies appropriated by the bill should be used for "the pay or supplies of any part of the army of the United States employed or stationed in any country or territory beyond the jurisdiction of the laws of the United States, or in going to or returning from points within the same." Senator Root objected that the amendment would encroach upon the President's powers as Commander-in-Chief, and it was defeated without a record vote. *Congressional Record,* 62nd Congress, 2nd sess., pp. 10,921–10,930. Ten years later the same situation occurred during President Harding's administration. Said Representative Mann of Illinois, regarding a proviso similar to that which Senator Bacon had championed: "Our power to limit appropriations is so conclusive that we can say that no money shall be given in this bill except to red-headed men. . . . I question the advisability of exercising this power, but the right is there." Representative Rogers of Massachusetts, on the other hand, denounced the proviso as both "unconstitutional and unwise" and, like its predecessor, it was rejected. *The New York Times,* March 23, 1922. A third effort of the sort occurred in 1928, and resulted similarly. An extract from the debate in the Senate states the issue in conventional terms:

"Mr. BLAINE: Mr. President, just one other question of the distinguished Senator from Idaho. I know that ordinarily he does not hedge. . . .

"I repeat; assuming that Congress has created an army and has created a navy, after that is all done, then may Congress not limit the uses to which money may be put by the President as Commander-in-Chief in the operation and in the command of the Army and Navy?

"The Senator has said that, of course, if we do not create an army and navy, then there is nothing over which the President has command. But we have an Army and Navy. Cannot Congress limit, by legislation, under its appropriation acts, the purposes for which money may be used by the President as Commander-in-Chief of the Army and Navy?

"Mr. BORAH: I do not know what the Senator means by 'purposes for which it may be used.' Undoubtedly the Congress may refuse to appropriate and undoubtedly the Congress may say that an appropriation is for a specific purpose. In that respect the President would undoubtedly be bound by it. But the Congress could not, through the power of appropriation, in my judgment, infringe upon the right of the President to command whatever army he might find. Congress might, by refusing to make an appropriation or by limiting it to a specific purpose, make it physically impossible for the President to discharge his duty in a particular instance. . . . But if the Army is in existence, if the Navy is in existence, if it is subject to command, he may send it where he will in the discharge of his duty to protect the life and property of American citizens. Undoubtedly he could send it, although the money were not in the Treasury." *Congressional Record,* April 20, 1928. See also *ibid.,* December 27, 1922; and 37 Stat. 913.

[50] It is on this ground that Attorney General Daugherty advised President Harding, September 13, 1923, that he was not authorized, in the absence of specific legislation giving him the power, to employ the Navy in enforcing National Prohibition, there being "no unlawful obstructions, combinations or assemblages of persons, or rebellion against the authority of the United States" rendering ordinary methods of enforcement impracticable. Daugherty found "but one instance in the history of the country in times of profound peace when Congress did authorize the use of naval vessels to enforce the civil or criminal statutes of the United States directed against individuals," and this was the Act of March 2, 1807, forbidding the slave trade from January 1, 1808. One provision of this measure made it "lawful" for the President to employ the Navy in its enforcement. 2

Stat. 426, 428. However, five years before this Congress had authorized the use of troops to expel intruders from the public lands (March 3, 1802, 2 Stat. 445), while by a provision that still remains on the statute books he is authorized to employ the land or naval forces of the United States, and the militia, to aid the execution of judicial process, in enforcement of the anti-peonage statutes, and to prevent the rescue of prisoners in the custody of the United States. U. S. Code, tit. 8, § 55. See also § 49.

Some other provisions of the same sort, enacted from time to time but apparently now lapsed, are listed in J. Reuben Clark, *Memorandum on the Right to Protect Citizens in Foreign Countries by Landing Forces* (United States State Department; rev. ed., 1912), pp. 32–38.

Notwithstanding the negative implication of such measures, the first Roosevelt was of the opinion, as was mentioned in the previous chapter, that he would have been authorized to use the Army to secure the operation of the Pennsylvania anthracite mines during the strike of 1904. *Ante*, p. 131. Also, Mr. Taft advances the theory in his volume on *The Presidency* that troops could be used to protect the treaty rights of aliens. *Ibid.*, pp. 82–83.

[51] Collateral to the subject discussed in the above section is the power of the President to repel invasions. By the Acts of 1795 and 1807 he is authorized to call upon the militia and to employ the armed forces of the United States not only in cases of actual invasion, but also whenever there is "imminent danger of invasion," a question to be determined exclusively by himself. *Martin v. Mott*, 12 Wheat. 19 (1827). President Wilson, in 1916, interpreted the power thus conferred as authorizing him to send punitive forces into Mexico in pursuit of the bandit Villa. Some of these forces proceeded as far as 400 miles from the American border, and remained on Mexican soil more than nine months. The Judge Advocate General ruled that the situation was technically "war," so that the soldiers involved were amenable only to military courts. *The New York Times*, October 22, 1916.

The question was raised as early as the War of 1812 whether the militia may be constitutionally sent out of the country and has continued to trouble commentators ever since. See Clarence A. Berdahl, *War Powers of the Executive in the United States*, pp. 131–134. Cited hereafter as Berdahl.

Sometimes it has been difficult to get the troops out of a state on account of the attitude of the local authorities themselves. Such a case occurred in 1907 when President Theodore Roosevelt responded to a call for aid from the Governor of Nevada. "The Governor," Mr. Roosevelt narrates, "became so well satisfied that he thought he would like to have them permanently." Ultimately the President notified him that "If within five days . . . you shall have issued the necessary notice to convene the Legislature of Nevada, I shall continue the troops during a period of three weeks. If when the term of five days has elapsed the notice has not been issued, the troops will immediately return to their former stations." *Autobiography*, p. 416. This proved effective.

[52] An illustration of the use of soldiers as police was furnished by the "slacker raids" in New York City and elsewhere in September 1918. *The New York Times*, September 6, 1918. The employment of soldiers for this purpose was, however, without authorization of the President, and was condemned by Attorney General Gregory as "unlawful" and "ill-judged." The raids themselves the Attorney General defended as legal and necessary. *Ibid.*, September 12.

[53] *Martial law* theoretically exists for the purpose of restoring civil government as soon

as possible; *military government* offers no such apology for its existence, and is a rela-
tively permanent order. The best example of the latter is furnished by the government of
conquered territory. See p. 196 *supra*.

54 Charles Fairman, *The Law of Martial Rule* (Chicago, 1930), pp. 20–22. This work
and Professor Robert S. Rankin's recent volume, *When Civil Law Fails* (Duke University
Press, 1939), are both excellent in their different ways and supplement each other at
important points.

55 *Law of the Constitution* (7th ed.) pp. 283–287.

56 See James F. Stephen, *A History of the Criminal Law of England* (1883), I, 203–
204, 213–215.

57 7 How. at 62, 70–75.

58 *Ibid.*, 45–46. Seven years before this John Quincy Adams had asserted in the House
that insurrection in a state was "war," and that if the United States entered a state for the
purpose of putting down such an insurrection it would be vested with the war power,
which was limited only by the laws of war. Citing, then, what had happened in South
America, he warned the slave states that in such a situation their slaves would be liable to
confiscation. "I lay this down," he continued, "as the law of nations. I say that the military authority takes for the time the place of all municipal institutions, and of slavery
among the rest; and that under this state of things . . . not only the President of the United
States, but the commander of the army has power to order the universal emancipation of
the slaves." *Congressional Globe*, XI, 429 (April 15, 1842).

It must be said that "Old Man Eloquent" was here indulging his penchant for baiting
the minions of slavery, at the expense of strict accuracy. Said Marshall, C. J., in 1833: "It
is very unusual, even in cases of conquest, for the conqueror to do more than displace the
sovereign and assume dominion of the country. The modern usage of nations, which has
become law, would be violated . . . if private property should be generally confiscated,
and private rights annulled." *United States v. Perchman*, 7 Pet. 51 (1833). He acknowledged, however, that enemy property could be confiscated by legislative decree, though
only thus. *Brown v. United States*, 8 Cr. 110 (1814).

59 4 Wall. 127. See also *United States v. Diekelman*, 92 U. S. 520, 526.

60 *Moyer v. Peabody*, 212 U. S. 78 (1909).

61 *Ibid.*, 84–85.

62 287 U. S. 378 (1932).

63 *Ibid.*, 400–401.

64 Art. I, §9, par. 2.

65 Taney's *Reports*, 246 (1861); McPherson, 154–158.

66 §§1338–1342; also to the same effect is 8 *Opins. A. G.* 365 (1857).

67 McPherson, 158–161.

68 *Ibid.*, 161–162. I have also had the use of a volume of contemporary pamphlets on
the subject in the Pierson Civil War Collection of Princeton University Library.

69 *Op. cit.*, 136–137.

70 14 Stat. 46 (1866). That Congress cannot indemnify for acts which it could not
have authorized in the first place is the doctrine of *Mitchell v. Clark*, 110 U. S. 633
(1884). If, therefore, suspension of the writ does not authorize arbitrary arrests in the
sense above indicated, then a statute of indemnity would not protect officers making
them. I know of no case, however, precisely on the point.

71 *Vd.* especially Hughes, C. J.'s, language in *Coleman v. Miller*. 307 U. S. 433, 454–
455 (1939).

72 On the rise and spread of this doctrine, and for an excellent criticism of it, see W. E. Hall, *International Law* (5th ed., Oxford, Clarendon Press, 1904), pp. 63–70. The doctrine had hardly been formulated when the factual basis of it was destroyed by the rise of conscript armies.

73 Earle, p. 143. This view was, even then, an illusion, arising from the fact that the American Revolution had been fought under the direction of the Continental Congress, which had no real governing power. Actually, when we turn to the state records of the period, we encounter a considerable mass of legislation which, though it had no direct reference to either recruiting or supply, was often stimulated by Congress and had the character of emergency measures meant to aid the prosecution of the war.

Thus on November 22, 1777, Congress recommended to certain of the state legislatures that they appoint commissioners "to regulate and ascertain the price of labour, manufactures, internal produce," and so forth. J. Reuben Clark, *Emergency Legislation,* pp. 211–212. A month later the same body further recommended "to the respective legislatures of the United States, forthwith to enact laws, appointing suitable persons to seize and take, for the use of the Continental Army of the said States, all woollen cloths, blankets, linens, shoes," and so on. *Ibid.,* pp. 214–217. Also, under date of October 2, 1778, Congress recommended laws for "the seizure of all grain and flour purchased up or engrossed" under such limitations as might be thought expedient. *Ibid.,* pp. 220–222.

Nor did Congress address only the state legislatures. In August and September, 1777, it resolved that "whereas the States of Pennsylvania and Delaware are threatened with immediate invasion from a powerful army . . . and whereas, principles of policy and self-preservation require all persons who may be reasonably suspected of aiding or abetting the cause of the enemy may be prevented from pursuing measures injurious to the public weal," "that the Executive authority" of the states in question apprehend, disarm, and secure all disaffected persons within their limits, and confine them "in such manner as shall be consistent with their respective character." It should be added that "these arrests were made with the knowledge and approbation of Washington. A writ of habeas corpus was issued at the instance of the prisoners, but it was disregarded by the officer in charge of them, and soon afterwards, on September 16, 1777, the Legislature [of Pennsylvania] passed a bill indemnifying the Executive Council and suspending the writ of habeas corpus." S. G. Fisher, *Trial of the Constitution,* pp. 223–225.

Likewise, when we turn to the statute books of the individual states during this period we find measure after measure enacted which entrenched upon the normal life of the community drastically: laws penalizing engrossing and forestalling, and trading with the enemy; laws forbidding the exportation of necessaries for limited periods; laws forbidding the distillation of whiskey and other spirits, in order to conserve grain supplies (Clark, pp. 250, 332, 380, 438, 497, etc.); laws fixing prices of labor and commodities, sometimes in the greatest detail (*ibid.,* pp. 420, 466, 535, 595, etc.); laws levying requisitions upon the inhabitants for supplies needed by the army (*ibid.,* pp. 482, 963, 969, etc.); in one instance a law impressing Negro slaves for labor on fortifications (*ibid.,* p. 280, Georgia); laws prohibiting auctions on account of their tendency to depress the currency of the United States (*ibid.,* p. 480 and *passim*); in one instance a law punishing dealers for withholding necessaries and refusing to take bills of credit of the state or the United States (*ibid.,* p. 466, Massachusetts); laws encouraging the manufacture of salt and of iron products; in one instance, a law for the erection of an arms manufactory for the United States (*ibid.,* p. 916, Virginia); and so on and so forth. Nor is this to mention the numerous acts of attainder, bills of pains and penalties, and confiscation measures which were passed by the states on their own initiative in the prosecution of their more or less private war upon the Loyalists. *Works of Charles Sumner,* VII, 59–64.

Thus, the actual prosecution of the War of Independence summoned into activity an immense range of legislative power. The fact, however, that this legislation came from the state legislatures whereas the war power was attributed to the United States in the Continental Congress served to obscure the fact that the former was really an outgrowth of the latter. Today, with the World War in mind, this lesson is clear.

74 Charles G. Fenwick, *Political Systems in Transition* (New York, 1920), pp. 90–92.

75 *Ibid.,* Chs. V–VII; Berdahl, Chs. VI, XI, XII. The extraordinary breadth of these legislative delegations of power is illustrated by the clause of the Lever Act which empowered the President to create "agencies" for carrying the act into effect (*ante,* Ch. III, note 11). Proceeding under this general authorization, President Wilson ordered Food Administrator Hoover to obtain charters under the laws of Delaware for two corporations, the "United States Grain Corporation" (1917) and the "Sugar Equalization Board, Inc." (1918). These organizations, the operating capital of which was furnished from funds which Congress had appropriated for the enforcement of the act, were treated as being endowed with the powers of ordinary business corporations in the matter of buying, selling, borrowing money, and so forth, although Congress had initially withheld such powers from the Food Administration. The borrowings of the Grain Corporation, whereby it was enabled through market operations to maintain grain prices, amounted at one time to $385,000,000. See generally, Harold Archer Van Dorn, *Government Owned Corporations* (New York, 1926).

76 *Hamilton, Collector v. Ky. Distils. and Warehouse Co.,* 251 U.S. 146 (1919); *Jacob Ruppert v. Caffey, ibid.,* 264 (1920). See also *Northern Pac. Ry. Co. v. No. Dak.,* 250 U.S. 135 (1919).

77 See especially *Schenck v. United States,* 249 U.S. 47 (1919); *Abrams et al. v. United States,* 250 U.S. 616 (1919).

78 245 U.S. 366 (1918).

79 The Court entirely ignored Mr. Hannis Taylor's striking brief as *amicus curiae* on this essential point. *Cf.* Maitland, *Constitutional History,* pp. 455–456.

80 *Block v. Hirsh,* 256 U.S. 135; *Marcus Brown Co. v. Feldman, ibid.,* 170 (1921).

81 The opinion of Chief Justice White in *United States v. Cohen Grocery Co.,* in which section 4 of the Food Control Act of August 10, 1917, as amended October 22, 1919, was set aside, perhaps militates against this view to some extent. But it should be noted that the decision came more than two years after the cessation of hostilities, and received on the constitutional point the approval of only six Justices. Chief Justice White's statement, therefore, in support of which *ex parte* Milligan is cited, that "the mere existence of a state of war could not suspend or change the operation upon the power of Congress of the guaranties and limitations of the Fifth and Sixth Amendments as to such questions as we are here passing upon," should be read with careful attention to the qualifications it contains. 255 U.S. 81 (1921).

"Sir, in the authority given to Congress by the Constitution of the United States to declare war, all the powers incidental to war are, by necessary implication, conferred upon the government of the United States. Now, the powers incidental to war are derived, not from the internal municipal sources, but the laws and usages of nations. . . . There are, then, in the authority of Congress and in the Executive, two classes of powers altogether different in their nature and often incompatible with each other—war power and peace power. The peace power is limited by regulations and restricted by provisions in the Constitution itself. The war power is only limited by the usages of nations. This power is tremendous. It is strictly constitutional, but it breaks down every barrier so anxiously erected for the protection of liberty and of life." J. Q. Adams, in *Register of Debates*, XII, 4037–4038 (May 25, 1831).

During the Civil War a state supreme court brought the doctrine of war necessity within the Constitution by the following argument:

"Under the Constitution of the United States all possible powers must be found in the Union or the States; or else they remain among those reserved rights which the people have retained as not essential to be vested in any government. That which is forbidden to the states is not necessarily in the Union, because it may be among the reserved powers. But if that which is essential to government is prohibited to one it must of necessity be found in the other, and the prohibition in such case on the one side is equivalent to a grant on the other." *Van Husen v. Kanause*, 13 Mich. 313.

That is to say, since it is inconceivable that the people intended to withhold from their governmental agents any power conducive to national self-preservation, the fact that the states are prohibited from engaging in war becomes an additional argument for considering the war power a plenary power inherent in the National Government.

[82] Berdahl, pp. 197–200, 211–212. It should be added that Mr. Hoover was appointed Food Administrator April 17, 1917, four months before the Food Control Act was passed. *Ibid.*, p. 205. Nor should all mention be omitted of the "heatless," "meatless," "sweetless" days, which represented the public's response to executive appeals to patriotism.

[83] *Ibid.*, p. 200; *War Cyclopedia*, pp. 112, 208. The status of German insurance companies and patent rights was eventually determined by the Trading with the Enemy Act.

[84] See my *President's Control*, pp. 152–156.

[85] James Hart, *The Ordinance Making Powers of the President*, pp. 92–96.

[86] For example, the Act of March 4, 1917, which empowered the President to commandeer munition factories and shipyards (see p. 134 *supra*), is still on the statute books as U. S. Code, tit. 50, §82b. Early in January 1940 a draft bill was sent to Congress by Secretary of the Navy Edison which would have vested the President with these powers in "an emergency." The idea was coldly received in Congress. *Newsweek*, January 15, 1940.

[87] The Sheppard bill (S. 25, 75th Congress, 1st sess.) is a sufficient sample of such proposals. By it the President would be authorized during a war, or a period of "imminence of war," to dictate production, prices, rentals; draft men between 21 and 31; control "industrial organizations"; require the registration of workers to be drafted into government service; and license industry.

Speaking with reference to this proposed measure, the late Senator Borah said:

"It is called a National Defense Act; it should be called the national assault act. How perfectly it would fit into a war situation. It transfers to one man practically all conceivable governmental powers. The businessman, the producer, the laborer, the civilian, and all walks of life would be regimented and every right of the citizen, as those rights have been known and enjoyed, would be subject to the arbitrary power of one man. If the bill were enacted into law we would have as complete a totalitarian state in many respects as they have in Germany and Italy. It is astounding that we have reached a point in constitutional thought when such a bill would even be proposed. But it is a war measure, and if war should come it would likely be overwhelmingly passed. But this is what war means under present economic conditions, especially so. War is always the eternal enemy of democracy, the friend of communism, and the father of fascism. Yet those who would drag us into all foreign controversies are the friends of just such measures as above referred to. While accentuating our supposed duties abroad, they would undermine and destroy our liberty as a people at home. Those who talk so glibly about our duty to crush nazi-ism in Europe, if they should have their way, would plant the brutal thing in the very heart of the American Republic." *Congressional Record,* March 29, 1938, Appendix.

An earlier, milder proposal drew from the late Newton D. Baker the sensible comment that:

"Laws passed in anticipation of war hampered more than helped the prosecution of the World War. What needed to be preserved was the implied power of the President, under the Constitution, to prosecute the war to the fullest extent in keeping with conditions obtaining at the time. Implied powers were seldom broadened, but rather restricted, by laws interpreting them." *The New York Times,* March 12, 1931.

[88] Berdahl, p. 135. During the War of 1812 the curious contention was advanced that the President could not delegate his power of command as to militia in the service of the United States. *Ibid.,* pp. 136–137.

[89] Rhodes, III, 581. See also *ibid.,* pp. 616–617.

[90] The feature of American military policy in the World War for which President Wilson was most criticized was the despatch of troops to Siberia and their retention there after the Armistice. Several resolutions of a censorious nature were introduced in Congress, but none was adopted in either house, showing, as Professor Berdahl puts it, "that even under the stress of bitter partisanship and despite all its mutterings and criticisms of executive policy, Congress will be slow to deny the power of the President as Commander-in-Chief to send and maintain troops of the army and navy abroad at his discretion, or to assert any definite claim of control for itself." *Op. cit.,* pp. 124–125.

[91] Art. I, §8, cls. 10 and 11. See also *Miller v. United States,* 11 Wall. 268 (1870), and *United States v. Arjona,* 120 U. S. 479 (1887).

[92] These activities, of course, illustrate the President's role also as organ of foreign relations. See next chapter.

[93] *Fleming v. Page,* 9 How. 603 (1850). *Leitensdorfer v. Webb,* 20 How. 176 (1857), however, shows a decided slant toward the conquest theory.

[94] *Fleming v. Page, supra;* The Insular Cases, 182 U. S. 1 (1901).

[95] *Cross v. Harrison,* 16 How. 164 (1853); *Santiago v. Nogueras,* 214 U. S. 260 (1909). His powers in conquered territory are measured only by the Laws of War as interpreted by himself. 182 U. S. 222, 231–232.

[96] See 15 *Opins. A. G.* 297 and note; 30 *ibid.,* 303. The early view was to the contrary. 1 *ibid.,* 233, 234 (Wirt).

[97] Note 17 *supra.*

[98] By the Act of May 18, 1917 (40 Stat. 83), Congress forbade the keeping or setting up of houses of ill fame in the vicinity of military stations. The provision was sustained in *McKinley v. United States,* 249 U. S. 397 (1919). Meantime it was supplemented by presidential orders or "requests" regulative of saloons in similar proximities. See New York papers of July 11 and August 18, 1917. Later, zones were created about certain naval stations from which saloons were banned entirely. *The New York Times,* March 8, 1918. See also *ibid.,* April 21, 25, and 29, for items showing federal intervention, or at least remonstrance, with the police authorities of Philadelphia and New York, in the interest of the health and morals of the troops in those vicinities.

99 See *Congressional Record* for December 3, 19, and 20, 1906, and January 19, 1907. Mr. Henry F. Pringle points out that in his *Autobiography* Roosevelt omits all mention of the Brownsville affair. *Theodore Roosevelt,* p. 464.

100 Congress did, however, during the World War confer power on President Wilson, acting with the consent of the Senate, to appoint for the period of the war to such grades as he might determine, in the case of general officers. Berdahl, p. 126. Polk was bitter because Congress would not create during the Mexican War the grade of Lieutenant General, in order that he might appoint somebody over the heads of Scott and Taylor. "My situation," he lamented, "is most embarrassing. I am held responsible for the War, and I am required to entrust the chief command of the army to a general in whom I have no confidence." *Ibid.,* p. 126. It is to be suspected that Polk's concern was largely of political motivation, Scott and Taylor both being Whigs. See the debate in the Senate, May 5, 8, 10, 12, 1848; the *Globe,* 30th Congress, 1st session.

101 See Chapter III *supra.* On the other hand, the President and the Senate have sometimes collaborated successfully to side-step the rules of eligibility laid down by statute. William Howard Taft, *Our Chief Magistrate,* pp. 127–128.

102 U. S. Code, tit. 10, §1590.

103 *Mullan v. United States,* 140 U. S. 240 (1891); *Wallace v. United States,* 257 U. S. 541 (1922).

NOTES TO CHAPTER VI*

1 At no point did the Framers depart more conspicuously from their materials than in dispersing among the President, Congress, and the Senate the powers most immediately touching the conduct of foreign relations—the war power, the treaty-making power, and the power to appoint ambassadors, etc. Blackstone, Locke, and Montesquieu were all in agreement in treating the direction of foreign relations as a branch of "executive," or royal, power. Said Blackstone:

"With regard to foreign concerns, the king is the delegate or representative of his people. It is impossible that the individuals of a state, in their collective capacity, can transact the affairs of that state with another community equally numerous as themselves. Unanimity must be wanting to their measures, and strength to the execution of their counsels. In the king therefore, as in a center, all the rays of his people are united, and form by that union a consistency, splendor, and power, that make him feared and respected by foreign potentates; who would scruple to enter into any engagement, that must afterwards be revised and ratified by a popular assembly. What is done by the royal authority, with regard to foreign powers, is the act of the whole nation; what is done without the king's concurrence is the act only of private men. And so far is this point carried by our law, that it hath been held, that should all the subjects of England make war without the royal assent, such war is no breach of the league. . . . The king therefore, considered as the representative of his people, has the sole power of sending embassadors to foreign states, and receiving embassadors at home." 1 *Commentaries* 252.

Locke expressed himself on the topic as follows:

"There is another power in every commonwealth which one may call natural, because

---

* *Chapter VI (Organ of Foreign Relations) begins on page 199.*

it is that which answers to the power every man naturally had before he entered into society. For though in a commonwealth the members of it are distinct persons still, in reference to one another, and, as such, are governed by the laws of the society, yet, in reference to the rest of mankind, they make one body, which is, as every member of it before was, still in the state of Nature with the rest of mankind, so that the controversies that happen between any man of the society with those that are out of it are managed by the public, and an injury done to a member of their body engages the whole in the reparation of it. . . . . This, therefore, contains the power of war and peace, leagues and alliances, and all the transactions with all persons and communities without the commonwealth, and may be called federative if any one pleases. So the thing be understood, I am indifferent as to the name. . . .

"Though, as I said, the executive and federative power of every community be really distinct in themselves, yet they are hardly to be separated and placed at the same time in the hands of distinct persons. For both of them requiring the *force* of the society for their exercise, it is almost impracticable to place the force of the commonwealth in distinct and not subordinate hands, or that the executive and federative power should be placed in persons that might act separately, whereby the force of the public would be under different commands, which would be apt some time or other to cause disorder and ruin." *Two Treatises on Civil Government* (Morley, ed.), Bk. II, §§145–146, 148.

Montesquieu's words are as follows:

"In every government there are three sorts of power: the legislative; the executive in respect to things dependent on the law of nations; and the executive in regard to matters that depend on the civil law.

"By virtue of the first, the prince or magistrate enacts temporary or perpetual laws, and amends or abrogates those that have been already enacted. By the second, he makes peace or war, sends or receives embassies, establishes the public security, and provides against invasions. By the third, he punishes criminals, or determines the disputes that arise between individuals. The latter we shall call the judiciary power, and the other simply the executive power of the state." *Spirit of the Laws* (Nugent tr.), Bk. XI, Ch. 6.

While these views were, of course, known to the Framers, their acceptance of them— so far as it went—was qualified from the outset by the allocation of the war-declaring power with Congress, where it had been lodged by the Articles of Confederation. *Cf.* Farrand, *Records,* I, 65–66, 70, 244, 292; II, 104; *Federalist* 75 (Hamilton); Elliot's *Debates* (1836), IV, 124.

For the later effect of the above view, and especially Blackstone's, on the Constitution's interpretation, see *infra*.

[2] "The War of Jenkins' Ear" commenced in 1739, seven years after the sanguinary cause of it occurred.

[3] For some particulars, see John Bassett Moore, *International Law Digest* (1906), VI, 651 ff.; Quincy Wright, *The Control of American Foreign Relations* (New York, 1922), pp. 18, 24, 25, 30, 60, 67, 206, 225, 229, 265; *United States v. Jeffers,* 4 Cranch, C. C. 704 (Fed. Cas. No. 15,471). While in attendance at the Paris Peace Conference President Wilson was forced to intervene through Secretary of State Lansing against certain legislative proposals in the California legislature having an anti-Japanese slant. *The New York Times,* April 11, 1919.

Indeed, presidential messages and less formal communications have at times disturbed good relations with foreign governments. As an example of the former, see the reference in Jackson's message of December 1, 1834, to the failure of the French Government to execute certain claims conventions. France protested, and was answered by Secretary of State Forsythe in the following words:

"The first reflection produced by Mr. Serurier's note is that it brings into discussion the propriety of a message of the President to Congress, for the contents of which, until the recommendations it contains are adopted by Congress, the United States are not responsible to foreign governments. . . . The President corresponds with foreign governments, through their diplomatic agents, as the organ of the nation. As such he speaks for the nation. In his messages to Congress he speaks only for the Executive to the legislature. He recommends, and his recommendations are powerless, unless followed by legislative action. No discussion of them can be permitted. All allusions to them, made with a design to mark an anticipated or actual difference of opinion between the Executive and legislature, are indelicate in themselves, and if made to prejudice public opinion will immediately recoil upon those who are so indiscreet as to indulge them. If they contain anything injurious to foreign nations, the means of self-justification are in their own power without interposing between the different branches of this government, an interposition which can never be made, even by those who do not comprehend the true character of the Government and the people of the United States, without forfeiting the respect of both." Richardson, III, 97, 100–105.

Eighty-six years later Ambassador Jusserand, acting under instructions from his government, expressed hurt surprise at references by President Wilson, in a letter to Senator Hitchcock, to "French militarism." *The New York Times,* March 12, 1920. Debates in Congress may once have excited foreign governments, but apparently do so no more. The houses were able in 1919 to pass resolutions favoring Irish independence without evoking an answering roar from the British Lion. Wright, *op. cit.,* pp. 33–34. And a year later 88 members of the House of Representatives cabled Prime Minister Lloyd George and the British Parliament a protest against the imprisonment without arraignment or trial of certain political offenders in Ireland, without producing any unfortunate repercussions on our diplomatic relations. See *The New York Times,* May 5, 1920.

The Dominion of Canada in 1925 requested our government to interpret a ruling of the Supreme Court bearing on the diversion of water from the Great Lakes by Chicago. Associated Press despatch, Ottawa, May 19, 1925. The fact that a foreign government may take cognizance at times of acts of American state legislatures does not prove that the latter have status as an organ of foreign relationship (*cf.* Wright, *op. cit.,* p. 30) any more than—for example—an American mob, of whose acts, too, a foreign government may take notice if they injure its citizens or subjects. See however note 12 below.

4 No. 64; Earle, pp. 418–419.

5 In No. 43 he wrote:

"The circumstances that endanger the safety of nations are infinite, and for this reason no constitutional shackles can wisely be imposed on the power to which the care of it is committed. This power ought to be co-extensive with all the possible combinations of such circumstances; and ought to be under the direction of the same councils which are appointed to preside over the common defence." Earle, p. 142.

6 *Ware v. Hylton,* 3 Dall., 199, 281 (1796).

7 On the general subject of the international obligation of the United States to enact legislation adequate to protect the treaty rights of aliens, see an informed note by Wright, *op. cit.,* p. 18, with citations. Illustrative of the general power of Congress to enact legisla-

tion in furtherance of the rights of foreign governments and of international comity, see *United States v. Arjona*, 120 U. S. 479 (1887). See also note 29 *infra*.

[8] 3 Dall. 54 (1795), especially at 80–81 (Patterson), and 91–95 (Iredell).

[9] 299 U.S. 304, 316–317 (1936). In the Philadelphia Convention, King of Massachusetts denied that the states had any international capacity whatsoever:

"The states were not 'sovereigns' in the sense contended for by some. They did not possess the peculiar features of sovereignty,—they could not make war, nor peace, nor alliances, nor treaties. Considering them as political beings, they were dumb, for they could not speak to any foreign sovereign whatever. They were deaf, for they could not hear any propositions from such sovereign. They had not even the organs or faculties of defence or offence, for they could not of themselves raise troops, or equip vessels, for war." Farrand, I, 323.

It is significant that nobody challenged this position.

[10] Attorney General Cushing argued to this effect in 8 *Opins. A. G.* 411 (1857).

[11] 14 Pet. 540.

[12] *Ibid.* 570–576. Taney accordingly concludes that the Framers "anxiously desired to cut off all connection or communication between a state and a foreign power"—a conclusion which is hardly borne out by the precise terms of Art. I, §10.

Two years prior to the Jennison Case, Daniel Webster had stated a very different doctrine in a letter to the Barings of London, as follows:

"Your first inquiry is, 'whether the Legislature of one of the States has legal and Constitutional power to contract loans at home and abroad?' To this I answer, that the Legislature of a State has such power; and how any doubt could have arisen on this point, it is difficult for me to conceive. EVERY STATE IS AN INDEPENDENT, SOVEREIGN POLITICAL COMMUNITY, except in so far as certain powers, WHICH IT MIGHT OTHERWISE HAVE EXERCISED, have been conferred on a General Government, established under a written Constitution, and exerting its authority over the people of all the States. This General Government is a limited Government. Its powers are specified and enumerated. All powers not conferred upon it still remain with the States and with the people. The State Legislatures, on the other hand, possess all usual and extraordinary powers of Government, subject to any limitations which may be imposed by their own Constitutions, and with the exception, as I have said, of the operation on those powers of the Constitution of the United States." W. O. Bateman, *Political and Constitutional Law of the United States* (1876), p. 211.

In point of fact, state governmental agencies do (even today) sometimes assume international significance temporarily. An instance is furnished by the action of the governors of Texas, New Mexico, and Arizona early in 1924 in according President Obregon of Mexico, in response to a request to that effect by Secretary of State Hughes, the right to transport troops from Naco, Arizona, to a point on the border between Texas and Mexico. Like permission was granted Carranza in 1915. News despatches of January 18 and 19, 1924. Nor should the following Associated Press despatch of August 20, 1924, from Geneva be overlooked:

"Philip S. Henry, bearing a signed and sealed document from Gov. Cameron Morrison of North Carolina, appointing Mr. Henry a special commissioner from North Carolina, arrived in Geneva today. League of Nations officials are somewhat puzzled over how to receive him.

"Mr. Henry has not yet presented his credentials, but it was said today the league officials were going to welcome him as a representative American, anxious to learn about the league, and particularly as the Governor's impressive document concludes with the words, 'I do hereby confer on him all rights, privileges and powers useful and necessary to the just and proper discharge of the duties of his appointment.' "

Governor Morrison later explained that he had given Mr. Henry his commission "more as an introduction than anything else."

[13] 299 U. S. at 318. See also The Chinese Exclusion Case, 130 U. S. 581, 604 (1889); *Fong Yue Ting v. United States,* 149 U. S. 698, 711 (1893); *Mackenzie v. Hare,* 239 U. S. 299, 311 (1915).

[14] Note 6 *supra.*

[15] I trace the history of judicial opinion on this subject in some detail in my *National Supremacy* (New York, 1913).

[16] 252 U. S. 416 (1920).

[17] *Ibid.,* 432–434; *cf.* argument of counsel, *ibid.,* 422.

[18] *University of Illinois v. United States,* 289 U. S. 48, 59 (1933). See also p. 238 *supra.* The "dual principle" has, nonetheless, even within recent years, furnished the State Department at Washington a pretext for declining to undertake international engagements the discharge of which would, to its way of thinking, obtrude upon "the police functions of the several states of the Union and which the Federal Government would not in consequence be capable of fulfilling." It was on this totally fallacious and deliberately specious reasoning that the United States based its declination to sign both the Geneva Convention of 1910 and that of 1921, concerning the traffic in women and children. Letter of the Undersecretary of State to the present writer, May 27, 1922.

Indeed as late as 1929 an American representative had the effrontery to base the refusal of the United States to assent to a convention for "equal treatment for foreigners and foreign enterprises" on the ground that it "proposed to give aliens the right to own real estate, which in the United States is a matter under the jurisdiction of the States." *The New York Times,* November 7, 1929. The truth is that the very first foreign treaty which the United States entered into under the Constitution, the Jay Treaty, dealt with this very subject. In short, the "dual principle" is still useful as a "stall."

[19] The classic statement of this principle was that made in Jackson's Veto Message of July 10, 1832 (*ante,* pp. 22–23). But the principle arose, it will be perceived, in the field of foreign relations.

[20] "Letters of Camillus," *Works* (Hamilton, ed.), VII, 556 ff.; Marshall, *Washington,* V, pp. 650–665; S. B. Crandall, *Treaties, Their Making and Enforcement* (Washington, D. C., 1916), pp. 170–171.

[21] The main purport of Madison's argument appears in the following passages from his speech in the House, March 7, 1796:

"It was an important, and appeared to him to be a decisive, view of the subject, that if the Treaty power alone could perform any one act for which the authority of Congress is required by the constitution, it may perform every act for which the authority of that part of the Government is required. Congress have power to regulate trade, to declare war, to raise armies, to levy, to borrow, and to appropriate money, etc. If, by Treaty, therefore, as paramount to the Legislative power, the President and Senate can regulate trade, they can also declare war, they can raise armies to carry on war, and they can procure money to support armies. . . .

"The force of this reasoning is not obviated by saying, that the President and Senate would only pledge the public faith, and that the agency of Congress would be necessary to carry it into operation. For, what difference does this make, if the obligation imposed be, as is alleged, a constitutional one; if Congress have no will but to obey, and if to disobey be treason and rebellion against the constituted authorities? Under a constitutional obligation with such sanctions to it, Congress, in case the President and Senate should enter into an alliance for war, would be nothing more than the mere heralds for proclaiming it. In fact, it had been said that they must obey the injunctions of a Treaty, as implicitly as a subordinate officer in the Executive line was bound to obey the Chief Magistrate, or as the Judges are bound to decide according to the laws. . . .

"He came next to the fifth construction, which left with the President and Senate the power of making Treaties, but required at the same time the Legislative sanction and cooperation in those cases where the constitution had given express and specific powers to the Legislature. It was to be presumed, that in all such cases the Legislature would exercise its authority with discretion, allowing due weight to the reasons which led to the Treaty, and to the circumstances of the existence of the Treaty. Still, however, this House, in its Legislative capacity, must exercise its reason: it must deliberate; for deliberation is implied in legislation. If it must carry all Treaties into effect, it would no longer exercise a Legislative power; it would be the mere instrument of the will of another department, and would have no will of its own. Where the constitution contains a specific and peremptory injunction on Congress to do a particular act, Congress must, of course, do the act, because the Constitution, which is paramount over all the departments, has expressly taken away the Legislative discretion of Congress. The case is essentially different where the act of one department of Government interferes with a power expressly vested in another, and nowhere expressly taken away: here the latter power must be exercised according to its nature; and if it be a Legislative power, it must be exercised with that deliberation and discretion which is essential to the nature of Legislative power." Benton, *Abridgment*, I, 650–651.

In the interest of strict accuracy it should be noted that Madison rejects the term "concurrent powers" as descriptive of his own position, as well as the view to which in the text I have applied this term. The latter he phrases as follows: "The Treaty Power and the Congressional power might be regarded . . . as each of them supreme over the other, as it may be last exercised." This position he repels as involving "the absurdity of an *imperium in imperio* of two powers, both of them supreme, yet each of them liable to be superseded by the other." *Ibid.*, 649. Actually this is the view which has come to prevail, it being today established doctrine that when a treaty and a statute conflict, the maxim *"leges posteriores priores contrarias abrogant"* applies in the same way that it would in the case of conflict between two treaties or two acts of Congress. *The Cherokee Tobacco*, 11 Wall. 616, 621 (1870); *United States v. McBratney*, 104 U. S. 621, 623 (1881); Head Money Cases, 112 U. S. 580, 599 (1884); *Whitney v. Robertson*, 124 U. S. 190, 194 (1888); *Botiller v. Dominguez*, 130 U. S. 238, 247 (1889); The Chinese Exclusion Case, *ibid.*, 581, 600 (1889); *Fong Yue Ting v. United States*, 698, 720–721 (1893); *DeLima v. Bidwell*, 182 U. S. 1, 195 (1901); *Johnson v. Browne*, 205 U. S. 309, 321 (1907); *Charlton v. Kelly*, 229 U. S. 447, 463 (1913); *Rainey v. United States*, 232 U. S. 310, 316 (1914); 6 *Opins. A. G.* 291 (1854); 13 *ibid.*, 354 (1870); 21 *ibid.*, 80 and 347. On the other hand, it is also true that treaty provisions which operate within the field of congressional enumerated powers generally contemplate supplementary action by Congress, and when this is so Congress is—to repeat—a free agent. "The House would not in any case consider itself under a constitutional obligation to appropriate money in support of a treaty the provisions of which it will not approve." James G. Blaine, *Twenty Years of Congress* (New York, 1884–1886), as quoted by Noel Sargent in *The New York Times,* November 18, 1928.

[22] *Ex parte* Grossman, 267 U. S. 87, 119–120 (1925).

[23] For a considerable list of treaty provisions affecting especially the war power and collateral powers of Congress, see a communication from Professor J. P. Chamberlain in *The New York Times* of December 11, 1927. Among others are mentioned the Treaty of Alliance of 1778 with France, which continued in formal effect till 1798 and contained a guarantee by the United States of French possessions in the West Indies; the Treaty of December 12, 1846, with Columbia by which the neutrality of the Isthmus of Panama was guaranteed; the Treaty of Paris of 1856 abolishing the right of privateering, to which President Lincoln offered to accede in 1861, notwithstanding Congress's power to issue "letters of marque and reprisal"; the Hague Convention of 1907 limiting the rights of belligerency, although the Constitution gives Congress the power to "make rules concerning captures on land and water"; etc. See further 155 Fed. 842 (1907).

[24] 2 Pet. 253 (1829).

[25] *Ibid.,* 309.

[26] *Oetjen v. Cent. Leather Co.,* 246 U. S. 297 (1918), and cases there cited.

[27] Benton, *op. cit.,* II, 466–467.

[28] Jefferson to Genêt, November 22, 1793, *Writings of Thomas Jefferson* (Mem. ed.), IX, 256; *Writings* (Ford, ed.), VI, 451. Note also his statement that "the transaction of the business with foreign nations is executive altogether." *Ibid.,* V, 162.

[29] Charles M. Thomas, *American Neutrality in 1793* (Columbia University Press, 1931), disposes of the persistent idea that the author was Chief Justice Jay. *Ibid.,* 43–49. The proclamation proceeded on the theory that violations of it would be subject to prosecution in United States courts for violation of "the Law of Nations," which was assumed to be embodied in "a common law of the United States"; and in the case of Gideon Henfield this theory was sustained by the federal circuit court at Philadelphia, though other federal courts rejected it. Charles Warren, *The Supreme Court,* I, 112–118.

[30] *Works* (Hamilton, ed.), VII, 76 ff.; My *President's Control,* pp. 8–15.

[31] The passage in question (*ibid.,* 10–12) reads:

"The second article of the Constitution of the United States, section first, establishes this general proposition, that 'the EXECUTIVE POWER shall be vested in a President of the United States of America.'

"The same article, in a succeeding section, proceeds to delineate particular cases of executive power. It declares, among other things, that the president shall be commander in chief of the army and navy of the United States, and of the militia of the several states, when called into the actual service of the United States; that he shall have power, by and with the advice and consent of the senate, to make treaties; that it shall be his duty to receive ambassadors and other public ministers, *and to take care that the laws be faithfully executed.*

"It would not consist with the rules of sound construction, to consider this enumeration of particular authorities as derogating from the more comprehensive grant in the general clause, further than as it may be coupled with express restrictions or limitations; as in regard to the cooperation of the senate in the appointment of officers, and the making of treaties; which are plainly qualifications of the general executive powers of appointing officers and making treaties. The difficulty of a complete enumeration of all the cases of executive authority, would naturally dictate the use of general terms, and would render it improbable that a specification of certain particulars was designed as a substitute for those terms, when antecedently used. The different mode of expression employed in the constitution, in regard to the two powers, the legislative and the executive, serves to confirm this inference. In the article which gives the legislative powers of the government, the expressions are, 'All legislative powers herein granted shall be vested in a congress of the United States.' In that which grants the executive power, the expressions are, '*The executive power* shall be vested in a President of the United States.'

"The enumeration ought therefore to be considered, as intended merely to specify the principal articles implied in the definition of executive power; leaving the rest to flow from the general grant of that power, interpreted in conformity with other parts of the Constitution, and with the principles of free government.

"The general doctrine of our Constitution then is, that the *executive power* of the nation is vested in the President; subject only to the *exceptions* and *qualifications,* which are expressed in the instrument."

32 *Ibid.,* 14.

33 *Writings* (Ford, ed.), VI, 338.

34 *Writings* (Hunt, ed.), VI, 138 ff.; *President's Control,* pp. 16–27. "He [Madison] therefore entered the lists against Mr. Hamilton in the public journals and in five papers under the signature of Helvidius, scrutinized the doctrines of Pacificus with an acuteness of intellect never perhaps surpassed and with a severity scarcely congenial to his natural disposition and never on any other occasion indulged." J. Q. Adams, *Eulogy on James Madison* (Boston, 1836), p. 46. Adams notes that Madison's "most forcible arguments are pointed with quotations from the papers of the *Federalist* written by Mr. Hamilton." *Ibid.,* p. 48.

35 *President's Control,* pp. 20–21.

36 The authoritative work for the subject, as it stood prior to the World War, is Charles G. Fenwick, *The Neutrality Laws of the United States* (Washington, D. C., 1913). Madison's cause was greatly aided of course by the breakdown of the theory that there was a common law of the United States for violation of which offenders could be prosecuted by the National Government even in the absence of statute. Note 29 *supra.*

37 7 *Opins. A. G.* 190, 209. Similarly, the President's power to nominate and, with the advice and consent of the Senate, to appoint "ambassadors, other public ministers and consuls" comprehends "all officers having diplomatic functions, whatever their title or designation." *Ibid.,* 192–193. For the expression of a different view, apropos of President J. Q. Adams's nomination, December 26, 1825, of three persons to be "envoys extraordinary and ministers plenipotentiary to the Assembly of American Nations at Panama," see Benton, VIII, 463–464; *President's Control,* pp. 56–57.

38 *Ibid.,* 24–25. In *The Federalist,* interestingly enough, Hamilton manifests no prevision of the potentialities of the power of reception. In No. 69 he writes:

"The President is also to be authorized to receive ambassadors and other public ministers. This, though it has been a rich theme of declamation, is more a matter of dignity than of authority. It is a circumstance which will be without consequence in the administration of the government; and it was far more convenient that it should be arranged in this manner, than that there should be a necessity of convening the legislature, or one of its branches, upon every arrival of a foreign minister, though it were merely to take the place of a departed predecessor." Earle, p. 451.

39 Moore, *Digest,* IV, 484–549. See especially *ibid.,* 507, for the case of Dupuy de

Lome, whose recall was demanded shortly preceding the war with Spain. For Bernstorff's dismissal February 3, 1917, see press despatches of this and following day; also *War Cyclopedia*, 37. J. Q. Adams introduced a bill in the Senate to authorize the President to dismiss foreign diplomatic representatives, arguing that, as such action was tantamount to a declaration of war, it was beyond his normal constitutional powers. The proposal was defeated by a vote of 74 to 24. Charles Warren, 10 *Boston University Law Review* 4 (1930), citing 9th Congress, 1st sess., March 3, 7, 1806.

⁴⁰ *Writings* (Hunt, ed.), VI, 266.

⁴¹ *President's Control*, p. 197. For a catalogue of congressional calls for documents, see *Senate Miscellaneous Documents*, No. 7, 52nd Congress, 2nd sess., pp. 232–272. For several instances of refusal of documents by the President, see Warren, article cited in note 39, at pp. 4, 8, 11, 12, 15, 16, 17, 29. Apropos of a resolution by Senator Penrose early in December 1906, "That the President be requested to communicate to the Senate, if not incompatible with the public interests, full information bearing upon the recent order dismissing from the military service of the United States three companies of the Twenty-fifth Regiment of Infantry, United States troops (colored)," Senator Spooner of Wisconsin said:

"Mr. President, I am opposed to the resolution offered by the Senator from Pennsylvania. My opposition to it is based entirely upon the form of it. This resolution does not, so far as the subject-matter goes, fall within the class of inquiries which the Senate has ever been accustomed to address to the President. It implies on its face, Mr. President, a doubt here which I think does not exist; as to whether the Senate is of right entitled to all the facts relating to the discharge of the three named companies or not. Always the Senate, in passing resolutions of inquiry addressed to Cabinet officers, except the Secretary of State, make them in form of *direction*, not *request*. It rarely has happened that a request has been addressed to any Cabinet officer where foreign relations were involved. Where such a resolution has been adopted it has been addressed to the President, with the qualification that he is requested to furnish the information only so far as, in his judgment, the transmission of it is compatible with the public interest.

"There are reasons for that, Mr. President. The State Department stands upon an entirely different basis as to the Congress from the other Departments. The conduct of our foreign relations is vested by the Constitution in the President. It would not be admissible at all that either House should have the power to force from the Secretary of State information connected with the negotiation of treaties, communications from foreign governments, and a variety of matters which, if made public, would result in very great harm in our foreign relations—matters so far within the control of the President that it has always been the practice, and it always will be the practice, to recognize the fact that there is of necessity information which it may not be compatible with the public interest should be transmitted to Congress—to the Senate or to the House.

"There are other cases, not especially confined, Mr. President, to the State Department, or to foreign relations, where the President would be at liberty obviously to decline to transmit information to Congress or to either House of Congress. Of course, in time of war, the President being Commander in Chief of the Army and Navy, could not, and the War Department or the Navy Department could not, be required by either House to transmit plans of campaign or orders issued as to the destination of ships or anything relating to the strategy of war. . . ."

In the ensuing discussion it was agreed that information had been sought from the

President from time to time on all sorts of subjects; that "we request the President and we direct the Cabinet officers"; that there had "been cases within comparatively recent years where Cabinet officers having been directed by resolution of the Senate to send certain information to it, had withheld entirely, or withheld in part, such information by order of the President"; and that there had been no remedy when this happened. *Congressional Record,* December 6, 1906.

President Hoover's refusal to furnish the Senate letters, cablegrams, minutes, memoranda, etc., with reference to the London Naval Treaty (*The New York Times,* July 12, 1930), evoked from Senator McKellar of Tennessee a claim of absolute right on the part of the Senate to such documents. The learned Senator said:

"Does anybody doubt that proposition of law, first, that the Senate and the President are co-equal partners in the business of treaty-making, and secondly, that the possession of one or all of the papers and documents in reference to a partnership matter makes them the joint property of all, and that they are all entitled to them? . . . He has the documents and we would have to take them away from him in order to get them. The law says they are the joint property of the two partners—namely, the Senate and the President —but the President withholds them." *The New York Times,* July 17, 1930.

The documents were not forthcoming.

[42] *Senate Documents,* No. 56, 54th Congress, 2nd sess., p. 9 note; Moore, *Digest,* IV, 462; *cf.* notes 46 and 56 *infra.* No doubt, the discarded practice was a left-over from Revolutionary days, when all such communications were sent to the Continental Congress.

[43] For debate on the act see *Annals of Congress,* December 27, 1798, to January 25, 1799, *passim.* The measure, amended by the Act of March 4, 1909, 35 Stat. 1088, is now U. S. Code, tit. 18, §5. See further "Memorandum on the History and Scope of the Laws Prohibiting Correspondence with a Foreign Government," *Senate Document,* No. 696, 64th Congress, 2nd sess. (1917). The author was Mr. Charles Warren, then Assistant Attorney General.

[44] *The New York Times,* October 19, 1920; *The Woman Patriot* (Washington, D. C.), May 1, 1922; *The New York Times,* June 22 and 23, 1930, and January 11, 1933. Mr. Ford's "Peace Ship" project early in 1915 did not of course fall within the purview of the Logan Act, not being intended "to influence the measures or conduct of any foreign government or of any officer or agent thereof, in relation to any disputes or controversies with the United States, or to defeat the measures of the government of the United States." A like enterprise would later on have appeared in a far different light.

[45] For Mr. Wilson's reaction to Grey's indiscretion see Washington despatches of February 5, 1920. For the exchange between Wilson and Harding see *The New York Times* of October 19, 1920. Mr. Hoover's invitation to Roosevelt was sent from Yuma, Arizona, November 13, 1932; and the latter's invitation to Sir Ronald Lindsay was sent January 28, 1933. An Associated Press despatch of December 23, 1920, mentioned two other breaches of official etiquette by foreign representatives. One was the action of the Guatemalan minister in discussing with Senator Moses a resolution introduced into the Senate by the latter with regard to the detention by Guatemalan authorities of former President Cabrera; the other was the action of the first secretary of the British embassy in sending direct to a Senate committee a denial of testimony before it to the effect that the British government censored cable messages from Great Britain to the United States.

[46] Presidential assertions of the principle have not always escaped a flavor of pedantry. In 1876 the governments of Pretoria and Argentina both sent congratulations to *Congress*

on the occasion of the Centennial, and the following January Congress adopted joint resolutions of "high appreciation," which, however, were vetoed by President Grant on the constitutional ground:

"The usage of governments generally confines their correspondence and interchange of opinion and of sentiments of congratulation, as well as of discussion, to one certain established agency. To allow correspondence or interchange between states to be conducted by or with more than one such agency would necessarily lead to confusion, and possibly to contradictory presentation of views and to international complications.

"The Constitution of the United States, following the established usage of nations, has indicated the President as the agent to represent the national sovereignty in its intercourse with foreign powers and to receive all official communications from them. It gives him the power, by and with the advice and consent of the Senate, to make treaties and to appoint ambassadors and other public ministers; it intrusts to him solely 'to receive ambassadors and other public ministers,' thus vesting in him the origination of negotiations and the reception and conduct of all correspondence with foreign states, making him, in the language of one of the most eminent writers on constitutional law, 'the constitutional organ of communication with foreign states.'

"No copy of the addresses which it is proposed to acknowledge is furnished. I have no knowledge of their tone, language, or purport. From the tenor of the two joint resolutions it is to be inferred that these communications are probably purely congratulatory. Friendly and kindly intentioned as they may be, the presentation by a foreign state of any communication to a branch of the Government not contemplated by the Constitution for the reception of communications from foreign states might, if allowed to pass without notice, become a precedent for the address by foreigners or by foreign states of communications of a different nature and with wicked designs." Richardson, VII, 431.

Earlier, on August 14, 1876, Grant had sent a special message to the House protesting against a clause of the diplomatic appropriations act for the ensuing year which directed the President to notify certain diplomatic and consular officers "to close their offices." "In the literal sense of this direction," he asserted, "it would be an invasion of the constitutional prerogatives and duty of the President." *Ibid.*, 377. Late in 1928 Congressman Britten of Illinois, Chairman of the House Naval Committee, sent Prime Minister Baldwin of Great Britain a proposal that the latter call a naval limitation conference. When the British Premier sought to reply through the State Department, the latter declined to transmit the reply. Subsequently Mr. Britten and Commander Kenworthy, a member of Parliament, exchanged correspondence looking to an "unofficial conference" on the same subject between American M. C.'s and British M. P.'s. United Press despatch, Washington, D. C., December 29, 1928. Nothing came of the idea.

"The very delicate, plenary and exclusive power of the President as the sole organ of the Federal Government in the field of international relations" is invoked by the Court in the recent case of *United States v. Curtiss-Wright Corp.*, 299 U. S. at 320.

[47] On the general subject of recognition, see *Senate Documents*, No. 56, cited in note 42 *ante;* Moore, *Digest*, I, 67–255 *passim; President's Control*, pp. 71–83.

[48] *Senate Documents*, No. 56, p. 30.

[49] *Ibid.*, 31.

[50] *Memoirs*, IV, 205–206.

[51] Benton, *Abridgment*, VI, 168.

[52] *Senate Documents*, No. 56, p. 36.

53 *Ibid.,* 41–43; Richardson, III, 266–267; Thomas Hart Benton, *Thirty Years View* (Boston, 1854–1856), I, 665–670.

54 *President's Control,* pp. 79–83; Warren, article cited in note 39 *supra,* 31–32.

55 *Senate Documents,* No. 56, pp. 21–22.

56 It should be noted, however, that Lincoln, in his message of December 3, 1861, asked for congressional approbation before recognizing "the independence and sovereignty of Haiti and Liberia." This deference may have encouraged Henry Winter Davis, April 6, 1864, to present the following resolution in the House apropos of Napoleon III's enterprise in Mexico:

"Resolved, That the Congress of the United States are unwilling, by silence, to leave the nations of the world under the impression that they are indifferent spectators of the deplorable events now transpiring in the Republic of Mexico; and they therefore think fit to declare that it does not accord with the policy of the United States to acknowledge a monarchical government, erected on the ruins of any republican government in America, under the auspices of any European power." McPherson, p. 349.

The resolution, which was voted unanimously, was transmitted to Dayton, our minister at Paris, by Secretary Seward, who at the same time took pains to indicate that it did not state the policy of the American government, that being "a purely Executive question" and one the decision of which constitutionally belonged "not to the House of Representatives but to the President of the United States." *Ibid.,* pp. 349–350.

Secretary Seward's despatch having been communicated by the President to the House at its request, Davis on June 27 made an elaborate report from the Committee on Foreign Affairs which concluded with the following resolution:

"Resolved, That Congress has a constitutional right to an authoritative voice in declaring and prescribing the foreign policy of the United States, as well in the recognition of new powers as in other matters; and it is the constitutional duty of the President to respect that policy, not less in diplomatic negotiations than in the use of the national forces when authorized by law; and the propriety of any declaration of foreign policy by Congress is sufficiently proved by the vote which pronounces it; and such proposition while pending and undetermined is not a fit topic of diplomatic explanation with any foreign power." *Ibid.,* p. 354.

The resolution passed the House in a somewhat diluted form, but failed to come to a vote in the Senate.

The residence of the power of recognition was found by Story, writing in 1833, to be still "open to discussion," but his own opinion evidently was that it belonged to the President alone:

"The constitution has expressly invested the executive with power to receive ambassadors, and other ministers. It has not expressly invested congress with the power, either to repudiate, or acknowledge them." 2 *Commentaries,* §1566. Story noted, however, the contrary opinion of Rawle, *On the Constitution.*

57 On this controversy see Washington despatches of September 4, 24, 25, and October 4, 1920; also Jesse S. Reeves, "The Jones Act and the Denunciation of Treaties," 15 *American Journal of International Law,* 33–38 (January, 1921). Congress has often passed resolutions denouncing treaties or treaty provisions, sometimes by the invitation of the President, and Presidents have "usually carried out such resolutions," though not always. Wright, *op. cit.,* p. 258. Late in 1922 Senator McKellar proposed two amendments to the Jones Act, one of which abrogated outright the twenty-one treaties affected by it,

and the other of which purported to notify the governments concerned. Washington despatches of December 26, 1922. Nothing came of these proposals. See also note 21 *supra*.

[58] Richardson, XVII, 7934. For a similar appeal by Wilson from Paris early in 1919 in support of the three-year naval building program which was then pending in the House, see Washington despatches of February 4, 1919.

[59] U. S. Code, tit. 22, §262.

[60] *Ibid.,* tit. 8, §213c. For the story of the passage of the provision, see George H. Haynes, *The Senate of the United States,* II, 648–651; *cf. ibid.,* 676, n. 3. On the relation of the measure to the "Gentleman's Agreement" of 1907, see Max J. Kohler, *The New York Times,* January 9, 1924. The constitutional question had been settled by the cases cited in note 13 *supra*.

[61] The Johnson Act is U. S. Code, tit. 31, §804a. Even in the absence of the principle of Congress's sovereignty in the external field, the act would be justifiable as a measure to implement Congress's power over property of the United States (Art. IV, §3, par. 2); the property in question being debts due the United States from certain foreign governments. On the Neutrality Act of 1937 (50 Stat. 121), see R. L. Buell, in *Foreign Policy Reports,* October 1, 1937, and James W. Garner in *American Journal of International Law,* July 1937, pp. 385–397. The text of the Neutrality Act of 1939 is conveniently available in *The New York Times* of November 4, 1939.

[62] James F. Green, "The President's Control of Foreign Policy," *Foreign Policy Reports,* April 1, 1939, pp. 17–18.

[63] *Ibid.,* p. 19; *The New York Times,* December 16, 1938; January 5, 1939; March 19 and 20, 1939.

[64] *Panama Refining Co. v. Ryan,* 293 U. S. 388, 421–422 (1934); *United States v. Curtiss-Wright Corp.,* 299 U. S. at 327–328 (1936). Among the questions which Representative Sam D. McReynolds of Tennessee, Chairman of the House Foreign Affairs Committee, addressed to Secretary Hull, December 6, 1937, respecting the Administration's policy toward the Sino-Japanese conflict, was the following:

"Is it a fact that the Department of State is using the Neutrality Act as an instrument of policy, as indicated by the following statements of the chairman of the Committee on Foreign Affairs on the floor of the House of Representatives on Nov. 17, 1937, to wit:

" 'I think it will aid Japan and aid the Fascist countries of Europe more by putting this law into effect now than by not putting it into effect.'

"And again:

" 'I am not saying that we should help China, but I want to stick a dagger in these countries that are trying to create dictatorship and trying to ruin the world.' "

To which Secretary Hull replied:

"With regard to the eighth question, the entering into force of the restrictive provisions of the Neutrality Act of May 1, 1937, is left to and is dependent upon decision of the President by a finding that 'there exists a state of war.' The policy of the Department of State in reference to this Act is dependent upon that decision. The Department of State keeps constantly in mind the fact that the principal purpose of the Act is to keep the United States out of war." *The New York Times,* December 7, 1937.

[65] *House Reports,* No. 1569, 68th Congress, 2nd sess., p. 10.

[66] *House Reports,* No. 1569, etc.

The attitude of Presidents toward such congressional expressions of opinion has naturally varied with circumstances—and also with the temperaments of Presidents. Monroe's cordiality toward congressional collaboration in the matter of recognizing the South

American republics was noted above. The same President also expressed his acquiescence in a resolution passed by the House February 28, 1823, requesting the President to enter upon negotiations with the maritime powers of Europe and America for the abolition of the slave trade. Richardson, II, 244. The Joint Resolution of April 27, 1846, requesting the President to give notice to Great Britain of the termination of the Convention of 1827, was approved by Polk—was, in fact, procured by him as a part of his efforts to disentangle himself from the embarrassment of his "Fifty-four Forty or a Fight" pledge.

Grant's and Wilson's response to congressional "interferences" was quite different, as we have seen. A further illustration of the latter's generally suspicious attitude is furnished by his letter of December 8, 1919, to Senator Fall anent a resolution which had just been introduced by the latter advising the President to sever diplomatic relations with Mexico. The letter reads:

"Thank you very much for your kind promptness in complying with my request that you send me a copy of the memorandum report of the sub-committee on Mexican affairs of the Committee on Foreign Affairs [sic]. I shall examine it with the greatest interest and care. What you told me of the investigation, on Friday last, prepares me to find it matter of the greatest importance.

"You ask an indication of my desire with regard to the pending resolution to which you and Senator Hitchcock called my attention on Friday, and I am glad to reply with the utmost frankness that I should be gravely concerned to see any such resolution pass the Congress. It would constitute a reversal of our Constitutional practice which might lead to very grave confusion in regard to the guidance of our foreign affairs. I am confident that I am supported by every competent Constitutional authority in the statement that the initiative in directing the relations of our Government with foreign governments is assigned by the Constitution to the Executive and to the Executive only. Only one of the two houses of Congress is associated with the President by the Constitution in an advisory capacity, and the advice of the Senate is provided for only when sought by the Executive in regard to explicit agreements with foreign governments and the appointment of the diplomatic representatives who are to speak for this Government at foreign capitals. The only safe course, I am confident, is to adhere to the prescribed method of the Constitution. We might go very far afield if we departed from it.

"I am very much obliged to you for having given me the opportunity to express this opinion.

Woodrow Wilson"

The New York Times, December 9, 1919.

Resolutions which were passed by the Senate and House separately in the 2nd session of the Fifty-third Congress, warning President Cleveland against the employment of force to restore the monarchy of Hawaii, probably saved his administration from a serious misstep. *Congressional Record,* 53rd Congress, 2nd sess., pp. 1814, 1825, 1838, 1879, 1942, 2000, 5127, 5499. Likewise, the once hotly debated "McLemore Resolution," requesting President Wilson "to warn all citizens of the United States to refrain from travelling on armed merchant vessels," while resented by him, did unquestionably afford him a valuable hint as to the state of the public mind, and one which he was quick to take. *House Reports,* No. 147, 64th Congress, 1st sess. Similarly, the *failure* of the Senate in August 1937 to adopt a resolution authorizing the loan of six superannuated destroyers to the government of Brazil saved Secretary Hull, the author of the proposal, from embarrassing our government's relations with Argentina.

[67] James M. Landis, "Constitutional Limitations on the Congressional Power of

Investigation," 40 *Harvard Law Review* (December 1926), 153–266. See also p. 444, note 88 *infra*.

[68] I am indebted in this matter to an unpublished thesis by Dr. James A. Perkins of Princeton University, entitled *Congress Investigates Our Foreign Relations* (Princeton University Library). The nice question arises whether a congressional investigating committee could be constitutionally authorized to require the Secretary of State to produce papers which the President had refused one or both of the houses on the ground of public interest. The point has never been determined or even resolutely pressed to an issue. A recent occurrence however, mentioned by Dr. Perkins, tends to negative the suggestion. I mean the refusal of Secretary Stimson to allow certain despatches to be read by Senator Johnson into the record of the investigation which the Senate Finance Committee, under the latter's chairmanship, conducted in 1931–1932 of the sale of foreign securities in the United States. *Senate Hearings on S. R. 19*, 72nd Congress, 1st sess. (December 1931 and January 1932). *Cf.* note 41 *supra*.

[69] *President's Control*, pp. 49–56.

[70] P. 75 *supra*.

[71] Pp. 123–124 *supra*. The maximum salaries of the different diplomatic grades were, however, often stipulated in early appropriation acts. Jefferson to Gallatin, February 19, 1804; *Works* (Mem. ed.), XI, 4–13.

[72] 10 Stat. 619.

[73] 7 *Opins. A. G.* 186 and 242.

[74] U. S. Code, tit. 22, §§1–231; §§31–40. The restriction as to ambassadors comes from the Act of March 2, 1909, 35 Stat. 672. In the face of this provision, when President Wilson sent Mr. Elihu Root to Russia on a special mission in May 1917, he conferred upon him "the rank of ambassador" and upon certain of his associates "the rank of envoy extraordinary." The mission was not authorized by Congress, nor were the names of its members referred to the Senate. President Harding imitated his predecessor to the extent of conferring the "rank of ambassador" upon the American delegates at the Washington Conference, but submitted their names to the Senate, despite the fact that some of them were Senators, and hence incapable of holding "any civil office under the authority of the United States" (Art. I, §6, par. 2). Later, too, Mr. Harding conferred "the rank of ambassador extraordinary where matters of diplomatic precedence are involved" upon his "High Commissioner" in Haiti, Brigadier General John H. Russell of the Marine Corps. Washington despatches of April 25, 1922.

The New York Times of February 14, 1940, carried the information that Mr. Myron Taylor, whose choice by President Roosevelt as a "personal representative" to the Holy See had been announced a few days earlier, would be accorded the status of "ambassador" by the Papal authorities.

It is interesting to note that as late as 1876 James A. Garfield contended that diplomatic offices were "constitutional offices," a view which was repelled by J. Randolph Tucker of Virginia. *Congressional Record*, August 15, 1876, 44th Congress, 1st sess., pp. 5685, 5688.

Whichever view be accepted, Congress's control over salaries would often enable it, if it chose, to force a practical severance of diplomatic relations, such as was threatened recently when the House came within three votes of cutting out of the State Department Supply bill the provision for the annual salary of the ambassador to Russia. *The New York Times*, February 8, 1940. For an earlier similar incident see note 46 *supra*.

75 *President's Control*, pp. 49–70; Wright, *op. cit.*, 328–334; Henry M. Wriston, *Executive Agents in American Foreign Relations* (Johns Hopkins Press, 1929). The great majority of such designations have been agents to conduct negotiations. Crandall, *op. cit.*, pp. 76–77, n. 52; *Senate Document*, No. 231, 56th Congress, 2nd sess.

76 Benton, *Abridgment*, XI, 221–222.

77 Richardson, I, 96–98.

78 *Congressional Record*, 53rd Congress, 2nd sess., pp. 127, 132, 196–197, 199, 205, 431–432; *Senate Reports*, No. 277, same Congress and session.

79 Note 37 *supra*.

80 Note 74 *supra*. Washington despatches of October 10, 1928, told of an agreement among twenty-two "career men" at the head of diplomatic posts of the United States not to follow precedent by resigning the following March 4th, at the beginning of Mr. Hoover's administration. President Coolidge demurred to the agreement on the ground that such heads of diplomatic posts were "primarily personal representatives of the President."

Henry L. Stoddard, in *It Costs To Be President*, gives the curious code which was sometimes used by Mr. Wilson and Colonel House in their correspondence with each other. *Ibid.*, p. 59. It was doubtless the product of the mystery-loving Colonel's mind. The President could hardly have had time for such nonsense.

81 Nos. 64 and 75. Speaking in the Senate in 1818, Rufus King, a surviving member of the Philadelphia Convention, said:

"In these concerns the Senate are the Constitutional and the only responsible counsellors of the President. And in this capacity the Senate may, and ought to, look into and watch over every branch of the foreign affairs of the nation; they may, therefore, at any time call for full and exact information respecting the foreign affairs, and express their opinion and advice to the President respecting the same, when, and under whatever other circumstances, they may think such advice expedient.

"There is a peculiar jealousy manifested in the Constitution concerning the power which shall manage the foreign affairs, and make treaties with foreign nations. Hence the provision which requires the consent of two-thirds of the Senators to confirm any compact with a foreign nation that shall bind the United States; thus putting it in the power of a minority of the Senators, or States to control the President and a majority of the Senate: a check on the Executive power to be found in no other case.

"To make a treaty includes all the proceedings by which it is made; and the advice and consent of the Senate being necessary in the making of treaties, must necessarily be so, touching the measures employed in making the same. The Constitution does not say that treaties shall be concluded, but that they shall be made, by and with the advice and consent of the Senate; none therefore can be made without such advice and consent; and the objections against the agency of the Senate in making treaties, or in advising the President to make the same, cannot be sustained, but by giving to the Constitution an interpretation different from its obvious and most salutary meaning." Farrand, III, 424–425.

Yet two years before this the first standing Committee on Foreign Relations asserted in a report to the Senate:

"The President is the constitutional representative of the United States with regard to foreign nations. He manages our concerns with foreign nations and must necessarily be most competent to determine when, how, and upon what subjects negotiation may be urged with the greatest prospect of success. For his conduct he is responsible to the Constitution. The committee considers this responsibility the surest pledge for the faithful discharge of his duty. They think the interference of the Senate in the direction of foreign negotiations calculated to diminish that responsibility and thereby to impair the best security for the national safety. The nature of transactions with foreign nations, moreover, requires caution and unity of design, and their success frequently depends on secrecy and dispatch." 299 U. S. at 319, citing *United States Senate Reports, Committee on Foreign Relations,* VIII, 24.

[82] Haynes, *op. cit.,* I, 62–67; *Journal of William Maclay* (Edgar S. Maclay, ed.), pp. 128–133; J. Q. Adams, *Memoirs,* VI, 427, where the story is told, on the authority of Crawford, that, as Washington strode out of the Senate chamber, he declared "that he would be damned if he ever went there again." The account given in Maclay seems to prove Crawford's anecdote to be apocryphal.

[83] Norman J. Small, *Some Presidential Interpretations,* etc., p. 69; Ralston Hayden, *The Senate and Treaties* (New York, 1920), Chs. II and III.

[84] *Ibid.,* Chs. VIII and IX.

[85] For this and other instances of prior consultation of the Senate, usually by message, see Crandall, *op. cit.,* pp. 67–72.

[86] Senator Cummins of Iowa introduced, December 2, 1918, a resolution in the Senate which, reciting the Senate's participation in treaty making, proposed that a Senate committee of four Democrats and four Republicans be sent to Paris to keep the Senate informed of proceedings there in connection with the making of peace. The proposal apparently did not come to a vote.

"He [the President] alone negotiates." Justice Sutherland, for the Court, in 299 U. S. at 319. The late Senator Lodge had stated this conclusion in an article in *Scribner's* in 1902. Hayden, *op. cit.,* p. 17.

[87] See especially "Treaty-making Powers of the Senate," *Foreign Policy Information Service,* IV, No. 16 (October 12, 1928); also, entry "Treaties" in Index to W. Stull Holt, *Treaties Defeated by the Senate* (Johns Hopkins Press, 1933). For the pro's and con's of senatorial participation in treaty making see Frank D. Fleming's *Treaty Veto of the American Senate* (New York, 1930), especially Ch. XII, and R. J. Dangerfield, *In Defense of the Senate* (University of Oklahoma Press, 1933). A well-balanced account of the classical struggle over the Treaty of Versailles is to be found in Professor Holt's work, cited above, where the defeat of the treaty is laid to "politics," and blame is equally awarded to Wilson and Lodge. *Cf.* note 98 *infra.*

[88] Crandall, *op. cit.,* p. 131; 19 *Opins. A. G.* 520.

[89] U. S. Code, tit. 19, §1351. For earlier precedents see Crandall, pp. 121–127.

[90] *United States v. Belmont,* 301 U. S. 324 (1937); *Altman & Co. v. United States,* 224 U. S. 583 (1912); *Field v. Clark,* 143 U. S. 649 (1892). In the face of these holdings such agreements are still sometimes attacked in Congress as of doubtful validity. Less than three years ago the late Senator Lewis expressed his strong disagreement with *Field v. Clark:* "I think the able court got very wrong and very far afield from the correct principles of government, and laid down the beginning of a very bad and wrongful policy." *Congressional Record,* February 25, 1937. See further Francis B. Sayre, "The Constitutionality of Trade Agreements," 39 *Columbia Law Review* 751 (May 1939).

[91] For the latter resolution see U. S. Code, tit. 22, §271. A vigorous attack was later

made on its constitutionality by Representative Tinkham. *Congressional Record,* February 5, 1935. Mr. David J. Lewis of Maryland, on the other hand, introduced in the House on March 19, 1934, a similar measure to end, as he declared, "the impasse which has for years enabled thirty-three Senators to delay final action upon American membership in the World Court." *The New York Times,* March 19, 1934. So far nothing has come of this suggestion. The War Debt funding agreements of 1923, which were entered into by a commission created for the purpose under the Act of February 9, 1922, were laid before Congress for acceptance, not before the Senate alone. Act of February 28, 1923, 42 Stat. 1326. Senator Walsh of Montana protested this legislation as unconstitutional. "Thereupon Senator McCumber of North Dakota retorted that anything done by treaty could be done by statute." Bertram D. Hulen, *The New York Times,* February 17, 1935. From 1866 to 1871 Congress declined to enact legislation to carry Indian treaties into effect, and in the latter year passed an act which "denied the right of any Indian tribe or nation to be recognized as an independent nation for treaty-making purposes," thereby transferring all Indian affairs to its jurisdiction. U. S. Code, tit. 25, §71: 16 Stat. 566. In connection with the Joint Resolution of July 2, 1921, see my article on "The Power of Congress to Declare Peace," 18 *Michigan Law Review,* 669–675 (May 1920).

[92] *President's Control,* pp. 117–120, 125, 151. The most remarkable example of an "executive agreement," at least the most remarkable one which to date has come to light, is the "agreed memorandum," dated July 29, 1905, of an exchange of opinion between Count Katsura of Japan and Secretary of War Taft, acting as personal representative of President Roosevelt. The document was discovered among Mr. Roosevelt's unpublished papers by Mr. Tyler Dennett, who described his find in an address before the Williamstown Institute of Politics, August 7, 1924, as follows:

"In the course of the conversation the American representative of President Roosevelt remarked to the Japanese, 'I suppose that you do not desire to take the Philippine Islands away from us.' The Japanese replied that he was glad to assure the American Government that Japan had no such desire or intention, and that Japan would be best satisfied to see the United States remain in the Philippines and establish and maintain a stable government.

"The Japanese representative then said in substance: 'You realize how difficult it is to preserve the peace of the Far East. There is danger that following the conclusion of the Russo-Japanese War, Korea will lapse again into a condition of anarchy. We are aware of the provision of the American Constitution which make alliances so difficult, but it seems to us as though it would be possible for the United States to enter into a secret agreement with Japan and England for the preservation of the peace of the Far East.'

"The American replied that under our Constitution such a secret agreement would be impossible. However, he thought he could assure the Japanese Government that the American people would be glad to act with the Japanese and British people for the preservation of the peace of the Far East.

"The Japanese representative then inquired of the American representative what, in his opinion, Japan should do with reference to Korea. The American replied that in his judgment Japan would be fully justified in establishing a military protectorate over Korea and in taking charge of her foreign relations.

"This document was approved by President Roosevelt only twelve days before the formal publication of the terms of the second Anglo-Japanese alliance and two weeks before the opening of the Portsmouth Peace Conference." *The New York Times,* August

8, 1924; also, Tyler Dennett, *Roosevelt and the Russo-Japanese War* (1925), pp. 112–114.

Nor, as Mr. Dennett further pointed out, did this action "stand alone." At the outbreak of the Russo-Japanese War, eighteen months earlier, Roosevelt had, according to a letter which also Mr. Dennett was the first to bring to light, "notified"—the words are Roosevelt's—"Germany and France in the most polite and discreet fashion that in the event of a combination against Japan to try to do what Russia, Germany, and France did to her in 1894, I should promptly side with Japan . . . to whatever length was necessary on her behalf." Dennett, *op. cit.*, p. 2. Undoubtedly, the exhumation of the records of such adventurings as these has aided the current agitation for the War Referendum proposal.

It took a treaty—the Nine Power Treaty of 1922—to end the Lansing-Ishii Agreement. *The New York Times*, March 31, 1923. The failure of the Senate to ratify the Treaty of Lausanne was repaired so far as our government was concerned by an executive agreement, entered into for the United States by Admiral Bristol, whereby diplomatic and consular relations with Turkey were restored. *Ibid.*, March 15, 1927. The Tariff Truce Pact of May 12, 1933, the parties to which agreed to forego for the time being "any new initiatives which might increase the many varieties of difficulties now arresting international commerce"—that is to say, agreed to forego exercising certain of their constitutional and legal powers—was an executive agreement. *Ibid.*, May 13, 1933.

An agreement which precipitated a heated discussion in the Senate was the one under which President Coolidge undertook, early in 1928, to supervise the Nicaraguan elections of that year. Senator Norris introduced a resolution calling upon the Foreign Relations Committee, after making proper investigation, to report on the following questions:

"1. What, if any, authority did the President of the United States have to accept such invitation on the part of the Nicaraguan Government to supervise an election in Nicaragua?

"2. If the Committee finds that the President of the United States did have such authority, then it is directed to report to the Senate whether, in its judgment, the same authority does not give the President of the United States the right to supervise any election in any foreign country?

"3. If the President of the United States does not possess authority to use the Army and the Navy of the United States to supervise elections in foreign countries, then the Committee is hereby directed to report to the Senate, by bill or otherwise, the necessary legislation that will prevent such illegal use of the armed forces of the United States in the future?

"4. If the President of the United States has authority, under existing law, to use the Army and the Navy of the United States to supervise an election in Nicaragua, has he not the same authority to use the same forces in the supervision of an election in any other foreign country?

"5. Will the use of the Army and Navy of the United States in supervising elections in foreign countries have a tendency to bring on war between our Government and foreign nations where such supervisory authority is attempted?

"6. If the President of the United States, under existing law, has authority to use the Army and the Navy to supervise elections in foreign countries, does he possess the same authority to use the armed forces of the United States to supervise elections in different States of the Union and would such use of the Army and the Navy of the United States be advisable in cases where the Senate has official information of corruption taking place

in State elections where members of the Senate and House of Representatives are elected?"
United States Daily, March 10, 1928.

While the Committee appears not to have taken any action, Senator Edge of New Jersey, a member of it, endeavored to meet Senator Norris's craving for information by citing several previous instances of the sort. Said he:

"Our Presidents have often acted as arbitrators in disputes between foreign governments. The right to do so seems to have been tacitly recognized although not definitely provided by either Constitution or law. I have never known of a President who asked Congress for authority in such a responsibility, and I am inclined to the opinion that it would be a deliberate trespass upon executive authority and responsibility to attempt by legislation to interfere." *Ibid.*

93 *Autobiography,* pp. 551–552; see also Bishop, *Roosevelt,* I, 433–434.

It was during this period that Roosevelt wrote to the British minister, Spring Rice:

"I am having my own troubles here, and there are several eminent statesmen at the other end of Pennsylvania Avenue whom I would gladly lend to the Russian government, if they care to expend them as bodyguards for Grand Dukes wherever there was a likelihood of dynamite bombs being exploded." Pringle, *Roosevelt,* p. 366.

94 Note 90 *supra.* See also *Tucker v. Alexandroff,* 183 U. S. 424, 434–435 (1902); *Altman & Co. v. United States,* 224 U. S. at 600–610 (1912); *Akira Ono v. United States,* 267 Fed. 359 (C. C. A.).

95 301 U. S. 330–331.

96 *Ibid.* 331–332. The Washington territorial court in 1870, speaking of the agreement of 1859 for joint occupancy by the United States and Great Britain of the island of San Juan, declared that, while not a "casting of the national will into the firm and permanent condition of law," nevertheless the instrument was in "some sort" an expression of the will of the people expressed through the political arm of the government; and that therefore it was incumbent upon the courts to permit its operation within reasonable limits even to the point of temporarily restraining or modifying statutes. *Watts v. United States,* I Wash. Ter. 288, 294.

97 *Constitutional Government in the United States* (Columbia University Press, 1908), p. 138.

98 *Ibid.,* p. 141. Elaborating upon the same idea he said further:

"Advisers who are entirely independent of the official advised are in a position to be, not his advisers, but his masters; and when, as sometimes happens, the Senate is of one political party and the President of the other, its dictation may be based, not upon the merits of the question involved, but upon party antagonisms and calculations of advantage.

"The President has not the same recourse when blocked by the Senate that he has when opposed by the House. When the House declines his counsel he may appeal to the nation, and if public opinion respond to his appeal the House may grow thoughtful of the next congressional elections and yield; but the Senate is not so immediately sensitive to opinion and is apt to grow, if anything, more stiff if pressure of that kind is brought to bear upon it.

"But there is another course which the President may follow, and which one or two Presidents of unusual political sagacity have followed, with the satisfactory results that were to have been expected. He may himself be less stiff and offish, may himself act in the true spirit of the Constitution and establish intimate relations of confidence with the

Senate on his own initiative, not carrying his plans to completion and then laying them in final form before the Senate to be accepted or rejected, but keeping himself in confidential communication with the leaders of the Senate while his plans are in course, when their advice will be of service to him and his information of the greatest service to them, in order that there may be veritable counsel and a real accommodation of views instead of a final challenge and contest." *Ibid.,* pp. 139–140.

It was rumored early in Mr. Wilson's first administration that, not content with reviving the custom of delivering his messages to Congress orally, he also planned to attend executive sessions of the Senate. The promise—or threat—was never fulfilled, although the Senate rules still provide for such a contingency just as in Washington's day.

[99] *Ante,* note 81.

[100] *Ante,* note 98.

[101] 135 U. S. 1, 64.

[102] 1 *Opins. A. G.* 566, 570–571.

[103] *President's Control,* p. 15.

[104] The most elaborate statement of this point of view, that by Mr. J. Randolph Tucker of Virginia as Chairman of the House Judiciary Committee (1887), relates to the incidence of treaty provisions on the revenue laws. 57th Congress, 1st sess., *House Reports* No. 4177; Henry St. George Tucker, *Limitations on the Treaty-Making Power* (Boston, 1915), Ch. XI. Judicial dicta, however, do not support the doctrine. Note 21 *supra.* See also *Willoughby on the Constitution,* I, 555–560.

[105] "Where a treaty is law of the land, and as such affects the rights of parties litigating in court, that treaty as much binds those rights and is as much to be regarded by the court as an act of Congress." Chief Justice Marshall, for the Court, in *United States v. Schooner Peggy,* 1 Cr. 103, 110 (1801). See also to the same effect *Foster v. Neilson,* 2 Pet. 253, 314 (1829). The principle was, in fact, assumed in the first case to come before the Court involving a treaty. *Ware v. Hylton,* 3 Dall. 199 (1796).

[106] Note 21 *supra.*

[107] Crandall, pp. 458–465; Wright, pp. 258–260. While treaties sometimes provide for their own termination upon notice to the other party, or upon the lapse of a certain period following notice, the presence or absence of such a provision seems not to have influenced the procedure of termination for the United States. Our earliest treaties, those of 1778 with the King of France, were "abrogated" by act of Congress, July 7, 1798, on the justification that they had been violated by France. Whether the act of Congress was formally brought to the attention of the French Government does not appear. In *Bas v. Tingy,* 4 Dall. 37 (1800), it was treated by some of the Justices as amounting to a partial declaration of war. In *Ware v. Hylton,* two years earlier, J. Iredell had expressed the opinion that a treaty of the United States could be cast off only in this way, namely, by a solemn declaration by Congress that the other party had violated it. 3 Dall. 260. In his message of March 1, 1879, vetoing a bill restrictive of Chinese immigration to the United States, President Hayes distinguished between outright termination of a treaty "by expressing the will of the nation no longer to adhere to it" and the power to modify an existing treaty. The former, he conceded, belonged to Congress; the latter, however, was lodged by the Constitution in the President and Senate. Richardson, VII, 514–518. Needless to say, the record of practice under the Constitution does not support this distinction. Note 21 *supra.* The broad power which Hamilton attributed to the President in connection with the interpretation and suspension of treaties (*ante,* p. 210) leads logically to conceding him the power to terminate them; and Jefferson's view as Secretary of State closely

approximated Hamilton's on this point. Moore, IV, 681. See also 229 U. S. 447, 473, where the question whether a treaty is still binding on the United States is held to be one for "the political branch of the government," by which is meant in this instance "the Executive." President Taft in 1911 headed off a resolution of Congress "directing" the abrogation of the Treaty of 1832 with Russia by giving notice "couched in a friendly and courteous tone" and inviting negotiations for a new treaty. *Our Chief Magistrate*, pp. 115–117; Washington despatches of December 18, 1911. Our extradition treaty with Greece, having proved of no aid in enabling us to get hold of Samuel Insull, was peremptorily denounced by the present administration without stimulation or assistance from either Congress or the Senate. Washington despatches, November 4, 1933. On the other hand, when the question arose of reviving the Patents Convention of 1909 with Germany, President Harding consulted the Senate, February 17, 1922, and that body gave its approval by a two-thirds vote. Haynes, *op. cit.*, II, 590.

The most recent instance of denunciation of a treaty was that of Treaty of Commerce and Navigation of February 21, 1911, with Japan, which was effected by the State Department's giving on July 26, 1939, the Japanese Government six-months notice, in accordance with the terms of the treaty. A proposal to the same end, offered by Senator Vandenberg, was at the time before the Senate Foreign Relations Committee. *The New York Times*, July 27 and 31, 1939.

[108] 229 U. S. 447, 472–474, and authorities there cited.

[109] I am indebted to Professor Zurcher for drawing my attention to this matter.

[110] For the above data, see Moore, *Digest*, II, 452–466. By the Act of May 27, 1921 (42 Stat. 8), "no person may land or operate in the United States any submarine cable directly or indirectly connecting the United States with any foreign country" without a written license from the President, who "may withhold or revoke such license when he shall be satisfied after due notice and hearing that such action will assist . . . in maintaining the rights or interests of the United States or of its citizens in foreign countries or will promote the security of the United States." U. S. Code, tit. 47, §§34–35.

[111] 30 *Opins. A. G.* 217.

[112] 37 Stat. 302, which has been superseded by the Act of June 19, 1934, 48 Stat. 1064 ff. Under the latter no station license can be granted any alien or representative, any foreign government or representative, or "any corporation organized under the laws of any foreign government." U. S. Code, tit. 47, §310.

[113] 30 *Opins. A. G.* 291; Richardson, XVII, 7962, 8006. Washington's Proclamation of Neutrality was, of course, a further illustration of presidential action in execution of a national duty under international law; and there have been numerous instances of the return by executive authorization of property of foreign governments or their citizens found, for some reason or other, within the confines of the United States. *Senate Executive Documents*, No. 123, 26th Congress, 2nd sess., pp. 379, 384, 853, 1288. The doctrine seems early to have been established, however, that the President may not deliver up fugitives from justice taking refuge in the United States except under an act of Congress or a treaty. This was on the ground that there is no such duty owing by the Law of Nations. 1 *Opins. A. G.* 509, 521 (1821); 3 *ibid.*, 661 (1841); Moore, *Digest*, IV, 245–246. And although President Lincoln delivered up one Arguelles, a Spanish subject, in 1864 upon the demand of the Spanish government, with which we had no extradition treaty at the time (*ibid.*, 249–250), the recent case of *Valentine v. United States*, 299 U. S. 5 (1936), approves the more generally accepted doctrine. *Ibid.*, 8.

[114] Pp. 193 and 273 *supra*. For expert authority urging such action by the President,

see *The New York Times,* March 5, 1917. Said Chief Justice Marshall, with reference to a seizure under the Act of February 9, 1799, suspending intercourse with France:

"It is by no means clear that the president of the United States whose high duty it is to 'take care that the laws be faithfully executed,' and who is commander in chief of the armies and navies of the United States, might not, without any special authority for that purpose, in the then existing state of things, have empowered the officers commanding the armed vessels of the United States, to seize and send into port for adjudication, American vessels which were forfeited by being engaged in this illicit commerce." *Little v. Barreme,* 2 Cr. 170, 177 (1804).

[115] *Works* (Hamilton, ed.), VII, 745–748; *President's Control,* pp. 133–135.

[116] See 2 Bl. at 659–660.

[117] 4 Blatch. 451, 454 (1860). The affair at Greytown is only one of a long line of similar episodes. See *Memorandum of the Solicitor of the State Department,* "Right to Protect Citizens in Foreign Countries by Landing Forces" (2nd revised edition, Washington, 1929).

[118] Richardson, X, 198.

[119] *Ibid.,* IV, 317–318.

[120] *President's Control,* pp. 158–163. Grant's Santo Domingo adventure was vastly improved upon by the first Roosevelt, both as to audacity and outcome, when late in 1903 he "took Panama." The debate on the matter, which was precipitated in the Senate early in January, 1904, when the Hay-Herran Treaty was laid before that body for ratification, centered upon a resolution which declared the President's course to have been violative of the Law of Nations, our treaty with Colombia, and the Neutrality Act. Said Senator Morgan:

"The President has paused in his usurpation of the war power, but not until he had gone to so great a length that he believed Congress would be compelled to follow the flag to save appearances and adopt a war that he was actually waging against Colombia under guise of treaty obligations to protect the transit across the Isthmus of Panama. . . . To obtain ratification of his excessive adventure he comes to the Senate and appeals to its special treaty-making power to join him in giving sanction to the war he had begun and is conducting with a display of war power at sea that is far greater than was mustered in the war with Spain, all under the pretext of protecting the isthmian transit. He asks the Senate to usurp the power of Congress to declare war, instead of making his appeal to Congress." *Congressional Record,* January 4, 1904, pp. 426–437.

[121] R. M. McElroy, *Grover Cleveland* (New York, 1923), II, 249–250.

[122] The referendum proposal upon which recent discussion has centered was introduced by Congressman Ludlow of Indiana. It came to vote January 10, 1938, on a motion to discharge the House Rules Committee. The motion was defeated by a vote of 209 to 188. At that time the proposed amendment read as follows:

"Section 1. Except in the event of an invasion of the United States or its territorial possessions and attack upon its citizens residing therein, the authority of Congress to declare war shall not become effective until confirmed by a majority of all votes cast thereon in a Nation-wide referendum. Congress, when it deems a national crisis to exist, may by concurrent resolution refer the question of war or peace to the citizens of the States, the question to be voted on being, Shall the United States declare war on —————?

"Section 2. Congress may otherwise by law provide for the enforcement of this section."

At the time of the adoption of the Constitution the New York and Rhode Island conventions urged amendments requiring that a declaration of war receive the concurrence of two thirds of both houses of Congress; and the Hartford Convention of 1815 suggested a similar proposal for all cases except actual invasion of the United States. From that time till the outbreak of the World War no amendment touching the war power seems to have been offered in Congress. Between 1914 and 1926, however, no fewer than seventeen such proposals were introduced in the one house or the other. Their usual sources were peace groups or German-American societies and their congressional sponsors came from Oklahoma, California, Washington, North Dakota, Wisconsin, and Missouri. Fourteen of these proposed amendments would have permitted Congress to declare war only in the event of imminent peril such as invasion, or after a majority of the people had declared in favor of war. One proposed by Senator Thomas of Oklahoma in 1924 stipulated that Congress could declare war only upon the concurrence of three fourths of the elected members of each house. Another, proposed by Senator Frazier of North Dakota in April 1926, and again in December 1927, read as follows:

"Section 1—War for any purpose shall be illegal, and neither the United States nor any State, Territory, association or person subject to its jurisdiction shall prepare for, declare, engage in or carry on war or other armed conflict, expedition, invasion or undertaking within or without the United States, nor shall any funds be raised, appropriated or expended for such purpose.

"Section 2—All provisions of the Constitution and of the articles in addition thereto and amendments thereof which are in conflict with or inconsistent with this article are hereby rendered null and void and of no effect.

"Section 3—The Congress shall have power to enact appropriate legislation to give effect to this article."

This proposal originated, Senator Frazier indicated, with the Women's Peace Union, of 180 Lexington Avenue, New York City. *The New York Times,* April 24, 1926. And see generally M. A. Musmanno, *Proposed Amendments to the Constitution,* pp. 124–126.

The most notable contribution to the discussion which was evoked by the Ludlow resolution was the Honorable Henry L. Stimson's letter in *The New York Times* of December 22, 1937. Mr. Stimson, a former Secretary of State, urged the tendency of such an amendment to weaken "our first line of defense," the "diplomatic one," which is drawn by the warnings of the President to other governments respecting our view of our own interests. He also urged "no more effective engine for the disruption of national unity on the threshold of a national crisis could ingeniously have been devised" than such a referendum.

Mr. George H. Gallup interpreted certain polls taken by his organization about a year ago as showing that "the people think that they should have the right, in a national vote, to say whether United States troops should ever be conscripted for fighting abroad." *The New York Times Magazine,* April 30, 1939. Such a right is probably the substance for which the great majority of the supporters of the War Referendum idea are contending, and it is by no means certain that the Constitution was originally thought to permit conscription for such a purpose. See Mr. Hannis Taylor's brief in the Selective Draft Cases, 245 U.S. (Record files). Indeed, a "correct" reading of the Constitution might make the War Referendum proposal altogether superfluous. Said C. J. Taney for the Court in *Fleming v. Page:*

"The genius and character of our institutions are peaceful, the power to declare war was not conferred upon Congress for the purposes of aggression or aggrandizement, but to enable the general government to vindicate by arms, if it should become necessary, its own rights and the rights of its citizens." 9 How. 603, 614 (1857).

It should be observed that this dictum was spoken in a case involving questions growing out of the war with Mexico.

A minor difficulty with all War Referendum proposals to date is the false emphasis they put on the "declaration" of war. As Professor Borchard has recently pointed out, "Most wars are undeclared." Address at South Orange, N. J., January 27, 1940. Nor is this any recent development, as Hamilton's words in *The Federalist* show: "The ceremony of formal denunciation of war has of late fallen into disuse." Earle, p. 156.

123 The significance of presidential initiative in the diplomatic field for the issue of war and peace is no recent discovery. As early as 1836 we find J. Q. Adams writing:

"However startled we may be at the idea that the Executive Chief Magistrate has the power of involving the nation in war, even without consulting Congress, an experience of fifty years has proved that in numberless cases he has and must have exercised the power. In the case which gave rise to this controversy the recognition of the French Republic and the reception of her minister might have been regarded by the allied powers as acts of hostility to them, and they did actually interdict all neutral commerce with France. Defensive war must necessarily be among the duties of the Executive Chief Magistrate." *Eulogy on Madison*, 47.

In his *Memoirs*, too, Adams animadverted upon "that error in the constitution which confers upon the Legislative Assemblies the power of declaring war, which, in the theory of government, according to Montesquieu and Rousseau, is strictly an Executive act." *Ibid.*, IV, 32.

Years later a Whig House of Representatives stigmatized the war with Mexico *ex post facto* as having been "unnecessarily and unconstitutionally begun by the President." *Congressional Globe*, 30th Congress, 1st sess., p. 95. And see James K. Polk's *Diary*, I, 233–234, 363–382 *passim*. (I am indebted for these references to Professor Zurcher.) Indeed, Adams underwent a revulsion of feeling on this point. See his speech of April 15, 1842, in 11 *Congressional Globe*, 428.

In his famous treatise on *Constitutional Law*, J. N. Pomeroy wrote a few years after the Civil War:

"The President cannot declare war; Congress alone possesses this attribute. But the President may, without any possibility of hindrance from the legislature, so conduct the foreign intercourse, the diplomatic negotiations with other governments, as to force a war, as to compel another nation to take the initiative; and that step once taken, the challenge cannot be refused. How easily might the Executive have plunged us into a war with Great Britain by a single despatch in answer to the affair of the Trent. How easily might he have provoked a condition of active hostilities with France by the form and character of the reclamations made in regard to the occupation of Mexico.

"I repeat that the Executive Department, by means of this branch of its power over foreign relations, holds in its keeping the safety, welfare, and even permanence of our internal and domestic institutions. And in wielding this power, it is untrammelled by any other department of the government; no other influence than a moral one can control or curb it; its acts are political, and its responsibility is only political." *Ibid.*, p. 565.

Never, however, have the potentialities of the President's initiative been much more richly illustrated than under the present administration. A partial chronicle of its *known* acts and utterances since the President's Chicago speech of October 5, 1937, suggesting "a quarantine on aggressors" to January 1, 1940, suffices to show this:

1937

December 13: The President took a hand in preparing a note demanding that Japan render reparation for the *Panay* incident.

1938

January 28: The President sent a message to Congress urging an $800,000,000 plan for expansion of the Army and Navy.

March 5: The President formally asserted the claim of the United States to Canton and Enderbury Islands and to Byrd's Land in the Antarctic.

August 18: In an address at Queen's University, Kingston, Ontario, the President assured Canada of our aid in case she was threatened by another empire.

September 25: The President appealed to Hitler and Benes to negotiate.

September 27: The President appealed to Hitler a second time.

November 14: The State Department summoned Ambassador Wilson home from Berlin for "report and consultation."

November 15: The President in his Press Conference strongly condemned Nazi anti-Jewish activities ("I myself could scarcely believe that such things could occur in a twentieth century civilization").

November 15: The President expressed himself as favoring arming for hemisphere defense.

December 15: The Export-Import Bank authorized a $25,000,000 credit to China.

December 15: The State Department sent note demanding that the Reich exclude American citizens from anti-Jewish decrees.

December 22: Assistant Secretary of State Welles bluntly rejected Nazi protest at Secretary of the Interior Ickes's Cleveland speech, saying it expressed American views.

1939

January 27: The President announced that he had approved the purchase of an undesignated number of fighting planes by France. (The statement followed the crash in Southern California of a bombing plane designed for the United States Army, and the rescue from the wreckage of a French officer. This episode was made a subject for secret inquiry by the Senate Military Committee.)

January 31: It was reported that the President, in his conference with the Senate Military Affairs Committee, whose members were sworn to secrecy, had located our defense frontier in France—a report which the President later denied as a "deliberate lie."

March 17: The State Department, in a statement agreed upon by the President and Assistant Secretary Welles, condemned the "wanton lawlessness" of the Nazi Government in absorbing Czecho-Slovakia.

March 18: The government increased the customs duties on German imports 25 per cent.

March 20: The State Department in a note to Germany flatly refused to recognize the conquest of Czecho-Slovakia.

April 8: Secretary Hull condemned Italy's invasion of Albania as "an additional threat to the peace of the world."

April 9: On leaving Warm Springs, Georgia, the President said, "I'll be back in the Fall if we don't have war," thereby again precipitating heated discussion of his intentions both in the Senate and elsewhere.

April 12: The President expressed approval of the barter of farm surpluses for needed war materials.

April 14: In an address to the governing board of the Pan American Union the President pledged the readiness of the United States to defend "the American peace," "matching force with force."

April 15: The President addressed a personal message to Hitler and Mussolini asking for a ten-year peace in exchange for world disarmament and an international conference on the subject of raw materials; also ordered the fleet to the Pacific.

July 26: The State Department formally denounced our commercial treaty with Japan, the denunciation to take effect January 26, 1940.

August 24: The President addressed a personal appeal to the King of Italy to exercise his influence for peace.

August 24: The President appealed to Hitler and the President of Poland to settle their differences by direct negotiation, arbitration, or conciliation.

August 25: The President sent a second appeal to Hitler.

August 28: With war impending the Treasury Department took unprecedented steps to delay the departure of the German liner *Bremen* from New York.

September 12: The President announced in press conference that the entrance of Canada into the war against Germany did not affect his pledge to that country of American protection against non-British domination.

September 15: The President summoned Congress to meet in extra session September 21 to consider revision of the Neutrality Act.

September 21: The President urged Congress to repeal the arms embargo provisions of the Neutrality Act as "the surest safeguard against the involvement" of the United States in the European War.

October 12: The United States appealed through its ambassador to Moscow in Finland's behalf.

October 18: The President issued a proclamation closing American ports and territorial waters against belligerent submarines, but admitting belligerent armed merchantmen.

October 19: Ambassador Grew asserted in a speech at Tokyo that American opinion deeply resented the "bombings, indignities and manifest interferences with American rights" in China at the hands of the Japanese army.

November 14: The President announced disapproval of transfer of eight United States Line ships to Panama registry.

November 29: Secretary Hull, with the President's approval, made a tender of the good offices of the United States to Russia and Finland.

December 1: The President condemned Russia's invasion of Finland as "a wanton disregard of law."

December 2: The President proclaimed "a moral embargo" upon the sale to Russia of United States planes and equipment that might be used in the bombing of civilians and open towns. (As early as June 1938 a similar embargo had been placed on the sale to Japan of airplanes, airplane equipment, and materials essential to airplane manufacture.)

December 5: The President disclosed plans for financial aid to Finland.

December 6: The President sent a cordial message to President Kallio on the 22nd anniversary of Finland's independence.

December 10: The United States, through the Export-Import Bank and the Reconstruction Finance Corporation, granted a ten-million-dollar credit to enable Finland to purchase agricultural surpluses and other civilian supplies here.

December 15: The State Department added aluminum and molybdenum to the list of materials under moral embargo to nations which bomb and machine-gun civilians and towns from the air.

December 18: The Navy Department yielded priority on deliveries to enable Finland to obtain more than forty of the latest and speediest American fighting planes.

December 20: Secretary Hull extended the moral embargo on munitions by announcing that a ban, aimed at Russia and Japan, on export of devices for improving aircraft fuel would apply to all countries whose forces bomb civilians.

December 23: President Roosevelt named Myron C. Taylor as his personal representative at the Vatican to work with Pope Pius XII, and called upon the Pontiff and Protestant and Jewish leaders to coöperate toward ending the war in Europe.

December 23: The United States Government and twenty other American republics issued a joint protest to France, Great Britain, and Germany against the battle involving the *Graf Spee*, and other "violations" of the safety zone around the Western Hemisphere.

[124] Last July Senator Nye proposed the creation of a joint committee by the two houses with which the executive should consult "in confidence on all major questions of foreign policy before final steps to decision are taken." *The New York Times*, July 30, 1939. Nothing came of the proposal at the time, but in his address of September 21 to the special session which was summoned to repeal the arms embargo, Mr. Roosevelt said:

"I am asking the leaders of the two major parties in the Senate and in the House of Representatives to remain in Washington between the close of this extraordinary session and the beginning of the regular session on Jan. 3. They have assured me they will do so, and I expect to consult with them at frequent intervals on the course of events in foreign affairs in this field, whether it be executive or legislative action."

In point of fact, the said leaders headed promptly for home, thus rendering the proposed enterprise of coöperation and mutual consultation with the President inoperative.

NOTES TO CHAPTER VII*

[1] F. D. G. Ribble, *State and National Power Over Commerce* (Columbia University Press, 1937), pp. 117–119. (The passage is quoted with the consent of the publishers.)

[2] Wilson, *Congressional Government*, pp. 6, 11, 23, 301.

[3] *Ibid.*, pp. 41–43 *passim*.

[4] *Ibid.*, pp. 44–45. It cannot be said that Wilson showed much discernment in this passage. For one thing, he entirely overlooks the way in which their labors in committee keep most Congressmen out of mischief much of the time.

[5] *The American Commonwealth* (New York, 1895), I, 61.

[6] *Ibid.*, 223–224. Lord Bryce's words reflect a conventional view, but the fact is that individual incumbents of an office are just as tenacious of its supposed powers as an assembly is of its supposed powers.

[7] *Ibid.*, II, 712–713.

[8] *Rise and Growth*, pp. 279–293 *passim*. It is, perhaps, worth noting that Ford was an editor, while Wilson and Bryce were academicians.

"In the strictest meaning of the term the [United States] federal government is a limited or constitutional monarchy, and the events of recent years have left it the only real monarchy of first-class importance in the world." Herbert A. Smith, *Federalism in North America* (Boston, 1923).

[9] *Congressional Government*, pp. xi–xii.

[10] *Constitutional Government*, pp. 67–73 *passim*.

[11] Black, *Relation of Executive Power*, etc. (Princeton University Press, 1919), Preface and p. 1.

[12] *Ibid.*, p. 62.

[13] The clause was probably suggested by a similar one of the New York constitution of 1777. Article 19 of this instrument declared it to be the "duty of the governor to inform the legislature, at every session, of the condition of the State, so far as may respect his department; to recommend such matters to their consideration as shall appear to him to concern its good government, welfare, and prosperity." Thorpe, V, 2633.

[14] See *ante*, pp. 18–19.

[15] No. 47; Earle, pp. 313–316.

[16] *Writings* (Ford, ed.), I, 160–165. See also *ibid.*, VII, 108.

[17] Sumner says that the incident gratified Jackson "more than any other . . . of the latter part of his life." *Andrew Jackson*, p. 367.

[18] *Autobiography*, p. 282.

[19] Mark Sullivan, *Our Times* (New York, 1926), I, 74.

[20] In his *Autobiography* Roosevelt calls the Washington correspondents "the most useful of all agents in the fight for efficient and decent government." *Ibid.*, p. 354. On "T. R.'s" popularity with the correspondents, see Oscar K. Davis, *Released for Publication* (New York, 1925), pp. 123–124.

[21] When in 1908 Congress had got entirely out of hand, Roosevelt is reported to have told a congressman that "he wished he had sixteen lions to turn loose in Congress with which august assembly he was just then having some difficulty." The congressman asked the President whether he thought they might not make a mistake. "Not if they stayed long enough," answered "T. R." Archibald Butt, *Letters* (New York, 1924), p. 104. I can testify of my own recollection to the wide-eyed amazement with which some students of

* Chapter VII (*Popular Leader and Legislator*) begins on page 255.

mine returned from an interview at the White House during the fight over the Hepburn bill. Mr. Roosevelt's characterizations of some of the Senators who resented his desertion of the Chandler *bloc* were uncomplimentary to a degree. On reaching Princeton the young men were met by telegrams asking them to consider what the President had said as confidential, but the caution came too late in some cases.

Late in his second administration the impression gained currency that Mr. Roosevelt was using the Secret Service to trail members of Congress, and a provision was inserted in the Sundry Civil Appropriation bill of 1908 limiting the activities of the Secret Service. This action the President condemned in his annual message the following December, thereby precipitating a mutually irritating wrangle with the House of Representatives. Richardson, XI, 1398 ff. (In this "revised" edition of Richardson, dated 1909, Vol. XI is paged continuously with Vol. X.)

That the Secret Service watched Senator Foraker at the time of the Brownsville affair and also tampered with his mail is asserted positively by Mrs. Foraker in her *I Would Do It Again* (New York, 1932), pp. 286–288.

22 *Autobiography*, pp. 382–383.

23 *Some Presidential Interpretations*, p. 182.

24 Mr. Wilson's appeal of October 24, 1918, read in part as follows:

"My Fellow-Countrymen: The Congressional elections are at hand. They occur in the most critical period our country has ever faced or is likely to face in our time. If you have approved of my leadership and wish me to continue to be your unembarrassed spokesman in affairs at home and abroad, I earnestly beg that you will express yourselves unmistakably to that effect by returning a Democratic majority to both the Senate and the House of Representatives.

"I am your servant and will accept your judgment without cavil. But my power to administer the great trust assigned to me by the Constitution would be seriously impaired should your judgment be adverse, and I must frankly tell you so because so many critical issues depend upon your verdict. No scruple of taste must in grim times like these be allowed to stand in the way of speaking the plain truth.

"I have no thought of suggesting that any political party is paramount in matters of patriotism. I feel too deeply the sacrifices which have been made in this war by all our citizens, irrespective of party affiliations, to harbor such an idea. I mean only that the difficulties and delicacies of our present task are of a sort that makes it imperatively necessary that the nation should give its undivided support to the Government under a unified leadership, and that a Republican Congress would divide the leadership.

"The leaders of the minority in the present Congress have unquestionably been pro-war, but they have been anti-administration. At almost every turn since we entered the war they have sought to take the choice of policy and the conduct of the war out of my hands and put it under the control of instrumentalities of their own choosing."

It will be noted that Mr. Wilson was not appealing to the people against Congress in behalf of a specific measure or program, but was asking the country for a vote of confidence for himself and party. His action is, therefore, in line with his own peculiar conception of the President as Prime Minister rather than with the Andrew Jackson–"T. R." procedure of endeavoring to bludgeon the President's own party. "F. D. R.'s" "purge" in 1938 was, of course, modeled on the latter procedure. See, e.g., his "Fireside Chat" of June 25, 1938, and his anti-Tydings speech at Denton, Md., September 5, 1938. *The New York Times,* June 26 and September 6, 1938.

On the other hand, Mr. Wilson repeatedly asked Congress during the War for what was in effect a "vote of confidence." Two items from *The New York Times* illustrate the point:

"Washington, July 23.—A virtual threat to veto the Administration Food Bill if the conferees retain the Senate amendment creating a joint committee to supervise war expenditures is contained in a letter sent tonight by President Wilson to Chairman Lever of the House Committee on Agriculture. The latter says the President would interpret 'the final adoption of Section 23 as arising from a lack of confidence in myself.' " *Ibid.,* July 24, 1917.

"Washington, May 15.—Three moves of prime importance were made today in connection with the aircraft controversy:

"President Wilson in a letter to Senator Martin, the Democratic floor leader, vehemently opposed the Chamberlain resolution for an investigation of the conduct of the war by the Committee on Military Affairs of the Senate. He said passage of the resolution would be 'a direct vote of want of confidence in the Administration,' and would constitute 'nothing less than an attempt to take over the conduct of the war.' The President called upon supporters of the Administration in the Senate to rally in his support." *Ibid.,* May 16, 1918.

Mr. Wilson got his way in both instances.

[25] *Theory and Practice of Modern Government,* II, 1034.

[26] *Congressional Record,* April 5 and June 19, 1906. On the latter occasion Senator Isidor Rayner became heavily sarcastic regarding Mr. Roosevelt's proceedings:

"Here we were day after day struggling with questions of constitutional law, as if we really had anything to do with their settlement, laboring under the vain delusion that we had the right to legislate; that we were an independent branch of the Government; that we were one department, and the Executive another, each with its separate and well-defined distinctions, imagining these things, and following a vision and a mirage, while the President was at work dominating the legislative will, interposing his offices into the law-making power, assuming legislative rights to a greater extent than he could possibly do if he were sitting here as a member of this body; dismembering the Constitution, and exercising precisely and identically the same power and control as if the Constitution had declared that Congress shall pass no law without the consent of the President; adopting a system that practically blends and unites legislative and executive functions, a system that prevailed in many of the ancient governments that have forever gone to ruin, and which today still obtains in other governments, the rebellious protests of whose subjects are echoing over the earth, and whose tottering fabrics I hope are on the rapid road to dissolution." *Ibid.* See also a speech of similar import by Representative Charles A. Towne, *ibid.,* June 11, 1906; and another by Senator Tillman, *ibid.,* March 16, 1908.

[27] See *ante,* pp. 36 and 339, note 48.

[28] *Public Papers of Woodrow Wilson* (New York, 1925–1927), I, 32. It is sometimes stated that Mr. Wilson delivered his messages as governor in person and orally, but the researches of Professor John E. Bebout seem to refute this belief. *Documents and Readings in New Jersey Government* (Copyright, Photo-Lithographers, 1931), p. 191.

[29] Tumulty, *Woodrow Wilson as I Know Him,* p. 176.

[30] Dr. Franklin Burdette tells the story in his excellent volume, *Filibustering in the Senate* (Princeton University Press, 1940), pp. 117–128.

[31] See J. S. Bassett, *Our War With Germany* (New York, 1919), pp. 117, 139–141, 150, 163, 173–177; J. B. McMaster, *The United States in the World War* (New York, 1920), pp. 36–37; Black, p. 58; Baker is singularly disappointing on such matters.

32 "The Future of the Presidency," *New Republic,* September 29, 1917; quoted in Black, *op. cit.,* pp. 38–39.

33 Robert Luce, *Legislative Problems* (New York, 1935), p. 260.

34 See also Binkley, *op. cit.,* pp. 236–257.

That Mr. Coolidge's constitutional views did not stand in the way of his drafting legislation to be laid before Congress is shown by the fact that in 1927 he drew legislation to apply the unexpended balance of the Deficiency Appropriation bill of July 3, 1926, to the prosecution of litigation to cancel the Fall-Sinclair-Doheny oil leases. *House Journal,* 69th Congress, 2nd sess., p. 194.

35 *Public Papers and Addresses of Franklin D. Roosevelt* (New York, 1938), III, 14 (cited later as *F. D. R.*).

36 *The New York Times,* November 13, 1932. On his western trip in 1937, Mr. Roosevelt remarked at Cheyenne that "it was part of the duty of the Presidency to keep in touch, personal touch, with the nation." *Ibid.,* September 25, 1937. See also his letter to Senator Barkley of July 15 of the same year: "On the Congress of the United States falls the primary responsibility for the adoption of methods, but on the President falls the responsibility of recommending objectives. This is in accordance with the Constitution."

37 *Ibid.,* November 15, 1936.

38 In a poll taken of the Washington correspondents between February and May 1936, during the concerted attack on Roosevelt by the Liberty League, the Hearst chain, etc., and before Landon had been nominated, the results were: Roosevelt—65.2 per cent; all Republican candidates—30.8 per cent. L. C. Rosten, *The Washington Correspondents* (New York, 1937), pp. 59–60. *Newsweek* for March 4, 1940, reported "A Periscope Survey" of political writers on the question: "Irrespective of his chances for nomination and election, who is the best qualified man for the next Presidency?" The President led with 54 votes. Runners-up were Secretary Hull with 36 votes, Senator Vandenberg with 29 votes, Attorney General Jackson with 26 votes, Mr. Hoover with 22 votes. After that the votes fell off rapidly.

39 This was when he was quoted as having said that "our frontier is on the Rhine," or words to that effect. See p. 421 *supra.*

40 It was at one time remarked that Mr. Roosevelt "had only to look toward a microphone" to bring a recalcitrant Congressman of his own party to heel.

41 This, of course, is not to say that Mr. Roosevelt invented the special message. Mr. Cleveland devoted his third annual message to the tariff. Richardson, VIII, 580. The first Roosevelt submitted special messages on Cuban reciprocity, naval armament, and other topics. Wilson comparatively early in his first administration had addressed Congress on tariff revision, currency reform, trusts and monopolies, and repeal of the Panama Tolls Exemption Act.

42 I am indebted to Mr. Turner Cameron for a list of the President's special messages and letters to chairmen of committees, compiled for the period March 4, 1933, to June 18, 1936, from *F. D. R.,* I–V, and as to later messages, from *The New York Times.* See also 31 *American Political Science Review,* 1083, and 32 *ibid.,* 1118.

Apropos of the "doubt however reasonable" letter (*F. D. R.,* IV, 297–298), see the memorandum by Attorney General Mitchell advising President Hoover that it would be proper for him to sign the Norris-La Guardia Act of 1932, restricting the equity powers of Federal courts, despite doubts as to the measure's constitutionality. The memorandum was attached to President Hoover's communication to Congress approving the act. *The New York Times,* March 24, 1932.

43 Charles A. Beard, "The President Loses Prestige," 42 *Current History*, 64 (April 1935); *cf.* the same writer, 43 *ibid.*, 64 (October 1935).

44 See *ante*, p. 404, note 41.

45 See President Cleveland's special message to the Senate of March 1, 1886, vindicating the Attorney General in refusing to comply with a demand for certain documents which bore on the suspension of one George M. Duskin from office (Richardson, VIII, 375ff.); also President Theodore Roosevelt's special message of January 6, 1909, setting out his reasons for directing the Attorney General not to reply to a resolution of the Senate asking whether or not certain proceedings had been instituted against the Tennessee Coal and Iron Company for an alleged violation of the Sherman Act, and if not, why not. The latter message reads in part:

"I have instructed the Attorney General not to respond to that portion of the resolution which calls for a statement of his reasons for non-action. I have done so because I do not conceive it to be within the authority of the Senate to give directions of this character to the head of an executive department, or demand from him reasons for his action. Heads of executive departments are subject to the Constitution, and to the laws passed by the Congress in pursuance of the Constitution, and to the direction of the President of the United States, but to no other direction whatever."

The Senate then tried to get certain documents bearing on the same matter from the head of the Bureau of Corporations, whereupon Roosevelt ordered that official to hand the papers in question to him, and defied the Senate to do its worst. Archibald Butt, *Letters*, pp. 305–306.

46 *Ante*, p. 379, note 89. A work of uncommon brilliance and insight on the subject of executive leadership in legislation is Émile Giraud's *La Crise de la démocratie et le renforcement du pouvoir exécutif* (Paris, 1938). While the argument is mainly directed against the deficiencies of the French constitution—now defunct—it is rich in observations of interest to American readers, as that the executive must direct the legislature, being the organ with "unity of thought," "capacity to acquire a view of the whole" (p. 110), and possessing, by virtue of its participation in administrative and diplomatic activities, adequate information (p. 115). M. Giraud systematically attacks the *laissez-faire* conception of democracy as "the organization of resistance to power" (p. 72, n. 2). To the contrary, he asserts, it is "a power of action and realization" (p. 99). "A feeble executive," he continues, "means a feeble state, one which fulfills badly its function of protecting the individual against political, economic, and social forces which, without the state, tend to swallow him up, to exploit and oppress him" (pp. 101–102).

47 On the foregoing paragraph, see Farrand, I, 21, 98, 103–104, 138–140; II, 71, 78–80, 104, 181, 298, 301, 568–569, 587. For the sources of the veto clause see the opinion of Judge Nott in *United States v. Weil*, 29 Ct. Cl. 538 (1894); also Thomas H. Calvert, *The Constitution and the Courts* (Long Island, 1924), I, 379–381.

48 See generally Edward C. Mason, *The Veto Power* (1891); and Clarence A. Berdahl, "The President's Veto of Private Bills," 52 *Political Science Quarterly*, 505–531.

49 Mason, 120.

50 In his veto of the Webb-Kenyon Act of 1913, which was promptly repassed over his objections and later upheld by the Supreme Court (242 U. S. 311), President Taft took the ground that his oath of office did not permit him to assent to an act of doubtful constitutionality. *Cf.* note 42 *ante*.

51 Musmanno, *Proposed Amendments*, pp. 67–70.

52 *Okanogan Indians v. United States,* 279 U. S. 655 (1920).

53 *Wright v. United States,* 302 U. S. 583 (1938).

54 See Justice Stone's separate opinion, 302 U. S. 598–609.

55 *Edwards v. United States,* 286 U. S. 482 (1932). The opinions of the Court in this and the Okanogan Case contain valuable historical data on the points decided.

56 The source of the Court's doctrine is *La Abra Mining Co. v. United States,* 175 U. S. 423, 453–454. Compare *The Cherokee Tobacco,* 11 Wall. 616, 621 (1871) for a similar example of judicial embroidery to fill up an admitted constitutional gap.

57 286 U. S. at 493.

58 "Arranging for the uninterrupted performance of his official functions during his proposed visit to Europe, President Wilson is represented as having reached an agreement with Vice-President Marshall, in his capacity as President of the Senate, and Representative Champ Clark, the Speaker of the House, under which these public servants would withhold their signatures from bills passed by the Congress until the President returns to this country, thereby delaying the presentation to him of such measures, and thus permitting him to exercise his power of veto when he is again established at the national capital." *The New York Tribune,* November 21, 1918.

59 The story is told by Dr. L. F. Schmeckebier in 33 *American Political Science Review,* 52–54. The important parts of the narrative are as follows:

"The House Calendar for June 20 under H. R. 8875 contains the following notation: 'Passed Senate, amended, June 18, 1936.' The same notation appears in the House Calendar for June 22, and in the final edition of the Calendar published about July 1. In the list of 'Bills and Resolutions which have become Laws' in the final edition of the House Calendar, no mention of the bill is made.

"Congress adjourned on June 20, with the bill on the Speaker's table. The record showed that the bill had been amended by the Senate, and that the House had not concurred in the amendments; therefore, on the face of the record, the bill was dead.

"After adjournment, the error was discovered and steps were taken to remedy it. According to a reliable source, this was accomplished through alteration of the House *Journal,* although it has been impossible to prove this, inasmuch as access to the manuscript *Journal* was refused. However, such an examination might not be conclusive, since if a few pages of the manuscript *Journal* were copied the alteration would not be apparent. However, the contemporary records cited above all point conclusively to alteration of the *Journal.*

"The entries relating to the bill in the *Congressional Record* were also altered. The entry regarding H. R. 8875 in the list of amended bills on page 10215 of the daily *Record* was deleted from the bound *Record;* a new entry for H. R. 8875 was added to the message from the Senate stating that certain House bills have been passed without amendment (bound *Record,* p. 10175).

"As the *Journal* now showed passage, the bill was enrolled. It is reported that it was sent by airplane messenger to the presiding officers, and was signed by the Speaker at Jasper, Alabama, on July 9, and by the Vice-President at Uvalde, Texas, on July 10. This was probably the first time that a bill had been signed by the presiding officers when not in Washington and so long after adjournment. On the face of the altered *Journal,* this procedure was regular enough, as House Concurrent Resolution 54 gave the presiding officers power to sign after adjournment. The place of signing was immaterial."

60 Berdahl, *loc. cit.,* pp. 508–511, including footnotes.

[61] Finer, *op. cit.,* II, 1033. The following item from *The New York Times* of May 23, 1934, disclosed an unusual facet of the veto power:

"Washington, May 22.—The Senate and House today by concurrent resolution recalled and amended at President Roosevelt's request the Equal Rights Nationality bill.

"This action followed a White House conference at which sponsors of the bill agreed that the bill should be so amended as not to penalize the children of American parents in order to benefit the children of American mothers married to foreign citizens. This bill had been awaiting Mr. Roosevelt's signature.

"The change resulted from a detailed study of the bill by the State Department which revealed that while it would extend citizenship to the children of American women married to foreign citizens, it would restrict privileges already enjoyed by the children of American citizens whose careers force them to live abroad permanently.

"President Roosevelt did not promise definitely to sign the bill when it is amended, but those at the conference gained the impression that he would do so, especially as it will be, when amended, exactly in line with a treaty drawn up at the Pan-American Conference at Montevideo in December."

In 1937 the obverse of the above situation occurred at Albany. Again the *Times:*

"Albany, June 5.—Governor Lehman signed today a bill establishing a Bureau of Narcotic Control in the State Department of Health. He had vetoed the bill on Monday.

"The Governor said that, since disapproving the measure sponsored by Senator McNaboe of New York, 'other facts have been submitted to me which, in my opinion, justify my now giving it my approval.' Senator McNaboe conferred yesterday with the Governor on the bill, and is understood to have submitted certain facts to the Executive which pointed to the necessity for enacting the bill into law." *Ibid.,* June 6, 1937.

[62] See the House proceedings in the *Congressional Record* for January 14, 1938, and appendix of the same issue; also *The New York Times* for January 6 and March 6, 1938. The President's request for this power read as follows:

"Appropriation item veto: An important feature of the fiscal procedure in the majority of our States is the authority given to the Executive to withhold approval of individual items in an appropriation bill, and, while approving the remainder of the bill to return such rejected items for the further consideration of the legislature. This grant of power has been considered a consistent corollary of the power of the legislature to withhold approval of items in the Budget of the Executive; and the system meets with general approval in the many States which have adopted it. A respectable difference of opinion exists as to whether a similar item-veto power could be given to the President by legislation or whether a constitutional amendment would be necessary. I strongly recommend that the present Congress adopt whichever course it may deem to be the correct one."

The constitutional issue was apparently conceded to turn solely on the matter of delegation.

In his earlier correspondence with Senator Vandenberg, who thought a constitutional amendment necessary, the President among other things remarked:

"I want you to know that I completely agree with your criticism of legislative 'riders' on tax and appropriation bills. Regardless of the merits or demerits of any such 'riders'— and I do not enter that phase of the discussion at the moment—the manifest fact remains that this practice robs the Executive of legitimate and essential freedom of action in dealing with legislation." *The New York Times,* January 6, 1938.

And again:

"About two months ago you wrote me in regard to the problem of the 'item veto.'

Since then I have talked with Alben Barkley and he agrees with us that riders are foreign to the objectives of appropriation bills or other specific subject legislation; that they constitute a bad practice and that the President ought to have, as many Governors have, the right to veto such a rider without having to veto the whole bill." *Ibid*.

It should be noted that the House proposal did not cover "riders." It would have given the President only the right to *reduce* appropriations, not the right to eliminate restrictions on their expenditure. Nor, to my way of thinking, would it be desirable to do the latter. "Riders" are frequently objectionable, but they may also be an indispensable means of checking the executive.

63 *Hollingsworth v. Virginia,* 3 Dall. 378 (1798).

64 253 U. S. 350 (1920).

65 In November 1919, Senator Lodge introduced a "concurrent resolution" in the Senate to declare the war with Germany at an end, and seemed considerably surprised when administration supporters informed him that President Wilson would veto it. Speaker Gillette, however, after reading Art. I, section 7, of the Constitution, opined that, while it was not customary to send concurrent resolutions to the President, apparently it would be necessary to do so in this instance. *New York Evening Post,* November 21, 1919. The resolution "died a-bornin'," but its fate did not deter its author from employing virtually the same idea quite extensively in the famous "Reservations" which he proposed to ratification of the Versailles Treaty.

The pending Connally bill would make deportations of aliens subject in certain cases to a concurrent resolution. *The New York Times,* June 30, 1940. And see generally *Senate Reports,* 1,335, 54th Congress, 2nd sess.

66 The vetoed measure fixed the first Monday in November as the meeting day of Congress and the second Monday of May as its time of adjournment; and the latter provision, the President argued, invaded both the prerogative of the houses to agree on a date of adjournment and the President's contingent prerogative, in the event of their not agreeing. Richardson, III, 231–232. The date of the message is June 9, 1836. There was considerable talk that President Wilson might have to employ this unused prerogative to get Congress officially adjourned in October 1914. *The New York Times,* October 24, same year.

67 The threat of an extra session has sometimes been employed by Presidents to speed compliance with their demands. Small, p. 181.

68 Speaking of President Roosevelt's relations with his first Congress, Professor E. Pendleton Herring, an excellent political observer, wrote in February 1934 as follows:

"His influence perhaps in greatest measure rested upon public confidence, together with his personal as well as official prestige. But for weathering the many political vicissitudes of putting through a complicated legislative program he was not forced to rely entirely upon these intangible factors. A second line of defense of undoubted significance was his control of patronage. In the distribution of jobs, the test of pre-convention support of Roosevelt was applied, but to this was added the query: 'How did you vote on the economy bill?' The President postponed all appointments except those that could not possibly be delayed, and owing to this (as one observer remarked) 'his relations with Congress were to the very end of the session tinged with a shade of expectancy which is the best part of young love.' His control of patronage was the only means that he had of touching individual members of Congress directly. The President could defy pressure groups and appeal to the country over the radio. But when he wished to marshal Congress behind his program and to persuade congressmen to risk the displeasure of important interests in their districts, he needed some means of strengthening their position at home. The dangers, the faults, and the limitations of this method are obvious. Yet the session indicated that the consummation of a national program of legislation is greatly aided by transmuting through patronage the localism of our politics into support of the Chief Executive." 28 *American Political Science Review*, 82–83.

Professor W. Y. Elliott expresses the view in his *The Need for Constitutional Reform* (New York, 1935) that "no President can surrender patronage unless he is given some other hold on Congress," and proposes in this connection that the President be empowered to dissolve both houses once during his term. *Ibid.*, 234–235. It is possible I am a bit overconfident in my position.

[69] Lindsay Rogers, *The American Senate* (New York, 1926), pp. 168–169.

[70] See generally Dr. Franklin L. Burdette's volume cited in note 30 *supra*. In a memorandum which he kindly prepared at my request Dr. Burdette lists the following Senate filibusters as having been directed against the President of the day or presidential policies.

1837 Brief obstruction against the resolution to expunge the Senate censure of President Jackson. Filibuster unsuccessful.

1846 Filibuster against a resolution to serve a year's notice of termination of "joint occupancy" of Oregon with obstruction eventually unsuccessful.

1846 (August 10) Filibuster of John Davis of Massachusetts, in effect against the Polk measure for an appropriation to be used for acquiring territory and in making peace with Mexico. Successful for the time. (See *The Diary of James K. Polk* [Chicago, 1910], II, 77, for the President's bitter complaint.)

1847 The same issue (an appropriation for peace with Mexico) was debated in the Senate from February 4 till March 1. Obstruction finally unsuccessful.

1863 (March 2–3) Democratic filibuster against a measure to "indemnify" the President for suspending the writ of habeas corpus. Obstruction unsuccessful because of arbitrary action of the chair.

1865 Filibuster of Charles Sumner and others against recognition of a reconstructed Louisiana. Successful.

1881 Final nominations of President Hayes were held in the Senate through factional Republican obstruction.

1893 Prolonged obstruction of President Cleveland's program for silver repeal. Eventually unsuccessful. For a detailed account of this filibuster see Jeannette Paddock Nichols, "The Politics and Personalities of Silver Repeal," *American Historical Review*, XLI (October 1935), 33.

1903 John T. Morgan filibustered in executive sessions against President Roosevelt's treaty with Colombia for the Panama Canal. A special session of the Senate was necessary to secure ratification.

1907 Democratic filibuster led by Edward W. Carmack against Republican ship subsidy legislation supported by President Roosevelt. Obstruction successful.

1911 Robert L. Owen filibustered in an effort to force admission of Arizona to the Union against the wishes of President Taft, who disliked Arizona constitutional provisions. The filibuster failed in its ultimate purpose, but it contributed toward the failure to admit New Mexico at that session.

1913 Taft's final appointments blocked by Democratic obstruction.

1913 Minor Republican obstruction delayed confirmation of Wilson's appointee to the position of Director of the Census. Republican threats of filibuster also served to postpone currency adjustments.

1914 Long debates on the Panama Canal Tolls, the Federal Trade Commission bill, and the Clayton Anti-Trust bill. It is doubtful whether these debates were genuine filibusters; and the President's program was eventually successful in each instance.

1914 President Wilson's Ship Registry bill was briefly delayed, but the President had his way.

1915 Republicans were successful in their filibuster against the Ship Purchase bill, supported by President Wilson.

1917 Republicans filibustered to delay business in order to force a special session and embarrass the administration. Obstruction continued from February 23 to February 28, but was abandoned when the Armed Ship bill was ready for consideration.

1917 Successful obstruction of the President's Armed Ship bill by "willful men."

1919 Republicans delayed business in order to force a special session "to keep representatives of the people closely in touch with peace negotiations in Paris."

1922 The Fordney-McCumber tariff supported by President Harding was long delayed.

1922–1923 Democrats successfully filibustered against a ship subsidy measure proposed by the Harding administration.

1926 A filibuster against adherence to the administration-supported World Court Protocol was broken by cloture.

1935 (May 21) Huey Long petulantly sought to prevent a joint session of Congress to hear President Roosevelt read his veto of the soldiers' bonus. The obstruction was unsuccessful.

1935 (June 12–13) Huey Long sought to force adoption of the Gore amendment providing for Senate confirmation of personnel under the proposed "skeletonized" NRA. This most celebrated of the Long filibusters was unsuccessful.

1939 Republicans and anti-administration Democrats won a technical though probably hollow victory by delaying a vote on renewal of the President's monetary powers until after their expiration at the end of the fiscal year.

On the other hand, the President has a few times been the intended beneficiary of a filibuster, as in the following instances:

1879 Republicans filibustered to defeat a Democratic rider to an appropriation bill intended to prevent use of Federal troops "as a police force to keep the peace at the polls." President Hayes had previously vetoed similar but more drastically worded legislation. Republican obstruction was finally abandoned when leaders became convinced that the ambiguous rider was really a Democratic retreat and therefore essentially a compromise. The rider was allowed to pass, and Hayes approved it.

1901 Thomas H. Carter, Republican, of Montana, defeated by filibuster a river and harbor bill. It was understood widely that the Montana Senator acted in accordance with the wishes of President McKinley in order to save the executive the possible embarrassment of a veto.

1936 Bennett Champ Clark and others obstructed Treasury and Post Office appropriations until the House finally agreed to a ship subsidy law supported by President Roosevelt.

Senate filibusters sometimes receive an adventitious justification from the fact that while the filibusterers are a minority in the Senate they represent a majority of the voters. Rogers, p. 175, n. 13. The theme that the Senate filibuster is indispensable as a check on the President was harped on continuously during the debate on the Ship Purchase bill of

1915, which succumbed to the filibuster against it. See 52 *Congressional Record,* pp. 904–4020 *passim* (January 4–February 18, 1915).

[71] U. S. Code, tit. 31, §15.

[72] Public No. 19, 76th Congress, 1st sess.

[73] The constitutional problem raised by such a statute was the theme of the following colloquy in the Senate a year or two since. The passage is worth rescuing from oblivion not only for its immediate relevancy, but also for the light which it throws on the inadequacy of judicial review in certain situations as a means of protecting and preserving the Constitution:

"Mr. BARKLEY. If we could abrogate or nullify by statute the constitutional right of each House to adopt its own rules in a particular case, such as the joint resolution referred to in the amendment now pending, we could by statute enact a law which would bind both Houses with respect to all their rules of procedure on any sort of legislation. Could we not pass a law making the rules of the House and the Senate identical with respect to all matters?

"Mr. NORRIS. Probably we could. Let us take the other side of the question. If we are to regulate the country by rule, could we not adopt a rule providing that when any bill comes to the Senate from the House it shall lie on the table for 30 days, then be referred to a committee, that the committee shall be powerless to report it for 30 days more, and that when the bill comes on the floor of the Senate it shall not be voted on for another 30 days, or 60 days, even though a statute fixed the procedure by which such matters should be considered?

"Mr. BARKLEY. I suppose that when the Constitution provided that each House should fix its own rules of procedure it took the chance that the Senate or the House might be foolish in the determination of its rules.

"Mr. NORRIS. No; I think it took the chance that it would not be foolish.

"Mr. BARKLEY. That is just what I was about to say.

"Mr. NORRIS. Yes.

"Mr. BARKLEY. Of course it would be possible for the Senate to provide by rule that a bill coming over from the House shall not be referred to a committee for 30 days, but shall lie on the table; that it shall then be held in committee for 30 days; and then it shall not be passed for 30 days more. That, however, would be a ridiculous exercise of the constitutional authority to establish rules.

"Mr. NORRIS. The same thing is true of any activity of Government. The Constitution makes the President the Commander in Chief of the Army and Navy. Everybody knows that with that power in his hands, in 30 days we could make war against all the world, or any part of the world. He could go so far that he could not get out of what he had done. Everybody knows that the Constitution says that we shall be the judge of the qualifications of our own Members. If a man came here who was a Democrat, we could say, 'We will not take him in because he is a Democrat.' We could keep him out because of his color or because of his nativity.

"We could keep him out by reason of his age. We could do any ridiculous or foolish thing we chose to do; but it is impossible to put together a government on paper without having all those possibilities. If power is to be given to anybody to do anything under a government, it is possible for him to misuse and abuse the power and make it disreputable and destructive.

"Mr. CONNALLY. Mr. President, will the Senator yield?

"Mr. NORRIS. I yield to the Senator from Texas.

"Mr. CONNALLY. I am very much interested in the Senator's discussion of the constitutional provision giving the Senate the power to make its own rules. That power is not in anywise limited or restricted. If the Senate should foolishly adopt a rule such as the one suggested by the Senator from Kentucky, providing that a bill shall lie on the table for 30 days, and then go to a committee for 30 days, no power on earth could prevent it.

"Mr. NORRIS. I agree with the Senator.

"Mr. CONNALLY. Any power which the Constitution gives to Congress, when properly exercised, is just as strong as the Constitution itself, is it not?

"Mr. NORRIS. Yes.

"Mr. CONNALLY. So if we should enact a statute providing the manner in which a bill should be considered, so long as the Senate observed the statute and did not adopt a rule contrary to it, of course, the statute would be a rule of this body. But if the Senate should decide, under its constitutional authority, to adopt such a rule, the Rules Committee could bring in a resolution providing the manner in which a bill should be considered, thus overturning the statute. Will not the Senator agree to that?

"Mr. NORRIS. Yes.

"Mr. CONNALLY. That is true, is it not?

"Mr. NORRIS. That is true. There would be a conflict.

"Mr. CONNALLY. And the constitutional provision would override the statute.

"Mr. NORRIS. We cannot change the Constitution, so far as I know.

"Mr. CONNALLY. Certainly not.

"Mr. NORRIS. There is no provision in the Constitution giving any Federal official anything to do which we could not disregard if we wanted to do so. Suppose a Governor appointed somebody who was only 15 years old to fill a vacancy in the Senate. The Senate is the judge of the qualifications of its own Members. It is supreme. There is no appeal. When the Senate decides such a matter, it is ended. The Constitution plainly states what the age must be. But suppose the Senate, in passing on the question, should say, 'We will accept this 15-year-old boy and make him a Senator.' What power could change it? Is there anybody in our Government who could change it? The Senate would have decided it. Everybody might say, 'The Senate itself has violated the Constitution.' What of it? The Constitution gives the Senate authority to pass upon the qualifications of its own Members. When the Senate decides such a question, that is the end of it.

"The Supreme Court is given certain authority under the Constitution. Suppose the Supreme Court should hold unconstitutional every act passed by the Congress. What could we do about it? It would be foolish, it would be silly; but the Supreme Court has the power to do it. So, in order to have power to perform the functions of their offices in a decent, methodical way, the Supreme Court must have power, which, if abused, might make them and the country ridiculous." *Congressional Record,* March 16, 1938.

74 See *Wilson v. New,* 243 U. S. 332 (1916). On the Profession's opposition to Mr. Brandeis's nomination to the Court, see *Senate Documents,* No. 409, 64th Congress, 1st sess.

75 See my *Court Over Constitution,* pp. 68–74.

76 For this paragraph see Warren, I, 185–214; II, 123–129, 313–316; III, 81–83, 102, 145, 171, 188–192, 214–216, 223; Carl B. Swisher, *Roger B. Taney* (New York, 1935), pp. 565–566.

77 On this episode see Sidney Ratner's well-known article, "Was the Supreme Court Packed by President Grant?" 50 *Political Science Quarterly,* 342–356.

[78] Mr. Alexander Sachs, in a letter to the present writer.

[79] Quoted from the late Senator J. T. Robinson's radio address of March 30, 1937. *The New York Times,* March 31, 1937. See also Mr. Pringle's *William Howard Taft* (New York, 1939), II, Index, "Supreme Court."

[80] In his Victory Dinner address of March 4, 1937, Mr. Roosevelt interpreted the election as meaning that the people expected the government to meet their needs "immediately." *The New York Times,* March 5, 1937.

[81] *F. D. R.,* V, 641–642; *The New York Times,* January 7, 1937.

[82] See Charles E. Fairman, "The Retirement of Federal Judges," 51 *Harvard Law Review,* 397–443. Nor is it surprising that "the man in the street" usually fastened on the age question as the main issue involved, as is shown in the following extracts from Richard Neuberger's amusing article in *Current History,* entitled "America Talks Court":

"Youthful service station operator: Sure the President ought to get rid of those old fossils. I've an uncle who is sixty-eight and I certainly wouldn't want him running the government. We have to help him around all the time, and he's never out of the doctor's office. He lives almost all the time on broth or milk toast. And by golly, he's younger than most of these Supreme Court justices.

"Young nurse: I didn't know whether to be for or against the President's plan until I saw a picture in a magazine showing the Supreme Court's dining room. All the judges had different knives and forks, and special salt and pepper shakers. That settled me. I've had enough experience with crotchety old patients to know that people who insist on all sorts of special favors sometimes aren't up to standard. If those judges can't use regular silverware and dishes, then they're too finicky and peculiar to run the government.

"Wife of a successful businessman: I know the President has never seen those dignified old men in their majestic black robes. If he had he would never propose such a terrible thing. When I was in Washington my husband took me to see the Court in session. It was the most wonderful sight I ever saw. It inspired me. If someone could only persuade the President to see the Supreme Court in that marvelous new hall, I know he would change his mind about the situation.

"A Townsendite: The President has no respect for the aged citizens of this country. He has made a political prisoner of their champion, Dr. Townsend, and now he claims that old people are not fit to serve on the Supreme Court. Providence will punish the President for this treatment of those who are old and gray. 'The hoary head is a crown of glory' says Proverbs, XVI, 31. Evil days will come on Americans if this Court plan is passed.

"Elderly lady: The founders of our country knew what they were doing when they provided for nine judges. If nine were good enough for President Washington, they should be good enough for President Roosevelt. I don't see why he needs fifteen.

"Young union man: I'll be for the bill if the President promises he won't appoint any more lawyers to the Court. The lawyers are the ones who have wrecked everything for the common people. If I had my way, no lawyers would be judges, Senators, or Congressmen." 46 *Current History,* 33–38.

[83] 301 U. S. 1, 548, 619. A common criticism of the Court for its recent decisions and the correct answer thereto are given in the following communication to the *New York Herald Tribune* by Mr. Roger Hinds of the New York Bar:

"In Mr. Archibald E. Stevenson's letter in your paper he said:

" 'I cannot help wishing that the Supreme Court, when it uncovers a long-standing mistake in constitutional interpretation, would forgo the satisfaction of correcting it itself. A better and more democratic plan, it seems to me, would be to let the people do it themselves in the manner prescribed by the amending clause.

"The suggestion, however, overlooks the fact that the judges have taken oath to uphold the Constitution, not to follow judicial precedents which are contrary to the Constitution. If any judge who conscientiously concluded that a precedent, no matter how long standing, was erroneous, should follow that precedent rather than uphold the Constitution, he would be unworthy to hold office and would deserve impeachment. In fact, the most effective opposition to the recent so-called court plan, was from those opponents who, conceding that the court had erred on important constitutional questions, held that the court could be trusted eventually to remedy its own mistakes, making 'packing' unnecessary. They refused to brand the court as incorrigible.

"There is no provision in our Constitution for judicial amendment. Under Mr. Stevenson's plan an erroneous judicial interpretation, after a sufficient lapse of time, would become part of the Constitution, in effect an amendment thereof, requiring a still further amendment to restore the Constitution to its original state, as intended by its founders. The Constitution does not prescribe amendment as the remedy for judicial error. Where the Constitution is all right as it stands, and the only fault is in its judicial interpretation, there is no occasion for amendment. The remedy should be applied to the interpretation, which is at fault, rather than to the Constitution which is not at fault.

"Not only is there no occasion for judicial amendment, accomplished through incorrigible adherence to erroneous precedents, but if we are first to make the unreasonable assumption that the judges are incorrigible, amendment by means of the amendment clause would be ineffectual to correct judicial error. The same judges who would flout the Constitution by consciously adhering to erroneous interpretations would be no more likely to obey the correcting amendments than to obey the original Constitution.

"If, for example, the court should now conclude that the Sixteenth Amendment means what it says, it is to be hoped that the court will candidly reverse its previous decisions to the contrary. Certainly it would unnecessarily and inartistically encumber our Constitution to adopt a new amendment stating that a previous amendment means what it says and not what the judges have erroneously said that it means.

"I think that we may properly assume that the judges are not only wise but are conscientious, and may be relied upon eventually to correct their own mistakes of interpretation, leaving the amending clause as a rarely used method for changing the Constitution itself.

Roger Hinds"

New York Herald Tribune, April 25, 1939.

Pertinent too—doubly pertinent, in fact—is the following passage from a speech by Senator William Jackson in the course of debate on the bill for abolishing the system of circuit courts which had been set up the year before. Answering the Federalist argument that the thing ought to be done by constitutional amendment, Jackson said:

"There is required first, then, two-thirds of both houses of Congress. Can this two-thirds be found now, or is there any probability of its being found for twenty years to come, who will concur in making the necessary alterations in the judiciary system that are now, or may hereafter, be required. . . . How, then, can we expect three-fourths of the legislatures of the several states to agree when we cannot agree among ourselves? There is, in fact, no amendment which could reach the case, and exhibit to view all requisite and necessary regulations for such an extent of the country. Such an attempt must form a volume, a Constitution by itself and after all fall short of the subject.

"I am clearly, therefore, of opinion that if the power to alter the judiciary system vests not here, it vests nowhere." Sen. William Jackson (Georgia). Judiciary Debate, January 1802, *Annals,* 7th Congress, 1st sess., col. 49.

[84] In a formal statement issued to the press, August 9, 1939, Mr. Roosevelt, with much justification, pronounced the objectives of his Court Reform bill "fully attained." He listed the objectives as follows:

"1. Extending to Supreme Court justices of retirement privileges available to other Federal judges.

"2. Ending the Court's 'narrow interpretations' which he blamed for impeding social and economic reforms, and the Court's 'assumption . . . of legislative powers.'

"3. Eliminating the Federal courts' congested dockets and delay in disposing of cases, and obtaining 'new blood' in the judiciary and additional judges.

"4. Obtaining greater flexibility in assignment of judges.

"5. Giving the Government the right to intervene in private cases involving constitutional issues.

"6. Providing direct and immediate appeal to the Supreme Court in cases involving constitutionality of Federal statutes.

"7. Reforming the administrative machinery of the courts."

[85] 4 Wall. 475 (1867). The scope of the argument in the case is indicated by the following extracts from Attorney General Stanbery's address to the court:

"If, when the President is here by a service of the subpoena, the court proceed in the case, and find it a case in which they are ready to order an injunction to issue to the President to command him not to execute those laws, and notwithstanding, the President goes on to execute them, what follows? That the court must now sustain its own dignity, for the court has a dignity and a power to be observed as well as the President. The next step here, then, is to move for an attachment, or a rule on the President, to show cause why an attachment should not issue against him; for what? For a contempt of this court; that whereas the court ordered him to abstain from proceeding further in the execution of these laws, in defiance of that order the President has gone on to do some acts in execution of the laws. He is therefore brought here by what kind of process? By process *quasi* criminal; by process of attachment to answer for a contempt of the court. . . .

"What sort of a spectacle have we? One great department of this government has arraigned another, and the executive department of the government, represented by the President, brought before the judicial department—for what purpose? To be punished criminally. . . .

"What then? The President deposed; the President made incapable of performing the duties of his office! Certainly a jail, or a dungeon it may be, is not a fit place to perform the duties and functions of President. You have made the President incapable of performing his duties. What is the effect of that? You have removed the President, for that is one of the conditions in which the President's office becomes vacant, that he is incapable of performing his duties. You have done it more effectually than by impeachment, for an impeachment does not deprive him of liberty; an impeachment sets him at large, and simply takes from him his official character; but the order of this court under these circumstances takes him as President and puts him in jail, and keeps him there until he performs what this court orders him to perform. . . .

"You leave the government without a head; you leave the office vacant, and the people must go about to get another President to perform these functions and these duties. In the meantime, until that is done, everything is at large, and there is not a law of the United States that can be executed, not an officer that can be appointed or an officer that can be removed. There is no one left to proclaim insurrection, if that shall happen. There is no one left to perform all the duties which for the safety of this people as a nation are reposed in the President. To correct a particular evil, to guard a particular individual or a particular State against the acts of the President, there is no way, according to the gentlemen, but to depose that President by a proceeding like this, and, for the correction of this lesser evil, to produce that enormous evil which affects not merely the State of Mississippi, but every other State of the Union and every individual." 4 Wall. 486–488.

The Attorney General's main reliance was on Jefferson's defiance of the *subpoena duces tecum*, which Chief Justice Marshall issued during the trial of Aaron Burr for treason, ordering the President to produce certain documents in court. Marshall's position was that the President could claim no exemption from the law save possibly on the ground that his official duties "demand his whole time," while in fact "this demand is not unremitting." Beveridge, *Marshall*, III, 444–447. Jefferson communicated his refusal to the United States Attorney for the district, George Hay, in a letter dated September 7, 1807:

"As I do not believe that the district courts have a power of *commanding* the executive government to abandon superior duties and attend on them, at whatever distance, I am unwilling, by any notice of the subpoena, to set a precedent which might sanction a proceeding so preposterous." *Writings* (Mem. ed.), XI, 365.

He had earlier commented on the possibility that he would be summoned in characteristic vein, as follows:

"Laying down the position generally, that all persons owe obedience to subpoenas, he admits no exception unless it can be produced in his law books. But if the Constitution enjoins on a particular officer to be always engaged in a particular set of duties imposed on him, does not this supersede the general law, subjecting him to minor duties inconsistent with these? The Constitution enjoins his constant agency in the concerns of six millions of people. Is the law paramount to this, which calls on him on behalf of a single one? Let us apply the Judge's own doctrine to the case of himself and his brethren. The sheriff of Henrico summons him from the bench, to quell a riot somewhere in his county. The federal judge is, by the general law, a part of the *posse* of the State sheriff. Would the Judge abandon major duties to perform lesser ones? Again; the court of Orleans or Maine commands, by subpoenas, the attendance of all the judges of the Supreme Court. Would they abandon their posts to them, to serve the purposes of a single individual? The leading principle of our Constitution is the independence of the legislature, executive and judiciary of each other, and none are more jealous of this than the judiciary. But would the executive be independent of the judiciary, if he were subject to the *commands* of the latter, and to imprisonment for disobedience; if the several courts could bandy him from pillar to post, keep him constantly trudging from north to south and east and west, and withdraw him entirely from his constitutional duties?" *Ibid.*, 240–241.

The principle of presidential immunity had been advanced at an early date. John Adams, Ames, and Maclay discussed the subject and the first two arrived at the conclusion that a President in office was answerable to no judicial process except impeachment. The President, they argued, was above "all judges, justices, etc.," and, secondly, that judicial interposition involving the President personally was liable to interfere with the operation of the governmental machinery. This, too, seems to have been Ellsworth's opinion, but Maclay thought decidedly otherwise. *Journal,* p. 167.

On the other hand, Jefferson's followers had made it one of their grounds of attack upon Justice Chase that he had refused to subpoena President Adams during the trial of Dr. Thomas Cooper for sedition. Beveridge, III, 33, 86. The inconsistency is the more glaring from the fact that Jefferson sought to extend his argument for exemption to his heads of departments. The incident referred to occurred in July 1806 during the trials of Smith and Ogden on indictments charging them with having aided Miranda in an attack on Caracas, Venezuela.

"They made affidavit that the testimony of James Madison, Secretary of State, Henry Dearborn, Secretary of War, Robert Smith, Secretary of the Navy, and three clerks of the State Department, was necessary to their defense. Accordingly these officials were summoned to appear in court. They refused, but on July 8, 1806, wrote to the Judges— William Paterson of the Supreme Court and Matthias B. Talmadge, district judge—that the President 'has specially signified to us that our official duties cannot . . . be at this juncture dispensed with.' " *Ibid.,* p. 436, n. 1.

Nevertheless, the idea that a President in office can be called to account judicially for his misdeeds reappears now and then. When in 1922 President Harding dismissed the director and twenty-seven chiefs of divisions in the Bureau of Engraving and Printing "for the good of the Service," Senator Caraway (Arkansas) moved an investigation of what he termed "an indictment" of the discharged employees "both as to honesty and efficiency," and in the course of urging his resolution, said:

"The immunity against malicious slander does not clothe the Executive. Wisely or otherwise, the Constitution clothes us with the right to express opinions in debate in the Senate and in the House and not be required to answer elsewhere, but such immunity does not run with the President of these United States; and I feel certain, Mr. President, that what never happened before in the history of this country is going to happen now— that one of these discharged employees is going to sue the President of these United States for wilful, malicious defamation of character, and the President, like any other citizen, is going to the bar of justice in a court room in the city of Washington and answer that charge. That is their last resort. They hoped that the President would have regard for their rights, and restore their reputations he so ruthlessly destroyed; but he says now: 'I will not do it, and I am not sorry for what I did.' " *Congressional Record,* February 23, 1923.

No such action was brought, nor did the Senator get his investigation. Nor did an Atlanta lawyer make better headway when, early in 1937, he petitioned the Supreme Court to put President Roosevelt "in his place" by holding him to be in contempt of court on account of his message of January 6, 1937. Associated Press despatch of January 23, 1937.

[86] In the Chase impeachment the prosecution advanced the doctrine that impeachment is "an inquest of office," a political process for turning out of office any official whom a majority of the House and two thirds of the Senate wished to be rid of. The failure of the impeachment went to establish the opposed view that it is essentially a criminal proceeding. Beveridge, III, 198–216.

The same issue was nevertheless raised at Johnson's trial by Manager Bingham, who at the outset defined an impeachable offense as follows:

"The result is, that an impeachable high crime or misdemeanor is one in its nature or consequences subversive of some fundamental or essential principle of government or highly prejudicial to the public interest, and this may consist of a violation of the Constitution, of law, of an official oath, or of duty, by an act committed or omitted, or, without violating a positive law, by the abuse of discretionary powers from improper motives or for an improper purpose." *Trial of Andrew Johnson* (1868), I, 147.

This position was rebutted with great acuteness by former Justice Benjamin R. Curtis, one of Johnson's counsel. Said Curtis, in part:

"In the front of this inquiry the question presents itself: What are impeachable offences under the Constitution of the United States? Upon this question learned dissertations have been written and printed. One of them is annexed to the argument of the honorable manager who opened the cause for the prosecution. Another one on the other side of the question, written by one of the honorable managers themselves, may be found annexed to the proceedings in the House of Representatives upon the occasion of the first attempt to impeach the President. And there have been others written and published by learned jurists touching this subject. I do not propose to vex the ear of the Senate with any of the precedents drawn from the middle ages. The framers of our Constitution were quite as familiar with them as the learned authors of these treatises, and the framers of our Constitution, as I conceive, have drawn from them the lesson which I desire the Senate to receive, that these precedents are not fit to govern their conduct on this trial.

"In my apprehension, the teachings, the requirements, the prohibitions of the Constitution of the United States prove all that is necessary to be attended to for the purposes of this trial. I propose, therefore, instead of a search through the precedents which were made in the times of the Plantagencts, the Tudors, and the Stuarts, and which have been repeated since, to come nearer home and see what provisions of the Constitution of the United States bear on this question, and whether they are not sufficient to settle it. If they are, it is quite immaterial what exists elsewhere.

"My first position is, that when the Constitution speaks of 'treason, bribery, and other high crimes and misdemeanors,' it refers to, and includes only, high criminal offences against the United States, made so by some law of the United States existing when the acts complained of were done, and I say that this is plainly to be inferred from each and every provision of the Constitution on the subject of impeachment.

"'Treason' and 'bribery.' Nobody will doubt that these are here designated high crimes and misdemeanors against the United States, made such by the laws of the United States, which the framers of the Constitution knew must be passed in the nature of the government they were about to create, because these are offences which strike at the existence of that government. 'Other high crimes and misdemeanors.' *Noscitur a sociis.* High crimes and misdemeanors; so high that they belong in this company with treason and bribery. That is plain on the face of the Constitution—in the very first step it takes on the subject of impeachment. 'High crimes and misdemeanors' against what law? There can be no crime, there can be no misdemeanor without a law, written or unwritten, express or implied. There must be some law, otherwise there is no crime. My interpretation of it is that the language 'high crimes and misdemeanors' means 'offences against the laws of the United States.' Let us see if the Constitution has not said so.

"The first clause of the second section of the second article of the Constitution reads thus:

"'The President of the United States shall have the power to grant reprieves and pardons for offences against the United States, except in cases of impeachment.'

" 'Offences against the United States' would include 'cases of impeachment,' and they might be pardoned by the President if they were not excepted. Then cases of impeachment are, according to the express declaration of the Constitution itself, cases of offences against the United States.

"Still, the learned manager says that this is not a court, and that, whatever may be the character of this body, it is bound by no law. Very different was the understanding of the fathers of the Constitution on this subject." *Ibid.*, 408–409.

This view must be regarded as having prevailed, not only on account of the failure of the impeachment, but because of the emphasis given by the House Managers themselves to the contention that Johnson was guilty of a breach of law, the Tenure of Office Act.

Johnson and his Cabinet were much concerned over rumors that it was the intention of his enemies in the House, following impeachment and pending the trial, to put him under arrest and/or suspend him from office. Welles, *Diary*, III, 21, 27, 50, 57, 60, 62, 151, 200, 235, 237, 238, 291, 313. But, of course, no such step was attempted. Several state constitutions contain provisions authorizing suspension from office in such a case; but when, late in the Philadelphia Convention, a motion was offered to this effect, Madison objected, as follows:

"The President is made too dependent already on the Legislature, by the power of one branch to try him in consequence of an impeachment by the other. This intermediate suspension will put him in the power of one branch only. They can at any moment, in order to make way for the functions of another who will be more favorable to their views, vote a temporary removal of the existing magistrate." Farrand, II, 612. The motion failed by a vote of 3 states to 8.

Is impeachment the *only* way in which Congress, or either house thereof, is constitutionally entitled to call the President to account for his conduct in office? So far as the Senate is concerned this question was answered with a most emphatic "yes" by President Jackson in his famous "Protest" Message of April 15, 1834, which was evoked by a resolution of the Senate asserting "That the President, in the late Executive proceedings in relation to the public revenue, has assumed upon himself authority and power not conferred by the Constitution and laws, but in derogation of both." Richardson, III, 69.

Said Jackson, among many other things:

"The Constitution makes the House of Representatives the exclusive judges, in the first instance, of the question whether the President has committed an impeachable offense. A majority of the Senate, whose interference with this preliminary question has for the best of all reasons been studiously excluded, anticipate the action of the house of Representatives, assume not only the function which belongs exclusively to that body, but convert themselves into accusers, witnesses, counsel, and judges, and prejudge the whole case, thus presenting the appalling spectacle in a free State of judges going through a labored preparation for an impartial hearing and decision by a previous *ex parte* investigation and sentence against the supposed offender." *Ibid.*, 76.

And not only, the President continued, was the Senate's action a usurpation of power on its part but of a most pernicious tendency, for should the example thus set be followed, "all the independent departments of the Government, and the States which compose our confederated Union, instead of attending to their appropriate duties and leaving those who may offend to be reclaimed or punished in the manner pointed out in the Constitution, would fall to mutual crimination and recrimination and give to the people confusion and anarchy instead of order and law until at length some form of aristocratic power would be established on the ruins of the Constitution or the States be broken into separate communities." *Ibid.*, 91.

"The resolution of the Senate," Jackson concluded, "contains an imputation upon my private as well as upon my public character," one which "must stand forever on their journals." This gloomy view of the matter was not borne out by events, for, as was mentioned in the text, the Senate itself finally "expunged" the objectionable resolution from its Journal, thereby affording Jackson his most sensational triumph over his political foes.

A similar question, but this time involving the House of Representatives, came up in 1860, when the House authorized the so-called Covode Committee to investigate: "whether the President of the United States or any other officer of the Government has, by money, patronage, or other improper means, sought to influence the action of Congress or any committee thereof for or against the passage of any law appertaining to the rights of any State or Territory; and, second, also to inquire into and investigate whether any officer or officers of the Government have, by combination or otherwise, prevented or defeated, or attempted to prevent or defeat, the execution of any law or laws now upon the statute book, and whether the President has failed or refused to compel the execution of any law thereof." Warren, 10 *Boston University Law Review*, 18; Richardson, V, 614.

Buchanan, who was the President in question, retorted that "the Constitution has invested the House of Representatives with no power, no jurisdiction, no supremacy whatever over the President" except in the sole matter of voting impeachments. "In all other respects," he continued, "he is quite as independent of them as they are of him. As a coordinate branch of the Government he is their equal. Indeed, he is the only direct representative on earth of the people of all and each of the sovereign States. To them, and to them alone, is he responsible whilst acting within the sphere of his constitutional duty, and not in any manner to the House of Representatives. The people have thought proper to invest him with the most honorable, responsible, and dignified office in the world, and the individual, however unworthy, now holding this exalted position, will take care, so far as in him lies, that their rights and prerogatives shall never be violated in his person, but shall pass to his successors unimpaired by the adoption of a dangerous precedent. He will defend them to the last extremity against any unconstitutional attempt, come from what quarter it may, to abridge the constitutional rights of the Executive and render him subservient to any human power except themselves." Richardson, V, 615.

Let Mr. Warren complete the story:

"This protest met with violent attack in the House. John Sherman of Ohio stated that the President could not claim exemption from investigation, and that the House had the 'right to examine into anything which may affect the conduct of any public officer under the Government from the Chief Executive down to the little page who runs your errands upon the floor. Everyone of the officers of this Government is subjected to the power of the House.' The Presidential doctrine, said he, was that of Charles I and Louis XIV—'The King can do no wrong.'—'L'Etat c'est moi.'—'This doctrine set up by the President of the United States is, in my judgment, the very worst that has been enunciated since the foundation of the Republic.' John B. Haskins of New York said that the question was: 'Shall we or shall we not maintain the Legislative power and independence of the House of Representatives which have been insulted this day by a Napoleonic decree coming here as a Message from the President?' Buchanan's Message was finally sent to the Committee of the Judiciary, which reported a Resolution, adopted by the House (June 8, 1860, by a vote of 88 to 40), stating that the House dissented from the President's doctrine, and that to abandon its well-established power to investigate would 'leave the Executive Department without supervision or responsibility and would be likely to lead to a concentration of power in the hands of the President dangerous to the rights of a free people.' The Covode Committee proceeded to investigate in secret sessions, not only the subject set forth in the original Resolve, but also actions of the President relative to domestic and foreign questions entirely within the Executive sphere of action. In continued protest against this usurpation of authority, Buchanan sent to the House another Message, June 22, 1860, stating that 'the Star-Chamber, tyrannical and odious as it was, had never proceeded like this Committee. . . . For centuries, there has been nothing like it in any civilized country, except the Revolutionary Tribunal of France in the days of Robespierre.' If its proceedings should be allowed to become a precedent, 'the Presidential office will be dragged into the dust.' He denied that the Constitution authorized 'this terrible, secret, inquisitorial power.' While stating that he made this protest, for the protection of his successors, he pointed out, however, that the Committee, in concluding its work, had reported no resolution for impeachment or censure and had made no suggestions as to any improper acts in the Executive Departments." *Loc. cit.,* 19–20.

Both Jackson's position in 1834 and Buchanan's in 1860 are high-flown in the extreme. There is certainly nothing in the Constitution to prevent either house from investigating any subject on earth or passing resolutions thereon, whether they happen to be complimentary to the President for the time being or not. That, on the other hand, a congressional investigating committee could not require the President to attend its proceedings, answer questions, or produce documents, is equally certain. See also note 88 *infra.*

[87] Ever since the time of the great leading case of *Marbury v. Madison,* 1 Cr. 137 (1803), heads of departments have occasionally been subjected to proceedings, brought usually in the first instance in a District of Columbia court, in which a writ of mandamus or a writ of injunction was sought, and such writs have now and then been awarded against them. See *e. g., Kendall v. Stokes,* 12 Pet. 524; *Decatur v. Paulding,* 14 Pet. 497; *Garfield v. United States,* 211 U. S. 249; *Smith et. al. v. Hitchcock,* 226 U. S. 53; *Morgan v. United States,* 304 U. S. 1. Two cases 130 years apart in which presidential orders were held by the court to be without legal warrant are *Little v. Barreme,* 2 Cr. 170 (1804) and *Panama Refining Co. v. Ryan,* 293 U. S. 388 (1934). See also *Ex parte Orozco,* 201 F. 106 (1912).

[88] See generally Marshall E. Dimock, *Congressional Investigations* (Johns Hopkins Press, 1926); M. Nelson McGeary, *The Development of Congressional Investigative Power* (Columbia University Press, 1940); and George B. Galloway, "The Investigative Function of Congress," 21 *American Political Science Review,* 46–70.

"A careful survey of the history of committee activity from 1789 to the expiration of the Sixty-eighth Congress in 1925 discloses that there have been, all told, about 285 investigations by the select and standing committees of the House and Senate. Only three Congresses have been barren of legislative inquests, while no administration has been immune. The high-water mark was reached during Grant's eight turbulent years, when incompetence and corruption ran riot through public life; between 1869 and 1877 Congress undertook thirty-seven different inquiries aimed at remedying bad conditions in the administration.

"Much American history can be gleaned from the reports of these nearly three hundred investigating committees. For the houses of Congress have employed the inquisitorial function over a wide range of governmental activity. Beginning with the inquiry into the defeat of General St. Clair by the Indians in 1792, and continuing down to the current investigation of the Tariff Commission, this device has been put to many uses. The record shows that the War Department has come most frequently under the inquiring eye. Congressional committees have scrutinized the conduct of all the wars in which the United States has engaged except the Spanish-American war, when President McKinley forestalled legislative inquiry by appointing the Dodge commission. They were responsible for the impeachment of President Johnson and Secretary of War Belknap. They have examined the conduct of the Treasury Department fifty-four times and of the Interior Department forty-one times, with attention centered most frequently on the Indian Bureau and the Pension and Patent Offices. The Government Printing Office has also been submitted to frequent inspection; likewise the Navy and Postoffice Departments. The President has been the subject of investigation twenty-three times, commencing with John Adams and ending with Woodrow Wilson. In fact, no department or activity of the government has escaped inquiry unless it be the Departments of Commerce and Labor since their separation in 1913." Galloway, *ibid.*, 47–48.

I ought to add that I know of no instance in which a head of department has testified before a congressional committee in response to a subpoena, nor been held for contempt for refusal to testify. All appearances by these high officials seem to have been voluntary.

[89] See e.g., George A. Graham, "Reorganization—A Question of Executive Institutions," *American Political Science Review*, XXXII, 708–718.

[90] Edwin E. Witte, *Report of the President's Committee* (Washington, D. C., 1937), p. 361.

[91] Article cited in note 89, at p. 710.

[92] Robert Luce, *Legislative Problems*, pp. 325–326.

[93] *Senatorial Report*, No. 837, 46th Congress, 3rd session (1881).

[94] Luce, pp. 327–330. See also W. R. Willoughby, *Principles of Legislative Organization and Administration* (The Brookings Institution, 1934) ch. XIII, for an elaborate criticism of the proposal.

"I have long believed that the official relations between the Executive and Congress should be more open and direct. They are now conducted by correspondence with the presiding officers of the two Houses, by consultation with committees, or by private interviews with individual members. This frequently leads to misunderstandings, and may lead to corrupt combinations. It would be far better for both departments if the members of the Cabinet were permitted to sit in Congress and participate in the debates on measures relating to their several departments,—but, of course, without a vote. This would tend to secure the ablest men for the chief executive offices; it would bring the policy of the administration into the fullest publicity by giving both parties ample opportunity for criticism and defense." James A. Garfield, *Works*, II, 483.

The Pendleton proposal was revived in Congress as recently as February 1935 by a member of the House and referred to the Committee on the Judiciary. *Congressional Record*, February 14 and 27, 1935.

A current suggestion for furthering collaboration between the President and Congress is the Legislative Advisory Council. At present nine states have such bodies. The Temporary Economic Committee, which is now functioning under Senator O'Mahoney as chairman, and which consists of three members of the Senate appointed by the President of that body, three members of the House appointed by the Speaker, and six members of administrative departments and agencies, may be taken as a transient embodiment of the same idea. And the six executive assistants, "with a passion for anonymity," who were authorized by the recent Reorganization Act, will doubtless be used to a great extent as "contact" men with the committees of Congress.

95 *Ante,* pp. 14–15.

96 See Professor Herring's reference to a "master-ministry" of Cabinet officers, congressional leaders, and others. 28 *American Political Science Review,* 853.

97 Speech at Hyde Park, November 4, 1938.

98 Writing of Jackson's relations with his Cabinet, Sumner says:

"Jackson introduced two innovations. He put the Secretaries back more nearly into the place in which they belong by the original theory of the law. He made them executive clerks or staff officers. The fashion has grown up of calling the Secretaries the President's 'constitutional advisers.' It is plain that they are not anything of the kind. He is not bound to consult them, and, if he does, it does not detract from his responsibility. Jackson, by the necessity of his character and preparation, and by the nature of the position to which he had been elected, must lean on somebody. He had a number of intimate friends and companions on whom he relied. They did not hold important public positions. They came to be called the 'Kitchen Cabinet.' The men were William B. Lewis, Amos Kendall, Duff Green, and Isaac Hill. If the Secretaries had been the 'constitutional advisers' of the President, their first right and duty would have been to break off his intimacy with these irresponsible persons, and to prevent their influence. Jackson's second innovation was that he did not hold cabinet councils. Hence his administration lacked unity and discipline. It did not have the strength of hearty and conscious cooperation. Each Secretary went his way, and gossip and newsmongering had a special field of activity open to them." *Andrew Jackson,* pp. 181–182.

Lincoln's relations with his Cabinet were equally haphazard, or even more so (*ante,* p. 322, note 51). And like Lincoln, the first Roosevelt failed often to keep his Cabinet informed of important decisions, consulting instead individual heads of departments and outsiders. Only Attorney General Knox knew that the Northern Securities suit was to be brought; and the taking of Panama was a similar surprise move. Mr. Oscar Straus describes Roosevelt's "Kitchen Cabinet" as consisting of "unofficial advisers who met round the luncheon and dinner table and afterwards in the White House study, where the President spoke without reserve on his executive problems, and read for our criticism and counsel his rough drafts of congressional messages, speeches, and notes to foreign governments." "This group," Mr. Straus adds, "served Roosevelt as energetically and loyally as if the grave responsibilities of state were upon their own shoulders." *Under Four Administrations* (New York, 1922), pp. 206–207. Likewise, Mr. Wilson regarded his Cabinet as a body of administrators rather than of political advisers. At no time were there more than two or three members whose opinions he valued on problems arising outside their departments. "When the Lusitania was torpedoed, it was dwelt on by the Washington correspondents that Mr. Wilson did not call together his Cabinet nor consult with any member of it, but, just as Lincoln had done, awfully communed with himself." Luce, p. 313. Nor did Wilson read his War Message to the Cabinet; and when Colonel House asked him why he had not done so he replied that if he had every man in it would have had some suggestion to make, and it would have been too picked to pieces if he had heeded their criticism. He said he preferred to keep it to himself and take the responsibility entirely upon his own shoulders. Charles Seymour, *The Intimate Papers of Colonel House* (1926–1928), II, 468.

Early in President F. D. Roosevelt's first administration the so-called "Brain Trust" rather put the Cabinet in the shade, and later some of the men brought into notice by the new Federal agencies, NRA, TVA, RFC, etc., did the same. And even when Mr. Roosevelt has had free recourse to his official family for counsel, he has turned to individual members of it quite as frequently as to the Cabinet as a body, and this on large questions of policy.

The following extracts from his *On Our Way* (New York, 1934) are illustrative:

"I discussed the banking situation with the Secretary of the Treasury and the Attorney General, asking them to be prepared the next day to outline a constitutional method of closing all banks."

"During these first five days, the Vice-President, the Cabinet, the Director of the Budget and I had been considering another vitally important factor necessary to the restoration of confidence [governmental economy]."

"Under the leadership of Secretary of Agriculture Wallace, we held many conferences with the leaders of farm organizations. . . ."

"Every day that went by . . . brought before me and the Cabinet and the Congress some new emergency which cried out for action."

"It took much courage on the part of Secretary of the Interior Ickes when he told me, about the middle of March, that he was ready to tackle a task which had baffled many others who had sought to limit production of oil to the needs of the consuming public. . . ."

"It was at this point that Secretary Woodin and I decided that the time had come to prevent the export of any more gold." *Ibid.*, pp. 1, 18, 38, 46, 49, 59.

99 It ought to be noted, in bringing this chapter to a close, that there are always people who seem to find the idea of the President as an autocrat most congenial and are willing to work overtime to scrape together the fragments of doctrine favoring their thesis, while of course they ignore statements of opposed tenor. See especially Charles A. Gardiner, "The Constitutional Power of the President," 28 *New York State Bar Association*, 269–292 (1905):

"Thus my ideal of the President coincides with the ideal of the people, a majestic constitutional figure uncontrolled by Congress, unrestrained by the courts, vested with plenary constitutional power and absolute constitutional discretion."

"How, then, is it possible for the President to exceed his express constitutional authority? What Federal act can he perform that he may not claim is in execution of his office and its attributes, of the Constitution and the laws, or of his executive powers?"

"Majesty is another attribute. It inheres in every sovereign, be he Czar or President. Imperium majestasque populi Romani."

"The President is invested with an office and the whole of it. . . . Who hath fixed its bounds? Who hath said, Thus far and no farther? No one has determined its illimitable extent; no one can determine it so long as the Republic endures." *Ibid., passim.*

This ecstatic theorizing was undoubtedly stimulated by certain acts and attitudes of Roosevelt I. For a rather pallid version of the same general point of view, which was meant to reflect certain aspects of Wilson's administration, see a speech by Senator Works of California. *Congressional Record*, January 5, 1917.

"As you know, I am as much opposed to an American dictatorship as you are, for three simple reasons:

"(A) I have no inclination to be a dictator.

"(B) I have none of the qualifications which would make me a successful dictator.

"(C) I have too much historical background and too much knowledge of existing dictatorships to make me desire any form of dictatorship for a democracy like the United States of America."

President Roosevelt to "My dear—," from Warm Springs, March 29, 1938. *The New York Times,* April 1, 1938.

NOTES TO RÉSUMÉ*

[1] "Indeed, the organization of the Executive Power in a republican form of government always presents the greatest difficulties. If its powers are defined with exact precision, events may at some critical juncture occur which will baffle all calculations. Then the republic will be placed between the danger of violating its fundamental law and the imperious necessities of public safety. Nor is it much to be feared that, in moments of imminent peril, the majority would decide in favor of usurpations of power, and suffer the Constitution to be sacrificed. The only means of avoiding these dangers is to mould the fundamental law so that the President, always prominent in times of crisis, may be able to stretch his privileges, in case circumstances shall absolutely require it. . . . Happily for the United States, the framers of the Constitution . . . vested certain powers in the President, but did not declare that these powers should form a limit to his authority. Besides, the prerogatives thus conferred upon him admit on certain occasions of an almost indefinite extension." Chambrun, *op. cit.,* pp. 153–154.

Cf. Upshur, pp. 23–24 *supra.*

[2] "An active and energetic foreign policy necessarily implies that the executive who directs it is permanent and clothed with powers in proportion to his vigor of action. At the same time, combinations with other governments can be of value only so far as they are upheld by an exhibition of adequate strength, or in other words, they cannot be formed without strongly organized land and sea forces.

"If, then, a passion for conquest and territorial acquisitions should take root and spread in the United States, it would soon and inevitably lead to an increase of the powers of the President." Chambrun, p. 284.

Cf. p. 262 *supra.*

[3] *Cf.* pp. 374–375 *supra.*

[4] The effect of the breakdown of States Rights in aggrandizing the Presidency became a theme for gloomy prophecy very early. Gouverneur Morris, in the great debate on the Judiciary Act of 1802, said in the Senate:

"While I was far distant from my country, I felt pain at some things which looked like a wish to wind up the general government beyond its natural tone; for I knew, that if America should be brought under one consolidated government, it could not continue to be a republic. I am attached to republican government, because it appears to me favorable to dignity of sentiment and character. . . . But if a consolidated government be established, it cannot long be republican. We have not the materials to construct even a mild monarchy. If therefore the States be destroyed, we must become the subjects of despotism." *Annals,* 7th Cong., 1st sess., pp. 15–16, 23.

Chambrun repeated the warning more than seventy years later in these words: "We may readily see that, should the autonomy of the States disappear, the Executive Power

---

* *The Résumé begins on page 309.*

would at once essentially change and assume inordinate proportions. It is to a great extent confined by State governments to that sphere of action prescribed for it by the Constitution. In fact, incessant conflicts would take place between the executive, which is independent within the scope of its constitutional authority, and the Legislature, with the increased powers that would almost necessarily attach to it on the destruction of the governments of the separate States. From that time one might foresee that the President, although a person of limited ability, would succeed in gaining the sympathy and influence of a majority of the people. Doubtless the latter might at times declare in favor of a deliberative assembly, but it would not be safe to depend on their permanent support. Called upon to choose between an abstract sovereignty and the concrete idea of power centered in one man, they would in the end almost always prefer the living personality, and recognize him as the elect of the nation, without scarcely remembering that they had also chosen their representatives." *Op. cit.*, pp. 233–234.

TABLE OF CASES

PAGE

INDEX

Page numbers from 1 to 316 refer to the text; page numbers from 317 to 449 refer to the notes.

PAGE

PAGE